Holt
Basic
Reading

Riders on the Earth

Bernard J. Weiss
Reading and Linguistics

Loreli Olson Steuer
Reading and Linguistics

Susan B. Cruikshank
Reading and Language Arts

Lyman C. Hunt
General Editor—Satellite Books

Level 15
HOLT, RINEHART AND WINSTON, PUBLISHERS
New York • Toronto • Mexico City • London • Sydney • Tokyo

ISBN 0-03-061398-1
2345   032   98765432

Acknowledgments:

Grateful acknowledgment is hereby made to the following authors, publishers, agents, and individuals for their special permission to reprint copyrighted material.

Atheneum Publishers, for "Forever," and "A Fishy Square Dance," from *It Doesn't Always Have to Rhyme* by Eve Merriam, copyright ©1964 y Eve Merriam. For "The Sappy Heasons," from *There Is No Rhyme for Silver* by Eve Merriam, copyright © 1962 by Eve Merriam.

Atheneum Publishers and Curtis Brown, Ltd., for an adaptation of a selection from *Maria's House* by Jean Merrill, copyright © 1974 by Jean Merrill.

The Bobbs-Merrill Company, Inc., and Brockhampton Press Limited for "Adventure in Naples," from *Voyage to Tasmania* by Richard Parker, copyright © 1961 by Richard Parker.

The Bobbs-Merrill Company, Inc., and Curtis Brown, Ltd., for "Music by the Minors" condensed from *Second-Hand Family* by Richard Parker, copyright © 1965 by Richard Parker.

The Christian Science Monitor for the poem "Post Early For Space," by Peter J. Henniker-Heaton. Copyright 1952 by The Christian Science Publishing Society renewed © 1980. All rights reserved.

Coward-McCann & Geoghegan, Inc., for "A Visit to Mars," adapted by permission of the publishers from *The Angry Planet* by John Keir Cross, copyright 1945 by Peter Lunn (Publishers) Ltd. Copyright 1946 by Coward-McCann & Geoghegan, Inc.

Crown Publishers, Inc., for "Mister Urian," taken from *Classical Songs for Children* by The Countess of Harewood and Ronald Duncan, copyright © 1964 by Marion Harewood and Ronald Duncan.

Thomas Y. Crowell Company and Collins-Knowlton-Wing, Inc., for "The Big Spring," from *Spring Comes to the Ocean* by Jean Craighead George, copyright © 1965 by Jean Craighead George.

Doubleday & Company, Inc., for "Pelops and Poseidon," from *Wonder Tales of Seas and Ships* by Frances Carpenter, copyright © 1959 by Frances Carpenter Huntington.

E. P. Dutton & Co., Inc., for "Mountain Fantasy" and "In a Million Years," from *Poems of Earth and Space* by Claudia Lewis. Copyright © 1967 by Claudia Lewis.

E. P. Dutton & Co., Inc., and Curtis Brown, Ltd., and Methuen & Company, Ltd., for "The Knight Whose Armor Didn't Squeak," from *Now We Are Six* by A. A. Milne. Copyright 1927 by E. P. Dutton & Co., Inc., copyright renewed © 1955 by A. A. Milne.

E. P. Dutton & Co., Inc., and William Heinemann Ltd., for "The Sea" from *The Wandering Moon* by James Reeves. Published 1960 by E. P. Dutton & Co. Inc.

Harcourt Brace Jovanovich, Inc., for "How Ologbon-Ori Sought Wisdom," from *Lode the Hunter and Other Tales from Nigeria* by Harold Courlander. Copyright © 1968 by Harold Courlander. For "The Dog of Pompeii," from *The Donkey of God and Other Stories* by Louis Untermeyer. Copyright 1932 by Harcourt Brace Jovanovich, Inc., copyright renewed © 1960 by Louis Untermeyer. For "Walter de la Mare Tells the Listener About Jack and Jill," from *Selected Poems and Parodies of Louis Untermeyer.* Copyright 1935 by Harcourt Brace Jovanovich, Inc., copyright renewed © 1963 by Louis Untermeyer.

Harcourt Brace Jovanovich, Inc., and Curtis Brown Ltd., for "Haiku" by Soseki, Shurin, and Meisetsu from *Cricket Songs: Japanese Haiku* translated and copyrighted © 1964 by Harry Behn.

Harcourt Brace Jovanovich, Inc., and Macmillan & Co., Ltd., for "Trouble in Camelot," adapted from *Half Magic* by Edward Eager. Copyright 1954 by Harcourt Brace Jovanovich, Inc.

Hastings House, Publishers, Inc., for "The Baseball Computer," condensed from *Ollie's Team and the Baseball Computer* by Clem Philbrook. Copyright © 1967 by Clem Philbrook.

Kay & Ward Ltd., for "Beowulf," from *Hero Tales of the British Isles* by Barbara L. Picard. Copyright © 1961 by Edmund Ward (Publishers) Ltd.

Alfred A. Knopf, Inc., for "Earth's Deep Frontier," adapted from *Ocean Harvest* by Helen Wolff Vogel and Mary Leonard Caruso. Copyright © 1961 by Helen Wolff Vogel and Mary Leonard

Caruso. For "Pretty Words," from *Collected Poems of Elinor Wylie*. Copyright 1932 by Alfred A. Knopf, Inc., copyright renewed © 1960 by Edwina C. Rubenstein. For "The Dream Keeper," from *The Dream Keeper and Other Poems* by Langston Hughes. Copyright 1932 by Langston Hughes, copyright renewed © 1960 by Langston Hughes.

Little, Brown and Company, for "The Subject Is People," from *The Story of People* by May Edel. Copyright 1953 by May Edel. For, "Extra! Extra!" adapted from *Me and the Terrible Two* by Ellen Conford. Copyright © 1974 by Ellen Conford.

Lothrop, Lee and Shepard Co., Inc., for "Signs and Symbols Around the World," from *Signs and Symbols Around the World* by Elizabeth S. Helfman. Copyright © 1967 by Elizabeth S. Helfman.

Macmillan Publishing Co., Inc. and McIntosh & Otis, for "Zeely," adapted from *Zeely* by Virginia Hamilton. Copyright © 1967 by Virginia Hamilton.

McGraw-Hill Book Company, for "Secrets of Minos," from *The Secrets of Minos* by Alan Honour. Copyright © 1961 by Alan Honour.

William Morrow and Company, Inc., for "The Language of the Bees," from *The Language of Animals* by Millicent E. Selsam. Copyright © 1962 by Millicent E. Selsam.

William Morrow and Company, Inc., and Laurence Pollinger Limited, for "Tidal Waves," adapted from *Waves* by Herbert S. Zim. Copyright © 1967 by Herbert S. Zim.

Harold Ober Associates Incorporated, for "Look Out over the Sea," from *The Big Wave* by Pearl S. Buck. Copyright 1947 by Curtis Publishing Co. Copyright 1948 by Pearl S. Buck.

Peter Pauper Press, for "Seascape Haiku," by Chiyo-Ni, Soseki, Kôson and Basho. Copyright © 1962 by Peter Pauper Press.

Random House, Inc., for "The Challenge of the Sword," adapted from *King Arthur and His Knights* by Mabel Louise Robinson. Copyright 1953 by Mabel Louise Robinson.

Rand McNally & Company, for "Young Ladies Don't Slay Dragons," adapted from *The Princess Book.* Copyright © 1974 by Rand McNally & Company.

Marie Rodell, as agent for the author, for "The Changing Year," adapted from *The Sea Around Us* (Junior Edition) by Rachel L. Carson. Published by Western Publishing Company, Inc. (Golden Press). Copyright 1950, 1951, renewed © 1958 by Rachel L. Carson.

William Jay Smith, for "Whale," from *Boy Blue's Book of Beasts.* Copyright © 1956, 1957 by William Jay Smith.

The Society of Authors, as representative of the Literary Trustees of Walter de la Mare, for "The Portrait of a Warrior," and "Echoes," by Walter de la Mare.

United Press International, for "Plane Crash Kills Roberto Clemente," which appears in the *Daily News*, January 2, 1973.

The Viking Press, Inc., for "Adventure in the Outer World," adapted from *The City Under Ground* by Suzanne Martel. Copyright © 1964 by The Viking Press, Inc.

Wesleyan University Press, for "The Base Stealer," from *The Orb Weaver* by Robert Francis. Copyright 1948 by Robert Francis.

Western Publishing Company (*The Golden Magazine*) for the poem "Stone," by Solveig Paulson Russell. Copyright © 1967 by the Western Publishing Company.

The Westminister Press and Faber and Faber Limited, for *The Forgotten Door* by Alexander Key. Copyright © 1965 by Alexander Key.

All material on evolution presented in this textbook is presented as theory rather than fact.

Other acknowledgments appear on opening pages of selections.

Art Credits:

Photo Credits:

Table of Contents

UNIT THREE
THE NEBULOUS DEEP

UNIT SIX
AGES FAR AWAY

11

Dear Reader,

Welcome to RIDERS ON THE EARTH. Many adventures and new ideas from around the world can be found in the selections in this book.

You will read ancient tales of knights and dragons, and modern-day stories of people all over the world. You will explore the depths of the ocean and meet its fantastic creatures by reading articles written by Jacques Cousteau and Rachel Carson. You will discover secrets of the past through story and legend, myth and folktale. You will venture into the possibilities of the future through science fiction. You will find that no matter when or where the story takes place people have problems to overcome, decisions to make and challenges to meet.

As you read each selection in the book try to identify the challenge or problem to be solved. Try to predict solutions to the problem before you reach the end of the story. Then compare your prediction to the way the character solves the problem. Predicting solutions to story problems will help you improve your comprehension of the selection.

You will read about many challenging situations in RIDERS ON THE EARTH. Think about the challenges as you read. But most of all enjoy the adventures that await you through reading.

Bernard J. Weiss

Reading makes a world of difference.

Unit 1 LANGUAGE IN ORBIT

Pretty Words

Poets make pets of pretty, docile words:
I love smooth words, like gold-enameled fish
Which circle slowly with a silken swish,
And tender ones, like downy-feathered birds:
Words shy and dappled, deep-eyed deer in herds,
Come to my hand, and playful if I wish,
Or purring softly at a silver dish,
Blue Persian kittens, fed on cream and curds.

I love bright words, words up and singing early;
Words that are luminous in the dark, and sing;
Warm lazy words, white cattle under trees;
I love words opalescent, cool, and pearly,
Like midsummer moths, and honied words like bees,
Gilded and sticky, with a little sting.

Elinor Wylie

A Visit to Mars

JOHN KIER CROSS

Martians!

We rose to our feet. Jacky moved over towards me, and I put my hand on her shoulder to calm her. We were all nervous. Why shouldn't we be? On the ridge above us, standing there gazing down at us, were creatures! They differed from anything any of us had ever known, but they were living creatures. They were Martians!

What did they look like? It is difficult to say. There was nothing in all of our experience on Earth to which we could compare them. They were small, varying in height from four to five feet tall. The one that seemed to be their leader was the tallest, about five feet six inches. Their bodies were slender, smooth, and round, somewhat like the trunks of medium-sized silver birch trees on

Earth. At the top, each trunk bulbed out slightly into what I can only call a head. Just below this "head" was the "face." On it were three, sometimes four, sometimes even five small bulges which glowed transparently. These were the "eyes." There were no organs of hearing or smell—at least we could see nothing that might be an ear or a nose. And there was nothing that looked like a mouth.

At the lowest part of the trunk was a mass of small, hard tentacles—the "feet." About a third of the way up the trunk, there was another mass of longer tentacles. These seemed to be the hands. They held, in their twining grasp, long spears or swords that seemed to be made of a sort of glass—Martian weapons!

These, then, were the creatures that stood before us that first morning on Mars. But their strange appearance was not the thing that astonished and upset us the most. It was the fact that their leader was addressing us, and that the language he was using was our own English.

"Who are you?" he said distinctly. "Who are you? What are you doing here?"

I looked wildly at Mac. He alone among us seemed to have calmed down. He looked up at the leader of the Martians and said, in a clear, slow voice:

"We are people. We come from Earth."

There was a rustling sound from the top of the ridge—a quivering of those hundreds of white, wormy tentacles. And the response came immediately—seemingly from several of the Martians at the same time.

"What are people? What is Earth? Explain, explain, explain. Who are you? Where do you come from? What are you doing here?"

The terrifying thing was that I could not imagine how the creatures were talking at all, let alone talking in English. Where was the sound coming from? And yet I knew, in my bones, that there was no sound, that I was not *hearing* what the Martians said! It was as if I were *thinking* the Martians' questions. It was as if their questions were forming by themselves in my brain!

"Mac," I cried, "for heaven's sake, what is it? How can they be speaking to us?"

Mac seemed confident and cool in the face of this mystery. He stood gazing up at the Martian leader, and without shifting his gaze, he now answered me.

"I don't know, Steve," he said quietly. "I do have a slight notion—no more than that yet. Give me time—just a little longer."

Then he addressed the Martian in the same loud, clear tones as before.

"Before I explain further who we are," he cried, "tell me who you are."

"We are the Beautiful People."

Quick as a flash, Mac turned round to us.

"Tell me, Steve, what did they say?" he asked.

"Why—'We are the Beautiful People,'" I answered dazedly.

"And you, Jacqueline, tell me what you heard them saying."

"I thought they said, 'We are the Lovely Ones,'" said Jacky.

"Ah! And you, Paul?"

"I agree with Jacky," said Paul.

"So do I," volunteered Mike. "That's what I heard them say—'We are the Lovely Ones.'"

Mac smiled.

"Steve," he cried, "I believe I've got it. Watch this. I'm going to ask them a question. I'm going to ask them if they knew we were here or if they came on us accidentally. *And you won't hear me saying a word.* Watch."

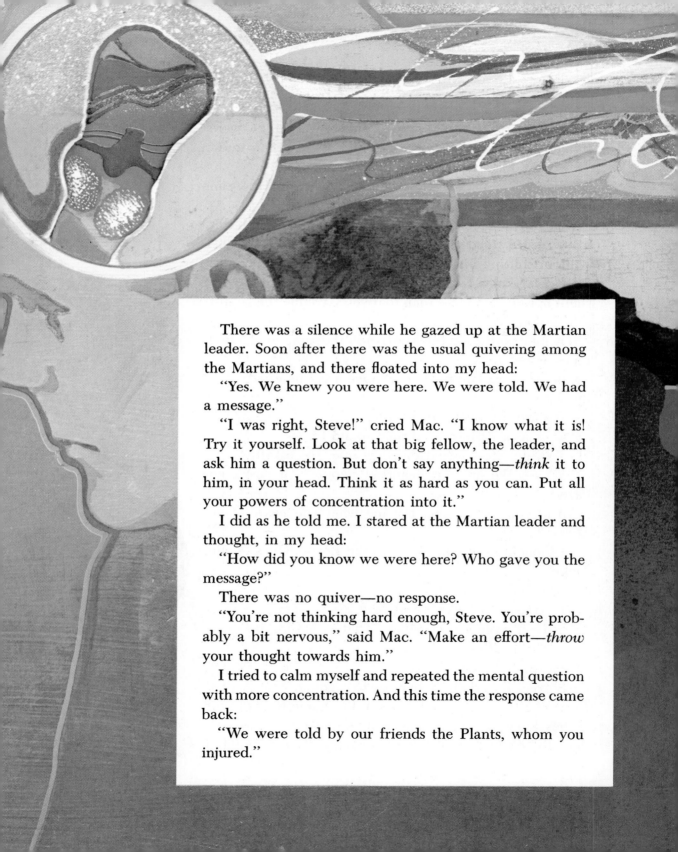

There was a silence while he gazed up at the Martian leader. Soon after there was the usual quivering among the Martians, and there floated into my head:

"Yes. We knew you were here. We were told. We had a message."

"I was right, Steve!" cried Mac. "I know what it is! Try it yourself. Look at that big fellow, the leader, and ask him a question. But don't say anything—*think* it to him, in your head. Think it as hard as you can. Put all your powers of concentration into it."

I did as he told me. I stared at the Martian leader and thought, in my head:

"How did you know we were here? Who gave you the message?"

There was no quiver—no response.

"You're not thinking hard enough, Steve. You're probably a bit nervous," said Mac. "Make an effort—*throw* your thought towards him."

I tried to calm myself and repeated the mental question with more concentration. And this time the response came back:

"We were told by our friends the Plants, whom you injured."

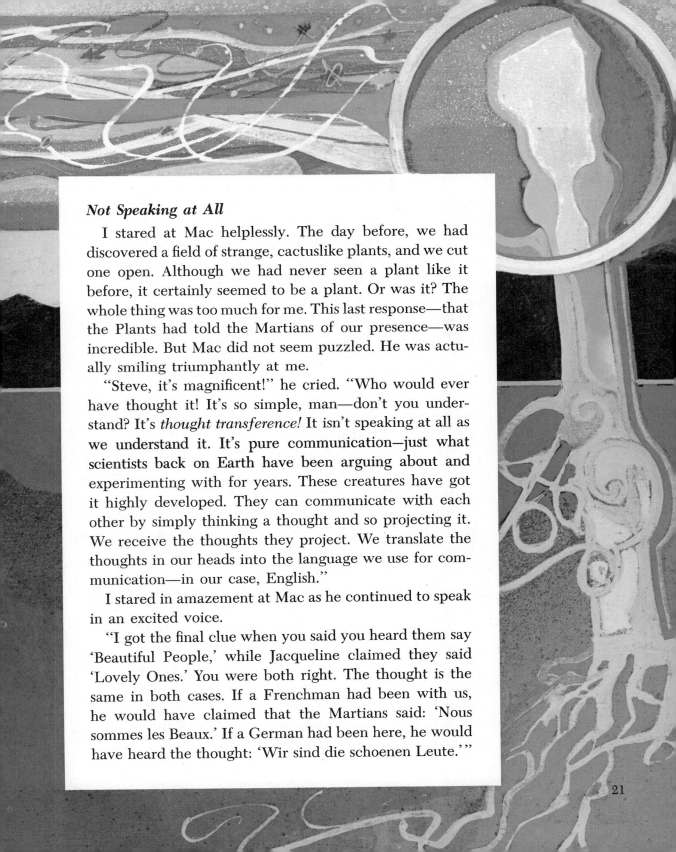

Not Speaking at All

I stared at Mac helplessly. The day before, we had discovered a field of strange, cactuslike plants, and we cut one open. Although we had never seen a plant like it before, it certainly seemed to be a plant. Or was it? The whole thing was too much for me. This last response—that the Plants had told the Martians of our presence—was incredible. But Mac did not seem puzzled. He was actually smiling triumphantly at me.

"Steve, it's magnificent!" he cried. "Who would ever have thought it! It's so simple, man—don't you understand? It's *thought transference!* It isn't speaking at all as we understand it. It's pure communication—just what scientists back on Earth have been arguing about and experimenting with for years. These creatures have got it highly developed. They can communicate with each other by simply thinking a thought and so projecting it. We receive the thoughts they project. We translate the thoughts in our heads into the language we use for communication—in our case, English."

I stared in amazement at Mac as he continued to speak in an excited voice.

"I got the final clue when you said you heard them say 'Beautiful People,' while Jacqueline claimed they said 'Lovely Ones.' You were both right. The thought is the same in both cases. If a Frenchman had been with us, he would have claimed that the Martians said: 'Nous sommes les Beaux.' If a German had been here, he would have heard the thought: 'Wir sind die schoenen Leute.'"

"But, Mac, it's fantastic. Does that mean they're listening in now to all this conversation of ours—these ideas that are flying back and forth between us in the form of language?"

"I doubt it. I think we must want to project our thoughts in their direction."

I was beginning to understand.

"My dear Steve," continued Mac, "it's perfect and beautiful. Language is a clumsy thing. Half the trouble in the world arises from people not understanding each other because language expresses thought so imperfectly. These creatures don't have to use language. They can exchange *pure ideas!* Think of it—sheer thought!"

I looked up at the creatures on the ridge. Throughout the long conversation between Mac and me, they had not moved. They still stood staring down at us quietly. I addressed the leader, putting all my concentration into the thought I was projecting.

"We are friends," I said (or, rather, thought). "We do not mean any harm to you."

And the response came:

"We know. If there had been evil intention in you, we would have felt it when you first looked at us. But you have not yet explained. Who are you? You are not like us. Where do you come from?"

I was puzzling in my mind how to answer this question simply when Mac said to me:

"Leave it to me. I've got a suggestion to make to them. I might as well speak aloud. That gets the thought over just as well, and it means we all know what is being said."

He turned to the Martian leader and said:

"Where we come from and who we are are difficult things to say. We shall be able to tell you in time, when

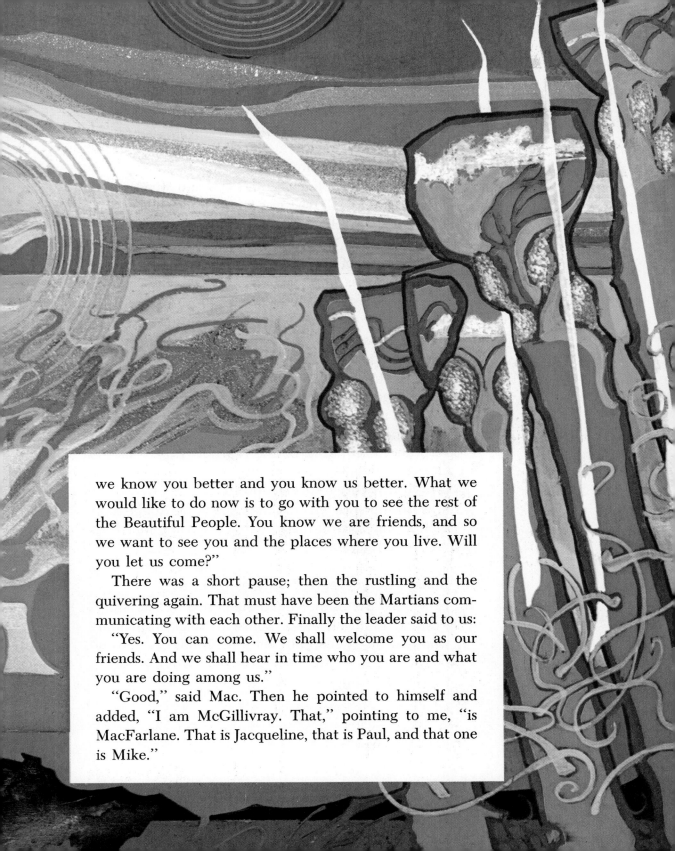

we know you better and you know us better. What we would like to do now is to go with you to see the rest of the Beautiful People. You know we are friends, and so we want to see you and the places where you live. Will you let us come?"

There was a short pause; then the rustling and the quivering again. That must have been the Martians communicating with each other. Finally the leader said to us:

"Yes. You can come. We shall welcome you as our friends. And we shall hear in time who you are and what you are doing among us."

"Good," said Mac. Then he pointed to himself and added, "I am McGillivray. That," pointing to me, "is MacFarlane. That is Jacqueline, that is Paul, and that one is Mike."

The leader of the Martians gestured to himself with his spear, and we heard in our heads:

"I am Malu—I am Malu the Tall, War Prince and Counselor of the Beautiful People."

Calmly, now, we climbed the slope and stood before Malu—Malu the Tall, who was barely a foot bigger than Mike! And so, surrounded by the strange and silent, but no longer sinister, Beautiful People, we set out on our Martian journey of exploration.

Reflections

1. What is the setting and the situation at the beginning of this selection? Where are the people and why, do you think, are they there?

2. How did the Martians communicate? What are the advantages and disadvantages of their system?

3. How do you explain the fact that, although all the Earth people spoke English, Mac and Steve interpreted the name of the Martian tribe as "the Beautiful People," but Jacky, Paul, and Mike interpreted it as "the Lovely Ones"?

4. Toward the end, why did Mac speak his suggestion aloud? Did voicing his message help the Martians or his companions?

5. At one point Mac said, "Language is a clumsy thing." Do you agree? Why or why not?

6. How does the author build suspense in this story?

7. Pretend that you are a space traveler from Mars who had never seen anything resembling a human being before. Write a letter to your family on Mars, describing a human boy or girl to them.

The Language of the Bees

MILLICENT SELSAM

Animals, including insects, do not have a language like ours. They do not talk to each other in words and sentences. But if we watch them, we can see that they do have ways of communicating with each other. Professor Karl von Frisch is a scientist whose experiments have thrown great light on the amazing ways honeybees communicate in their dark hives.

News of Food

Professor von Frisch had worked with bees for many years. He was puzzled by something he had observed again and again. When he placed little dishes of scented honey on a table, he attracted bees. As soon as one bee discovered the honey, many more came to it in a short time. It seemed that one bee was able to communicate the news of food to other bees in its hive. How was this possible? To find out, Von Frisch built special hives, containing only one honeycomb. He built a glass wall through which he could watch what went on inside. Because he wanted to tell the bees apart, he painted some bees with little spots of color.

25

When a marked bee returned to the hive from the feeding table, Von Frisch watched through the glass. To his amazement, the bee began to perform a dance on the surface of the honeycomb. First she made a circle to the right, then to the left. She repeated these circles over and over. But that was not all. The dance seemed to excite the surrounding bees. They trooped behind the first dancer, imitating her movements. Then the bees left the hive and went to the feeding place. The circle dance seemed to communicate news of food. But what else?

Communicating Distance

Von Frisch wanted to find out whether the dance told how far away the feeding place was. He set up two feeding places. One was close to the hive. The other was much farther away from the hive. He marked all the bees that came to the nearby feeding place blue, and all the bees that went to the faraway place were marked red.

CIRCLE DANCE   WAGGING DANCE

When the bees came back to the hive, Von Frisch saw a curious sight. All the bees that had been at the nearby place were doing the circling dance. All the bees that had been at the distant feeding place were doing a completely different dance, a wagging dance. The dancer ran in a straight line, wagging from side to side. Then she turned in a semicircle, ran straight again, and turned in another semicircle to the opposite side. She kept repeating the "steps" over and over. It was clear now. The circle dance meant that food was near. The wagging dance meant that food was far away.

But then another question came up. Did the wagging dance tell the bees how far away the food was? To answer this question, Von Frisch and his co-workers set up a feeding place close to the hive. Then they slowly moved it farther and farther away. Back at the hive they watched the wagging dance closely. With a stopwatch, they counted how many times the bees repeated the dance during one minute. They discovered that the farther away the feeding station was, the slower the dance was. The slower the dance was, the fewer the times it could be repeated in a minute. So another amazing fact came to light. The number of wagging dances per minute told the distance to the feeding place.

27

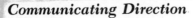

Communicating Direction

Next Von Frisch thought that bees needed to know more than just the distance to a faraway place. He thought they needed to know the direction to it. He set out to discover whether the wagging dance showed direction. He put a glass dish with sugar water scented with honey to the west of the hive. A marked bee fed from the dish and returned to the hive. Soon, the bees in the hive flew out. They flew right to the dish. Then Von Frisch moved the dish to the east of the hive and waited for a marked bee to feed. Again the bees flew right to the dish. How did the bees know exactly in which direction to fly?

Von Frisch watched the wagging dance very carefully. He noticed that the straight part of the dance was different in the morning from what it had been in the afternoon. It soon became clear that the straight part of the dance shifted with the sun's position. If the feeding place was toward the sun, the dancer headed straight upward during the straight part of the wagging dance. If the feeding place was away from the sun, the straight part of the wagging dance pointed downward. The wagging dance of the honeybee, therefore, did show the direction of a feeding place.

A Kind of "Language"

What can we decide about bees from the experiments of Professor Karl von Frisch? Are bees intelligent? Do they have minds that figure out direction and distance? There is no scientific reason to say so. All we can say is that bees do communicate with each other. Their dances are a kind of "language." But the world of the honeybee is just beginning to be opened to us. Someday we may be able to understand how bees developed their amazing "language."

Reflections

1. What were the three problems that Professor von Frisch wanted to solve?
2. What did he learn from each experiment? Outline the steps in one of these experiments.
3. One dictionary defines *intelligent* as "revealing or reflecting good judgment or sound thought." On that basis, would you say that bees are intelligent? Give your reasons.
4. What scientific experiment could be made to learn whether bees ever "forget" their messages? Describe the experiment you would set up.
5. Some scientists believe that dolphins have a "language" and can communicate with each other. Find out about this subject using magazines and reference books. Write a report to present to the class.

Over the wintry
forest, winds howl in a rage
with no leaves to blow.

—Soseki

A cloud shimmering
on the still pool . . . a fish stirs
under the water.

—Shurin

Haiku

俳句

30

A river leaping,
tumbling over rocks roars on . . .
as the mountain smiles.

—Meisetsu

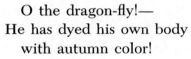

O the dragon-fly!—
He has dyed his own body
with autumn color!

—Lafcadio Hearn

O the thin shadow
of the dragon-fly's wings in
the light of sunset!

—Lafcadio Hearn

Yoózookee he
Oosookee tonbo no
Hah-kahgeh-kahnah

31

Around the World with English

DONALD LLOYD

Almost everywhere you travel in the world, you will find someone who uses English. As far back as 1828, Noah Webster predicted that in the future 300 million people would be using English. Today approximately 400 million people in the world use English for communication.

In the United States, the United Kingdom, Australia, New Zealand, Bermuda, the Bahamas, Canada, and parts of Africa, English is the major language. But in each of these places, people have their own kinds of English. For example, speakers of British English pronounce the word *hot* as though it were spelled *hawt*. They use words like *underground* instead of *subway*, *telly* instead of *television*, *chips* instead of *French fried potatoes*, and *lorry* instead of *truck*. British spelling is often different from American spelling.

American Spelling	British Spelling
color	colour
curb	kerb
tire	tyre
jail	gaol

In Australia, a ranch is called a *station*. And to say one might *bot some oscar from a cobbler* means one might "borrow some money from a pal." *Kangaroo* and *boomerang* are Australian words that Americans have adopted. Even with such differences in pronunciation. vocabulary, and spelling, people whose major language is English are able to communicate well with each other.

English as a Second Language

But English is used not just in places where it is the major language. People living in other areas where English is not the native language sometimes learn English in school. Learning a second language helps them to communicate with English speakers and to read literature written in English. Non-English speakers also learn English in order to talk with other people for whom English is a second language too. For example, when a person from India and a person from Sweden meet, they both can use English. More and more, English is becoming the language of international communication.

Sometimes English finds its way into other languages and becomes part of them. English has become so popular that more and more non-English speakers are borrowing English words. However, when you hear or see some of these English words, you may not recognize them at first because non-English speakers may not say or write them exactly as you do.

Do not be surprised if you hear a German boy talking about being able to *dribbeln* when he plays basketball or *kicken* when he plays football. French boys and girls may tell you how much they enjoy *le camping*. And French girls and boys may talk about *le week-end, le snack-bar,* and *le sandwich.*

The Russians, the Japanese, and speakers of Swahili have also borrowed words from English. In Russian a basketball player is a *basketbolist,* baseball is *bezbol,* and a goal is a *gol.* Russians do not spell words with our alphabet, however, because they have their own.

The American way of life and American English have had a great influence in Japan. A Japanese *chiineijya* (teen-ager) looks at *terebi* (television). He sees a baseball hitter make a *hoomurun* (home run), and rides the *busu*

(bus). The *chiineijya* also listens to a *disuku jokii* (disc jockey) playing a favorite *rikuesuto* (request). *Sutereo* (stereo) is popular. And people can hear the *riibapuru saundo* (Liverpool sound) on the *jyukubaaksu* (jukebox). Japanese people may eat in a *guriru* (grill or restaurant). And they may enjoy eating *baniira aisu kurimu* (vanilla ice cream) or *chakoreto* (chocolate). A department store is *depaato,* a hotel is *hoteru,* and an elevator is *erebata.* The Japanese writing system is different from ours, but some of the Japanese people learn to write in our alphabet.

Another language which contains English words is Swahili. You may recognize some English words or their parts in *hospitali* (hospital), *tikiti* (ticket), *picha* (picture), *motaboti* (motorboat), and *daktari* (doctor). The Swahili language is written in the same alphabet we use for English.

As you have seen, English has traveled all over the world. If you look back a few hundred years, you can trace the spread of English from the British Isles to our country and to other places. When British merchants and colonizers traveled, they carried their language with them. Their language revealed the unique ideas, ways of life, and achievements of their nation.

In recent times tourists, military and business people from the United States have carried American English to other places. Today American English is finding its way into other languages more and more. In addition, many visitors from other countries—for example, India, Japan, and European countries—are studying English in the United States. American economic and political power

and American achievements in the fields of science, the arts, and recreation have caused American English to become popular throughout the world.

As bigger and faster airplanes make travel easier, English will continue to travel around the world. Television, communications satellites, radio, newspapers, magazines, and books will also help the spread of English. Even as words from other languages are added to English, so will English words be added to many other languages. People called *linguistic geographers* study the spread of English. They make maps to show where English is spoken and to show the different kinds of English used.

In today's world English is a very important language. In the future it may become the language most commonly used for communication among all the different peoples of the world.

Reflections

1. Name some countries where English is the major language. Are there other kinds of English besides the one you know? Give some examples.
2. If you know some people who learned English as a second language, ask them why and how they learned English. Make a report based on what they say.
3. Name some of the present-day means of communication that will help spread the use of the English language among the peoples of the world.
4. Why do people all over the world adopt so many American English words? Write a paragraph stating your opinion and give reasons for it.

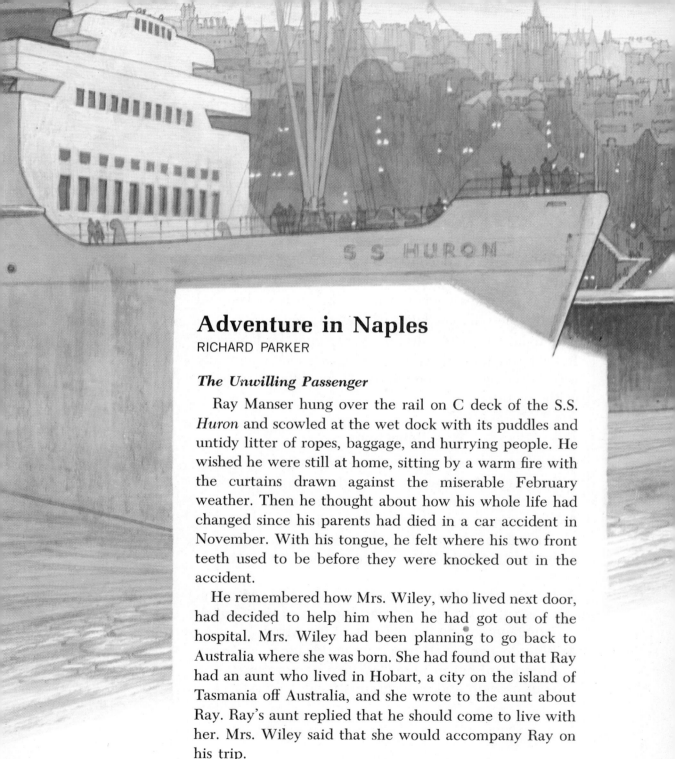

Adventure in Naples

RICHARD PARKER

The Unwilling Passenger

Ray Manser hung over the rail on C deck of the S.S. *Huron* and scowled at the wet dock with its puddles and untidy litter of ropes, baggage, and hurrying people. He wished he were still at home, sitting by a warm fire with the curtains drawn against the miserable February weather. Then he thought about how his whole life had changed since his parents had died in a car accident in November. With his tongue, he felt where his two front teeth used to be before they were knocked out in the accident.

He remembered how Mrs. Wiley, who lived next door, had decided to help him when he had got out of the hospital. Mrs. Wiley had been planning to go back to Australia where she was born. She had found out that Ray had an aunt who lived in Hobart, a city on the island of Tasmania off Australia, and she wrote to the aunt about Ray. Ray's aunt replied that he should come to live with her. Mrs. Wiley said that she would accompany Ray on his trip.

Now Ray was on a ship about to take him to an aunt he had never even seen, one who lived in a strange city in a strange land. At the thought of it, he pressed his mouth so hard that he almost cried out with the pain. Then, suddenly, he realized that the ship was moving away from the dock. He stared at the lights getting smaller. Then he noticed the smoky haze over London glowing with an orange light from the streetlights and the neon signs. He wondered if he was ever again going to see the streets and houses he knew. With a shiver, he turned away from the rail and headed down towards his cabin.

On the deck below, Ray came upon a group of children. They were speaking to him, and all he could hear was a jumble of sounds. He decided that the children must be foreign, and he walked past them toward his cabin.

A boy who seemed to be about Ray's age was standing right in front of the door to Ray's room. When he saw Ray coming, he moved aside and smiled slightly. Ray tried to smile back, but somehow his face felt stiff and immovable. He stood in the doorway, and the two boys looked at each other for what seemed to be a long time. Then the boy pointed his finger toward himself and said, "Anti. Anti Pyrheinen."

Ray guessed this must be the boy's name, so he repeated it. The boy nodded, pleased. Then he pointed at Ray.

"Ray. Ray Manser," said Ray.

"Ray?" said Anti. When Ray nodded, Anti's face broke into a wide smile, and the first thing Ray noticed was that two of his top teeth were missing. So then he grinned broadly, too, and showed his own bare gums. In a moment they were both grinning and laughing and pointing at each other as if it were the funniest thing in the world that both of them should have gaps where their top front teeth ought to have been.

Later that evening Ray was lying facedown on the pillow in his bunk. He felt terrible. Earlier Mrs. Wiley had sent him to fill her teapot with boiling water. He did not know how to work the tap for boiling water and, as a result, had scalded his hand. Now it was red and blistered. Ray let his injured hand hang over the side in the air from the blowers so that it did not hurt quite so much. He dozed off almost at once and woke again with a start a few seconds later. Someone was knocking on the cabin door. It was the cabin steward. He poked his head in and said, "I came by to ask if you'd do me a favor."

There was a silence, and then very slowly Ray raised his head and turned it to face the steward. "What favor?" he asked faintly.

"One of these Finnish families," said the steward. "They're in trouble. The purser has made a mistake and put five in a four-berth cabin. One of the children hasn't got a bed."

Ray lifted his head off the pillow. "Why not use the spare bunk in here?" he said. "I don't mind."

"I was hoping you'd say that," said the steward. "If you wouldn't mind one of the kids spending just one night here, that would solve it."

"All right," said Ray, and the steward left.

Ray waited for a long time. Then when he was almost ready to drop off to sleep again, a figure wearing a bright, green bathrobe came shyly through the door. It was Anti. He grinned when he saw Ray. Then he jumped forward, grabbed Ray's hand, and shook it vigorously. Ray was taken by surprise, and the sudden pain in his scalded hand made him cry out and try to snatch it away. Anti jumped away as if expecting a blow and retreated to the far corner of the cabin.

"Sorry," said Ray. "It's my bad hand. I scalded it."

Anti walked back toward Ray and stared at the blisters. Then, muttering something in Finnish, he darted away. He was soon back again with a small tube of ointment. Anti showed the tube to Ray, but as the writing was also in Finnish, seeing the words didn't help. Then Anti squeezed some of the ointment onto the back of Ray's hand and, very gently with one fingertip, smeared it over the sore places. In ten seconds the pain had gone.

"It's better!" exclaimed Ray, holding up his hand and wiggling his fingers. "It's better already!"

Anti did not understand a word of this, but he seemed to guess what was meant. He smiled with pleasure. After screwing the top of the tube on again, he placed it on the table. He pointed to it and then to Ray's hand.

"Thank you," said Ray, speaking slowly and clearly. "Thank you very much."

"Sank you muk," said Anti with another bob of his head. Then he climbed up to the other bunk and sat there grinning and showing the empty space between his teeth. Ray grinned back in the same way. It was almost as if it were a secret sign of some sort.

Ashore in Naples

From that night on, Ray and Anti were always together on the ship, jabbering away in bits of English and bits of Finnish and lots of sign language. It was amazing how the two boys managed to get along even when they didn't speak the same language.

When the ship reached Naples for a stopover, Mrs. Wiley asked Ray, "Will you come with us on a bus tour of the city?"

"I'd rather stay on board," Ray told her. "I like it on the ship. I wish the voyage could go on forever. I don't like it when we go somewhere. It reminds me about Hobart."

"But Hobart's lovely," said Mrs. Wiley. "And anyway, this is Naples."

But Ray still would not go.

By lunchtime the ship was almost deserted since many of the passengers had left to tour the city. Feeling hungry, Ray went down to the dining room and found Anti at his table. Anti seemed depressed. Ray wondered what was wrong but knew it was no use asking Anti. As it happened, a man who knew both Finnish and English came over to the table and started talking to Anti. Their conversation went on for some time. Then, as the man was leaving, Ray asked, "Is anything wrong?"

"Well, wrong in a way," said the man. "Anti was going ashore with his family, but Mrs. Pyrheinen got sick at the last moment, so they couldn't go. Of course, Anti's very disappointed."

Ray smiled at Anti to show that he sympathized.

During the afternoon both boys found themselves wandering back to the end of the gangway and standing with their eyes fixed on the distant town. Some of the passengers were already returning to the ship, although it was not due to sail until six o'clock. By half-past three, Ray had begun to feel that he might just as well have been walking around the town. He looked at Anti and wondered how the Finnish lad was feeling; then, making a sudden resolution, he walked to the gangway. He turned back and beckoned to Anti, who hesitated only a second and then scrambled after him.

When Ray and Anti emerged from the dock gates, they crossed a wide roadway. They turned to the right along a big street. Apart from the queer words written over shops, there wasn't anything very foreign or strange. They walked until they came to a cobbled street which climbed steeply up a hill. Here there were a few shops with goods for sale on trays or rough tables. At one shop there were fruit and a jar of immense doughnuts.

Ray began to feel quite hungry. He pointed to the doughnuts. "Shall we try one?" he asked Anti. Anti rubbed his middle by way of reply. Ray approached the shopkeeper, who looked about his own age.

"Two of these, please!" he said.

The boy did not understand, so Ray took the top off the jar and lifted out two doughnuts. Then he took six dates out of a tray and put them beside the doughnuts. "How much?" he asked.

The boy thought for a moment and then said something which Ray and Anti could not understand. Ray held some coins out for the boy to take, but the boy called out across the street to a carpenter's workshop. A man came out wiping his hands on his apron, crossed the street, and stared at the money in Ray's hands.

"Inglis money?" he inquired.

"It's all I have," said Ray.

The man gave his hands an extra hard wipe, took two more dates and put them with the six Ray already had. Then he took only a sixpence out of Ray's hand.

"Thank you very much," said Ray, picking up the paper.

"Okay," said the man, backing across the street to his work. *"Grazie!"*

"That must mean thank you," said Ray to himself. *"Grazie! Grazie* very much, " he said.

Ray and Anti went on, munching happily, to an open square where a street market was being held. Stalls covered with flowers, fruit, and bright scarves made the square seem to glow. As the boys stood looking, a lady came over to them. She carried a gray silk parasol, and she wore white net gloves. There was something oddly old-fashioned about her, as if she had stepped out of an illustration in an old book. In very clear English, she said, "You look English."

"I'm English," said Ray. "My name is Ray Manser. This is my friend, Anti Pyrheinen. He's from Finland."

"My name is Mrs. MacLaren, and I'm from England," said the lady. "I thought you might like to know that if

you go up to the old fountain and turn right, you'll be in the oldest street in Naples. I live in the brown house on the corner. You must go and look."

She bobbed her head at them and walked on.

Ray did not care very much about the oldest street in Naples, but he did not like to hurt people's feelings. Nudging Anti, he started off in the direction the lady had indicated.

The boys had been walking for a few minutes when, suddenly, they heard the unmistakable sound of a ship's siren. "The ship!" cried Ray. "What's the time?"

Neither of them had a watch, and there were no clocks in sight. The boys looked at each other, appalled. What happened when the ships were ready to leave? Did they wait for people? In any case, no one knew they had gone ashore. As if thinking the same thing, Ray and Anti bolted toward the direction of the siren.

It seemed miles before they reached the dock. It was empty.

"It must be the wrong place," Ray cried out.

But it wasn't. This was where the *Huron* had been tied up, and now there was no sign of her at all. Ray stared out into the harbor, giving his eyes a hard rub to make sure he was seeing properly. And right out, beyond the mouth of the harbor, was the familiar shape of the S.S. *Huron* making for the open sea.

No English Spoken Here

When Ray dragged his eyes away from the disappearing *Huron,* he felt lonely and helpless. People in the street would not even be able to understand him, let alone help him. And what did people do when they'd been left behind in a foreign country?

He turned to Anti and felt annoyed that his friend could not understand English. It would have been a comfort to have someone to talk to. Anti was, in fact, wiping his eyes on his sleeve. Ray was too near crying himself to feel any sympathy.

"We'll think of something. We'll find somebody who can help. We'll ask a police officer or someone else," said Ray.

Anti could not have understood all of Ray's words, but he must have gotten the idea, for he gave a gigantic sniff and then managed a shaky grin.

Ray wondered how leaders of famous expeditions felt at a time like this. "Let's push on. We must allow no obstacle to stand in our way. Forward, men!" he said.

Together the two boys faced the strange city. Just at the end of the dock stood some official guides and some tourists waiting to begin a tour of the city. Ray went up to the nearest guide.

"Excuse me," he said, "but do you speak English?"

"Much English," the man said.

"We should have been on that ship that just sailed—the S.S. *Huron,*" said Ray. "I was wondering if you could tell us what to do?"

The man pushed back his cap and scratched his head. "Have you try government tourist office?" he asked.

"No. Where is it?" answered Ray.

Pointing to the large modern building on the side of the dock, the man said, "In there. But no open until nine tomorrow morning."

"Thank you very much," said Ray.

"Sank you muk," said Anti.

Then Ray saw a police officer come through the gate. He was about to approach him to ask for help when he began to think that maybe he and Anti had committed some crime by getting left behind. Suppose they were arrested or something? After all, it was a crime to be a stowaway on a ship, and now they were like stowaways on land. "You know," he said aloud, "I don't think it's such a bright idea to ask a police officer. Let's just walk past and have a look around. Something might turn up."

The shops were beginning to close. People coming out of the large office buildings were on their way home. They were not likely to be much help. Two or three shops had notices in the windows saying that English was spoken there, but in each case the doors were locked and the blinds down.

"I'm afraid it's tomorrow morning at the tourist office," Ray said. "At least we know they open at nine. The only thing is, we'll have to find somewhere to sleep tonight." The idea was making him shiver, for now that the sun had gone down, it was not at all warm. "We'll have to find a place somewhere and light a fire. Wood and matches, that's what we need!"

Ray found an open stand that sold papers and magazines and bought some matches there. Then he and Anti began to wander and collect handfuls of rubbish. Finally they made camp in an empty lot. Here they were sheltered from the wind and were hidden from view. They built a fire in the spokes of a wheel from a broken-down

cart they found. They used other wood from the cart to keep the fire burning.

"That should do," said Ray, looking at the fire with pride. The boys crouched on either side of it and grinned at each other across the flames. For the first time since they had seen the *Huron* halfway out of the harbor, they felt fairly happy.

But the night lasts a long time for those who do not sleep. In a warm bed the morning seems only a few moments later than the night before. But when you crouch over a fire in the open air, with the bare sky above you and the cold wind on your back, then every single minute of the night stretches its fullest length. Talking can make the time pass, but Ray and Anti could not talk because they could not understand each other.

"I wish I could understand Finnish better or you could understand English!" Ray exclaimed.

Anti said something in Finnish which probably meant the same thing.

Then Ray had an idea. If Anti did not understand English well enough to have a conversation, then the thing to do was to teach him! After all, he was going to Australia, and everybody there spoke English, so he would have to learn sooner or later. Better to start learning now. And they had the whole night before them!

"Fire!" said Ray, pointing to it. And so the first lesson began. "Dark," said Ray, "sky, wood, earth, wheel."

And Anti repeated the words after him, obviously approving of the idea and eager to learn.

Very Nars Lady

At daybreak Ray said, "Time for the tourist bureau." The boys crawled out of their camp and went back toward the tourist bureau. When they reached the dock gates,

Ray caught hold of the bars, shook them, and gave a polite cough to get the attention of the police officer who was looking out towards the horizon. The officer turned and stared at the boys, but he did not open the gate.

"Can we come through?" Ray asked, with a smile.

"Pass, please!" the officer said.

Ray thought at first he meant they must pass the gate. Then he realized the police officer wanted to see their passes.

"We haven't got a pass," Ray said. "We want to go to the tourist bureau."

The officer shook his head. "No pass, no come," he announced.

It was useless to stay at the gate any longer, so the two boys moved away. Ray sat down on the edge of the pavement and put his head in his hands. Tears began to trickle through his fingers and drip into the dust. Anti tugged at Ray's sleeve, but Ray shook him off. He did not want the Finnish boy to look at him while he was in this state. "I'm all right," he muttered. "Just leave me alone, can't you?"

"Ray," said Anti. "Come! Pliz! Look!" His voice was so urgent that Ray looked up, forgetting the tear marks he had been hoping to hide.

"All right," he said, getting to his feet. He looked in the direction Anti was pointing. There, about two short blocks away, was Mrs. MacLaren, the English lady! Ray suddenly awakened to what Anti was after. "Anti," he cried, "you're a genius!"

And with that they headed towards Mrs. MacLaren, calling her name as they ran. She turned, and when she saw the boys approaching, she smiled with delight. Ray, out of breath from running, told her their story, and Mrs. MacLaren threw up her hands in horror. "All night in the open by yourselves!" she exclaimed. "If only I'd known. Why didn't you think of coming to me right away? But never mind, you found me in the end. Come home with me, and then we'll see about getting you back. Are you hungry?"

They were and said so. When they reached Mrs. MacLaren's house, the boys washed and sat down to a breakfast that seemed big enough for six people.

"Now you start eating while I go and get busy on the telephone and straighten this trouble out for you," said Mrs. MacLaren.

Before the boys had finished their breakfast, she came back. "Well," she said, "I've talked to a lot of people."

"What's going to happen to us?" Ray asked. "Has there been any fuss about our missing the ship?"

"Has there been a fuss? I'll say there has. The shipping office had a cable from the *Huron* telling them to search for you, and they've had people out on the job just about all night. I persuaded the shipping office to cable the

Huron telling your people that you'd been found. I arranged for you to travel on the S.S. *Sioux,* which will be sailing at six this evening. It's a fast boat. It should reach the next stopover just about the same time that the *Huron* does."

"That's wonderful," said Ray.

Mrs. MacLaren smiled. "Since the ship doesn't leave until this evening, I'm inviting you to be my guests for the day. Are you ready?"

"Ready for what?" asked Ray.

He soon found out, for Mrs. MacLaren took the boys on an exciting tour of Naples. They drove to the volcano Vesuvius. Then they had lunch on the veranda of a restaurant and went swimming at a beautiful beach.

Finally Mrs. MacLaren took them to the S.S. *Sioux.* As the boys were about to board the ship, Ray said, "Would you let me write to you when we get to Australia—just to let you know we're all right? You don't need to answer, of course. . ."

"I'd love you to write," said Mrs. MacLaren. "And I shall certainly answer. It will be nice to have a friend on the other side of the world."

Ray and Anti stood at the top of the gangway and watched Mrs. MacLaren's car until it was out of sight.

"Well, that was a nice day," said Ray.

Anti said slowly, "Very—nars—lady!"

"Nice," said Ray.

Anti nodded. "Nars," he repeated.

"It's time I gave you some more lessons in English," said Ray.

The boys smiled at each other and walked onto the ship.

Reflections

1. How did Ray and Anti first become friends? What events strengthened their friendship?
2. Whom did Ray and Anti meet in the market square? Why was this meeting fortunate for the boys?
3. How clearly was Ray thinking when he decided not to ask the police officer for help? Give reasons to support your opinion.
4. Why did Ray decide that the night was the perfect time to teach Anti English?
5. Why might it be desirable to learn a second language even if you had no definite plans for foreign travel? Give three possible reasons.
6. How were Ray and Anti different? How were they alike? Write an essay comparing the two boys.

The Sea

JAMES REEVES

The sea is a hungry dog,
Giant and gray.
He rolls on the beach all day.
With his clashing teeth and shaggy jaws

Hour upon hour he gnaws
The rumbling, tumbling stones,
And "Bones, bones, bones, bones!"
The giant sea-dog moans,
Licking his greasy paws.

And when the night wind roars
And the moon rocks in the stormy cloud,
He bounds to his feet and snuffs and sniffs,
Shaking his wet sides over the cliffs,
And howls and hollos long and loud.

But on quiet days in May or June,
When even the grasses on the dune
Play no more their reedy tune,
With his head between his paws
He lies on the sandy shores,
So quiet, so quiet, he scarcely snores.

William Jones: Language Detective

BERNARD WEISS

Whom do you look like? Your answer is probably someone in your family—maybe your mother or father or grandmother or grandfather. Maybe it is your eyes that show the resemblance, or maybe it is the shape of your face. You will probably be surprised to learn that languages also show family resemblances. Below is a chart of words in six languages. It is no accident that the words in these languages resemble each other. The languages are related; that is, they belong to the same language family. The language family is called Indo-European.

English	German	Dutch
mother	Mutter	moeder
father	Vater	vader
three	drei	drie

Latin	Spanish	French
mater	madre	mère
pater	padre	père
tres	tres	trois

One of the first people to discover resemblances and relationships among languages was William Jones. He was born in London, England, in 1746, just thirty years before the American Revolution. As he grew up, he became interested in science, literature, law, and politics. He also wanted to learn as much as he could about people all over the world; therefore, he began to study their languages. He learned twenty-eight languages during his lifetime. Many of them he taught himself, and he enjoyed learning them all!

As William Jones studied various languages, he noticed words in several languages that resembled each other and had the same meaning. He wondered if there was a reason for all the likenesses. They probably were not accidental because there were too many. Slowly he began to suspect that the languages containing similar words were all descendants of one language. That language must have existed very long ago and was no longer spoken anywhere in the world.

In 1794 William Jones died. He is given credit for being a clever language detective who made an important discovery about the history of certain languages and, therefore, also about the history of civilization. His discovery of word similarities encouraged other language scholars to continue his work after he died.

The language scholars, called linguists, decided that William Jones had been on the right track. One language was the ancestor of certain other languages. The linguists called the ancestor language Indo-European because its descendants reached from Europe across to India.

Mother

ater

Linguists could only guess what the ancestor language looked and sounded like because no one has found any evidence of it in writing, and no phonograph records or tapes existed to record it.

Linguists guessed that the speakers of Indo-European were members of a small tribe that lived in north-central Europe at the end of the Stone Age, about 3000 B.C. The members of the tribe were not primitive cave dwellers. They lived in houses, raised cattle and sheep, farmed, and

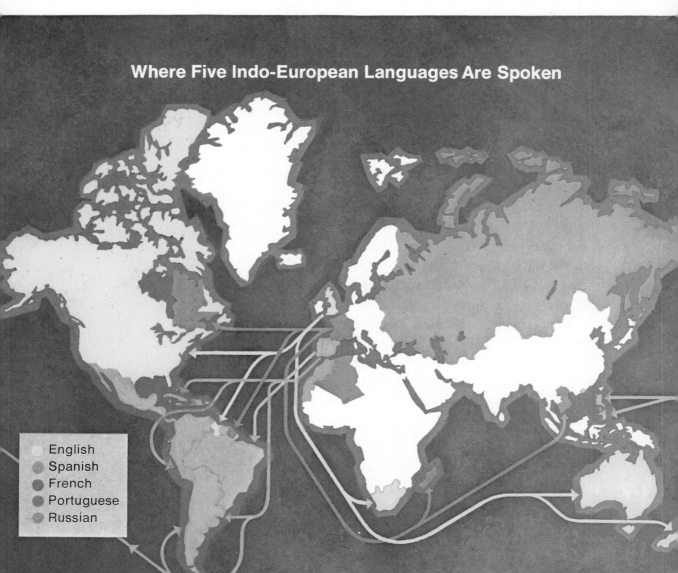

Where Five Indo-European Languages Are Spoken

- English
- Spanish
- French
- Portuguese
- Russian

knew how to spin and weave. When the tribe grew too large for its territory, some members wandered off to other places.

As time went on, the wanderers no longer spoke Indo-European exactly as it had been spoken before. Their language changed. Sometimes it became mixed with words from languages spoken by people whom the wanderers met. Sometimes the wanderers had to make up new words for new plants and animals they found. The result was that Indo-European developed into different languages in different places—for example, Greek, Latin, and Old English. As time passed, even these different languages changed—for example, Old English became Modern English, the language we speak today. But some resemblances between the current languages and Indo-European still remain.

It took William Jones, a clever language detective, to discover resemblances among languages and to begin the work of tracing languages back to their source.

Reflections

1. What do we mean when we say that certain languages are "related to each other"?
2. Why did the scholars call the ancestor language Indo-European?
3. What languages belong to the Indo-European family?
4. Why was the discovery about the relationships of languages also a discovery about the history of civilization? What guesses did it lead other scientists to make about human history?
5. Why do many people find the study of language and languages fascinating? In an essay, give as many reasons as you can.

The Sappy Heasons

EVE MERRIAM

In the skue-bly sprays of ding
When yaffodils are dellow,
And tragnolia mees are mellow;
Then I feel a fively lellow,
Fively lellow.

In the good old tummer-sime
When lovers spike to loon,
And molden is the goon;
Then I hum a tappy hune,
Tappy hune.

When the autumn teaves are lurning
And there's lost upon the frand,
Still Thanksgiving's hose at cland;
So I'm feeling grimply sand,
Grimply sand.

When the winter blorms are stowing
And the snow is hiling pigh,
And nothing dreems to sy;
Then I'm glad that ug am snI,
Ug am snI.

Signs and Symbols
Around the World
ELIZABETH S. HELFMAN

Signs and Symbols for Today

Today, more than ever before, we need some sort of international language. More and more people are traveling. Some go to live in faraway places for long periods of time. All over the world people must communicate with other people who speak different languages. If they can neither talk together nor read the same things, there is little understanding between them. One of the most important jobs in international communication today is to develop signs and symbols that everyone will understand immediately.

Some international events, such as world exhibitions, have developed signs of their own. A set of signs was designed for the Olympic Games. Here are some.

SHOWER   DINING ROOM   LUNCHROOM   FIRST AID

Also for the Olympic Games, signs were designed to indicate different sports. How many can you identify?

EXPO 67 in Montreal, Canada, later called Man and His World, provided twenty-four signs without words for visitors from all over the world. Here are four of these signs and their meanings.

DON'T TOUCH   DON'T LITTER   BUS STATION   COFFEE SHOP

Signs and Symbols for Tomorrow

Many organizations are working to develop signs that are so clear that people everywhere can learn them easily. Here are four such signs from the International Council of Graphic Design Associations. They are only part of a set of signs.

INFORMATION   AIRPORT   HOTEL   DOCTOR

These signs are just one attempt to create useful signs for the future. New signs will have to be tested all over the world before they are finally accepted for use.

Attempts at creating an international sign language have established a new use for an old word, *glyphs,* meaning "signs and symbols." It is part of the word *hieroglyph.* The word *glyphs* comes from the Greek verb *glyphein,* which means to carve. In the early days of our history, many glyphs were carved in stone. Today the word *glyphs* is used to mean those signs and symbols that have been accepted around the world. Numerals, letters, mathematical signs, musical signs, punctuation marks, and scientific symbols are examples of glyphs. All of these have been developed and accepted over a period of many years.

The United Nations considers glyphs very important for international communication. In 1965 the United Nations used glyphs as part of its program for International Co-operation Year. Here is the United Nations symbol for International Cooperation Year.

A sign is a small thing in this big world—often small enough to be drawn or printed on an ordinary piece of paper. Yet signs and symbols have a big job to do. They can contribute much to better understanding among the peoples of the world.

Reflections

1. Look back at the signs that were designed for EXPO 67. Why do you think these signs and the signs for the Olympics are alike?
2. In what kinds of situations would symbol writing be most useful?
3. Do you think the signs for *information, airport, hotel,* and *doctor* are clear? If not, how would you change them?
4. Look up *hieroglyphics* and *runes* in the encyclopedia. What are they? Which peoples used them and for what purpose?
5. Do you think signs and symbols can ever replace English or another alphabetical language? Write a paragraph giving reasons for your opinion.

Baseball Signalers

Have you ever been to a professional baseball game? Did the third base coach look nervous? His hands are always moving—touching his cap, clapping, removing the cap and scratching his head, wiping his forehead, even blowing his nose. Many of these movements are signs which tell the players what to do. Others are there just to confuse the opposing team.

The batter, seeing the coach scratch his head, now knows that the baserunner on first will try to steal second. The baserunner will start toward second as the pitcher throws the ball. The batter must swing at it to distract the catcher and slow his attempt to throw the base stealer out.

The catcher on the other team also sends out signals. He gives hand signals that tell the pitcher whether to throw a fastball or a curve. He sends a series of them—pointing two fingers down, then three, then pounding his fist into his glove. He has told the pitcher beforehand that the second sign will tell him which pitch to throw.

Thinking that the runner on first base will try to steal second, the catcher has called for a fastball. This will give him a little extra time to throw the runner out. Unfortunately for him, the batter, swinging to protect the base stealer, drills the ball into the stands for a homerun. The runner in front of him crosses homeplate easily. All that headscratching by the third base coach and all the signing by the catcher have been wasted.

Frank Robinson *(above),* star of the Cincinnati Reds and the Baltimore Orioles, is the only one to win the Most Valuable Player Award in both major leagues. He became player-manager for the Cleveland Indians.

Sandy Koufax *(above),* outstanding fastball pitcher for the Los Angeles Dodgers, is tied for the record for pitching the most no-hit games. He led the National League in Earned Run Average for five years in a row.

Joltin' Joe DiMaggio *(right),* also known as "The Yankee Clipper," was an outstanding batter from 1936 to 1951. He still holds the record for hitting safely in 56 consecutive games. His number, 5, has been retired and no one else on the New York Yankees may use it.

The Base Stealer

ROBERT FRANCIS

Poised between going on and back, pulled
Both ways taut like a tightrope-walker,
Fingertips pointing the opposites,
Now bouncing tiptoe like a dropped ball
Or a kid skipping rope, come on, come on,
Running a scattering of steps sidewise,
How he teeters, skitters, tingles, teases,
Taunts them, hovers like an ecstatic bird,
He's only flirting, crowd him, crowd him,
Delicate, delicate, delicate, delicate—now!

The Baseball Computer

CLEM PHILBROOK

A Bold Prediction

It was the final game of the Tom Thumb League World Series, Willowdale, Pennsylvania. There were two away—last of the sixth, with the bases loaded. The count was three and two. Oliver Scruggs was well aware of the score as he stepped out of the batter's box. His team was three runs behind. His desperate teammates were silent behind him on the bench. The crowd was hushed. It was so quiet, you could have heard a fly ball drop.

Yet Ollie had never been more sure of himself in his life—so sure that he lifted his right arm and pointed toward the right field fence.

A gasp rose from the crowd and swelled from one end of the bleachers to the other. There could be no mistaking that gesture. Ollie was boldly predicting a home run.

The pitcher's mouth tightened. He checked the runners, reared back, and fired a fast ball right across the plate. Ollie stepped into the ball with perfect timing. At the instant his weight shifted to his forward foot, the bat met the ball cleanly. Ollie had a nice feeling from the tips of his fingers to the ends of his toes.

The fleet right fielder was off at the crack of the bat. Back, back, back he raced—but Ollie smiled to himself as he rounded the bases to the roar of the Willowdale fans. No one was going to get that ball. It was long gone.

Suddenly Ollie fell out of his glorious daydream with a mental thud. It was quite a jolt to find himself back in the sixth-grade room at Willowdale Elementary School. Miss Carmody was picking up the class magazine.

"All right, class, time for current events," she said. "Let's turn to page three and start with an article on the growing use of computers and their effect on our society."

"My father programs computers," Ollie announced proudly.

Miss Carmody smiled. "It would be nice if he could program boys to raise their hands when they wish to talk. Do you think he might do that, Oliver?"

Ollie grinned and raised his hand.

"Yes, Oliver. I am sure the class would like to hear more about your father's profession."

"Well, my father has an IDIOT."

"He sure has," Bruce Dodge snickered. The class laughed at this.

Miss Carmody rapped on her desk. "Order, please," she commanded.

Ollie calmly went on speaking. *"IDIOT* stands for International Data Integrating Organization Tabulator. It can be used by a lot of different people who share the

cost of using it. This is called time-sharing in computer language."

"You certainly have learned a lot about computers," Miss Carmody said. "Can you tell us more, Oliver?"

The class was listening closely now.

"Customers are linked to the IDIOT at a data center. They communicate with the IDIOT by pushing keys on a keyboard something like a typewriter's. If customers push wrong keys, the computer tells them. Then they can correct, or debug, it and start over again."

"Brrr," the dismissal buzzer sounded, bringing Ollie's talk to a sudden end.

"Thank you, Oliver," Miss Carmody said. "We will have to continue our discussion of computers at another time."

As Ollie left school, he was again dreaming about baseball. There was to be another game that evening at six thirty. Maybe this time his team, the Red Sox, would win. Then he remembered. This evening the Red Sox, better known as the Red Flops, were playing Bruce Dodge and his Braves—and they were the toughest team in the Willowdale League. They already had three straight official wins, and they had clobbered the Red Sox in the season opener. The next two of the Red Sox's official games had been rained out.

The Red Sox's only claim to fame was that they had a lady coach—Miss Carmody, Ollie's teacher. The team came in for a lot of ribbing because of this, but Ollie thought it was not fair. There was nothing in the regulations prohibiting a lady coach, and Miss Carmody knew baseball from top to bottom. She came from a long line of baseball fans and had even been a softball star in college. Still, the Red Sox had lost all their preseason games. What really ailed them, thought Ollie, was that every player was unhappy with the position he or she was playing. The first baseman thought he should be playing second base. The second baseman thought she should be playing shortstop. And the shortstop thought he should be playing third base. Everyone on the team was sure he or she would make a great pitcher.

Nobody wanted Ollie's job. He was the catcher.

The Red Sox-Braves game started at six thirty sharp. Ollie's father was umpiring. At six thirty-eight the Braves had the bases loaded. At six thirty-nine Bruce Dodge stepped up to the plate and proved that not all pitchers are poor hitters. He swung from the heels at a fat pitch and blasted it out of the park. At six forty-one the Braves had a four-run lead and a player on base.

Ollie walked out to the mound. "You want me to take over?" he asked Dusty.

Dusty glared at him. "Beat it! I'll settle down."

The rest of the team stood silent, staring in Dusty's direction. Ollie knew they were all thinking the same thing he was—that they could do a better job pitching than Dusty. Then Gary Allen hit a towering fly toward right field. Second baseman Sue Turner and right fielder Larry Donovan each waited for the other to catch it. The ball dropped between them with a dull plop. By the time Sue got a hand on the ball, grinning Braves were on first and second bases. There was nobody out.

"You should have taken it, Larry," Miss Carmody said. "The player coming toward a fly ball should always make the catch if possible." Ollie did not see how Larry could forget a rule like that. Still, Larry was another one who thought he should be pitching. Probably that was why he forgot.

By the time the sun set, the Red Sox had lost another game, by a score of twenty-eight to zero.

"Last time they beat us thirty-one to zero," Herbie piped up. "Tonight it was only twenty-eight to zero. We're getting better, huh?"

His cheerfulness was met with stony glares as the players gathered up their equipment. They glared at Ollie's dog, Sir Winston, too. He was stretched out under the bench, snoring away.

"Some mascot," Larry mumbled. "The least he can do is stay awake and bark once in a while."

"Your fielding is enough to put anyone to sleep," Sue Turner pointed out.

Miss Carmody pushed her baseball cap to the back of her head. "Another miserable performance," she said with a sigh. "What's wrong with this team, anyway?"

Ollie's father smiled. "I think I know what ails them."

"That's easy," grumbled Dusty. "None of us can play baseball."

"You *won't* play baseball," Mr. Scruggs corrected. "From the griping I heard during the game, I'd say all players feel they are playing the wrong position. There's no teamwork. The result is confusion. In my line of work, I have learned how important it is to have the right person in the right job. In fact, we work out aptitude tests for industry to help them do just that. We process the tests through a computer."

Belief in an IDIOT

It was later that evening before Ollie's brainstorm struck. An aptitude test to match baseball players with their positions—that was the answer! "Why not?" he thought. If his father could match the right person to the right job by computer, he could match the right players to the right positions on a baseball team. Certainly the players would believe an IDIOT.

Ollie's heart pounded double time as he dashed from the kitchen table to talk to his father. He could just see newspaper headlines! "Automation invades our national game. Surging Willowdale Red Sox first data-processed team in world!"

After mulling over Ollie's idea, Mr. Scruggs admitted that it might work. If Miss Carmody agreed, he would meet with her the next evening to work out an aptitude test for the team. If the players would take the test, the data could be processed. Then all the players would find out the positions they should be playing.

The following morning Ollie pledged all the Red Sox players to secrecy when he rushed out to the playground and called them into a huddle. Everyone was excited about the idea. Dusty summed it up nicely. "How can we miss?" he asked. "Computers don't make mistakes."

Ollie felt very smug as he faced the class later that morning. Every time he looked at Bruce, he had all he could do to keep from laughing. Boy, would Bruce wipe that smirk off his face if he knew what the Red Sox had up their sleeves!

The next evening Mr. Scruggs handed the tests to the team. "Your answers to the questions on this test will give us profiles of you as individuals," he explained. "We will learn about your interests and personalities. The IDIOT then will select your position for you according to the data you give. Begin now."

The aptitude test contained such multiple-choice questions as, "Infielders are more important than outfielders," "Pitchers are more important than catchers," "The coach is the most important member of a team." The players had to circle "Agree," "Neutral," or "Disagree." There were other questions with answers like these to be circled: "A. Usually calm," "B. Usually active and energetic."

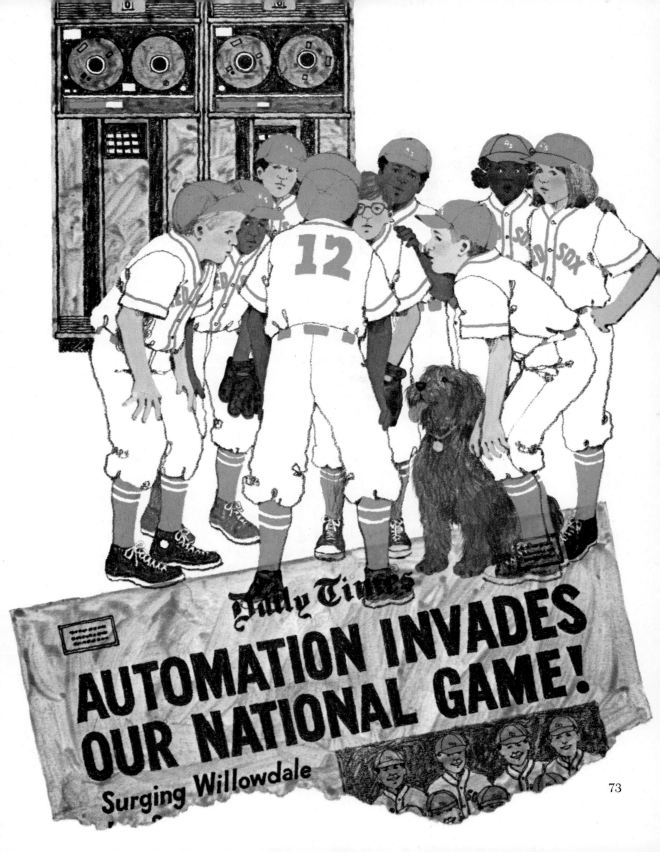

On Friday afternoon Ollie's father read the computer results before practice. The computer put Ollie exactly where he was—behind home plate. Barney was best suited to first base, Sue to second, Herbie to shortstop, and Billy to third base—the same positions they were already playing. There was a change in the outfield. Tony Girard went from center to left field, Patty Finnegan from left to right, and Larry Donovan from right to center. But that was it. Everything else stayed the same. Dusty was still the top pitcher, with Tony second, and Patty next.

When Mr. Scruggs was finished reading the results, Miss Carmody said, "Well, you asked for it, gang. The Red Sox have been data-processed by the latest in computer equipment. Let's hope you will now stop crabbing and settle down to business."

Ollie's father grinned. "Anybody want to question my computer?"

"How do you argue with a computer?" Barney asked. "If it says I'm a first baseman, then I must be a first baseman."

"I'll buy that," Sue agreed, "and I've got a lot to learn about second, too."

Herbie drove his right fist into his glove with a loud smack. "Hey, Coach, how about giving us a few pointers?"

"Don't think I won't," Miss Carmody answered. "You all have a lot to learn—things like making the right play in the blink of an eye. If you hesitate, you are lost. This is a game of split-second timing."

She paused to let her words sink in. Then she said, "There is only one way to learn—practice. We are going to drill and drill and drill—until making the right move will be automatic. There's no time like the present; so take your positions." She picked up the bat and squared off at the plate.

That was the beginning of better things. What followed was the liveliest practice session of the year. Oh, they were not suddenly transformed from Willowdale's worst team into the best, Ollie realized. But there was a real change in their attitudes.

Even Sir Winston seemed to sense their mood. For the first time he stayed awake and watched the action, barking his approval.

"I begin to see a glimmer of hope," Miss Carmody said as practice drew to a close. "At least you are trying."

"You certainly are," Mr. Scruggs agreed. "You are probably the most trying baseball team in the state."

Miss Carmody smiled as the team gathered in a circle around her. "Seriously, I'm proud of you, and I have a strong hunch you will give a good account of yourselves in tomorrow's game against the Yankees."

"We'll be right here to help you," said David Miller and Elmira Bisbee, two of Ollie's younger neighbors who had been watching the team practice.

"We have some new baseball jokes, haven't we, Elmira?" asked David.

"What do you know about baseball?" interrupted Ollie.

"Oh, we know a lot. We've read many baseball books, and we play, too," answered Elmira and David.

Then Elmira said, "Tell me, David, why does it take longer to go from second base to third than from first base to second?"

David's brown eyes sparkled. "Because there's a *short stop* in between."

The two children burst into giggles. Ollie cringed. Dusty held his nose.

Then David winked at Elmira. "Tell the team what baseball stockings are, Elmira."

"Why certainly, David. Baseball stockings are stockings with runs in them!"

Ollie glanced at Dusty with disgust as Elmira and David burst into giggles.

The Big Game

On Saturday afternoon every player on the field was determined to do well when Mr. Scruggs called, "Play ball!" The team looked as though it meant business. Uniforms had been altered, cleaned, and pressed. The boys and girls wore them with pride.

No one was more determined to make good than Ollie. He had spent hours studying a book about baseball. A catcher must be right on the ball at all times, Ollie decided.

"Ho, ho, what do you know?" he sang out as he started the ball on a final trip around the diamond. "The Red Sox are ready to go-go-go!"

The Yankee lead-off smirked as he strolled up to the plate. "Hey, hey, what do you say?" he answered. "The Yankees will beat your team today."

By the end of the game, the Red Sox proved that Ollie was right. Final score: Red Sox, thirteen; Yankees, eleven.

Coach Carmody called her team together after the customary three cheers had been given. "That was more like it," she said. "If you keep playing that brand of ball, we may stand a chance." She smiled at Ollie's father, who had just joined them. "I think we all owe a vote of thanks to Mr. Scruggs. It was not easy to make out that aptitude test and process the data."

A rousing "yeaaa" was heard for Mr. Scruggs, who grinned in return. "Believe me, it was well worth it," he told them. "Never have I seen such a change in a team. I predict that you will win the league championship because you have been scientifically selected by an IDIOT. Data-processing will triumph again."

"What's this all about?" demanded Nosy Newman, elbowing his way through the group. If anyone could smell out news, Nosy could. He covered sports for the weekly *Courier*. He was tall and hawklike, with dark eyes behind horn-rimmed glasses. He peered at Mr. Scruggs. "What were you saying about data-processing?"

Mr. Scruggs and Miss Carmody looked at each other. Finally Miss Carmody said, "Oh, well, I guess you might as well know. Some of my players felt they were placed in the wrong positions. Mr. Scruggs offered to devise a questionnaire—a kind of aptitude test—which the team filled out. Then the data were fed into one of Mr. Scruggs's computers, which analyzed each player and suggested what position he or she was best suited for."

Nosy whipped out his notebook and pencil. "And it really worked!" he squeaked. "What a story! What a miracle! What an idea!" He frowned at Miss Carmody. "And whose idea was it, by the way—yours or Big Ollie's?"

Miss Carmody shook her head. "Neither one. The idea was young Oliver's."

Yes, Ollie decided, he was proud of his idea. It had turned out to be a blockbuster. Best of all, it had enabled the Red Sox to break out of their slump.

"The IDIOT has debugged the Red Sox," he told Dusty on the way home. "Bruce and his old Braves had better watch out. We'll give them a run for their money next time we meet."

Almost everyone in town was at the Tom Thumb League field for the final game between the Red Sox and the Braves. Sir Winston was hitched to his post by the Red Sox bench. David and Elmira were telling jokes and giggling. They wore red sweaters and caps. Nosy Newman was there, too. His articles about the data-processed Red Sox had created a lot of interest. The Red Sox had now won four games in a row. In the meantime the Braves had gone into a slump and lost two. The two teams were tied. People realized that this game would be a real battle.

And it was—from Dusty's very first pitch, which Toby Baker lined into left field for a triple. Gary Allen bounced one off the right field fence for a double. One after another, the Braves hit a single, a double, and another single, each hit coming on Dusty's first pitch.

"Let's settle down," Miss Carmody called. "Fire hard in there!"

Dusty finally got the range and fanned three batters in a row. Sir Winston, who had started to yawn, perked up and began to bark when the team came trotting in to the bench.

"That's more like it," Miss Carmody told them. "Now let's get back a few of those runs."

They got back very few. Bruce gave up hits the way a miser gives up gold. In the first three innings the Red Sox eked out four hits for a grand total of two runs. In the meantime Dusty was getting better, too. He held the Braves to a total of two runs in the next three innings. The Red Sox came up to bat in the last of the fourth with a six-to-two score staring them in the face.

"Let's go, you IDIOTS!" yelled a fan.

"What happened to your computer?" heckled a Braves fan. "I thought you guys were supposed to be data-processed."

"Their computer must have developed a short circuit," chimed in another. .

The Braves supporters cackled in glee. Ollie's ears burned at the insults. "Remember, we haven't lost a game since we were data-processed," he reminded the team. "Let's show them what a computer can do!"

Filled with determination, Ollie whacked a clothesline drive into right field for a single. Then Tony Girard singled to left field. The Red Sox fans came to life, sensing a rally.

Sue Turner kept their hopes alive by bunting in front of home plate for a perfect sacrifice. She was out, but the runners advanced to second and third. Patty Finnegan stepped up to the plate and smote a terrific triple. Ollie and Tony scampered home to narrow the gap six to four.

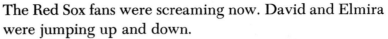

The Red Sox fans were screaming now. David and Elmira were jumping up and down.

That was the end of the rally. Patty died on third as Bruce set down two batters in a row. The Braves picked up a run in the fifth, while the Red Sox went scoreless. Dusty bore down hard in the top of the sixth and slammed the door in the Braves' faces. The Red Sox came to bat in the bottom of the sixth and final inning on the short end of a seven-to-four score. They needed three runs to tie, four to win.

"You're playing great ball, gang," Miss Carmody said. "Now let's go! Dusty, you're up. Barney, on deck!"

No one could say they didn't give their all, Ollie thought as he watched Dusty and Barney Sawyer spark another rally. Dusty helped his own cause by banging a grounder between first and second for a single. Barney dropped a mean one into short left for another. Bruce started to show the strain and walked little Herbie Snell to load the bases. Then he got stingy again and fanned the next two batters.

Ollie came up to the plate like someone walking in a dream. In fact, it was just like that dream he had in class, which seemed a long time ago. When the count went to three and two, it was exactly like the dream. There were two men away, last of the sixth with the bases loaded. His team was three runs behind. Even his desperate teammates were silent behind him on the bench. The crowd was hushed. It was so quiet you could have heard a fly ball drop.

Yet Ollie had never been more sure of himself in his life. He smiled, stepped out of the batter's box, lifted his right arm, and pointed to the right field fence. There could be no mistaking that gesture. Ollie was boldly predicting a home run.

A gasp rose from the crowd and swelled from one end of the bleachers to the other.

Bruce's mouth tightened. He checked the runners, reared back, and fired a fast ball right across the plate. Ollie stepped into the ball with perfect timing. At the instant his weight shifted to his forward foot, the bat met the ball cleanly. Ollie had a nice solid feeling from the tips of his fingers to the ends of his toes.

The Braves' right fielder, John Tuck, was off at the crack of the bat. Back, back, back he raced—but Ollie smiled to himself as he rounded the bases to the roar of the Red Sox fans. No one was going to get that ball. It was long gone.

When the tumult died down, Nosy Newman interviewed Miss Carmody and her beaming team. "What a miraculous age we are living in!" he said. "I remember when these players all had two left feet and no hands. Who would have believed that a computer could transform them from a bunch of also-rans into champions?"

Miss Carmody smiled at her team. "It didn't," she replied.

Ollie looked at her, jaw sagging. "Of course it did," he corrected. "We didn't win a game until we were data-processed. Then we filled out these questionnaires, and the computer told us where we should play."

"*I* told you where you should play," Miss Carmody said. "Your father and I didn't like the results the computer showed. Actually, you have all been playing exactly the same positions you had before you filled out those questionnaires—except for shifting the outfield. The difference is that you have been playing those positions with enthusiasm and confidence, instead of complaining and lying down on the job."

She put a hand on Ollie's shoulder. "What it all proves is this—if we just accept the duties we are assigned and do our very best, we can accomplish wonders."

Ollie scratched his head. One big question remained unanswered. "Why didn't you like the results the computer showed?"

Miss Carmody looked at Mr. Scruggs and winked. "The IDIOT showed that every player on the squad should be a pitcher," she replied.

Reflections

1. Why were the Red Sox in trouble?
2. Do you think Ollie's solution to the Red Sox's problem was a good one? Tell why or why not.
3. How was the Red Sox team changed by being data-processed?
4. How are questions fed into a computer? In what form do the answers come from the computer?
5. What caused Ollie's daydream to come true?
6. If you had been Ollie's father, what would you have done with the computer results?
7. What do you think Nosy said in his final news story? Put yourself in his place and write an account for the *Courier*. Write it in newspaper style.

RUNNING, JUMPING, SPINNING

Dorothy Hamill *(top left)* won a gold medal in figure skating in the 1976 Olympics at Innsbruck, Austria.

Wilma Rudolph *(bottom left),* won three gold medals for the United States in the 1960 Olympics. While performing for Tennessee A&I, this runner broke record after world's record.

Billy Mills *(above),* an American Indian from South Dakota, set an Olympic record in the 10,000-meter run in Tokyo in 1964. In 1976 he was elected to the National Track and Field Hall of Fame.

83

Roberto Clemente Dies In Plane Crash

San Juan, P.R., Jan. 1 (UPI) Baseball great Roberto Clemente and four other persons were killed New Year's Eve when the DC-7 the Pittsburgh Pirate idol had chartered crashed into the Atlantic. The plane was on a mercy flight to the earthquake-ravaged country of Nicaragua.

Roberto Clemente

The airplane developed engine trouble after take-off from San Juan. It was trying to return to the airport when it went down in 80 feet of water about a mile off the coast. A United States Coast Guard cutter and a Navy helicopter reported finding bits of wreck-age, life jackets, luggage, and boxes filled with relief supplies.

Headed Relief Committee

Clemente was the head of a local committee which gathered tons of relief supplies for victims of the recent earthquake in Nicaragua. The city of Managua, capital of this Central American republic, was nearly leveled by the earthquake.

Clemente, 38, was a national hero of Puerto Rico, where three days of national mourning were proclaimed.

Clemente was the star of the 1971 World Series. In the Series, Pittsburgh defeated the Baltimore Orioles in seven games. He was named to the National League All-Star team 12 times. And he won the National League batting title four times.

Somoza Sends Cable

Anastasio Somoza, former president of Nicaragua, sent a cable to the Clemente family. He said, "Clemente died as a hero, leaving his family in order to aid humanity."

Rafael Hernandez Colon, Governor-Elect of the Commonwealth, postponed a "people's" reception.

"Roberto died in moments in which he was serving his fellow man. Our youth loses an idol and an example. Our people loses one of their glories," Colon said.

Roberto Clemente at bat as a pinch-hitter in the ninth inning against the Chicago Cubs.

Reflections

1. In the first paragraph of most news stories, you will find the answers to five questions: Who? What? Where? When? Why? Read the first paragraph of the story. *Who* is the story about? *What* happened? *Where* did it happen? *When* did it happen? *Why* did it happen?

2. The remaining paragraphs of a news story give more details. What additional facts about the plane crash does the second paragraph give? What additional information do you find in the third paragraph?

3. In a news story, the most important facts are given first. Can you think of some reasons for this?

4. Write a news story about something that has happened recently in your school or community. Try to follow the pattern of the article on Roberto Clemente.

Extra! Extra!

ELLEN CONFORD

For as long as she could remember, Dorrie Kimball had been after her father to put her picture in his weekly newspaper. But he had always refused. He said that would be nepotism. Nepotism, he told Dorrie, is when you do a favor for a relative, even when they don't deserve it.

Mrs. O'Neill, Dorrie Kimball's sixth-grade teacher asked her class to form committees. Each group was to prepare a special project for Children's Book Week. Charles, Haskell, and Serena were on Dorrie's committee.

Dorrie and Her Committee

I woke up the next morning with the most fantastic idea for our project. I couldn't imagine where I'd gotten it. I hadn't been able to think of anything before I fell asleep. It just came to me, out of no place, as I was getting out of bed.

I dashed down the stairs. My father and mother were at the breakfast table. "Dad," I began, after he had had two cups of coffee. "We have to do a project for Children's

Book Week. Now I have this terrific idea for my committee—did you know I'm the head of the committee?"

"Your mother told me."

"Oh, well, see the thing is, I need some help."

"What do I have to build?" he asked suspiciously.

"No, nothing like that. Anybody could do that."

"Uh oh. I smell something big and expensive coming up."

"Well," I said meekly, "I don't know how expensive it would be, but it is kind of big."

"You'd better stop trying to break it to me gently. What is it?"

"A newspaper," I said eagerly. "I want to know if you could print us up a newspaper."

"A newspaper! But that's a very big—"

"Well," I said defensively, "I told you it might be big."

"But, Dorrie, you're supposed to be doing the project."

"We will! We'll do all the writing and the pictures and everything. All you have to do is print it. Would that be very expensive?"

"All I have to do is print it," he repeated, shaking his head. "You'd better tell me more."

So I did. I told him all my ideas, and while he listened, he began to smile. I could see that he thought it was a good project.

"You're sure it will be only four pages—"

"Oh, sure," I said excitedly. "Only four pages."

"Well, I guess I could—"

"Oh, thank you! Thank you!" I yelled. I flung my arms around him just as he put down his coffee cup.

"DORRIE!" he howled. His cup overturned and coffee splashed all over the table and dribbled down into his lap.

"I'm sorry," I said feebly, backing out of the way as he leaped up from his chair. He glowered at me.

Dorrie's committee got together after school to talk about their project. Dorrie waited impatiently till the others were finished.

"All right," I said eagerly. "Here's my idea. It's a newspaper. My father will print it up for us himself, and it'll look really professional. All we have to do is write the stories and draw some pictures."

"What kind of a newspaper?" Charles asked curiously.

"A special edition of the *Leader,* put out just for Book Week."

"Oh, no, you mean with book reports in it?" Charles asked.

"No, nothing like that," I said. "This will be putting famous books into news stories, with headlines and pictures and things. Like for instance, take *Alice in Wonderland.* The headline would say, 'Girl Falls Down Rabbit Hole. Alice Tells of Strange Adventures.' Then you could have a news article underneath it, and I thought it could end, 'She is now under examination at the county hospital.' "

"That's not bad," Charles said thoughtfully. "But could we fill up a whole newspaper with that stuff?"

"Sure we could. It'll only be four pages, and we could do drawings and things if we run out of ideas."

"I think it's a great idea," said Serena. She sounded interested for the first time since we began the project.

"We might," said Haskell suddenly, "do classified ads too. For instance," he went on with a little grin, "Lost, flock of sheep. Owner heartbroken. Generous reward. Call Bo-Peep."

"Or," Charles suggested, "Real Estate: Large house with 14 bedrooms desperately needed. Contact old woman in shoe."

"And we could have the Recipe of the Day," Serena broke in. "Blackbird pie. Take four and twenty blackbirds and a very big pie plate—"

"Can anyone besides me type?" I asked. "We have to make neat copies for the printers."

"I can type," Charles volunteered. "But not fast."

"That's okay," I said, relieved. "We can divide up the typing between us."

"And I can do the pictures," offered Serena.

Putting the Paper Together

The weeks ran together like a blur. The only thing I could think about was our Book Week newspaper. I would be in the middle of watching television, and an idea would come to me. Or I'd be brushing my teeth and all of a sudden I would think, "Piper's Son, Tom, Steals Pig. Escapes Police Dragnet."

There didn't seem to be enough time to work on our project during school, so I began to call committee meetings for after school at my house.

A couple of times my father sat in on our meetings, and explained to us about counting paragraph inches and leaving enough space for pictures, and making headlines fit the columns and setting up a dummy page.

"I didn't realize," Serena said at one of these meetings, "how much work this was going to be."

"Neither did I," I admitted.

Charles and I began typing up the stories. Time was running out and even as we began to type up our final copies for the printer, we kept thinking of new ideas for articles.

TOM SAWYER HOLDS PAINT-IN
YOUNGSTERS FLOCK TO TAKE
PART IN STREET BEAUTIFICATION PROJECT

Serena drew picture after picture, till she had one for almost every story we'd written. Then we made up captions for them: "Little Women who want to do their bit for the soldiers. Meg, Jo, Beth, and Amy knit stockings."

The Wednesday before Book Week we met at my house and made our final choices of articles and pictures. We did a rough layout, as my father had explained, to get an idea of where we'd put everything, and how the paper would look when it was finished.

On Thursday morning, my father took all our material to the office with him. The printers were going to set up the galleys, and he would bring the proofs home in the afternoon.

That day the committee had its final meeting. We had to proofread everything to check for mistakes and correct the few we found. Then we had to cut stories out of the long sheets of paper that were the galley proofs and paste

them onto a dummy sheet the same size as our newspaper.

My mother made franks and beans for everyone so no one would have to go home for dinner. We didn't finish the paper until seven-thirty.

When it was finally done, my father checked it over one last time while we slumped, exhausted, on the living room floor.

"This is a fine job," he announced at last.

"Thank goodness!" Serena sighed with relief.

Haskell gave a weak cheer, and slapped hands with Charles.

"Now how many copies should I make up?" my father asked.

"I never thought of that," I realized. "I guess one for

everybody in the class, and an extra one for Mrs. O'Neill."

"You know, once the type is set it's as easy to make a hundred as it is to make twenty-five," he said.

"Then why don't we make enough for the whole school?" Serena suggested eagerly. "Mrs. O'Neill wants to display the projects and have the other classes come in and see them. She said we would do things the whole school could enjoy—"

"So you'll need about a thousand?"

"Will that be too expensive?" I worried.

"No, it's all right," he assured me. "With the free advertising you gave me, it's worth it."

On the front page, in a little box, we had set up a plug for my father's paper. It read: "The *Book Week Leader* is grateful to the *Brockton Center Leader* for printing this special edition. For news of the real world, read the *Leader* every Thursday."

At first my father hadn't wanted to put it in, being against nepotism and everything. But the committee insisted. We said if he made us leave it out, it would be censorship. If there's one thing my father hates more than nepotism, it's censorship; so he finally agreed to let us do it.

I couldn't wait for school to be over on Friday. My father was going to bring the finished paper home with him, and I was a nervous wreck all day, wondering how it would turn out.

My father came home just before dinner, and I flung myself at him when he was barely over the threshold.

"Let me see it! Did it come out okay? How does it look?"

"Here," he said, handing me a bunch of papers. "See for yourself. I think it came out beautifully."

My mother came up behind me and reached for a copy. "I've been waiting all day for this. Oh, Dorrie! It's beautiful!" She sat down on the couch and began to read it. She turned the pages eagerly. Every once in a while she smiled or laughed, and pointed out something she especially liked to my father.

It was beautiful. It looked just like the *Leader*, but it had only four pages. *Book Week Leader* was in the same kind of type my father uses for *Brockton Center Leader* on the top of the front page. Serena's pictures had come out perfectly.

I smiled as I re-read the stories and headlines that I already knew practically by heart.

R. CRUSOE LOST AT SEA

TORNADO RIPS HOUSE FROM KANSAS FARM
Girl, Dog, and House Vanish During Killer Storm

QUICK-THINKING YOUNGSTER PLUGS DIKE
Saves Holland from Flood Disaster

"Oh, it's gorgeous, gorgeous!" I cried. "Isn't it? Oh, it's just the way I pictured it. No, it's better!"

> *When Dorrie woke up Monday morning, it was snowing. And her throat hurt. She felt terrible.*
> *Just as they were about to leave, Dan, Mr. Kimball's photographer, and Haskell showed up. It was a good thing. They could help carry the cartons of newspapers into the school.*

The Big Day

My father parked in front of the main entrance to the school, and we each carried in a carton. They weighed about a ton apiece, and we practically staggered up the steps and inside.

Charles and Serena were already there, waiting for us.

Serena grabbed a paper from one of the cartons. "Oh, it looks great!" she exclaimed, holding it a little away from herself like she was admiring a painting.

"You can look at it later," Charles said, hoisting a pile of papers up to the Lost and Found table. "Let's get set

up before the kids start coming in. We have two other
entrances to cover."

Serena had made three posters which read: *BOOK
WEEK LEADER* FREE! TAKE ONE! She'd already
taped one to the Lost and Found table, pushing aside the
stray gloves, hats, scarves, and gym shirts so we'd have a
place to put the papers. The other two posters were for
the other doors to the school, where she and Charles were
going to hand out papers to the kids who came in that
way.

"Before you go," my father said to Charles and Serena,
"let's have Dan take a picture of the committee in back of
the poster. We'll have copies made up for all of you; then

you'll always have something to remind you of how hard you worked on this."

"Oh, I'll never forget that," Serena groaned.

Haskell, Serena, Charles, and I grouped ourselves behind the table and held up a copy of the *Book Week Leader.*

"Don't all stare at the camera," my father advised. "Dorrie, open the paper and everybody pretend to be reading it."

So I did, holding it up so the front page would show in the picture.

"Now look at the paper. Don't look at Dan."

"Got it!" Dan said as the flashbulb blazed.

"Okay," my father said. "We've got to get to a town board meeting now. I'll have those pictures made up for you in a couple of days."

"So long," I said, patting his arm. "Thanks a lot, Dad."

"It was fun," he said. "Sort of. Good luck!"

We spent most of the morning setting up our projects around the room. All of the committee leaders described their projects and how they were done. I don't even remember what I said, because by that time I really felt awful, and I was sure I had a fever of about 109°.

But I didn't want to go down to the nurse's office and be sent home. Not today. Even if I was on the verge of pneumonia, I was enjoying myself more than I ever had in school. I didn't want to miss one minute of this day.

While I don't remember what I said about our project, I remember very well what Mrs. O'Neill said.

"This is a marvelous, original idea. You did a beautiful job. I just don't see how you could have made it any better."

And in the afternoon, although I still felt sick, I enjoyed hearing the kids in the other classes, whom Mrs. O'Neill had invited to see our projects, exclaim, "Oh, there's the paper!" It had been pasted up on the outside of the classroom door.

But by three o'clock I was glad that it was time to go home. I was too tired to think straight.

Is It Nepotism?

My father came home very late on Thursday.

"How are you feeling?" he asked, coming into my room with my mother.

"A little better," I said.

"Hal," my mother said, "will you please—"

"What's the matter?" I asked.

"Oh, your mother's very worked up about something she saw in the paper," he grinned.

"In what paper? The *Leader?*" There's usually only local news in my father's paper, and I can never find anything in it to get worked up about. Maybe they were raising town taxes or building a swamp across the street from our house.

"What is it?" I asked curiously.

"Oh, nothing," he said carelessly. He handed me the paper, opened to an inside page. "Just that."

The headline and picture leaped out at me from the page.

STUDENTS PUBLISH SPECIAL ISSUE OF LEADER
Book Week Project Surprises Parkview School

And next to the story was the picture Dan had taken of us. I was holding up the *Book Week Leader,* with Charles, Serena, and Haskell reading it over my shoulder.

I just sat there with my mouth open, unable to say a

word. I touched the picture with my fingertips, trying to convince myself that it was real.

"Dorrie Kimball," it said under the picture, "with her committee, Serena Blood, Charles Abbot, and Haskell Conger, reading the hot-off-the-presses *Book Week Leader.*"

"You put my picture in the paper," I said at last. "You really put my picture in the paper.

"I can't believe it," I breathed. "I just—I mean, nepotism and all—"

"This isn't nepotism," my father objected, grinning broadly. "You did something newsworthy. I told you, all you had to do to get your picture in the paper was—"

"OHH!" I shrieked, leaping up onto my bed and flinging the paper into the air. "I'm in the paper! I'm famous!"

I hurled myself at my parents, hugging both of them so hard, I nearly knocked their heads together.

"Dorrie!" they gasped, hugging me back. "Please!"

Reflections

1. Which stories or poems can you identify from the headlines?
2. What were some of the things the committee had to do to prepare the newspaper?
3. Were Dorrie's parents proud of her? What evidence can you give?
4. Do you agree with Mr. Kimball that nepotism is a bad thing? Why or why not?
5. Write an article for the *Book Week Leader*. For your subject, choose a book you have read recently. Be sure to include the answers to the questions Who? What? Where? When? and Why? in your first paragraph. Write a snappy headline for your story.

ON A NEWSPAPER

If you like to write, have a nose for news, and can work under pressure, there may be a job for you as a reporter. Or if you like to work with computers or machines, your place may be in the bustling composing room or in the pressroom.

The newsroom of a daily paper is one of the noisiest, busiest rooms on earth. As deadline time approaches, the room is filled with the ringing of telephones and the rising voices of **editors** and **reporters.** Here *(top)* an editor and two reporters talk over a story.

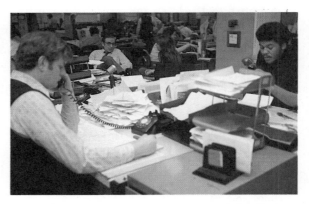

(center) A **rewrite reporter** takes notes from a reporter who is phoning in her story from where it is all happening.

Next the story is typed on a computer terminal keyboard *(bottom)* with the text displayed on a video screen. The story is stored in the computer's memory until an editor recalls it to edit it.

Once the final command is given to the computer, the photo-composing machine produces long columns of type on photosensitive paper. Editors make dummy pages showing where stories, headlines, and photographs are to appear. **Layout technicians** go to work pasting the stories into position *(top)* on the page.

Next, each completed page is photographed. From the negative a plastic plate is made which is used in the printing process.

In the pressroom, **printers** fasten the plates to cylindrical presses *(bottom)*. Some presses can produce a stream of about 120,000 copies an hour. Huge machines print and fold the papers. **Drivers** and their trucks are waiting. Tomorrow's newspaper will soon be on the streets.

PRINT AND SPEECH

Our writing system, based on the Greek and Roman alphabets, depends on arranging lines of writing from left to right, one after another on pages. It depends on orderly spelling, on space between words, on punctuation, and on capitalization. A writing system is a code designed to capture the sounds of spoken language.

Here are some exercises, using our own alphabet, to show you how some other writing systems work. Study each exercise. Figure out what is happening. Then copy your solution to each on a sheet of paper.

1. THEROMANSUSEDONLYCAPITALLETTERSTOWRITE
   THELATINLANGUAGEBECAUSETHESMALLLETTERS
   HADNOTBEENINVENTED.EARLYROMANWRITINGDID
   NOTSEPARATEWORDSWITHASPACEBETWEENTHEM.

Do you think you would be a better reader if we used only capital letters? Give reasons for your answer. What are the advantages and disadvantages of the old Roman system of writing?

2. VERYEARLYINTHEHISTORYOFGREEKWRITING
   OTTFELMORFENILENOETORWSKEERGEHT
   RIGHTANDTHENEXTLINEFROMRIGHTTO
   ETARAPESOTECAPSESUTONDIDYEHT.TFEL
   WORDS.THEYOFTENOMITTEDVOWELSINWRITING.

   THSLNHSNVWLSCNYSPPLTHMNDBRKTHSCD

What are the advantages and disadvantages of the early Greek way of writing?

103

3. The people of Japan do not use an alphabet. They have developed a different kind of writing system. This exercise uses our alphabet, but the words are arranged as they would be in one kind of Japanese writing. Can you figure out what is happening here?

```
T   U   T   D   A   T   B   Y   T   I
H   N   H   O   N   H   Y   O   A   F
E   T   E   W   D   E       U   U
    I   N   N           S       G   Y
B   L           W   U   T   W   H   O
O       M   O   O   P   A   O   T   U
T   E   O   N   U   P   R   U
T   N   V   E   L   E   T   L   I   H
O   D   E       D   R   I   D   N   A
M   I       C           N           D
    N   L   O   R   R   G   R   J
L   G   E   L   E   I       E   A   B
E       F   U   A   G       A   P   E
F   A   T   M   D   H       D   A   E
T   T       N       T           N   N
```

Do you think that there are advantages or disadvantages in this arrangement? Why? Explain how it differs from the arrangement of words in written English.

How Writing Captures Sound

Written language makes no sounds. Language as we speak it is partly sound, partly gesture and expression. When you read, you match the sounds you make or think with written letters or combinations of letters.

The following exercise will show you how this can work with three sounds: the sound shown by *k* in *keep*, the sound shown by *u* in *flu*, and the sound shown by *sh* in *ship*.

Copy *keep*, *flu*, and *ship* on the first line of a sheet of paper. Then rearrange the words below under the three key words, paying attention to the underlined parts. Be sure to match the words with the proper sound.

cash	rule	acquaint
canoe	account	fruit
ship	Bacchus	grew
maneuver	flue	character
tack	group	tissue
ocean	two	move
biscuit	machine	sacque
special	barbeque	keep
nauseous	mansion	sugar
schnitzel	mention	conscience

How many ways do we spell the *u* sound shown by *u* in *flu?* the *sh* sound in *ship?* the *k* sound in *keep?*

The good reader masters the relationship between sounds and the letters used to show them. You will improve in reading as you learn more and more about the connection between spoken sounds and written letters.

Unit 2 ALL OF YOUR DREAMS

The Dream Keeper

Bring me all of your dreams,
You dreamers,
Bring me all of your
Heart melodies
That I may wrap them
In a blue cloud-cloth
Away from the too-rough fingers
Of the world.

Langston Hughes

The Forgotten Door
ALEXANDER KEY

He Is Lost and Found

It happened so quickly, so unexpectedly, that Little Jon's cry was almost instantly cut short as the blackness closed over him. No one knew the hole was there. It hadn't been there the day before, and in the twilight no one had noticed it.

At the moment it happened, the first shooting stars were crossing the sky—they were beginning to stream across like strings of jewels flung from another planet—and everyone was watching them. The smaller children were exclaiming in delight, while the older ones stood silent and enthralled. Here on the hill, where the valley people often came to watch the glittering night unfold, you could see the whole magic sweep around you, and you felt close to everything in the heavens. Other people, you knew, were standing on other hills on other worlds, watching even as you watched.

Little Jon, whose eyes were quicker than most, should have seen the hole, but all his attention was on the stars. Small for his age, he had moved away from the rest for a better view, and as he stepped backward, there was suddenly nothing under his feet.

It was astonishing at that moment to find himself falling swiftly into the hill at a spot where he had walked safely all his life. But in the brief seconds before the blackness swallowed him, he realized what must have happened: there had been a cave-in over the old door—the door that led to another place, the one that had been closed so long.

He cried out and tried to break his fall in the way he had been taught, but the effort came an instant too late. His head struck something, and darkness engulfed him.

Long later, when Little Jon was able to sit up, he had no idea where he was or what had happened. Memory had fled, and he ached all over. He would have been shivering with cold, but his thick jacket and trousers and heavy, woven boots kept him warm.

He seemed to be in a narrow cleft of broken rock. There were mossy stones around him, and just ahead he could make out a bed of ferns where water trickled from a spring. He was still too dazed to be frightened, but now he realized he was thirsty, terribly so. He crawled painfully forward and lay with his face in the water while he drank.

The coldness of the water startled him at first, but it was wonderfully sweet and satisfying. He bathed his face and hands in it, then sat up at last and looked around again.

Where was he? How did he get here? He pondered these questions, but no answers came. He felt as if he had fallen. Only—where could he have fallen *from?* The rocky walls met overhead, sloping outward into a tangle of leafy branches.

There was another question his mind carefully tiptoed around, because it was more upsetting than the others. Whenever he approached it, it caused a dull aching in his forehead. Finally, however, he gave his head a small shake and faced it squarely.

"Who am I?"

He didn't know. He simply didn't know, and it made everything terribly wrong.

All at once, trembling, he got to his feet and fled limping toward a shaft of sunlight ahead. Thick shrubs barred his way. He fought blindly through them, tripped, and fell sprawling. Fortunately he missed the boulders on either side and landed in a soft bed of old leaves under a tree. He scrambled up in panic, started to run again, then stopped himself just in time.

This wasn't the sort of country where you could run. There were steep ledges here, and below them the ground sloped sharply downward for a great distance. All of it was covered with a wild tangle of forest. Little Jon rubbed his eyes and looked around him with growing wonder and fright.

Nothing here was familiar. He was *sure* of that. He had never seen trees quite like the ones around him. Many of the smaller trees were in bloom, covered with showers of white blossoms—these were *almost* familiar, as were the ferns and lichens on the rocks. But there was a differ-ence. But what the difference was, he was unable to tell.

Carefully he worked down to an open area below the ledge and stood listening. The *sounds* were familiar, and hearing them made him feel a bit better. Birdsong, the gurgling of hidden springs, the faint clatter and fuss of a rushing stream somewhere. And there were the hesitant steps of wild creatures that came pleasantly to his sharp ears. Without quite realizing his ability, which was as natural as breathing, his mind reached toward them and found nothing strange in them—except that they were afraid. Afraid of him!

"Don't be afraid," he told them, so softly that his lips barely moved. "I'd *never* hurt you."

After a minute two of the creatures—they were a doe and her fawn—moved hesitantly down the slope and stood looking at him curiously. Little Jon held out his hands, and presently the doe came close and nuzzled his cheek with her cold nose.

"Where am I?" he asked her plaintively. "Can you tell me?"

The doe couldn't answer, and all he could gather was that she was hungry and that food could be found in the valley below.

"Lead the way," he told her. "I'll follow."

The doe and the fawn started down through the tangle. Little Jon went scrambling and limping behind them. Walking was difficult, for both his knees were badly bruised, and one ankle pained with every step. Soon, however, they reached a winding game trail, and the going was much easier. Even so, it was hard to keep up with the doe, and several times in the next hour he had to beg her to stop and wait for him.

It did not seem at all strange to be following her. Her presence was very comforting and kept the unanswered questions from troubling him.

As they wound down near the bottom of the slope, the trees thinned and they passed through an open gate. Ahead he could see bright sunlight on a small greening field. Around a corner of the field ran a clattering

stream—a stream different from the one he had heard earlier.

At the sight of the field, Little Jon caught his breath. Fields and cultivated things were familiar. There would be people near. Soon he would meet them and find out about himself.

The doe paused at the edge of the field, sniffing the air currents. Little Jon could feel her uneasiness, though he could not understand it. He sniffed, too, but all he could smell were the pleasant scents of fresh earth and blossoms and the richness of the forest behind them. He was disappointed that he couldn't make out the scent of humans near, but maybe this was because the air was flowing down from the mountain, away from him.

As the doe stepped daintily into the field and began to nibble the young plants, Little Jon unconsciously did what he should have done earlier. His mind reached out, searching hopefully. He had no thought of danger. The sudden discovery that there *was* danger was so shocking that he could only spring forward with a strangled cry.

The doe whirled instantly and leaped, just as the sharp report of a rifle shattered the peace of the morning.

Little Jon had never heard a rifle shot before, but he was aware of the hot slash of pain across the doe's flank, and he could see the weapon in the hands of the man who rose from his hiding place at the edge of the stream. He was a lean man in overalls, with one shoulder higher than the other. The harsh features under the cap showed surprise and disbelief as he stared at Little Jon. Then the thin mouth twisted in fury.

"You ruint my aim!" the man roared, striding forward. "What you doin' in my field?"

Little Jon could make nothing of the words. The language was strange, but the hate-driven thoughts behind it were clear enough. For a moment he stood incredulous, his mind trying to fight through the shock of what had happened. Surely the man approaching was a being like himself. But why the intent to kill another creature? Why the sudden hate? How could anyone ever, ever . . .

The anger that rose in him was a new thing. It was something he had never experienced before, at least in this measure. His small hands balled into fists, and he trembled. But just as quickly, he realized that he couldn't quench hate with hate and that now there was danger to himself. He turned abruptly and fled.

"Stop!" the man bellowed, close behind him. "I know you—you're one o' them Cherokees from over the ridge! I'll teach you to come meddlin' on my land!"

Little Jon tried to lighten his feet and put distance between himself and his pursuer. Ordinarily he might have managed it in spite of his pains, but he knew nothing of barbed-wire fences. The rusty wires were hidden by the shrubbery until he was almost on them. When he attempted to slide through them, the barbs caught his jacket. The tough material refused to tear. In another second he was squirming in the man's firm grasp.

The man dragged him roughly back to the field, then turned at the sound of an approaching motor. Presently a small farm truck whirled around the bend of the creek and stopped close by. A large woman, wearing faded overalls, got out and came over to them. She had a full face, with small, shrewd eyes as hard and round as creek pebbles.

Little Jon had never seen a woman like her. Though he was repelled by her, she drew his attention far more than the truck, which was equally strange.

"I declare!" she muttered, staring. "What you got there, Gilby?"

"Not what I was aimin' at," the man growled. "The thievin' varmint spoiled my shot."

"Just as well, I reckon, or he'd tell someone. Whose kid is he?"

"Dunno, Emma. Figured 'im for a Cherokee, but—"

"Pshaw, *he* ain't no Indian," she interrupted, peering closer.

"Got long, black hair like most of them. Could be half an' half."

"H'mp! Look at them *clothes!* Seems more foreignlike. Gypsy, maybe. Where you from, boy?"

Little Jon clenched his teeth and looked stonily back at her. Though her speech was strange, the rising questions and her ugly thoughts were easily understood. She was a person to be avoided, and he wouldn't have answered her even if he had known how.

"You better answer me! Cat got your tongue?" she snapped.

As the woman spoke, Jon drew back abruptly to avoid her unwelcome inspection and curious questioning. As he did so, the man unclenched his hand to get a better grip on him. Immediately Little Jon twisted free and ran.

This time he was able to lighten his feet and went over the fence in a bound. He heard gasps of astonishment behind him, then shouts, and the man's pursuing footsteps. Presently these sounds faded, and the forest was quiet.

Little Jon ran on until he was nearly exhausted. He would have followed the doe and the fawn, but they had gone over a ridge where the way was too steep for his throbbing ankle.

Finally he huddled by a fallen log, removed one boot, and rubbed his swollen ankle while he gained his breath. Tears rolled down his cheeks. He missed the doe terribly. She was his only friend in all this strangeness.

Suddenly he dug his knuckles into his eyes, drew on his boot, and struggled to his feet. He couldn't stay here all day. It solved nothing. He had to keep moving, keep searching . . .

Resolutely he began limping around the curve of the slope, taking the easiest course. Somewhere there must be other people—people unlike those behind him. But when he found them, he would have to be very careful.

He heard the soft slither of the snake ahead before he saw it, even before it rattled its deadly warning. Its sudden rattle astonished him. He stared at it with more curiosity than fear. What a strange creature, legless and covered with scales, and with a rattle on the end of its tail! It seemed he had heard of such things, vaguely, just as he had heard of the odd kind of vehicle the woman had driven. But where?

Troubled, he limped carefully around the snake. With the thought that there might be other dangers here, dangers he knew nothing about, he drew a knife from his belt and cut a staff from the shrubbery. The small knife felt so much a part of him that he hardly questioned it till he had finished using it. It was only a tool—it seemed that someone had given it to him long ago—but he couldn't remember any more about it.

The staff made walking easier for a while, and he trudged painfully on, stopping at times to rest or to drink from one of the many springs. The sun, which he could glimpse only at intervals through the trees, began to sink behind him. He was very hungry, and his eyes searched continually for food. There ought to be berries. He had noticed some earlier, growing near the barbed-wire fence where the man had caught him.

Edible things, he decided finally, must grow in the open places, lower down.

Warily, slowly, he began to angle toward the valley. He reached the bottom of the slope much sooner than he had expected, only to discover that the valley had vanished. Another slope rose immediately ahead. In sudden alarm he realized he could no longer see the sun. With every step the gloom was deepening. The forest had chilled, and for the first time he saw the gray mist creeping down from above.

The gloom, the chill, and the creeping mist in this strange and bewildering land, together with his growing hunger and lameness, were almost too much. A sob broke from his lips, and he began to tremble with a black dread. He couldn't go much farther. What would he do when darkness came?

Then, like a glow of warmth in the chill, he felt the comforting knowledge of wild creatures near. They were friendly, but timid. He was on the point of calling to them when he heard the distant sound of a motor.

He stiffened, his hands clenched tightly on his staff. Memory of the angry man and harsh woman rose like a warning. He shook off the thought of them. He *had* to go on. It was the only way . . .

Abruptly he began plunging toward the sound, following the narrow gully that curved away on his right.

A half hour later he broke through a tangle of evergreens and stared in amazement at the scene ahead.

He was on the edge of a steep bank that dropped down to a winding gravel road. Beyond the road a broad valley opened. The valley was ringed by wave on wave of blue and purple mountains that rose to the clouds. The valley was in shadow, but he could make out the farms with their little white houses and see animals grazing in the pastures.

The motor he had heard earlier had passed, but a second one was approaching. Instantly his mind went out to it, exploring. There were several people in the vehicle, and they were very different from the ones he had met—but not different in a way that mattered. As the machine swung into sight, he allowed himself only a curious glimpse of its bright newness before he cowered back into the tangle.

The shadows deepened in the valley and began to creep over the distant mountains. Three more vehicles passed, and once a man on a horse went by. The horse sensed his presence and whinnied. Little Jon liked the horse, but he fought down the urge to call to it, for the man filled him with uneasiness.

It was nearly dark when he heard the final motor. This time, aware of the friendliness of its occupants—and something beyond friendliness—he did not hesitate. It was a small truck, and as it swung around the bend in the road, he slid quickly down the bank to meet it.

He Gains a Home

As his boots struck the edge of the road, his bad ankle gave way under him, and Little Jon fell in a heap. For a moment he was afraid the truck would go past without anyone noticing him. Its headlights were on, but the beams were sweeping beyond him around the curve.

He managed to struggle upright for a moment, then sank weakly to his knees. He had dropped his staff and found that he could hardly stand without it.

The truck braked suddenly and stopped. A man leaned out and said in quick concern, "Hey there, young fellow! What seems to be wrong?"

Little Jon opened his mouth soundlessly and raised one hand. He heard a woman's voice say, "For heaven's sake, children, let me out—I think the boy's hurt!"

Both doors of the truck flew open. The man stepped out of the driver's side, and a boy and a girl tumbled from the other, followed by the woman. Little Jon saw that the girl was about his own size. The boy was much larger, but he seemed no older than himself. Both wore jackets and blue jeans, like the woman.

Though the man was nearer, he moved with a slight limp, and the woman reached him first. "My goodness, honey," she said, stooping and raising him gently, "your face and hands are all scraped. Did you have a fall?"

He nodded, and the man asked, "Are you hurt badly?"

Little Jon shook his head. His eyes swung quickly from one to the other. The woman wore a green scarf around her bright hair. There were freckles across her lean cheeks, and small laughter creases at the corners of her eyes and mouth. The man had a thick shock of dark hair graying at the temples; his face was ruddy, but deeply lined.

The man said, "Can you tell us where you live, sonny?"

Little Jon shook his head again. There was sudden silence. The woman bit her lip, then asked quietly, "Can you understand what we are saying?"

Again he nodded, and she said, "Thomas, I believe he's had a bad shock that keeps him from speaking. I—I hate to take him to the hospital. I think all he needs is a hot meal and some rest."

"We're taking him home with us," the man said definitely. "If he's been lost in the mountains all day, he's had it." He jerked his head at the boy and girl. "Sally, you and Brooks ride in the back of the truck. Mary—"

"I'll carry him," she said. "He hardly weighs what Sally does."

"Mommy," said Sally, speaking for the first time. "Where do you think he's from?"

"I can't guess, but it doesn't make any difference. He needs help and that's all that matters. All aboard!"

She swung Little Jon into the truck and settled him on the seat beside her. The two children scrambled into the back, and the man slid behind the wheel.

While the truck wound along the road, Little Jon sat with his hands clenched, trying to suppress the sudden tears of thankfulness that ran down his cheeks. It was so wonderful to find people who were, well, like people should be. If only he could talk to them and explain . . .

He tried to fit their spoken words to the thoughts he had felt in them. Their names he knew: Thomas, Mary, Sally, Brooks. His quick ears had already picked out scores of words for his eager memory to hold, but fitting them to the right thoughts would take time. He wished they would speak more, but they said little during the drive.

Even so, he was aware of questions in all of them. The man: "Odd—never saw a boy like him. Can't be from around here." The woman: "There's something very strange about him. It's not his long hair. We're used to that. His features are so—so sensitive. And his jacket— where in the world can you find material like that?"

The truck slowed presently, and the headlights swept a small brown building with a sign that read "Bean's Rock Shop, Smoky Mountain Gems." The truck turned into a lane beside it and climbed in second gear to a house nearly hidden by evergreens. There was a barn some distance behind the house, and Little Jon was aware of animals there, waiting. A dog barked furiously at them until he gave it an answering thought of friendliness.

They got out, and the woman carried him to the door, which the man opened with a key. Lights came on, and he was placed on a couch by a fireplace. It was a comfortable room, paneled in brown wood. He was aware of a flicker of pride in the man, who had built this home with his own hands.

The man said, "Brooks, you and Sally unload the groceries, then look after the stock."

"Aw, Dad," Brooks grumbled. "Please, can't we—"

"Do as I say, and I'll handle the milking later. There'll be plenty of time to get acquainted with him. And if your mother will whip up some supper for us, I'll build a fire and play doctor. This boy needs attention."

While the man kindled a fire, Little Jon removed his woven boots and carefully rolled his trousers up above his knees.

The man, turning, saw the bruises and whistled softly. He examined them carefully. "You sure got banged up, young fellow, but I don't believe any bones are broken. Some of the Bean family liniment ought to do the trick. Good for all types of ailments from hornet stings to hair loss."

At that moment, as Brooks and his sister were bringing in the last of the groceries, a truck turned into the lane outside. Little Jon sat up quickly, his lips compressed. There was no mistaking the particular sound of that truck.

Brooks peered out of the window. "I think it's Mr. Gilby Pitts, Dad."

Thomas Bean frowned. "Wonder what Gilby—" He stopped and exclaimed, "Hey, young fellow, what's come over you?"

Little Jon was on his feet, trembling, trying to limp away. It was not fear that made him tremble, but a sudden return of the morning's shock, when he had met an evil that was beyond his understanding.

Mary Bean, entering from the kitchen, put her arm around him and asked softly, "Have you had trouble with Mr. Pitts, dear?"

At his tight face and nod, she frowned at her husband. "Thomas, he's afraid of Gilby. I don't know what's happened, but I don't like—"

"Take him into our bedroom and close the door," Thomas Bean said quickly. "Knowing Gilby, I'd just as soon not—"

Save for the forgotten boots near the sofa, the room was clear when the knock sounded.

After an exchange of greetings, Gilby Pitts entered.

"You folks just git home, Tom?" he asked.

"Oh, a short while ago."

"See anything kinda unusual on the way back?"

"Saw a nice sunset. Why?"

"H'mp! I don't pay no mind to sunsets." Gilby shuffled toward the fireplace, rubbing his unshaven jaw against his high shoulder. His narrow eyes darted about the room. "There's queer things goin' on around here, Tom. I don't like it. You still got that bloodhound you raised?"

"No. Traded it to Ben Whipple over at Windy Gap for a calf. Trying to train another dog, but he's a tough one. About got me licked."

"Sure wish you had that hound. I got a mind to go over to Whipple's an' borrow him."

"What on earth for?" Thomas Bean looked at Gilby curiously.

"Might as well tell you, Tom. There's a wild boy loose in this country. Seen 'im with my own eyes. Emma can tell you. I caught the little varmint, but Emma an' me couldn't git nothin' out of him. While we were tryin' to make 'im talk, he tore loose an' took off like a streak. Never seen nothin' like it! Cleared a fence like—like—"

"A wild boy!" Thomas exclaimed. Then he asked softly, "What was he doing when you caught him, Gilby?"

"Trespassin'. An' I got signs up. I—"

"Oh, come now. No one worries about trespassing signs except in hunting season. You know that. We cross each other's land all the time. Saves miles of travel by the roads. I do it all the time when I'm out rock-hunting."

"This is a heap different. I been missing things. I—"

"Did it ever occur to you," Thomas Bean interrupted, "that this boy you're talking about could be lost and in need of help? Why, he could be badly hurt—"

"*He* weren't hurt! You shoulda seen 'im jump!"

"Then you must have frightened him badly. Why did you frighten him?"

"The varmint come sneakin' down to that west field o' mine with the deer. He—"

"With the *deer!*"

"That's what I said. *With the deer.* Just like he was one of 'em!"

Thomas pursed his lips, then said dryly, "You wouldn't have been taking a shot at one, would you, Gilby?"

Gilby Pitts spat angrily into the fireplace. "Fool deer been ruinin' my field. Man's got a right to scare 'em away."

"But the boy—"

"He took off an' got tangled in the barbed-wire fence, or I'd never a caught 'im. Acted like he didn't know the barbed wire was there. But he knowed it the second time, when he busted loose. Sailed right over it like he had wings. I tell you he's wild. Wild as they come." Gilby stopped. In a lower tone he added, "An' that's not all.

He ain't natural. I don't like *unnatural* things around. If there's more like 'im, we ought to know about it."

There was a moment's silence. In the adjoining bedroom, where every word of the conversation could be heard, Mary Bean had opened the liniment bottle and was rubbing Little Jon's bruises. There was wonder in her eyes as she whispered, "Is that true about the deer? You were—friendly with them?"

He nodded, and struggled to fit new words to thoughts. But the words were too few.

"You're an odd one," she whispered. "I wish you could remember your name. Try real hard."

"J—Jon," he said. The name came unbidden to his lips. There was more to it, but the rest would not come.

They fell silent, for Thomas Bean was talking.

"Gilby," said Thomas, "if I were you, I'd go sort of easy about this. Suppose a stray kid from over at the government camp got lost. If he fell and hurt himself, he could wander around in a daze, not even knowing who he was. If you actually found him and scared him away instead of trying to help him, you'd be in for a lot of criticism."

"Well, mebbe . . ."

"What's more, this isn't hunting season, and you'd be in for more trouble if people thought you were trying to sneak some venison."

"Now lissen to me, Tom—"

"I'm only telling you the truth, Gilby. Anyway, it's quite possible that some Cherokee boys from the reservation came over this way on a hike. You know how they are in the spring."

"Aw, I dunno. Emma didn't think he was no Cherokee." Gilby shuffled around, and suddenly muttered, "I declare. Them's queer-lookin' boots yonder."

In the bedroom Mary Bean stood up quickly, alarm in her blue eyes. She went to the door and started to slip into the hall, but at that instant Sally darted past her from the kitchen.

"Hello, Mr. Gilby," Sally chirped brightly, scooping the boots from under Gilby Pitts's nose. "My goodness, Mommy will scalp me if I don't get the mud off these." She skipped back into the kitchen, calling, "Mommy, when are we going to have supper? I'm *hun*gry!"

"Coming in a minute, dear," her mother answered.

Gilby Pitts scowled, rubbed his chin on his high shoulder, and finally shambled toward the door. "Reckon I'll be goin', Tom. Let me know if you hear anything."

"Sure will. Be seeing you."

No one said a word until Gilby Pitts's truck was safely down the road. Then Thomas let out a long breath. "That Gilby!" he muttered.

"Do you think he suspected anything?" Mary said, bringing Little Jon back into the room.

"Probably not. He's just nosy. I only wish he hadn't seen the boy this morning—but maybe I've calmed him down enough so he won't do anything." He grinned suddenly at his daughter. "Thanks, Sally, for snatching the boots. That was quick thinking."

"I deserve a dime for that," Sally said pertly, holding out her hand. "Fork over!" she demanded. "Don't be a stingy-puss."

"Mercenary wretch," he said teasingly, giving her the dime. He stooped and kissed her.

"I'm *not* mercenary," she said. "See, I can give as well as receive." She pressed the dime into Little Jon's hand. "It's yours—and—and I hope you stay with us a *long* time."

Brooks Bean, who had temporarily forgotten his chores, watched the exchange with interest. Abruptly he burst out, "Say, guy, didn't you ever see a dime before?"

"His name is Jon," said Mary Bean. "Like short for Jonathan. His name is all he can remember right now."

"But—but, jumping smoke," Brooks persisted, "a dime's a dime. Don't you know what money is, Jon?"

Little Jon shook his head.

"But you must know English, or you wouldn't know what we're saying," Brooks went on, baffled. "So you must know about *money!*"

Mary Bean said firmly, "We've questioned him enough for one evening. After all, if you had a bump on your head as big as his, you wouldn't know which way was up. Jon's had a pretty bad day. What he needs is something to eat and a good night's rest. Tomorrow's Sunday, and there'll be plenty of time to talk."

There was only one other surprise that evening. They had scrambled eggs for supper, along with some of Mary Bean's home-canned vegetables, generous slices of baked ham, and some fried chicken left over from the day before. Little Jon ate ravenously of everything but the ham and chicken, which he refused to touch.

He began to nod at the table and was sound asleep before he could finish undressing for bed. He shared Brooks's bed that night and wore a pair of old pajamas, much too large for him, that Brooks had outgrown.

He Learns a New Language

In the morning Little Jon felt nearly as well as ever. Save for the bump on his head, which was better, all his swellings had gone down during the night, and the ugly bruises had almost vanished. There was hardly a sign of the scratches that had marred his hands and face. He could walk easily.

"I can't understand it," Mary Bean said at breakfast. "I *never* saw anyone heal so fast. I've heard of fast healers, but . . ."

"Oh, it's only our special Bean liniment," Thomas said lightly, carefully hiding his own surprise. "Jon, it's an old Indian concoction. Supposed to cure everything but poverty and rabies. If it wasn't for the poverty restriction, I could sell it in the shop and make a fortune on it."

"Aw, Dad," Brooks began, but Sally said brightly, "Why don't we rub some on Jon's head? Maybe it would bring back his memory!"

Little Jon laughed. He knew she meant it, which made it all the funnier.

The others laughed with him, then looked at him curiously.

Thomas Bean said, "It's good to hear you laugh, Jon. That means your voice will be coming back soon as well as your memory. Then we can locate your folks." He paused, frowning. "What I can't understand is why there was no mention of you on the radio this morning. Ordinarily, in this mountain country, if anyone gets lost, you hear about it first thing on the local station, and search parties go out. But there wasn't a word."

Mary Bean murmured, "I hope it wasn't like what happened over beyond the gap last summer."

Brooks said, "Jon, some tourists drove off the mountain, but nobody ever knew about it for a week. Some hikers just happened to stumble over their car. Everybody in it was stone dead."

"Brooks!" his mother scolded despairingly. "You shouldn't—"

"Aw, *he* didn't wander off from any wrecked car," Brooks told her. "I know. I asked him about it while we were getting dressed. Jon doesn't know any more about cars than he does about money."

Thomas Bean blinked. "Is that true, Jon?"

"Yes," said Little Jon, using his first English word.

"He spoke!" Sally cried, delighted. "Maybe some of the liniment got on his tongue."

Neither Thomas nor Mary laughed. They glanced at each other, their eyes shadowed with questions. Mary Bean said, "Thomas, I won't go to church this morning. I'll stay home with Jon. Why don't you go on with Brooks and Sally and sort of nose around. . . ."

"Um, okay. I follow you. I'll see what I can pick up—without saying anything."

"Right. Now, Brooks," she said, "you and Sally listen to me carefully. I don't want either of you to mention a word about Jon to a soul. Understand?"

"Yes, ma'am," said Brooks. "I'm not dumb."

"But why shouldn't we mention him?" Sally asked. "I think Jon's *nice*, don't you?"

"Of course he is, dear. And we want to protect him. Remember how Mr. Gilby was last night?"

"Oh, *him!*" Sally wrinkled her nose in distaste.

"So you see how it is, dear. There are too many things about Jon that people like Mr. Gilby can't understand—and they could make all kinds of, well, difficulties. Will you promise to keep Jon a secret?"

"I promise, Mommy."

"That's my girl," said Thomas, smiling at her. "Better get ready, you two. We don't want to be late."

When they were gone, Mary Bean went to the radio and tuned it carefully to the local station. She listened to the next news report, then shook her head.

"Do you know about radios?" she asked.

Little Jon was not deceived by the casual tone of her voice. The question was important to her, for behind it were those troubling thoughts about cars and money.

"Yes," he replied. Then he remembered the politeness word and said, "Yes, ma'am."

"Wonderful!" she exclaimed. "It's coming back. Is it hard to talk?"

"It is hard—now. But—it is coming." He liked her bright hair and her quick blue eyes that were almost green. Sally looked much like her, but Brooks resembled his father.

"Well, we'll take it easy," she said. "Maybe I shouldn't talk to you at all for a day or two. You may have a concussion or something—I don't know too much about those things, but you've still got that bump on your head. Does it hurt this morning?"

"Only—when I—touch it. Please—talk. It—helps."

"Okay. We'll talk up a storm. I'm the biggest talker in seven counties—when I have the chance." She laughed. "Poor Thomas is too busy trying to keep the money coming in to listen to me half the time."

"Money?" he said. "Why?"

"There we go again! Money. You *must* know what money is! Everybody has to have it. You can't eat without it—though we manage pretty well, what with a garden and the stuff I can from it, plus chickens and a cow. They call this place a farm—but no farmer could possibly make a living from it these days, no matter how hard he worked. And we all work hard. Thomas is no farmer—but he prefers country life. So he studied geology after the war and managed to buy this place and start the Rock Shop. That's where our money comes from—mainly during the summer from tourists."

She stopped, her eyes crinkling. "Am I talking too much?"

"Oh, no! Please—please talk more."

"All right. About money. Are you absolutely certain you've never seen any before?"

"Absolutely certain."

"And the same for automobiles?"

"They are—strange to me."

"And you're getting stranger to me by the minute."

Mary Bean sat down, and he was aware of her growing bewilderment as she stared at him. His own bewilderment matched hers, but he fought it down while his mind sorted the dozens of new words he was learning. Words were used in patterns, and they had to match the patterns that thoughts came in. It was very easy—but it took time.

Suddenly she jumped up. "Jon, I'm going through the house and point out things. I want you to tell me whether they are familiar or strange. You know about radios, so you should know about TV also."

"It is like radio—but has—pictures?"

"Yes, television. We don't have a set—we've been using our extra money for books—but we hope to get one soon."

"Television—it seems familiar."

"Good. What about books?" She waved to the shelves of books flanking the fireplace.

"Familiar," he said instantly.

"Can you read this one?" She handed him a copy of one of Sally's books.

"No. I cannot read—this."

"That's strange. I get the feeling you're older than you look. Anyone who speaks English ought to be able to read this. Oh, dear, I didn't realize—maybe English isn't your language."

"There *is* another language I—I seem to know."

"Now we're getting somewhere!" she exclaimed happily. "If you could speak a little of it, maybe I might be able to recognize it."

Little Jon looked out of the window and let his mind rove over the greening valley in the distance. Suddenly he began to hum a little song about valleys. The humming changed to singing words. He wondered where he had heard it.

Mary Bean clapped her hands. "That was beautiful, Jon! Beautiful!" Her bewilderment returned. "I thought I knew something about languages—my father taught them in school. But this is a new one. How long have you known English?"

"I don't know it yet. I only began—last night."

She shook her head. "Say that again?"

"I—I am learning it from you, now," he said and instantly wondered if he should have told her. She didn't believe him. It was strange that she couldn't understand thoughts, even strong ones—but nobody here seemed to be able to. Only the animals . . .

"Jon," she said very patiently, "do you know the difference between truth and—and falsehood?"

"Truth? Falsehood? Truth is—is right," he managed to say. "Falsehood is—not truth. There is another word for it—but you have not spoken it yet."

"The word is *lie*," she said softly. "When you are not telling the truth, you are telling a falsehood—a lie."

His chin quivered a moment, then stiffened. "You think I am not telling you the truth—but—but I *must!* You are as strange to me as—as I am to you. Yesterday—in the morning—I woke up—on a mountain—far away from—from here. I hurt all over. I felt as if—as if I had fall—fallen. I did not know my name until last night when you asked me. Everything was strange. The mountain, the trees, everything . . . only the deer. I—" He stopped, all at once aware of the dog he had glimpsed last night.

The dog was thirsty. It was almost a hurt to feel the dryness of its throat, the craving for water.

He told Mary Bean about the dog, but she shook her head. "Oh, I'm sure he was taken care of. Thomas would never forget Rascal. Anyway, how could you possibly—"

"But he *did* forget the water. How could Rascal think a lie?"

"Jon!" There was something like fright in her eyes. "Are you trying to tell me that you can—" She shook her head, and said, "We'll go out to Rascal's pen and see—"

They had started through the doorway when they heard a car coming down the road. Instantly she drew him back inside and closed the door. They stood waiting for the car to pass. It slowed, then went on.

"The Johnsons," she said. "They would have stopped if they'd seen us. Thank goodness they didn't."

Almost in the same breath she said firmly, "Rascal will have to wait. Jon, since Mr. Gilby will be looking for someone with long hair, I'm going to cut yours. I'll also give you some different clothes, so that you'll look as much like other boys as possible. It's terribly important."

"I don't mind," he said, giving Rascal a quieting thought. "I'm sorry to—to make so much trouble."

"I don't mind it in the least. In fact, if I can only get used to you, I believe I'm even going to enjoy this. But getting used to you . . ."

She got scissors and a comb and started to cut. She found the nearly hidden clip holding his hair together at the nape of his neck. "O-o-oh!" she gasped. "What work-manship! Thomas will be interested in this."

She put the clip carefully aside and very expertly cut his hair. "I'm the family barber," she explained. "You'd be surprised what it saves. Costs a dollar-fifty in town, and nearly double that in cities. That's six dollars a month for Thomas and Brooks. Now, let's see. Clothes. Most of Brooks's old things went to the charity collection, but I saved the best for Sally to play in. They ought to fit you."

When he was finally dressed in faded jeans, a fairly good shirt, and a light jacket with a zipper, she surveyed him critically.

"We're short on shoes," she said, "but I think your boots will pass, if you keep your trousers pulled over them. Next, we've got to think up a story to explain your presence here. I know—Thomas had a pal in the Marines named Jimmy O'Connor. He married a French-Moroccan girl when he was stationed in North Africa. They were both killed in the trouble there recently—so who's to know if they didn't have a son about your age? You do look, well, a bit foreign. I don't see why we couldn't call you Jon O'Connor and say we'd sort of fallen heir to you for the time being."

"But—but that would not be telling the truth," he said, wondering.

"You're right, of course," Mary said, sighing. "And we do try to be honest. But, Jon, in this day and age, with the way things are, truth—the exact truth—is sometimes a hard thing to manage. There are times when it could cause needless trouble and suffering."

"Things must be—very wrong if—if truth can cause trouble," he replied simply.

She sighed again. "You're right—but that's the way the world seems to be. Even in little things, we often tell small lies to save people's feelings."

"Small lies?"

"Well, take Mrs. Johnson. She makes her own clothes, just as I do. But she's never learned to sew well, and she makes the ugliest dresses in the community. Still, I wouldn't hurt her feelings by telling her how ugly they are. I usually think of something nice to say about them."

Little Jon was puzzled. "But that's not right. How can she learn? It's wrong to make things ugly. Why, if she's wrong, should her feelings—"

Mary Bean shook her head. "Her feelings are important. Listen, dear. To avoid trouble, I'm afraid you'll have to be Jimmy O'Connor's boy—until we can find out more about you. I don't dare tell the Johnsons or the Pitts or some other people that—that you're a strange boy from nowhere, who has curious clothes that won't tear and curious ideas that don't fit, who has never seen money or cars before, and who can talk to—" She stopped, and again he was aware of the flicker of fright in her mind.

Quietly she said, "Let's go out and see if Rascal really is thirsty."

Rascal was a huge brown mongrel, with a wide head and heavy jaws. He snarled as they approached the enclosure and lunged to the end of his chain. The iron pan that held water was empty. Mary Bean frowned at the pan. She turned on the hose and filled it from a safe distance. Rascal quieted and drank greedily.

"How you ever knew about that pan—" she began. "Anyway, I'd better warn you about Rascal. Thomas is always picking up stray dogs and trying to train them—but this creature was a mistake. He won't let anyone but Thomas go near him. We've got to get rid of him. If he ever broke that chain . . ."

"He—he won't hurt you."

"I happen to know better. He's as vicious as they come, and even Thomas—No! *Don't open that gate!*"

He hardly heard her, for he had slipped quickly through the gate, and all his attention was on Rascal. He held out his hands, and the big dog came over to him, uncertain, then whining in sudden eagerness, trembling. As he spoke silently, he could feel the blackness and the lostness fade away from the creature that now sprang upon him.

Thomas Bean, returning, glimpsed the two from the foot of the lane. He sent the truck roaring up to the house and jumped out, calling, "Hey, you crazy kid! Get out of there before—"

His voice died with recognition. Shaken, he limped over to Mary, followed by Brooks and Sally. "Didn't know him with a haircut and those clothes," he muttered. "Lord preserve me, how did he *ever* make up to Rascal?"

"I'll try to tell you later," she whispered, "but you won't believe it. Incidentally, I've decided that he's Jimmy O'Connor's boy. We—we've got to explain him somehow."

Thomas nodded slowly. "A good choice. People around here wouldn't be about to check up on it."

"Did you learn anything at church about a missing boy?"

"Not a thing. I was surprised to see Gilby and Emma there. They don't belong to our church."

"They must have come with the Macklins—they're related, you know."

"Well, the Macklins were all there. They sang as loud as anybody—and they looked well fed on Bean hams."

"Thomas! You don't *know* that they stole our hams."

"No, I certainly couldn't prove it. Anyway, I drove through town afterward, listened around a bit, and got all the papers I could find. Atlanta *Journal*, Asheville *Times*, and a couple others. There's bound to be something in one of them about a lost boy."

"Want to make a bet on it?"

"But, Mary, he had to come from *somewhere!*"

Little Jon called from the enclosure, "Please, may—may I take Rascal out? He—he hates the chain."

"Why, say, you're getting your voice back!" Thomas exclaimed. "You're really progressing, young fellow. Er, I don't know how you made up to Rascal, but I think you'd better leave him where he is."

"He—he promises to be good."

"Oh, he *promises*, does he?" Thomas chuckled. "Well, some dogs can break promises just as some people do. Maybe tomorrow . . ."

Little Jon turned away to hide his disappointment. "He doesn't understand," he silently told Rascal. "But he will. Be patient, and tomorrow we will play together."

He heard Thomas say to Mary, "Thank heaven he's able to talk to us. Seems like a pretty bright kid, so it shouldn't be too hard to find out a few facts about him."

"Thomas," Mary whispered, "I have something to tell you about his speech. Get a double grip on yourself and come into the house."

He Makes a Discovery

The next morning, as soon as Brooks and Sally had gone to meet the school bus, Thomas Bean said, "Let's all get down to some facts and see what we can figure out."

A study of the papers had yielded not the slightest clue, and it had been decided to save all further questions until this time, when they would have the morning to themselves. Little Jon had looked forward hopefully to this moment, yet he approached it with misgivings. His memory still told him nothing. And the Beans, much as he was beginning to love them, were still as strange to him as he was to them.

"Let's start with your clothes," said Thomas, limping over to the table on which Mary had placed them. "They should tell us a lot. Is everything here?"

"All but my boots—and my knife and belt," he said. "I'm still wearing them."

Mary Bean said, "His boots are woven of the same material as the rest of his clothes, only thicker. Even the soles."

"No leather?" said Thomas.

"Thomas," she said, "there isn't a scrap of leather in anything he owns."

Leather was a new word. Little Jon asked about it and was shocked when he learned. "But how—how can you kill another creature for its skin?" he exclaimed.

"At first to keep warm, young fellow," Thomas said. "But now, Jon, some people are beginning to think the way you do about that." As he spoke, Thomas started jotting down all that they had so far discovered about Jon. "I learned in the Marines," he said, "that if you get enough facts together, no matter how queer they may look alone, they'll always add up to something."

The pencil in Thomas Bean's hand moved swiftly as he intoned, "No leather. Doesn't believe in killing things. Will not eat meat. Seems to know how to—to communicate with animals. H'mm. Clothes, all handwoven. Some material like linen . . ."

"It's a hundred times stronger than linen," Mary hastened to say. "The soles of his boots hardly show a sign of wear."

"Vegetable fiber," Thomas mumbled, writing. "Tougher than ramie. Dove gray. Designs on hem of jacket in tan and blue. Could be Indian or Siberian—"

"But they're not," said Mary, "and I see no sense in writing all that down when I know the answer."

"And what *is* the answer, Madame Bean?"

"I—I'm not ready to tell you," she said. "You should be seeing it for yourself. I think Jon sees it. Do you, Jon?"

He was startled by her thought. "You could be right," he told her slowly. "I almost believe you are—but I'm not sure yet. You're better able to judge. You have your memory."

"Hey, what's all this?" Thomas asked curiously.

"Skip it," Mary told him. "You're the fact finder. Have you listed his English as one of the facts?"

"I'm listing it as a language that he knows."

"That's not what I mean, Thomas."

"Oh, come on. It takes years to learn English the way he speaks it. Jon's picked it up somewhere—he'd forgotten it temporarily. That crack on the head—"

"No," said Little Jon. "Your language is new to me. I'm sure I never heard it until you spoke it. But I find it—easy."

"Oh, I don't doubt your word," said Thomas Bean, "but English just *seems* strange to you. There isn't a living soul who can pick it up in a day or two. That's absolutely impossible. The thing is, you're able to sort of know our thoughts before we speak them. That's an unusual ability—though I've heard of people who can do it. Anyway, it's an ability that's helping you to relearn English as fast as you hear it. Doesn't that sound right to you?"

Little Jon shook his head. "No, sir. I—I don't *think* in English. There's another language I—"

"We'll come to that in a minute. It's all adding up."

"What about cars and money?" Mary Bean asked quickly. "Can you add those up with the rest of it?"

"Certainly," said Thomas. He was pacing back and forth with his awkward step, one hand rubbing his deeply lined face while he frowned at his notes. "It's beginning to make sense. Even the fact that he knows about radios and nothing about some other things. How's this:

"Jon was raised in a foreign country, in a very remote district. He learned to speak the language of that area— probably before he learned English. Because it was a primitive sort of place, there was no money, and all trade was by barter. Naturally they had no cars there. But his folks had a radio, so they could keep in touch with the outside world. Wouldn't be surprised if his folks were missionaries. Sound right to you?"

Mary said, "Why must you be so—so reasonable, Thomas? But go ahead. Name some places like that."

"Oh, that's easy. I've been in a number of them. Parts of India, the Middle East, North Africa, and even South America. Those clothes could have been woven by Indians in the Andes."

"Nonsense," Mary said. "Those people weave only with animal fibers and cotton. The material in Jon's clothes didn't come from any of the places you mentioned."

"Well," Thomas asked, "where *did* it come from?"

"Not from any place you know about—and while you're thinking of places, you might consider *how* he got here. That really stumps me."

"He must have flown, Mary."

"In what kind of plane, Thomas?"

"Oh, a small private one, I'd say—one that hasn't been missed yet. It *has* to be that. There's no other solution. You see, when we found him, he was still wearing the clothes he must have put on when he left home. He'd hardly be wearing such odd-looking things if he had been in this country long enough to change them. I wish I'd thought of this earlier! He must have come in a plane, and it must have crashed somewhere here in the mountains. We'd better organize a search—"

Mary was shaking her head. "No, Thomas. Jon has never seen a plane in his life. He saw pictures of some in one of our magazines yesterday and asked me what they were."

Thomas stared at her, then turned. "Is that true, Jon?"

"Yes, sir. I'm certain I've never been in a plane, Mr. Bean."

"But your memory, Jon—"

"My lost memory doesn't keep me from knowing familiar things," he said earnestly.

"H'mm. Well, what *is* familiar to you?"

"Radios are familiar, sir. Books are very familiar. Deer and—and singing birds and birds like chickens—are all familiar. And dogs."

"Cows and horses?"

"Horses, yes. But I'm sure I never saw a creature quite like a cow before or machines like planes and automobiles. Of course, the *idea* of all those machines is familiar, and some of them seem familiar, like spaceships and—"

"*Spaceships?*"

Mary Bean said, "He saw some drawings of spaceships in one of the magazines."

"But I've never been in one," Little Jon hastened to say. "It's just that I feel I've seen them. They are not strange like—like snakes and cows and—and the language you speak."

Thomas Bean sat down. He began snapping his fingers, his face blank. Speech seemed to have deserted him.

Mary laughed. "You wanted facts, Mr. Sherlock Holmes Bean. We'll toss a couple more at you. Jon, show him your knife. I'll get the clip."

The clip was gold filigree, set with a blue stone. The knife, which had been entirely hidden by its woven sheaf, was small, with a short, thin blade that looked like gold.

Its handle was of finely carved wood, with a blue stone set in the golden hilt.

"Well?" said Mary after Thomas had been examining the articles silently for several minutes. "You've been around, Mr. Bean. You're supposed to know something of gems and jewelry. Where were those things made?"

Thomas shook his head. "I've never seen such work. If these stones are real—but, of course, they can't be. Star sapphires like these . . . h'mm." He picked up a sliver of wood from the fireplace and sliced it with the knife. "Sharp as a razor! Must be a special gold alloy."

Suddenly he stood up. "Let's go down to the shop. I'd like to test these stones."

As they went down the lane, Little Jon heard Rascal bark and was aware of the eager question in it. "Soon," he called to Rascal. "I have not forgotten."

He watched Thomas unlock the shop door and followed him inside. "Why do you keep the door—locked?" he asked, peering curiously and with quick interest at the rocks cramming the shelves and heaped in the corners and at the glass case full of trays of gems.

Mary said, "Locks are to keep out thieves."

"Thieves? Thieves?" It was another new word with a confusing thought behind it.

"A thief is a person who steals," she explained. "We have a lot of valuable things here in the shop. If the windows weren't barred and the door didn't have a good lock on it, somebody might break in and take everything we own—even the safe."

"B-but why—"

Thomas asked, "Don't people steal where you're from?"

"Of course not! Why would they? It seems so stupid. They—"

"Go on!" Mary urged. "You're remembering."

"I—" He shook his head. "I almost thought of something, but it's gone. I only know that stealing is—stupid and foolish. I'm sure I've never heard of people doing it. Why would they?"

"It's one way to make money—" Thomas began dryly, "if you don't mind risking jail. Some people will do anything for money. They'll even start a war."

"Jail? Money? War?"

"Here we go again!" said Mary. "You see, Thomas, English *is* strange to him, because it contains *ideas* that are strange."

Little Jon listened carefully, holding back his astonishment, as she proceeded to explain. One subject led to another. She had finished about war and was touching upon government and rulers and power when they were interrupted.

A man on horseback was approaching. It was the same rider who had gone by on the road Saturday evening, before the Beans appeared in their truck.

"That's Angus Macklin," said Mary. "He lives up the road beyond the Johnsons. I hope he goes on."

But Angus Macklin, seeing the door open, stopped, dismounted, and came in. He was a short, thick man with round, blinking eyes and an easy smile. Little Jon was not deceived by the smile, though he was fascinated by the repulsive wad of tobacco Angus was chewing.

"Howdy, folks! Howdy!" Angus said heartily. "See you're open for business. Ought to be gettin' some customers if the weather holds."

"Little early for tourists," Thomas told him. "How are things, Angus?"

"So-so. Ain't seen Tip an' Lenny around, have you?"

"Not this morning. Why aren't they in school?"

141

"Aw, you know kids," said Angus Macklin. "School's out tomorrow, an' it's kinda hard to make 'em go. When they heard about that wild boy, they just took off. Gilby told me about it yesterday after church. Soon's we got home, my kids lit out to hunt 'im. They lit out again this morning—pretended they was going fishin', but I know better. Mighty queer about that crazy wild boy. Gilby tell you how far he jumped? Near forty feet!"

"Nonsense!" Thomas said shortly. "Gilby was probably imagining things. Perhaps he saw a stray Cherokee boy."

"Oh, I dunno," said Angus, scratching under his cap and blinking owlishly at Little Jon. "That thing he saw was plumb wild and unnatural. I've seen some queer things myself in these mountains. Lights where there shouldn't be no lights. Heard music where there shouldn't be no music. My kids can take care of themselves, but all the same, that wild thing could be dangerous." He paused. "Nice-lookin' boy you got here. Ain't noticed him around. He visiting you folks?"

Thomas nodded. "Jon O'Connor. Son of an old friend of mine in the Marines."

Angus smiled meaninglessly and grunted. "Well, I'll go along. You see them fool kids o' mine, tell 'em I want 'em home."

They watched him ride away. Thomas said, a little angrily, "So, the news is out. I should have known Gilby would tell somebody like Angus. It's going to spread all over the mountains and get wilder every time it's told."

He drew forth the knife and clip he had hidden under the workbench. As he studied them again, he began to whistle softly through his teeth.

"Out with it," said Mary. "Are the gems real?"

"They're real. I can't quite believe it. Jon, have you any idea what these things are worth?"

Little Jon looked at him intently. "They are not worth what you think they are, Mr. Bean. You're thinking they're worth more than your house and everything in the shop—but that's all wrong. Anyway, a thing shouldn't have two values."

"*Two* values?" said Thomas, raising his eyebrows.

"Yes, sir," he said seriously. "You're judging the value of my knife by the amount of money you could sell it for. But that has nothing whatsoever to do with its real value."

Thomas whistled softly. "I know what you mean, Jon. But it's a good thing we're not in business together, or we'd never make a profit."

"But—but doesn't the idea of a profit seem wrong to you?"

"It's part of our free enterprise system, Jon," Thomas answered. "If Mary and I couldn't make a little profit on the things we sell, we'd soon go broke and wouldn't have enough to eat."

Again the dreadful feeling of lostness poured over Jon. He was sure of the answer now. Mary Bean had guessed it. He was a long way from home.

Suddenly he turned, peering out of the back window as he heard Rascal barking. Rascal was lost, too, though in a different way, chained in a world where everything seemed, if not wrong, at least very different.

"Please," he begged, "may I take Rascal out of his pen? I promise he'll be good."

Thomas frowned, but Mary said, "Let him try it, Thomas. I'm sure he can manage Rascal."

"Um—okay. We'll chance it this once. And here's your knife, unless you want me to keep it in the safe. You don't want to lose anything like this."

"Oh, I won't lose it, sir. I'll need it to—to—"

"Go on," Mary said quietly. "You need it to—to do what with it?"

"I don't know. Maybe it will come back if I run with Rascal. I think running will help."

As he darted out the door, Mary said, "He's upset, Thomas. I think he sees the truth. Can't you see it, too? You've got facts enough—or is it that you just don't want to face the facts?"

"But, Mary, they don't make sense. I simply can't—"

"Look at him!" she gasped, staring through the rear window. "Thomas—*look!*"

In his eagerness to release Rascal, Little Jon was racing up the steep lane. Unconsciously he had made his feet light, so that his boots hardly touched the ground. Only a deer could have equaled his upward bounds.

"You win," Thomas said finally, expelling a long breath. "I don't know how he got here, and I can't understand why some things are so familiar to him—but he didn't come from this world."

"Of course not. What are we going to do?"

"H'mm. Seems like the important thing is to find out *how* he got here, if we can. I'm afraid I see trouble ahead."

He Remembers Something

Sleep did not come easily that night. For a long time Little Jon lay motionless beside Brooks, thinking of the day while he listened to the sounds beyond the window— the familiar and unfamiliar sounds of a world he didn't belong in.

Somehow, by some accident, he had been lost on a planet that was not his own. It had been hard for the Beans to admit that to him, but, of course, there wasn't any other answer. Only, how did he get here—and why did so many of the wild creatures seem familiar?

Thomas had a theory about the wild creatures and life on other planets. As they puzzled over it that afternoon, Thomas had said, "The latest belief among astronomers is that our earth wasn't made by chance. It's the result of certain exact conditions. There are other suns just like ours, and the same laws affect them. So there are bound to be other worlds like ours—with life developing on them in almost exactly the same way. If there are people like Jon on them, then naturally—"

"I won't dispute you," said Mary, "but that doesn't solve Jon's problem."

That was when Thomas suggested they get some help.

"Oh, good heavens, no!" she exclaimed. "How could anyone really help us? Don't you realize what a mess it would be if people started buzzing around? The papers would get it, and we'd have reporters and half the world swarming all over the place. Honestly!"

"Um—guess you're right. Thank Pete someone like Angus Macklin didn't find you, Jon. It was lucky we happened on you when we did."

"No, it didn't happen that way, sir. I picked you." He explained to the Beans how he had waited for them by the side of the road.

"That settles it," said Thomas. "If you picked us to help you, we're sticking by you. Now, here's the crazy thing to consider: Our civilization is pretty advanced—the most advanced on earth—yet we're just beginning space travel. No human being has landed on distant planets yet. So— how did you, whose civilization seems to be behind ours, ever reach us? You must have—"

"Thomas," Mary interrupted, "you're starting off wrong. Can't you *see* how wrong you are?"

"But, Mary, I'm judging by what I see. Jon's people haven't progressed beyond barter and the handloom. They must be tribal, for he knows nothing of money, laws, cities, and government."

"Thomas, cities come and go. Governments fall, and money becomes worthless. Is there a mill on this earth that can produce anything as wonderful as Jon's jacket?"

"Well, if we had that kind of fiber—"

"But we haven't. Can anyone on this earth learn a language as quickly as he learned ours—and read our thoughts the way he does?"

"No."

"Can anyone *move* the way he does?"

Thomas shook his head, his lips compressed.

"Thomas," she went on, "if all the people on this earth—everybody—were *absolutely* honest, would we need laws and jails—and armies and bombs and things? Therefore, doesn't it seem obvious that Jon's people are actually *far* in advance of us?"

"They're certainly mighty intelligent . . ."

"So intelligent that they could easily have all the expensive and complicated things we have, if they wanted to. But they must not want them. They don't value them. I'm sure they've progressed way beyond them—and value other things more. Thomas, how long do you think it will take us to do away with crime and war?"

Thomas Bean shook his head. "I hope I'm wrong, but at the rate we're going, we'll need another million years."

"Then there's our starting point. If Jon's people are a million years ahead of us, they've long known about space travel, and they've simplified it. They seem to have simplified everything else. My goodness, Thomas, they could have worked out something as simple as stepping through a door from one room to another."

"That sounds a little farfetched," said Thomas. "But maybe I *am* a million years behind. Does it make any sense to you, Jon?"

Something moved in his mind. "From one room to another," he repeated. "Door—door—It seems familiar—the idea, I mean."

"Think!" Mary Bean urged. "Think hard!"

It was no use. The thought, whatever it was, remained in hiding.

When Brooks and Sally came home from school, he spent the rest of the afternoon helping Brooks in the garden. Already they had begun to accept him as Jon O'Connor.

Lying awake in the night beside Brooks, he searched again for the hidden thought. It seemed important, the most important of all the hidden thoughts; but the harder he searched, the farther it seemed to retreat from him.

He dozed finally and long later awoke suddenly. Rascal was barking, warning of wild creatures crossing the pasture. Deer.

Instantly, silently, he was out of bed, telling Rascal to be quiet while he drew on his clothes. In another minute he was outside, running with lightened feet to the pasture fence and bounding over it.

But the deer had been frightened by Rascal's barking. They had gone back up the forested slope and refused to come down again.

Disappointed, Little Jon paused and automatically glanced upward.

For the first time since his arrival, he saw the wonder of the stars. Here in the open pasture, above the black bowl of the surrounding mountains, they blazed in uncounted millions. Even as he stared at them, one streaked like a flaming jewel across the sky.

A shooting star! There had been shooting stars when—when something happened. Shooting stars—and a door.

He raced back to the house, excited. It was nearly dawn, and the Beans were already stirring. As he burst into the living room, he saw Thomas, still in pajamas, lighting a fire in the fireplace.

"There was a door!" he cried. "I can remember that part . . ."

"A door?" said Thomas as Mary hastened in from the kitchen. "What kind of door?"

"I don't know. But it seems that I was standing somewhere, looking at the stars, and I fell. And as I fell, I remembered something about a door . . ."

"Go on," Mary urged.

"That—that's all I can remember, as if it were part of a dream. Just stars, and thinking of a door."

"Could you have been in a ship?" asked Thomas. "You might have fallen out of one in some way."

"No—no—it wasn't like that. I suddenly fell *into* something—and when I woke up, I was here on a mountain, and it was morning."

Thomas stood snapping his fingers, frowning. "Mary," he said finally, "it's possible you've hit on the right idea. Jon, as soon as we've finished the chores and had breakfast, we're going hunting. I want to see that spot where you found yourself."

After breakfast Brooks and Sally went down to catch the school bus, and Thomas got out a knapsack for Mary to fill with lunch. When it was ready, he thrust an odd-shaped hammer into his belt and started for the truck.

Little Jon looked curiously at the hammer. "That tool—it seems familiar. Do you—chip rocks with it?"

"It's a rock hound's hammer, Jon. Thought I'd take it along and examine a few ledges while we're out. Might find a thing or two for the shop. How did you know what it's for?"

"I had the feeling I knew how to use it. Have you another I may take?"

"Why shore, podner, we'll jest go prospectin' together."

Thomas found a second hammer, and they were returning to the truck when a car with a star on the side turned into the driveway. The car stopped behind them, and a lean, gray-haired man got out.

At the sight of him, Little Jon was aware of sudden worry and alarm in Mary Bean, who stood watching from the steps. The man approached, studying them carefully with his hard, observant eyes. His nose was slightly hooked, and he made Little Jon think of a hawk he had seen the day before—a hawk searching for prey.

"Mr. Bean?" said the man in a grating voice. "I'm Deputy Anderson Bush, from the sheriff's office." He opened his coat and showed a badge.

"Glad to know you, sir," Thomas said easily, extending his hand. "I've seen you around, but . . . This is Mrs. Bean, and my young partner here is Jon O'Connor. What can we do for you?"

"Like to ask a few routine questions, if you don't mind."

"Sure. Fire away."

Deputy Bush said, "Where were you Saturday?"

"In town most of the day. Er, is anything wrong?"

"We'll get to that. I understand you have two children. Were they with you?"

"Yes."

"All the time?"

"Well, most of the time, except when they were in the movies. I knew where they were all the time, if that's what you want to know."

149

The deputy wrote something in a notebook, then looked down at Little Jon. "What about this boy?"

"He didn't arrive until Saturday evening."

"Where was he before that?"

"Traveling—on his way here."

"His parents bring him?"

"No." Thomas lowered his voice and added, "Both Captain O'Connor and his wife were killed recently, and Jon's been pretty badly upset. Must we . . ."

The deputy finished writing in his notebook before he spoke. "Mr. Bean, I only want to know where the boy was all day Saturday and Sunday. That also goes for your boy. I believe Brooks is his name."

"Yes. You see, this is Jon's first trip to the mountains. Took him all day to get here. He arrived about supper-time. Sunday he stayed home with Mrs. Bean, and I took my kids to church."

"And Sunday afternoon?"

"We were all here. No one left the place. What's this about?"

Deputy Bush made some more entries in his book. Again he glanced sharply at Little Jon. "Mr. Bean, have you heard anything about a wild boy in this part of the mountains?"

"Er—yes, I have," Thomas replied slowly. "Gilby Pitts told me about it, but I'm afraid I don't take much stock in it. Do you?"

"Mr. Bean, I don't know what Mr. Pitts saw, but it seems to be very unusual. My job is to check up on the story. Have you noticed any strange boy around?"

"I certainly haven't seen any boy that looks wild to me," Thomas answered, smiling. "Is he accused of any crime?"

Deputy Bush carefully closed his notebook and returned it to his coat pocket. "No one," he said, "is being accused of anything yet. Do you know the location of Dr. Holliday's summer place?"

"Of course. Dr. Holliday is an old customer of mine. Gilby Pitts takes care of the place while he's away. What about it?"

"Someone broke into it—either Saturday or Sunday. Mr. Pitts didn't learn about it until yesterday morning when he went over to finish some work he'd started last week. Some things were stolen."

"And you think a boy did it?"

"No question of it. There are footprints and other signs. It was a boy about the size of this one, for he squeezed through a narrow window that a larger person couldn't have entered. He may have had a helper. Now, Mr. Bean, don't take any of this personally; I have to check on every boy in the area. Thank you for your help. Good day, sir."

"Good day, Mr. Bush."

Thomas stood, snapping his fingers, after the deputy left. "Of all the things to happen!" he burst out angrily.

"Thomas," Mary began worriedly, "do you think it likely that Anderson Bush could find out the truth about—about this wild boy thing?"

"He certainly could! He's no fool. I've never talked to him before, but I know his reputation. He's a born ferret and a stickler for the law—that's why he'd sure give us trouble. He sure had me going with those questions. If only he doesn't get too curious and start asking more. Wish I didn't get this uneasy feeling whenever I have to talk to outsiders about Jon."

"There's no reason for him to," Mary said. "It should not be hard to find out who broke into Holliday's."

"Oh, he'll find out—but that's not what worries me. It's pretty obvious who did it. Only he doesn't know certain people like we do—he hasn't been here long enough. It'll take time to narrow things down and find out who's lying. Oh, confound Gilby Pitts for bringing up that tale."

"But he had to, Thomas. After all, when there's been a robbery . . ."

"Oh, I suppose so. Well, the thing's happened, and there's nothing we can do about it now." Thomas sighed and turned back to the truck. "Let's get on with our hunting, Jon."

He Is Recognized

The truck wound down toward the lower valley and stopped briefly at the spot where Little Jon had crouched in hiding on Saturday.

"As nearly as I can guess," Thomas told him, "you must have walked ten or twelve miles through the mountains to come out here. That's all National Forest. You were heading east most of the time. Which way did you head earlier when you were following the deer to that field of Gilby's?"

"I don't know, sir. We wound around a lot. And we went over one low ridge before we got down into the valley."

"H'mm. Have you any idea how long it took you to reach the field?"

"It's hard to judge, sir. You see, I hadn't learned to count the time the way you do. And I felt so bad—it was all I could do to keep up with the doe. It may have been an hour, or even more. How far can you walk in an hour?"

Thomas chuckled. "In *this* country there's no telling. But let's say you walked a mile and a half, and mostly in an easterly direction. Gilby's place is in a pocket where the valley curves—and it isn't the same valley as this one. So what we'll do is drive past his land and hike up the mountain to the first cove. If we can't find a spot you recognize, we'll come back tomorrow and start in below Gilby's."

The truck moved on, going up and down and winding in many directions. Finally it crossed a bridge and turned into another valley. They drove past a farm and several summer cottages that faced a noisy creek bordering the road. The next farm was nearly hidden by the dense growth of poplars along the fence.

"That's Gilby's place," said Thomas, jerking his head as they went by. "Dr. Holliday's property is about a quarter of a mile farther on. We'll stop between the two."

At the first wide spot in the road, the truck was run as far over to the edge of the creek as possible, and they got out. "There's no bridge near," Thomas told him. "We'll have to wade."

"I'll jump," said Little Jon, and without thinking he made his feet light and cleared the stream in a bound. Turning, he saw the expression on Thomas Bean's face. After Thomas had splashed awkwardly over, Little Jon said apologetically, "I—I forgot. You're afraid someone might see me do that."

"I'd hate for Anderson Bush to catch you at it."

Thomas stamped water from his boots and squinted at the forested slopes rising on three sides of them. "By the roads, we're nearly fifteen miles from home. Bet you can't tell me in what direction home is—and no fair peeking in my head for the answer!"

"I already know the answer," Little Jon told him, pointing instantly to the south. "It's a short distance over that ridge yonder. You see, I've been watching the way the roads and the valleys curve."

"I'll be jiggered! There's not a man in a hundred would guess that, unless he'd been raised around here. It's only two miles through a gap back of the Holliday place—if you know the trail."

"Oh!"

Thomas Bean frowned at him. "What's worrying you, Jon?"

"I was wondering why Mr. Macklin's boys would steal—and why Mr. Macklin would let them."

"Great guns, how'd you ever get such an idea?"

"Well, you've been *thinking* they did, and Mr. Macklin *knows* they did, because yesterday when he stopped at the shop, *he* was thinking about it." Little Jon paused and looked up earnestly. "Please, Mr. Bean, you mustn't believe that I'm always looking into other people's heads. It isn't—" He groped for a word. "It isn't polite or even right. The only reason I've been doing it is so I could learn. I *had* to do it. And sometimes you have thoughts that are so strong, they—they seem to jump out at me. It goes with the way you feel. It was that way with Mr. Macklin. Yesterday he was thinking about his boys carrying things over the gap, from a house on this side. It didn't mean anything to me then, but now I understand why the thought was so strong."

"Good grief!" Thomas muttered, staring at him. He began snapping his fingers. "What a thing to know—and we can't say a word about it."

Thomas gave a worried shake of his head and adjusted the knapsack over his shoulder. "Let's forget about the Macklins and see if we can find the spot we're after. It's

getting more important all the time." He thrust through a tangle of laurels and began limping up a narrow ravine that opened through the trees.

Little Jon followed him easily. He could have climbed twice as fast had Thomas been able to manage it. It was too bad, he thought, that people here couldn't make their feet light and save themselves so much trouble in getting around. It was such a simple thing. A way of thinking. But it was like so many other things that should be simple—like agreeing on something that was right, instead of trying to make it right some other way. That was why Thomas Bean limped. He had been wounded in a place called Korea, Brooks had said. Many men had died there, and still no one agreed on the right or wrong of the war.

They topped the first ridge, and Thomas Bean stopped to rest. "See anything around here that looks familiar to you?"

"I don't believe I came this way," he said, studying the shadowed cove below them. "If I'd felt better Saturday, I'm sure I could have remembered everything exactly. But my head hurt, and I was so confused . . ."

"Don't apologize. This isn't going to be easy. I've known people to be lost for days in these mountains—and all the time they were within a half hour of a road. Let's start working east."

They followed the cove, crossed another ridge, and tramped for a winding mile or more through dense forest. By noon Little Jon had seen nothing he recognized. Finally they sat down on a mossy outcropping of rock, and Thomas opened his knapsack. Little Jon had finished a sandwich and an apple when he suddenly whispered, "The doe—she's near!"

All morning he had known that many wild creatures were watching them from a distance, and several times he had seen deer go bounding away. He had not tried to call to them. But aware of a friend, he spoke silently, urging her to come nearer. She refused.

"What doe?" Thomas whispered. "I don't see—"

"She's way up yonder to the right—the one I followed Saturday. She knows me, but she won't come out. She's afraid of you. Mr. Pitts shot at her and hurt her—it wasn't a bad hurt because I spoiled his aim—but it makes her very afraid."

Thomas growled under his breath, "Had an idea something like that happened. That Gilby Pitts!"

"I couldn't tell you at the time—I didn't yet know the words. Anyway, we're getting close, Mr. Bean. The doe proves it."

"But I don't see how. These deer range for miles over the mountains."

"Yes, but she has a fawn that can't travel far, and she's still on the trail she used Saturday, only higher up. There are some—some vines she eats when she can't get anything else."

"Wild honeysuckle. Do you know the direction of Gilby's land from here?"

"Of course. It's straight over yonder." Little Jon pointed. "But we'll have to go way around, then curve to the left."

"Let's get going! I don't know how you keep these directions straight, but with a head such as you have, I suppose . . ."

They found the doe's trail easily, and now Little Jon led the way. For Thomas Bean the next half hour was difficult. Many times Little Jon had to help him over tumbled faces of rock, slippery with green moss and running water. When they reached better ground, Thomas glanced back and grumbled, "I'm a fair mountain man in spite of my foot—but when we head for home, it won't be *that* way."

"We won't have to, sir. The road's much closer from here. We just turn left—north. Oh—I know this place! Yonder's where I first saw the doe."

He darted ahead, suddenly excited, then stopped to look slowly about him, searching.

"Was it here?" asked Thomas, limping over to him.

"It must be. It's where—no, there was a spring. I drank from it. After that I crawled . . ."

"There are springs all around here. You say you crawled—from where?"

"It was from a sort of dark place."

"You mean a cave?"

"It must have been. I hadn't realized till now—but there's no cave here."

"Let's try higher up," said Thomas, starting upward through a tangle of rhododendrons. "There seems to be a ledge . . ."

There was a ledge. And there was a break in the strata, marking what seemed to be a shallow cave behind the tangle. Near the mouth of it, water trickled into a small pool.

"This is the place!" Little Jon cried. "I drank from the spring—see the marks of my hands? I woke up in there, where it's flat."

They crawled inside. Thomas Bean took a flashlight from his knapsack and sent the beam slowly about. The cave was much larger than it had appeared from the entrance.

"There's been a fall of rock in here recently, Jon. Funny-looking stuff. Looks igneous—but only on one side."

"Igneous?"

"Volcanic. But no volcano ever melted this." He chipped experimentally with his hammer. "It's what we call metamorphic granite—old, old rock that's changing. And something has seared one side of it, a long time ago. I'll be jiggered!"

Thomas went farther back and straightened up. "This place is like the inside of a bottle. We've certainly found something—but don't ask me what. Think, Jon! Think about that door idea! Could this be part of it?"

"I—I don't know, sir. This place, it makes me feel sort of—tingly all over, as if something . . . but I can't yet remember."

He was aware of Thomas Bean's rising excitement as he chipped off flakes of fallen rock and examined them. Finally Thomas thrust the pieces into his knapsack and turned the light on his pocket watch. It was later than either of them had realized.

"Pshaw!" Thomas growled. "Hate to leave—but it'll be nearly dark when we get back, and there are things to do. We'll return first thing in the morning."

They left reluctantly, their thoughts leaping as they talked of their discovery. As the shadows deepened in the forest, they fell silent and began to hurry. Little Jon led the way, following the doe's trail to the valley. At the fence he turned, skirting Gilby Pitts's land, and went through the woods to the creek.

He crossed the creek as before, though not until he had made sure that no one was around to see him.

The truck was several hundred yards around the bend ahead. They were in sight of it when Little Jon heard a car approaching. It was almost inaudible above the clatter of the creek, yet his sharp ears recognized the sound.

He clutched Thomas Bean's arm in sudden uneasiness. "Mr. Bush is coming," he said. "I—I ought to hide."

"There's no reason to. He's already met you. What makes you afraid?"

"I don't know. Something . . ."

There was no place to hide here. The creek fell away on their left, and on their right the rocky slope rose sharply. And suddenly the car with the star on the side was swinging around a curve.

It slowed as it came near them and stopped. Gilby Pitts was sitting in the front with Anderson Bush.

"Howdy, Tom," said Gilby, his eyes sliding interestedly over Little Jon. "Heard you had a visitor. This him?"

"Yes. We've been doing a bit of rock-hunting together. How are matters up at Holliday's?"

"Been tryin' to make a list of what's been took. Some pretty valuable things. The doctor's pet target rifle—he paid over three hundred dollars for it. Then there's some expensive fishin' rods . . ." Gilby Pitts rubbed his chin over his high shoulder and leaned out of the car window, squinting downward. "Them boots . . ."

All at once Gilby was out of the car and stooping swiftly. Little Jon knew what was coming even before Gilby's clutching hand gave his trouser leg a jerk to expose the top of the boot. And he was aware of Thomas Bean's desperate thought, "If you'll just keep quiet, Jon, and not say a word, I'll handle this."

Thomas said, "What's come over you, Gilby?"

"Them's the boots I seen at your house Saturday night," Gilby Pitts said accusingly.

Thomas laughed. "What of it?"

"This kid was there all the time I was there! You never told me . . ."

"That we had a visitor? Why should I? Jon had had a hard day traveling, and we'd put him to bed. What's got into you, Gilby?"

"Them boots," snapped Gilby. "Ever since I seen 'em there, I been wonderin' where I seen 'em before. It's come to me. That wild boy was wearin' 'em!"

Thomas laughed again, but Gilby said hoarsely, "You been hiding 'im! You cut his hair an' changed his clothes, but you ain't changed his face. I'd know that peaky face anywhere! This here's the ornery little varmint that done the breakin' in and stealin'!"

"Gilby," Thomas said quietly, but with an inner fury that only Little Jon was aware of. "Take your hands off Jon—and stop accusing him before I lose my temper."

"Hold it!" ordered Anderson Bush, who had already stepped from the car and was standing, frowning, behind Gilby. "Mr. Pitts," he said in his grating voice, "are you absolutely sure this is the same boy you saw the other day?"

"I got eyes!" snapped Gilby. "I'd know 'im anywhere!"

"You would be willing to swear to it?"

"On the Bible!" Gilby said emphatically.

"That's all I need to know." Anderson Bush looked hard at Little Jon, and his eyes narrowed as he turned to Thomas. "Mr. Bean, I'm afraid you haven't been honest with me. You said this boy had never been in the mountains before and that he arrived at your place Saturday night."

"So I did."

"Why is it he was seen over here Saturday morning?"

"Pshaw!" said Thomas. "This thing's getting ridiculous. Who knows what Gilby really saw over here?"

"I know what I saw!" Gilby Pitts cried. "An'—*I know them boots!*"

"You see, Mr. Bean?" the deputy went on, his eyebrows raised. "I'm sure Mr. Pitts is a reliable witness. Those *are* very unusual boots the boy is wearing—and the boy himself is, well, different looking. I'm sure I'd never forget either the boots or the boy if I'd seen them before."

"Look here," said Thomas, his voice tighter, "this whole thing started because of a robbery that Jon couldn't possibly have had anything to do with. Are you accusing him of being a thief?"

"Mr. Bean," replied Anderson Bush, with a sort of deadly patience, "I'm only an investigating officer looking for facts. I've run into some very peculiar facts that need an explanation. We're due for another talk, Mr. Bean, so I think you'd better go home and wait for me. I'll be right over as soon as I drop off Mr. Pitts."

He Is Accused

It was nearly dark when they reached the house. Little Jon glimpsed Brooks and Sally running from the barn to meet them, and he could hear Rascal whining impatiently in the enclosure, eager to see him and yet reproachful at being left alone all day. He wished suddenly that he had managed to take Rascal with them. The big dog would have loved it. Maybe tomorrow . . .

"Remember," Thomas was saying, as he set the brakes and turned off the motor, "if Bush insists on asking you questions, let me think the answers before you tell him anything. He can't make us answer—only a court can do that. But I don't want him dragging us into court."

"Hi, Dad!" Brooks called. "School's out! Yow-ee!"

"Mommy said you'd gone rock-hunting," Sally said eagerly, running ahead of Brooks. "Did you find any pretty stones?"

"A few. Where's your mother?"

"Here, Thomas," said Mary Bean, appearing from around the side of the house. "What kept you so late?"

"Trouble," Thomas said hastily. "We ran into Gilby and that deputy on the way back, and Gilby recognized Jon. Bush is on his way over to ask more questions. Keep Sally and Brooks in the kitchen. Jon, you might stay out of sight in the living room—but close enough to hear. I'll talk to Bush on the porch. Hurry—here he comes."

It was a warm evening, and the windows had been opened. Little Jon, huddled in a chair in the darkened room, heard the deputy's feet on the porch and Thomas Bean's polite voice offering him a seat.

"Would you care for some coffee, sir?" Thomas asked. "I think Mrs. Bean has a fresh pot ready."

"No, thanks," came the deputy's grating reply. "I just want to talk to that boy. Will you get him out here, please?"

"I don't see any real reason to, Mr. Bush. I'll answer your questions."

"Mr. Bean, by your own admission, you didn't see that boy until Saturday evening. How can you tell me what he was doing the rest of the day?"

"I know where he was," Thomas said. "I know he's no thief, and I don't care to have him questioned about a matter that doesn't concern him."

"You told me his parents are dead, Mr. Bean. Are you his legal guardian?"

"I have charge of him for the time being."

"Then I gather you're *not* his legal guardian. Will you kindly tell me who is?"

Thomas stood up, and Little Jon could feel the rising anger in him.

"Mr. Bush, the only thing that concerns you is to clear up that theft. You're not going to clear it up by wasting your time here. There are other boys in this area you should be investigating."

"Mr. Bean," said Anderson Bush in his deadly patient voice, "you're being very evasive. When people are afraid to answer questions, that means they have something to hide. What are you trying to hide, Mr. Bean?"

"I'm trying to protect an innocent boy who's had a very bad experience."

Little Jon could almost see Anderson Bush shaking his head. "You're making a mistake, Mr. Bean. I've investigated all other possible suspects and checked them out. This boy—this Jon O'Connor—is the only one left who could have done it. He was seen, under very strange circumstances, near the Holliday place early Saturday. He's small enough to have squeezed through that window, and there are prints in the dust that could have been made by his boots."

The deputy paused and went on slowly. "I realize how you feel, Mr. Bean. It's never pleasant to have anyone connected with you accused of a thing like this. But if it's his first offense and all the stolen property can be recovered, we don't have to be too hard on him. If you'll call that boy out here and let me talk to him, you'll save yourself some trouble."

"No!" Thomas said firmly. "I'll not have him questioned! He had nothing to do with this!"

But Little Jon was already coming through the door. Thomas, he realized, could protect him no longer without making things worse than they were. He thrust his small hands into his pockets to hide their unsteadiness and shook his head at Thomas Bean's silent urging to leave. How strange, he thought, looking intently at Anderson Bush, that people here would want to make life such an ugly sort of game. Somewhere, wherever he had come from, there couldn't be this ugliness or any of these secret hates and desires that darkened everything . . .

"Now, Jon," Anderson Bush was saying with pretended friendliness. "I'm glad you decided to come out and clear this thing up. We don't like to see young fellows like you in danger of being sent to reform school. So, if you'll tell me where you put those things you took the other day from Dr. Holliday's summer house . . ."

"Mr. Bush," he said, "mind if I ask you a question?"

"You'd better start answering questions instead of asking them," the deputy said testily.

"I only wanted to ask you where Mr. Macklin said his boys were Sunday afternoon."

"You can't blame this on the Macklin boys. The whole family was in town all Saturday, at church the next morning, and at Blue Lake with friends all Sunday afternoon. I checked it."

Little Jon turned to Thomas. "Mr. Bean, do you remember when Mr. Macklin rode by Monday, looking for his boys? Can you tell Mr. Bush what he said?"

"Let me think," said Thomas. "H'mm. He said Tip and Lenny had skipped school and were out hunting that wild boy. Gilby Pitts had told him about it at church. He said—" Suddenly Thomas sat up and snapped his fingers. "I'd entirely forgotten it, but Angus said his boys were away all Sunday afternoon doing the same thing. That means Angus was lying if he said Tip and Lenny were with them at Blue Lake."

In the darkness it was hard to see the deputy's face.

But his voice was cold as he spoke. "You have a very convenient memory, Mr. Bean. It proves nothing, and it doesn't explain what this boy—this Jon O'Connor as you call him—was doing when Gilby Pitts caught him Saturday. Just who *is* this boy, Mr. Bean? You've admitted you're not his guardian. Who brought him here—and why is he staying with you?"

"Blast your nosiness!" Thomas exploded. "He's the orphaned son of Captain James O'Connor of the Marines, who was killed in North Africa three months ago. The boy has lost his memory, and he was brought here by regular Marine channels because he needs a quiet place to recuperate. I happen to be O'Connor's friend and his former commanding officer. Enough of that. The only thing that concerns you is the robbery. If you don't believe what I've told you about Macklin, you'd better go over there and have it out with him!"

"We'll all go over," Anderson Bush snapped back. "Get in the car, you two."

It was less than a half mile up the valley. The deputy drove grimly through the night. Little Jon could feel the coiled danger in him, and he wished Thomas hadn't lost his temper and told the lie. He loved Thomas for trying to protect him, but the lie was a mistake. There were old hates in Anderson Bush, ugly things of the past that made the man the way he was now. Little Jon wished the thoughts were not there to be seen, but they leaped out as strongly as if the deputy had shouted them aloud. Anderson Bush had been in trouble in the army, and he hated all officers because of it. Later there had been trouble over a son . . .

The car stopped with an angry jerk before a weathered farmhouse. Anderson Bush slid out, and they followed him up to the dim porch where a hound backed away.

The door opened, spilling light upon them, and Angus Macklin stood there blinking. As Angus recognized the deputy, Little Jon was aware of a flicker of uneasiness in him.

"Why, it's Mr. Bush!" said Angus, smiling. "Thought you was Gilby at first."

"Are you expecting Gilby Pitts?"

"Yeah. He phoned about that wild boy, said—" Angus stopped, his eyes widening as he saw Little Jon behind Thomas. "Tom, I declare, is that really him?"

Thomas Bean ignored him. "There's Gilby coming now," he growled as lights swung up the road. "Going to be a nice party!"

The approaching truck stopped behind the deputy's car. Gilby and Emma Pitts got out and came up on the porch. "There's that boy!" Gilby whispered hoarsely.

And Emma said, "I want to see 'im—I want to see 'im in the light!"

They followed Angus into the big ugly living room, where a single glaring bulb hung from the ceiling. A pinched woman, with her hands wadded nervously in her apron, stared at them from the back hall. Little Jon guessed she must be Mrs. Macklin. He was wondering about the Macklin boys when Emma Pitts suddenly grabbed his arm and jerked him under the light.

She was dressed in overalls just as he had seen her in the field that first morning. He forced himself to look steadily into her hard pebble eyes and was surprised to see the sudden dawn of fear in them.

All at once she was backing away, exclaiming, "That's 'im! You cut his hair an' changed his clothes, Tom Bean, but you ain't hidin' what he is! He's that same wild boy, an' there's something mighty queer . . ."

"He ain't natural!" muttered Gilby Pitts.

"He sure ain't," said Angus Macklin, backing away. "I can see it in his face! Anything that runs with wild critters—and jumps like 'em . . ."

Thomas burst out in angry disgust, "For Pete's sake, Jon's not going to bite any of you—but it would serve you right if he did! Mr. Bush, I'll thank you to settle this business and take us home. We haven't had supper yet."

"Hold your horses," Anderson Bush ordered. "Mr. Macklin, where're Tip and Lenny?"

"Round the barn somewhere," Angus replied. "They got chores."

Little Jon tugged at Thomas Bean's sleeve and whispered the thing that Angus was worried about. Thomas straightened. "Angus," he demanded, "do those chores take your boys as far over as the Johnson place?"

"How come you say that, Tom?"

"Because we just came by the Johnson place. It's not too dark to see a couple of boys crossing your pasture, if you happen to be watching. Couldn't make out what they were carrying—but it's not hard to guess."

The smile had frozen on Angus Macklin's face. "You don't sound very neighborly, Tom."

"I missed too many hams last winter to be in a very neighborly mood," Thomas snapped back, finally sure of his ground. "You told Bush you'd taken Tip and Lenny to Blue Lake Sunday, but you told me they were out hunting that wild boy."

"You heard me wrong! I never said no such—"

"Pipe down!" Thomas' voice had a military ring that made Angus flinch. "I'm settling this right now! Your kids ran off Sunday and swiped that stuff from Holliday's. Lenny went through the window—he's small enough. They thought they could blame it on that so-called wild boy. But with the law buzzing around all day, you got to worrying about having stolen property on the place. So tonight you sent Tip and Lenny off to hide the things near the Johnsons'."

Thomas swung determinedly toward the door. "Come on, Bush. Get your flashlight. We don't need a search warrant for this. I'll bet those things are hidden on the edge of Johnson's woods. They won't be hard to find."

"You're taking a lot on yourself," Anderson Bush said coldly. "You'd better be sure what you're doing."

Emma Pitts cried, "If you find them things in the woods, it'll be because that wild varmint put 'em there! You've got a lot of nerve, Tom Bean, trying to blame it on Angus's boys!"

"There'll be fingerprints," Thomas reminded her and limped outside.

Reluctantly Anderson Bush got a flashlight from his car, and they started across the pasture below the house. A mist was settling down from the ridge, making the night darker than it had been. After a hundred yards the deputy stopped.

"Mr. Bean," he grated, "I've heard enough lies for one night. It would have been impossible to have seen anyone out here when we drove by. What kind of trick are you trying to pull?"

Little Jon tugged at Thomas Bean's sleeve. "Over there," he said, pointing into the mist.

The deputy swung his light, and Thomas called, "Tip! Lenny! Come here!"

Two vague forms materialized in the beam of the light. They started to run, then halted as the deputy shouted. Slowly they came over, two slender boys in soiled and patched jeans, with something secretive in their knobby faces that reminded Little Jon of Mrs. Macklin. Suddenly he felt sorry for Mrs. Macklin and for Tip and Lenny.

Anderson Bush demanded, "What are you boys doing out here?"

"We got a right to be here," Tip, the taller one, said defiantly. "This here's our land."

Thomas said, "You were coming from Johnson's woods. Take us back the way you came."

"What for? We ain't been over there."

"You were seen over there. Get going!"

"You never seen us!" cried Lenny. "It musta been that wild boy."

Tip said, "We was coming back from the barn when we thought we seen something out here. Bet it was that wild boy!"

"Get going!" Thomas Bean repeated. "Take us where you hid those things."

There were loud denials. Tip cried, "How you think we gonna find something in the dark we don't know nothing about?"

They were approaching the lower fence. Poplar thickets and brush loomed dimly on the other side. Anderson Bush began moving slowly along the fence, directing his light into the brush. Once Little Jon plucked silently at Thomas Bean's sleeve and pointed. Thomas nodded and whispered, "Wait. We don't want this to look too easy."

They reached the corner near the road, and the deputy turned back. Now he crawled through the fence and very carefully began scuffling through the brush as he swung his light about. Thomas and Little Jon followed him, but Tip and Lenny stubbornly refused to leave the pasture.

The mist settled lower, and presently it became so thick that the power of the light beam was lost after a few yards.

Anderson Bush said, "It would take a hundred men to find anything out here tonight—*if* there's anything for them to find."

"Let me have the light a minute," said Thomas. "I thought I saw something gleam way over in yonder."

Thomas took the light and, guided by tugs of Little Jon's hand on his sleeve, plunged deeper into the woods.

Little Jon stopped suddenly before a clump of small cedars growing close to the ground. There was nothing

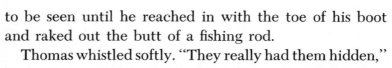

to be seen until he reached in with the toe of his boot and raked out the butt of a fishing rod.

Thomas whistled softly. "They really had them hidden," he muttered. "Bush will never believe we didn't know where they were. Careful—don't touch anything with your hands."

Thomas raised his voice and called the deputy.

Little Jon watched while Anderson Bush carefully drew two fishing rods, a tackle box, and an expensive target rifle from under the cedars. The deputy remained grimly silent until he had tied the fishing rods and the tackle box together with his handkerchief and looped the gun strap over his shoulder.

"Mr. Bean," he said at last, "you not only have a very convenient memory, but you and that boy have an exceptional ability to locate things you claim you have no knowledge of. But I'll ask you no more questions. I'll leave that to the court."

"Very well," snapped Thomas, "if that's the way you want to play it. But make sure you check all the fingerprints on those things—and in the house as well."

"You can depend on that, Mr. Bean."

He Is Summoned

Rascal was whining forlornly when they got back, begging for Little Jon to take him out. Little Jon went over and petted him, quieting him with a promise for tomorrow, then followed Thomas into the house. It had been a long and difficult day, and he knew that Thomas was badly upset by all that had happened. That was the worst of it—knowing how Thomas felt and knowing it had all come about because the Beans were trying to help him.

Tonight, if it would have made matters any easier for the Beans, he would not have hesitated to go away. He could leave his knife in payment for Rascal, and he and the big dog could take their chances in the forest. But it was too late for that. It solved nothing, and it would only make things harder for Thomas.

Sally and Brooks were still eating when they reached the kitchen. They were bursting with questions, but Mary Bean silenced them. "You look beat," she said anxiously to Thomas. "What happened up at Macklins'?"

Thomas told her. "So," he finished wearily, "the cat's about out of the bag. Or it will be soon—if Bush has his way."

"Why do some people want to make so much trouble?" Mary asked. "But we'll talk about it after you eat. You two get washed and come to the table."

They cleaned up and ate silently. Finally Little Jon said unhappily, "I'm awfully sorry about all this, Mr. Bean. I wish I could do something to—to—"

"Sorry? Why should *you* be sorry?"

"Because of the trouble I'm causing."

Thomas sat up. "If there's any apologizing to be done, *I'm* the one to do it. I apologize for the stupidity and meanness of some of the people you've met here. Actually, there are some pretty nice people in this world—only there aren't enough of them. It's just too bad that the troublemaking kind keeps all the rest of us on the jump and makes things the way they are. Maybe nature intended it that way—to keep prodding us so we'll learn faster. I don't really know." He spread his hands. "I wish I knew what Bush is going to do."

"When he left," said Little Jon, "he was thinking about the Marines and finding out about Captain O'Connor."

Mary Bean gasped. "Oh, no! That would tie it."

Sally, helping with the dishes, said, "Jon, how did you know what Mr. Bush was thinking?"

"I—just knew."

Sally wrinkled her nose at him. "I know how you knew." In a stage whisper she added aloofly, *"You read minds."*

Brooks gaped at her. "You're crazy as a hoot owl!"

Mary said, "Sally!"

But Sally went on quickly, "Jon can! I've known it since yesterday. It's, oh, lots of little things—like always passing me the right dish at the table before I ask for it." She made a face at Brooks. *"You* didn't know it, smartie. That proves girls are smarter than boys—except that Jon's smarter than any of us. I think it's wonderful. I wish *I* could do what he can."

"Thank Pete you can't," Brooks said with feeling. "Life wouldn't be worth living around here." He stared at Little Jon. "Sally's only kidding, isn't she?"

Thomas Bean said, "It's true, Brooks, but stow that down your hatch and keep it battened." He frowned at Mary. "If Bush finds out about the O'Connors, that's all he needs to know. Fingerprints won't matter. He'll haul us into court, and we'll be forced to tell everything."

Thomas began snapping his fingers. Suddenly he lurched to his feet. "I'm going to call Miss Josie and arrange a private talk with her. She's the only really understanding person around here, and if she knows the facts ahead of time, she'll—What's the matter, Mary?"

Mary was shaking her head. "I've already tried to get her on the phone. I got so worried while you were up at Macklins' that I had to do something. Miss Josie is away tonight. Tomorrow she's got a busy morning in court, and she's flying to Washington immediately afterward. She won't be back till Monday."

Thomas sat down and began snapping his fingers again. Little Jon asked, "Who is Miss Josie?"

"She's Mrs. Cunningham," Mary told him. "Judge Cunningham, really. But everyone calls her Miss Josie. She handles all juvenile cases. I wish we could talk to her!"

She looked knowingly at Thomas. "Did you have any luck this morning—rock-hunting?"

"Yes. Very good luck. I'm taking Jon back first thing tomorrow. It may help his memory."

"Hey, can I go with you?" Brooks asked. "School's out, and—"

"No," Thomas said firmly. "This is too important. Jon's *got* to recover his memory. His best chance is to start over there on the mountain, where he first found himself. We can't have anyone along."

"It's way past bedtime," Mary reminded them, "and it's been a day. Everybody scoot."

Little Jon awoke to a misty morning with a threat of rain over the ridges. The rain notwithstanding, he and Thomas set out on foot at daybreak, taking the shortcut through the gap that led to the other valley. This time Rascal went with them. To Thomas's amazement the big dog behaved himself and kept quiet even when deer were sighted.

It started to pour when they reached the cave, but neither cared. There was something to be learned here if they could find it. While Thomas crawled about in the dim interior, chipping experimentally with his hammer, Little Jon sat down and tried to think.

Thomas, glancing at him once, said, "Maybe you'd better not *try* to remember. Sort of let your mind go blank. It might come to you easier."

He did as Thomas suggested. Even being here was exciting. Shadows of thoughts seemed to be crowding into the background of his mind. While he waited for them to take

form, he drew out his knife and idly began to carve a twisted piece of root that lay near the cave entrance.

The thought shadows refused to take form that morning, but the piece of root did. When Thomas Bean saw it, the rain had stopped, and the root had become the striking head of a man—a man with a curious cap over his long hair, and one hand clenched under his chin as if he were lost in thought.

Little Jon was surprised that Thomas should make such a fuss over it. "But doesn't everybody do things like this?" he asked.

"Hardly. It would take a genius like Rodin to produce such a head. Here, look what *I* found. It was under that fall of rock."

Thomas held out a woven cap much like the one in the carving. Little Jon put it on. It fitted him.

"The cap," said Thomas, "proves—at least to me—that you landed here in the cave. It was probably knocked off when you fell and covered up. It's a wonder you weren't killed. Anyway, the cap also proves that Mary's idea of the door is correct. You see, something had to happen in here to *make* that rock fall on your cap. It isn't the kind of rock that ever splits and breaks into fragments like this—unless a force as strong as a lightning bolt hits it. Now, there's no mechanism in here or anything that moves. That means that the door, and whatever it is that makes it work, is on the other side—I mean in that distant place where your people are."

He was sure Thomas was right. He wondered, with a longing he could not express, if he had a father and mother beyond the door and if he would ever see them again.

Thomas said, "Let's get back. I want to show Mary these things."

Mary Bean's eyes were stormy when they returned.

"It's started," she snapped before they could show her the cap and the carving. "The phone's been ringing all day. Thomas, did you know we've been hiding a wild boy that spits fire, jumps a hundred feet, and eats live rattlesnakes? That's how the tale has grown. I'd like to choke Gilby—and stuff Anderson Bush down his throat!"

She paused for breath. "That's only the half of it. There was a reporter here about an hour ago. I told him he'd been hearing a lot of nonsense and that we only had the young son of a friend of ours visiting us. I don't think he believed me, and I'm sure he'll be back, because he wants pictures. He had hardly left when *this* came."

Angrily she thrust out a stiff folded paper.

"What is it?" Thomas asked.

"A summons! To the juvenile court. Monday at ten."

Thomas whistled. "Bush has found out that the O'Connors didn't have any children. I'll bet he got on the phone first thing and called the Marine personnel office in Washington. Jon was right. We should never have made up that story. All we can do is keep Jon out of sight—and pray that his memory comes back."

"Did you make any progress today?" she asked.

"Some." Thomas opened the knapsack and took out the cap. He explained about it. "It proves you're right about the door idea—and it tells us some other things." He looked around. "Where are Brooks and Sally?"

"I sent them out to pick wild strawberries, where nobody can see them. That reporter caught Sally in the yard and tried to question her."

"Well, we mustn't let Brooks, Sally, or anyone—even Miss Josie—know about the cave. If it's ever so much as mentioned, the news of it will spread, and there'll be a thousand people hunting for it. It'll be torn apart and blasted and the pieces probably sold for souvenirs. But if it's never mentioned, it'll never be discovered. You can walk right by it and not know it's there. We've got to keep it that way. It's Jon's only means of getting back where he came from."

"But how—"

"How does it work? Mary, only Jon's memory can tell us that. We're just guessing, but we figure it's a sort of threshold—a place where you land when you step through from the other side. My compass goes haywire in there, so I suppose the earth's magnetism has something to do with it. From the looks of it, it hasn't been used for ages."

Thomas paused, then added, "When you think about it, there's no reason why it should ever be used again—except to get Jon back."

Little Jon asked, "Why do you say that, Mr. Bean?"

"Just this: If your people are as advanced as we believe they are, what have we to offer that they'd be the least bit interested in?" Thomas laughed. "I'll bet they took one look at us and decided we were best forgotten. They probably thought more of our wild creatures—wouldn't be surprised if they carried some young ones home with them, before we finished killing them all off."

Thomas took the carving from the knapsack.

"Have a look at this, Mary. Jon made it while I was poking around."

Mary Bean studied the carving. She said nothing for a minute, but Little Jon was aware of her amazement, the quick turning of her thoughts, her sudden conviction.

"You—you think it looks like me!" he exclaimed. "That it could be my—father."

"Yes, Jon, I do. It would almost have to be. And being what he is, I'm almost sure I know what he's doing this very minute—he's moving heaven and earth to get that *door* thing repaired so he can find you."

Thomas snapped his fingers. "Of course! Jon's here by accident—and if the door were usable, he'd have been found before he left the cave. There's been no change in the place, so it means the thing hasn't been repaired yet."

Suddenly Mary asked, "Jon, can you write in your language?"

"I don't know. I haven't tried."

"Try it now. It's important. If your people came looking for you, they wouldn't know what had become of you—unless you left a message in the cave."

"But if they are like I am," he told her, "they would only have to call—and I'm sure I would hear them, even miles away. Still, if I were asleep . . ."

He sat down at the table with paper and pencil and tried to remember symbols that might stand for thoughts. He doodled and made marks on the paper, but they were not marks with meaning.

"I'm afraid I've forgotten how," he said.

"But you must know your language," Mary insisted. "Remember the little song you sang the other day?"

"I remember that—but I can't put it on paper. Do you suppose if I learned to write your language, that it would help bring back the other? Brooks was showing me the alphabet the other night, and I can print that already. Maybe if you'll show me how to make words with it . . ."

The writing lesson was interrupted by the telephone and later by the return of the reporter.

Little Jon hid in the front bedroom while Thomas spoke to the man. The reporter was not easily turned away this time.

"Mr. Bean," he said stubbornly, "you ought to be glad to get a little free publicity. It'll help your business. You'd be surprised at the people who'll come out to your Rock Shop to—"

"I'm quite aware of it," said Thomas, "and I don't want it. Mrs. Bean has already told you about the boy. I can't help these crazy tales that are going around, but I'd advise you to be very careful what you print."

"But at least you can let me take a picture of him, Mr. Bean. I know there's nothing in the tales, and I'd soft-pedal all that. But he's news, and I could do a nice little human-interest story that would help you a lot here."

"Sorry," said Thomas, showing him the door. "No pictures, please."

"Okay. But there'll be plenty of pictures taken when Monday comes."

"What do you mean by that?"

"Mr. Bean, it's already common knowledge that the boy's a juvenile delinquency case. Of course, we're not allowed to print anything like that—but the wild boy angle is something else. You can't stop news, Mr. Bean—and that boy is *news*. I'll see you Monday."

He Goes to Court

It was five days till Monday, and Little Jon dreaded it more each day. The phone rang almost constantly at first. Cars filled with curious people began to creep along the road. To escape prying neighbors, and the probability of more reporters, he and Thomas spent long hours at the cave.

None of this helped his memory.

When Monday finally came, Thomas and Mary took him to the courthouse in the center of town and tried unsuccessfully to slip through the rear entrance without being noticed. A lurking photographer spotted them. Suddenly two cameras were flashing, and they were surrounded by a small crowd of ogling townspeople. Thomas thrust through into the hall, where they were rescued by a policeman.

"In yonder, Mr. Bean," said the policeman, pointing to a door. "Back, everybody! You know these hearings are private."

"Hey, Mr. Bean," a man called, "can that kid really jump a hundred feet?"

The door closed behind them, shutting out the racket. Thomas, Little Jon saw, had timed their arrival carefully. The others were all present, sitting in a semicircle of newly varnished chairs facing a desk. The small room seemed overflowing with eight other people besides himself and the Beans. As he sat down on one side between Thomas and Mary, he could feel every eye upon him.

Angus Macklin and his two boys were sitting over on his left. Angus was smiling, and Tip and Lenny looked stubbornly defiant. Gilby and Emma Pitts were behind them. Anderson Bush, his hands full of papers, was talking in a low voice to a large, square-faced woman in the corner. With the woman was a long-nosed man in glasses. The man seemed aloof and officious.

Little Jon glanced uneasily at the square-faced woman. She kept staring at him as if he were something unpleasant. Mary whispered, "That's Mrs. Groome. She's in charge of welfare. The man with her is Mr. McFee, the probation officer."

The door on the other side of the desk opened, and a respectful hush fell over the room. Judge Cunningham entered. She was small, gray, and precise. There was no nonsense about her, but behind her quiet, thoughtful eyes Little Jon sensed all the qualities of a friend.

As she took her seat, she smiled quickly at Thomas and Mary. "I've been wanting to visit the Rock Shop again, Thomas, but I haven't had time lately."

Thomas was already on his feet. "Miss Josie," he said, thrusting a folded sheet of paper across her desk, "before this thing gets any more out of hand, there are some points that I feel you—and you alone—should know about. I've jotted them down here."

"Thank you, Thomas." Judge Cunningham smoothed the paper out on her desk and quietly surveyed the room. "Why are you here, Gilby?"

Gilby Pitts gave a nervous twitch of his high shoulder. "Me an' Emma are witnesses, Miss Josie. I got charge of Dr. Holliday's place where all them things was stolen. An' we seen that wild boy yonder when he—"

"That's enough, Gilby!" The judge's voice had the sting of a whip. "You'll not use that expression in this room. If you are asked anything, you'll stick to facts, and facts only—and you'll not repeat them when you leave here."

She turned to Anderson Bush. "Mr. Bush, I've been back in town for three hours, and I've heard nothing but preposterous gossip about this case. Juvenile cases of this nature are *not* for the public. When children get in trouble, they need help, not foolish gossip and publicity. Yet I find our town full of talk and the courthouse full of curious people. It's disgraceful and disgusting."

The deputy's face had darkened, but he said smoothly, "I'm sorry, Miss Josie, but the talk had already started before I entered the case. Naturally, when someone catches a strangely dressed boy trespassing under the, er, most unusual circumstances—and then discovers that there's been a robbery . . ."

"Let's not waste time, Mr. Bush," she interrupted. "You were ordered to investigate a simple matter of breaking and entering and theft—obviously committed by one or more boys. Stick to that and tell me exactly what you learned about it."

Anderson Bush began. He told of Gilby Pitts's discovery of the forced window in the Holliday house, the small footprints inside, the missing articles, and their high value. Then he related what Gilby had told him about catching a strangely dressed boy in the field. The deputy paused and said, "Dr. Holliday's place is only three hundred yards from the spot where Mr. Pitts caught this boy Saturday morning. It was Monday morning before the theft was discovered, and naturally our suspicions centered on this strange boy. I'd like to read you a description of that boy as I got it from Mr. and Mrs. Pitts and tell you a few facts about him I've uncovered. He—"

"That's unnecessary at the moment," said Judge Cunningham. "Confine yourself to the theft."

The deputy shrugged. "Yes, ma'am. As I was saying, this strange boy seemed the logical suspect. All the same, I investigated three possible suspects in Mr. Pitts's area and checked them out. That left only the boys living in Mr. Bean's valley. Now, there's a gap behind the Holliday place, which makes it an easy hike from one valley to the other, if you happen to know the way."

"I know about the gap," said Judge Cunningham. "I've lived in this country sixty-four years. Proceed."

"Well, on Mr. Bean's side there's only Mr. Bean's boy— and this, er, strange boy he has with him—and the two Macklin boys up the road. I checked out the two Macklin boys. Witnesses prove they were away all Saturday and Sunday, which is the only period the theft could have happened. I also checked—"

"Pardon me," said Thomas. "You are leaving out something, Mr. Bush. I told you Tuesday night what Mr. Macklin told Mrs. Bean and me at the shop—that his boys had been out all Sunday afternoon looking for that strange boy."

Angus burst out, "I never said no such a thing! We were at Blue Lake! We—"

"Quiet, both of you," Judge Cunningham ordered. "Mr. Bush, did you check a second time at Blue Lake and get the names of those witnesses?"

"I did, ma'am. Mr. Macklin and his family were visiting a Mr. and Mrs. Hinkley all Sunday afternoon. The Hinkleys swear to it."

"Mr. Bush," said Judge Cunningham, "did you know that Joe Hinkley and Angus Macklin were half brothers?"

Anderson Bush stiffened. "No, ma'am."

"It takes time to learn all these local relationships, and you've been here only five years. Proceed with your story."

"Well, ma'am, as I was saying, I checked out Mr. Bean's boy, Brooks. That left only Mr. Bean's visitor, this boy he calls Jon O'Connor. When I questioned him about Jon O'Connor, Mr. Bean was very evasive. He told me that Jon O'Connor was the orphaned son of Captain James O'Connor of the Marines, who was killed recently in North Africa. He said further that the Marines had brought Jon O'Connor to his house Saturday evening and that the boy could have had nothing to do with the theft. Yet Tuesday evening Mr. Pitts saw this Jon O'Connor and positively identified him as the strange boy he had caught in his field. Later Mrs. Pitts identified him as the same boy—the Beans had changed his clothes and cut his hair to make him look more normal—"

"But he's the same sneaky boy!" Emma Pitts exclaimed. "I'd know 'im anywhere. He ain't natural!"

"Quiet, Emma!" the judge snapped. "Be careful what you say in here. Mr. Bush, this is all very interesting about Jon O'Connor, but at the moment we are concerned only with the theft. I understand that the stolen articles were recovered that very evening when you took Mr. Bean over to the Macklins'. Tell us about that."

"Yes, ma'am." The deputy pointed to a table in the corner. On it were two fishing rods, a tackle box, and a rifle. "Those are the articles, ma'am. When we got to the Macklins', Mr. Bean insisted he'd seen the Macklin boys crossing their pasture, carrying what appeared to be the stolen things. He also insisted that Tip and Lenny were going to hide the things over in Johnson's woods, so they wouldn't be found on their own place." The deputy paused.

"Well?" said Judge Cunningham.

"It was a pretty dark night," said Anderson Bush. "I've got good vision, but I didn't see Tip and Lenny crossing the pasture. However, Mr. Bean insisted that we immediately search the edge of the woods. We started across the pasture and met Tip and Lenny returning. That struck me as rather odd, and I didn't get an explanation out of them till later. Anyway, I searched the edge of the woods very carefully and found nothing."

The deputy stopped again and glanced at Little Jon.

"Go on," said the judge. "Who found the things?"

"Mr. Bean and that boy yonder did. They found them in less than five minutes. The articles were hidden far back under a cedar clump, where they couldn't have been seen even in daylight. It would have been almost impossible to find them at night unless you knew exactly where they were."

"Were there fingerprints on them, Mr. Bush?"

"Yes, ma'am. The fingerprints belonged to Tip and Lenny. When I questioned the Macklins about it afterward, they finally said their boys had found the stolen articles during the afternoon when they were playing in the woods. They'd taken them to the barn. Mr. Macklin says when he learned about it, he made the boys return the things to the cedars and hide them exactly as they'd found them. He says he was afraid they might be accused of the theft if they reported it."

Judge Cunningham asked, "Did you find any of Jon O'Connor's fingerprints on the stolen articles?"

"No, ma'am. But they could easily have been rubbed off by so much handling from other people."

"Did you find Jon O'Connor's fingerprints in the Holiday house?"

"No, ma'am. I did find Tip's and Lenny's prints in there—but Mr. Pitts tells me the boys had been in the house a number of times. The doctor had them do odd jobs about the place."

"I see. Now, what have you learned about Jon O'Connor?"

Anderson Bush smiled. "There is no such person, Miss Josie. I checked with the Marines. It is true that there was a Captain O'Connor, that he was Mr. Bean's friend, and that he was killed recently. But he had no children."

"Very well," said the judge. "That states things clearly. Thomas, what have you to say?"

Thomas Bean swallowed. "It's true that I lied to Mr. Bush. But I had good reasons. Miss Josie, before I try to explain, I wish you'd read those notes I gave you. They'll prepare you—"

Little Jon clutched his arm. "Please—not yet. Miss Josie," he spoke earnestly, "before you read that, will you let me say something first?"

She nodded. "Yes, Jon. We want your side of it."

Little Jon took a long breath. This was not going to be easy. Because of Anderson Bush, he was forced to say and do certain things he abhorred. But, if only for Thomas's sake, he had to go through with it.

"Miss Josie," he began, "Mr. Bean has been trying to protect me ever since he found me Saturday evening over a week ago. I cannot remember anything that happened before that day. I had been in some kind of accident, for I was badly bruised. And I was frightened, because I didn't know what had happened or where I was—except that I was somewhere on a strange mountain. I followed a doe and her fawn down to Mr. Pitts's field, trying to find someone to help me. Mr. Pitts tried to kill the doe, but I spoiled his aim, an'—"

"That's a lie!" Gilby cried. "I never shot at no doe!"

"Gilby," Judge Cunningham said icily, "hold your tongue, or I will fine you. Jon, please continue."

"Mr. Pitts caught me, but after Mrs. Pitts came, I broke away and ran. I wandered all day through the mountains until I came out on the road where Mr. Bean found me."

"Jon," said the judge, "during your wanderings that day, did you find the Holliday house and enter it?"

"No, ma'am. I haven't yet seen the place. Besides, I was looking for someone to help me." Little Jon smiled. "I would hardly have expected to find any help in two fishing rods, a heavy tackle box, and a rifle. I knew nothing about such things at the time, and I couldn't have carried them if I'd wanted to. I needed a stick to walk."

He paused to plan his next move. Over in the corner he saw Mr. McFee, the long-nosed probation officer, whistle softly and shake his head. "I've heard some wild ones in my day," McFee said under his breath to Mrs. Groome, "but this kid's tale has 'em all beat."

"Mr. McFee," the judge said coldly, "keep your opinions to yourself. Jon, you've just told me you knew nothing of fishing rods and rifles. For a boy of today, I find that a very strange statement."

"I'm sure you do, Miss Josie. But it's true. You see—"

"Jon," she asked suddenly, "how old are you?"

"I don't know, ma'am."

She studied him a moment, puzzled, then said, "Well, continue your story."

"That's about all, Miss Josie, except for finding the stolen things. After being taken to Mr. Macklin's house that night, I knew exactly where they were."

Judge Cunningham raised her eyebrows. "You did?"

"Yes, ma'am. Here is how I knew. Will you think of a number, Miss Josie? I believe it will be better if you think of a large one."

"Very well. I've thought of one. What about it?"

"The number is three million, seven hundred and forty thousand, nine hundred, and seventy-six."

The judge opened her mouth, closed it, then sat perfectly motionless while she looked at him. The room had become deathly still.

Little Jon said, "I'm not sure my pronunciation is right. I haven't known English very long, and Mrs. Bean has had so much trouble with people interrupting her lately that she hasn't had time to teach me certain things. Is the number I gave correct?"

She nodded, her lips compressed.

"Do you want to try another number, Miss Josie—or something else?"

"It isn't necessary," she answered, almost in a whisper. "It's obvious, Jon, that you can read my thoughts."

"Yes, Miss Josie. It is very unpleasant to have to tell you this, but the thoughts of everyone in this room are so—so loud, they might just as well be shouting. So how can I help but know what the Macklins have done?"

"I don't believe it!" Anderson Bush grated. "This smooth-talking kid is full of more lies than any kid I ever—"

"Please, Mr. Bush," Little Jon said quickly, before the judge could speak, "I'd rather not have to say any more. But if you won't take numbers for proof, I'll have to convince you another way. Years ago you were in the army. You were ordered to drive a truck somewhere. On the way you had a bad accident. You—" Little Jon swallowed. "Must I tell what you did and what happened to you afterward?"

The deputy's jaws were knotted; his face had paled.

"No!" he said hoarsely. "I've heard enough." He glared at Angus Macklin. "What about it, Macklin? Have you been stringing me along all this time?"

"No—no—honest I ain't!" Angus had lost his smile. His hands were shaking. "My boys wouldn't—"

The deputy snapped, "You crazy fool, this kid really is a mind reader! Don't you realize what that means? You can't keep a secret from him. *Nobody* can!"

Emma Pitts suddenly cried, "I *told* you that kid's unnatural! Let me out of here—I don't want nothin' to do with no mind reader!" She and Gilby were on their feet, backing away. There was fear in their faces.

The room was in an uproar. From somewhere in a drawer, Judge Cunningham produced a gavel. She pounded it vigorously on the desk.

"Sit down!" she ordered. "Quiet, all of you!"

When the room was restored to order, she said, "Angus Macklin, I've known you all my life, and I happen to remember things about you I'll not mention here. Let's have the truth. Did Tip and Lenny break into the Holliday place and take those things?"

Angus swallowed and nodded. "Y-yes, ma'am."

"Where did they hide them?"

"In the barn at first. Then—then I got to worrying about it and had 'em take the things over in the cedars."

187

"I see. You thought all the blame would fall on this strange boy everyone was talking about. Angus, this is a very serious matter. The value of those stolen articles is over five hundred dollars. I want you and Tip and Lenny to go home and think about how serious it is. Tomorrow I have a full day, but Wednesday I want you all back here at ten o'clock, and I'll decide what to do about you. I'm afraid Tip and Lenny are badly in need of corrective measures. You, Angus, could be prosecuted."

She turned and glanced at Mrs. Groome and Mr. Mc-Fee. "Does what I'm doing meet with your approval?"

Mr. McFee nodded; Mrs. Groome started to speak, then nodded also.

The judge said, "All right, Angus. You and the boys may go. Gilby, you and Emma may go. But let me warn all of you not to say one word of what you've heard in this room this morning."

When they were gone, Mrs. Groome spoke first.

"Miss Josie," she began disapprovingly, "I don't know what to make of this boy. He may be a mind reader, but I'm not at all convinced he's telling the truth. He sounds entirely too clever for someone his age. I just wonder. Furthermore, if he's really lost his memory and doesn't know where his home is, then he's a welfare case, and I should be the one to handle him."

She looked coldly at Thomas. "Mr. Bean, I think you've taken a lot on yourself. Why didn't you come to me in the first place when you found this boy?"

Thomas said, "Mrs. Groome, I did what I thought was best for Jon. If Miss Josie will read what I've written for her, I'm sure she will agree with me."

Suddenly Little Jon found the judge smiling at him.

He smiled back, loving her. "I think you'll find it easier to understand now, Miss Josie," he said.

He Is Threatened

Judge Cunningham took her glasses from her bag, wiped them and put them on, and unfolded the paper. It was filled with Thomas's small, neat handwriting, the facts carefully arranged as if he were making an official report. As she read, her mouth opened slightly, and she bit down on her lower lip. Other than that, she gave no indication of the shock and astonishment that Little Jon knew she felt.

Thomas had listed all that the Beans knew about him— the way he had learned English, his ability to speak to animals, his strange clothing, his total ignorance of some things, and his familiarity with others. It was a long list, and Thomas had even given the value of the gems in Little Jon's knife and clip. Nothing had been omitted but the cave.

Thomas had headed the paper:

"Secret—This is for Judge Josephine Cunningham's eyes only."

At the bottom he had added:

> After exhausting all possibilities, we are convinced that Jon is an accidental visitor from another planet. He is sure of this himself. A few scraps of returning memory give proof of it and indicate how he arrived and how he may be returned. We are working on that now. Our main problem is to avoid further publicity and give him a chance to get his memory back. Our one fear is that some government agency may learn of his abilities and take him away and hold him for study. We feel this would be a tragedy. Please help us all you can.
>
> Thomas Jamieson Bean

Judge Cunningham read the paper a second time. Anderson Bush crossed and recrossed his legs; Mr. McFee began tapping his fingers impatiently on the table beside him. Mrs. Groome seemed to be swelling momentarily. Little Jon knew that she was burning with both resentment and curiosity.

Suddenly Mrs. Groome said, "Miss Josie, if this boy— whatever his name is—is a welfare case, I have a right to know whatever there is to know about him."

The judge ignored her. Before saying anything, she carefully folded the paper and put it in her handbag with her glasses. She looked thoughtfully at Thomas; then her eyes met Little Jon's. He smiled back at her and knew he had another conspirator on his side.

"Thomas," she murmured, "it's fortunate I've known you as long as I have. You did a lot of Intelligence work in the Marines, didn't you?"

"Yes, Miss Josie."

She turned to Mrs. Groome. "Jon is not a welfare case," she said quietly.

"But—but of course he is!" Mrs. Groome protested. "He's a lost boy—he doesn't even know who he is."

"He was lost for one day," said Judge Cunningham.

Mrs. Groome seemed to swell even larger. "Miss Josie, I don't understand this at all. What right have the Beans to keep a boy like this—"

"Jon happens to be visiting the Beans," replied Judge Cunningham firmly. "That's all that is necessary for anyone to know."

"Well! This is certainly *very* strange. If the boy's parents are unknown, who gave him permission to stay at the Beans'? I think this should be looked into. I also think there should be a medical report on the boy. I think I have a right to insist—"

"Mrs. Groome," Judge Cunningham interrupted quietly, "I understand your feelings about the matter. But much more is known about Jon than can ever be told here. He has every right to visit the Beans for as long as they wish. It is very unfortunate that he happened to be drawn into the public eye when so much depends upon—secrecy."

The judge uttered the last word as if she were touching on high matters of state. It had an immediate effect upon her audience. Anderson Bush and Mr. McFee blinked, and Mrs. Groome was visibly deflated.

"So I must insist," Judge Cunningham went on, "that all of you say nothing whatever about what you have learned here—not even the fact that Mr. Bean has done Intelligence work. Your silence is extremely important. There'll be questions, and you can help by making light of this—and saying it was all a mistake. And it was a mistake—a terrible one."

She stood up. "Thomas, I'll be out to see you as soon as I possibly can. Mr. Bush, please escort the Beans outside and keep those foolish people away from them."

It was over, this part of it at least, but the rest of it was just beginning. Little Jon knew that as they started for home. The judge had ordered secrecy from everyone, though not for an instant had she believed no one would talk.

Money was bound to make someone talk. That thought had been in the judge's mind when they left.

Little Jon said to Thomas and Mary, "I'm sorry for what happened in the courtroom. But I couldn't think of any other way to solve things."

"You had to do it," said Thomas. "There wasn't any other way."

Mary said, "You certainly gave Anderson Bush a jolt—and the rest of them, too. Anyway, you prepared Miss

Josie for what Thomas had written. She was able to make up her mind quickly and decide what to do. She's a remarkable woman. I wish we'd gone to her when we first found you."

"That was our mistake," Thomas mumbled. "But we had no idea something like this was going to happen. Now too many people know Jon's a mind reader."

"Oh dear," said Mary. "If the papers ever get it . . ."

"They'll get it. The first reporter that waves some cash under Gilby's nose will learn all about it—with trimmings. The same goes for Angus—in spite of the trouble he's in."

They turned into the driveway at last. It was good to be back and hear Rascal barking a greeting. Little Jon got out and started happily for the enclosure, then stopped as the kitchen door flew open and Brooks and Sally raced toward them.

Something was wrong. Sally looked frightened. Brooks was angry.

"Hey, Dad! Look what somebody threw on our porch a few minutes ago!" Brooks thrust out a crumpled piece of wrapping paper. "It was folded around a stone."

After his lessons, Little Jon had no difficulty reading what was on the paper. Thomas held it for all to see. Crudely written in large letters were the words: "This is a warning. Get rid of that wild boy and do it quick."

He heard Mary's gasp and was aware of Thomas's sudden fury. "Mr. Bean," he said before Thomas could speak, "if I stay here, I might be a danger to all of you. Maybe it would be better if I went to—to that place we found. I could camp there with Rascal—"

"No!" snapped Thomas. "This is your home. I'll be hanged if I'll let any bunch of cowardly characters drive you away from here! Brooks, did you get a look at the person who threw this?"

"No, Dad. Sally and I were in the garden when it happened. We heard Rascal bark; then the stone hit the porch. There wasn't anybody in sight. But a little later I heard a car start up somewhere down by the fork. Did you pass anybody on the road?"

"No. He must have taken the west fork when he drove away, after sneaking up here through the trees. It had to be Angus or Gilby, or a relative. There's a bunch of them, counting the Blue Lake people, and they're all related. And they're all afraid now." Suddenly Thomas laughed. "After Jon's exhibition in court this morning, they all know what he can do, and they're scared to death of him."

Mary said worriedly, "I don't see anything funny in this, Thomas. Some of those people have things to hide. They could be dangerous."

"If they threaten us again, I'll have to show them that Jon and I can be more dangerous than they can."

"Daddy," said Sally, "did Jon read minds in court this morning?"

"He sure did, honey. That's why those people are afraid."

Sally laughed. "They'd be a great deal more afraid if they knew he came from Mars or someplace, wouldn't they?"

"Sally!" Mary exclaimed. "What ever—"

Brooks said, "I told you it couldn't be Mars, Sally. There's not enough air on it. It has to be a planet like ours. Isn't that right, Jon?"

"I think so," Little Jon answered. "But since I can't remember—"

Thomas was staring hard at Brooks, and suddenly Brooks burst out, "Aw, Dad, stop trying to hide it from us! Sally and I have had plenty of time to figure it out.

Why, anybody who can do all the things Jon can just couldn't be from *our* planet! He's too smart."

"Okay, son. You know the answer—but keep your hatch battened on it. Too many things are being learned about Jon already, and tomorrow the papers may be full of it. Before anything else happens, he's got to get his memory back."

Little Jon thought of the cave. He was anxious to return to it, but it was too late to start and get back before dark. He and Thomas would have to wait until morning.

Every visit had produced something, if only another carving. He had done three: the head of a man older than the first and another of a woman who Mary Bean believed was his mother. He hoped so. She was so beautiful, and she seemed so wise. Strange how his fingers seemed to remember things that his mind couldn't. But the thought shadows were always there. Soon they would take form. He was sure of that.

Rain was slashing down in torrents the next morning. Little Jon stared out at it in dismay. Thomas said, "It ought to pass in an hour or so. We'll get ready and leave the moment it clears a bit."

It was barely daybreak, and they dawdled over breakfast. They were hardly finished when the telephone rang.

Little Jon answered it. Judge Cunningham was calling.

"Jon," she said, "I don't suppose any of you have seen the morning papers yet."

"No, ma'am. Mr. Bean doesn't take a daily."

"Well, I've just seen two, and I'll try to get more. I think we'd better have a conference. Tell Mary I'm inviting myself to lunch. It's the only time I can get away."

In spite of the rain, it was a busy morning. Two cars containing out-of-town reporters and photographers came. Thomas had an unpleasant but firm session with them on the porch. They left the house but refused to leave the area. Long-distance calls began coming over the phone. A publishing syndicate wanted exclusive rights to Jon O'Connor's story. A theatrical agent offered a staggering amount of money for two weeks of personal appearances and mind reading. By the time Judge Cunningham's car spun into the lane, Thomas was fit to be tied.

The judge said, "I wish I weren't in such a rush, but everything seems to be happening at once for all of us. Thomas, look at these."

She spread an Atlanta paper and two others on the table. On the front page of two papers were pictures snapped at the courthouse. Under them were long stories. One was headed: "Mind-reading genius discovered in mountains." Another began: "Wild boy reads minds, clears self of theft charges." The one without pictures had a two-column box headed: "Who is Jon O'Connor?" All the known facts had been printed. These were filled in with highly colored rumors and questions.

Mary gasped. "It's worse than I ever—"

"It's what I was afraid of," said Judge Cunningham. "And it's only the start." She looked at Brooks and Sally. "How much do they know?"

"Everything," said Thomas. "We didn't tell them—they guessed it."

"If they guessed," she said, "others will, too, in time. Jon, have you any idea how valuable you can be to some people?"

Little Jon was shocked by what she was thinking. "I—I didn't realize that this country has enemies. You believe they might—is *kidnap* the word?"

"Yes. I'm just looking ahead, Jon. Nothing at all may happen, but we'll have to plan for the worst. There are some smart people in this world, and some of them can be dangerous. You said one thing in court yesterday that didn't worry me at the time, but it frightens me now. Somebody was bribed to tell it; it's in all three papers. Here it is: 'The thoughts of everyone in this room are so loud that they might just as well be shouting.' Thomas, I think we'd better hide Jon. For his own safety, I think we should get him away from these mountains to some-place where he won't be recognized."

Little Jon said, "But I can't leave, Miss Josie. I *have* to stay here."

"Why, Jon?"

Thomas said, "Let me explain. Miss Josie, he doesn't dare leave here, or he'll never get back where he came from. There's a—a connection in this area, something magnetic, that forms his only means of return. He has to regain his memory here and be close by when his people come looking for him—and from what we've learned, we're sure they will."

"Oh my, this does complicate things." She frowned and looked at Little Jon and said almost absently, "I wish you had your memory and that I had hours to talk with you, not minutes. I must have read what Thomas wrote about you a hundred times last night. It gave me a glimpse of what a peaceful and wonderful place your world must be—and how strange and terrible ours must look to you. Jon, the awful part of it is what people here would do to you if they could. They'd use you and pay no attention to the good you could give; they'd use your mind to help fight their secret battles. And no matter which side got you, nothing would be changed. It would still go on . . ."

The judge shook her head suddenly. "I've got to think of something. Thomas, there's a legal side to this that worries me. By law, you and Mary have no real authority to keep Jon. Before some agency tries to take him away,

I'd better have papers drawn up giving you temporary custody of him."

She stopped and stared out of the front window. "Oh, no! Look at those cars on the road. Silly people coming to gape. This settles it, Thomas. You'll have to have a guard here."

Brooks said, "Miss Josie, I think we need a guard. Look what someone threw on the porch yesterday." He showed her the piece of wrapping paper with the warning on it.

Her face tightened as she read it. "I don't like this, Thomas."

"What can they do?" said Thomas. "One of Gilby's bunch wrote it, I'm sure. They're just scared. Still—" Thomas paused and began snapping his fingers. "After what's in the papers, someone may try to use them. They're fools enough to let some clever person . . ."

"Yes," said Judge Cunningham. "That's exactly why they're dangerous. Thomas, I'm going to send a deputy out here this afternoon and try to get another one for night duty. I'm not sure I can manage a night man—you know how our sheriff is: if he smelled smoke, he wouldn't believe there's fire unless it burned his nose. Anyway, I'll fix up those papers as soon as possible."

That afternoon a young deputy drove out, parked his car near the edge of the lane, and stood waving traffic on while he barred the lane to visitors. His presence, however, did not prevent a television truck from stopping under the trees at the far side of the road. Its crew set up a camera on a high platform and began taking pictures of the growing traffic and everything happening on the Bean property.

When the young deputy went off duty that evening, no one came to take his place. He had been gone hardly ten minutes when a stone crashed through one of the front windows. Wrapped around it was a piece of paper covered with another crudely lettered warning: "Get rid of that wild boy—we mean business."

"Where's this thing going to end?" Thomas muttered angrily as he nailed a board over the broken pane.

He Is in Danger

The next day started badly. They had planned to leave early for the cave, but when Thomas went out to the barn at dawn, he discovered that his one milk cow was missing. She had gone back into the pasture the night before; this morning the pasture was empty, and the gate to the road at the far end of it was open.

It was obvious that the cow had been stolen, and most certainly for spite. Little Jon knew that Thomas never expected to see her again. The road was jamming with cruising sightseers, and the young deputy, back on duty, was having trouble keeping a fresh batch of reporters out of the yard.

The deputy had brought Mary a paper from town. There were pictures in it showing the Bean place and the deputy standing in the lane. The story was captioned: "Mystery boy's fame spreads, house guarded." In a separate column a new question was asked: "Is mind reader from Mars?"

Thomas glanced worriedly at the headlines and glared at the passing cars through the unbroken window. Little Jon, watching him, was sick at heart.

"I'd better phone Miss Josie," said Thomas.

It was past noon when Thomas managed to get Judge Cunningham at her home. While Thomas talked, Little Jon tried to think. Everything was so unbelievably tangled on this world, with their laws and money and their hates and their fighting for power. He could see only one solution that might help the Beans.

Thomas hung up at last. He shook his head. "Miss Josie's trying to work out something, but all this publicity has stirred up a hornet's nest. Mrs. Groome is making trouble, and if the government steps in and claims Jon . . ."

"But, Thomas," Mary cried, "they just *can't* take him away."

"I'm afraid they can, honey. If this were Jon's world and Jon's country, it would be an entirely different matter. And if Miss Josie had more time and could give us a chance to adopt Jon legally as our son, we'd have some rights. But there isn't time. Jon, you and I will go to that place we discovered. No one can find you there—and it's mighty important that you be there anyway. Mary, get us some blankets while I fill the knapsack. Jon, maybe you'd better change into your own clothes—we've nothing to compare with them for camping."

There was no changing Thomas's mind. In a very short time they were slipping out past the garden fence, carrying their equipment. Rascal trotted beside them.

They edged around the barn, skirted the pasture, and reached the road a quarter of a mile beyond the house. They crouched in the brush until no cars were in sight, then hurried across. In the woods on the other side, they began angling up the slope toward the gap trail.

They were still some distance from the gap when Little Jon stopped at a warning from Rascal. "Mr. Bean," he whispered, "we're being followed."

Thomas froze. "It must be more nosy reporters," he muttered.

"No, it's Mr. Pitts and—some strangers. Men I haven't met or seen around. I—I should have known about this earlier, but there were so many people on the road . . ."

His mind went out, searching, and his small hands clenched as he became aware of the danger they were in—Thomas especially. The pursuers would kill Thomas to get Jon O'Connor. It shocked Jon to realize that such a terrible value was placed on his mind-reading ability.

He said quietly to Thomas, "They've been watching the house with—with field glasses, waiting till we left. They can't see us here, but they saw us cross the road. Mr. Pitts thinks we're heading for the gap."

"If we hurry," Thomas whispered, "we can lose them on the other side."

"No—they've stopped, waiting for others to come. There are four—five in all. Mr. Pitts is talking to them. He's telling them we're bound to get away, once we cross over. He's going back and get a dog—that bloodhound you once had. If the others can't catch us, they'll wait for him at the gap. He—he thinks they're some sort of government men he's helping."

Muscles knotted in Thomas's jaw. "A fool like Gilby would swallow that. They've got us checked. We can't go to the cave. That bloodhound could trail us anywhere."

There was nothing to do but circle back as quickly and as quietly as they could and return to the house.

The sun had gone down over the ridge when they finally slipped in through the kitchen door. Mary paled when Thomas told her what had happened.

"You'd better call the sheriff," she urged. "That young deputy has gone home for the night, and Jon's got to have some protection. This is nothing less than an attempted kidnapping."

Thomas made several calls, all without result. The sheriff was away from town, and there were no deputies immediately available.

Thomas locked the doors and began limping about the room, snapping his fingers. Once he disappeared into the bedroom and came back with a pistol thrust into his pocket. Jon knew Thomas hated weapons, that he had thought, after the war, he would never use one again.

Little Jon studied the road through the windows. The twilight was deepening. A knot of coldness gathered in him as he considered what might happen to the Beans. As long as he was with them, Brooks and Sally and all of them would be in danger. Danger was out there; it wasn't close yet, but it would surely come upon them after dark. The road would be clear, and the one remaining car containing watching reporters would be gone.

Already the unknown men with Gilby had discovered that he and Thomas had not taken the gap trail. The house was in their thoughts, and they were waiting . . .

He wished he could understand what they were planning. But they were scattered about, and there were more men gathering. So many thoughts were confusing . . .

Thomas came over beside him. "Jon," he said softly, trying not to show his growing worry, "what's going on outside? Any idea?"

"I'm trying to find out."

It was hard to concentrate. Something was stirring in his mind. He tried to thrust it away, for at the moment it didn't matter. All that mattered was to draw danger away from the Beans.

As he studied the twilight again, he was aware of Rascal's uneasiness. Suddenly he knew that Gilby Pitts was somewhere over on the edge of the pasture, in the shadows. Gilby had Angus Macklin with him and some of their friends. They were going to help the outsiders as soon as dark came . . .

What was their plan?

He tried to reach Gilby's thoughts, but other thoughts kept intruding. There seemed to be a whispering in his mind.

"Little Jon! Little Jon! Where are you?"

All at once he gasped and stood rigid as understanding came.

Mary, seeing him, cried, "Jon! What's wrong?"

"The door—it must be open!" he managed to say. "My people—they are here—they are calling me . . ."

He Escapes

"Can you hear them?" Thomas exclaimed. "In your mind, I mean? They've come for you?"

"Yes—they've come through that place—it really is a sort of door . . . I can almost see it . . . it was broken on the other side, but they've got the power working, and the door is open . . . it's a shimmering spot, and you step right through it as if space were nothing . . ."

His hands were suddenly trembling; he clenched them and closed his eyes, listening to the silent voices calling eagerly to him. He answered and told them about the Beans and what had happened. "Stay where you are," he begged. "There is danger here. The Beans are in danger because of me. I must help them."

He opened his eyes and looked at Thomas and then at Mary. "They are over on the side of the mountain, waiting for me. My father is with them, and my mother, too . . ."

"Oh, Jon, I—I'm so happy for you!" Mary's chin was suddenly trembling; there were tears in her eyes.

Thomas said, in a voice that was not quite steady, "Jon, can you—is it possible—for you to make a break for it now and reach them safely?"

Little Jon bit his lip. Alone, he could do it easily; even Rascal couldn't catch him.

"Yes," he said. "But what about you?"

"Don't worry about us," said Thomas. "We'll be okay."

"But you wouldn't—nothing here would ever be all right. If I disappeared, you couldn't explain what had happened to me. No one would believe you. There'd be all kinds of trouble . . ."

Suddenly Thomas turned pale. "I didn't realize . . ."

Thomas knew now. Mary did, too. Sally and Brooks would be in danger. They might even be taken and held to be exchanged for Jon O'Connor. Life for the Beans would never be the same. There would be questions and trouble for years. Little Jon knew they had no near relatives, no one they could turn to.

And time was getting short. It would soon be dark. They had only minutes to decide something . . .

He looked at them—Thomas, Mary, Brooks, and small Sally with her frightened eyes and brave chin. He loved them all, and he didn't want to leave them.

"I don't remember what it's like where I came from," he told them. "But I *know* it isn't like this. I'm sure, just from listening to what they are saying to me now, that we live in small groups and help one another. There are not too many of us, but we have great knowledge, and we've made life so simple that we don't have laws or even leaders, for they aren't needed any more than money is needed. I think we make things—everything—with our hands and that life is a great joy, for we have time for so much . . ."

They were staring at him, and Mary whispered, "Jon, what—what are you trying to tell us?"

"I—I'm trying to tell you that you'd like it there and that I want you to come with me. I've been talking to my people, explaining what's happened to us and telling them that I can't leave you. They—they've agreed that you must come with me."

They gasped. He read their sudden confusion. How could they drop everything? . . . They needed time to think, to plan . . .

"There's no time left," he hurried to say. "You won't need anything from here—just flashlights to see your way through the woods . . ."

Suddenly Sally said, "Oh, Jon, I think it would be wonderful to live in a place where all the animals were friendly, and nobody hunted them. Please, Daddy—"

"Yes," said Mary.

Thomas said, "Okay, Jon. How do we manage to get away from the house?"

"After I leave, wait a few minutes," he told them. "When you hear shouts out in the pasture, get in the truck and drive as fast as you can up to the gap trail. Then climb to the gap. I'll meet you up there."

Before they could ask questions, he darted to the kitchen door, unlocked it, and raced outside.

He reached the enclosure in two bounds and released Rascal. "Stay behind me," he ordered. "Keep quiet."

Where was Gilby now? His flying feet took him across the garden and over the pasture fence. As he touched the pasture, he heard a shrill whistle from the road and an answering whistle ahead. It was still twilight, and he had been seen already. It was better than he had hoped for.

He slowed, pretending to be undecided. In the shadows ahead he could make out Gilby and Angus and several others. He realized that they planned to fire the barn and draw attention from Jon O'Connor. But Jon O'Connor was here—and he could see Angus, who carried an oil can, gaping at him in astonishment and disbelief and fear.

There was a quick clattering of shoes over the stones along the edge of the pasture. Other men were coming in a rush.

As he turned to dart away, a man called hoarsely, "Head the boy off! Don't let him get past! Hit him with something—but watch out for that dog!"

A hurled stone went past his head. He leaped easily beyond the frightened Angus and saw Rascal spring growling at a second figure that tried to block his way. He listened for the sound of Thomas's truck. The way was clear, and the Beans should be leaving . . .

A rock grazed his shoulder, and another struck his back with such force that he stumbled and almost went sprawling. He gained his balance, but too late to avoid the next stone. There was an instant when he saw it coming, and abruptly there was the stunning impact of it across the top of his head.

Consciousness did not leave him as he fell. He heard men shouting, the pounding of approaching footsteps—and a man's sudden scream as Rascal slashed into him. The big dog was all at once a whirling, snarling fury, his charges sending men tumbling as his fangs ripped cloth and flesh.

Little Jon heard all this, but as his hands clutched the pasture grass, it seemed for a moment that he was somewhere else—far away on a hill at home . . . Memory flooded over him, and he saw again the valley people on the hill and the glittering wonder of the shooting stars they had come to watch . . . Then he had fallen into the hill—into the crumbling chamber with its old machine. The machine spun a force that bridged space in an instant. You stepped through the shimmering door it made—and the threshold on the other side was something else, another world.

He struggled to his knees, aware of the fury that was Rascal, of a man crawling away in pain . . . This wasn't home. This was the strange world that he had stumbled into—Thomas Bean's world. Once, his people had visited here, but the door to it had long been closed . . .

He heard the sudden roar of Thomas's truck, and he sprang up with a glad cry. This was no longer Thomas Bean's world—the Beans were leaving . . .

He began to run. Behind him Rascal made one final charge, then raced to overtake him. There was pursuit, but his pursuers might have been following the wind. He and Rascal cleared the road together and went bounding upward through the darkening woods.

He met the Beans on the trail and led them on to where his people waited. They all carried glowing lights that made a radiance in the forest. But presently, one by one, the lights vanished. The forest grew still again and empty save for a wandering doe and her fawn.

The Bean house stands empty. All through the mountains people whisper of it and shake their heads. When the first investigators came, there was still food on the table, untouched. Everything the Beans owned was there, and nothing had been taken, even from the shop. Thomas Bean's truck was found up the road, abandoned. The family had simply vanished, empty-handed, without the least sign to indicate what had happened. And the strange boy, Jon O'Connor, had vanished with them. Men searched the mountains for days.

So the Bean place stands empty, and the pasture and the fields are overgrown. Gilby Pitts never goes by there if he can help it. Angus Macklin has moved away. Judge Cunningham went there once. She found three curious carvings on Thomas Bean's desk, which no one else had eyes for. She treasures them and often wonders about them when she is alone, but she has never mentioned her thoughts to anyone.

Across a threshold and somewhere far beyond, there is a hill where the valley people often gather when the day's work is done. From it you can watch the glittering night unfold and see the whole magic sweep when the shooting stars begin to stream like jewels across the sky.

Even the deer come out to watch, unafraid.

Reflections

1. How is the setting important to the plot? Do you think that the story could happen in a large city? Explain why or why not.

2. What do you think made Jon so unusual? To what extent did each of the following affect his person-ality: his strange looks, his special abilities, his set of values? What would he have been like had he been born to the Bean family?

3. What does the word *prejudice* mean to you? Now look the word up in the dictionary to check your definition. How do prejudices affect the actions of several of the characters?

4. Which characters seem real (come alive) to you? What does the author say about them or have them do that gives them life? Which ones would you want to live with you in your world? Why?

5. How is Jon's problem resolved? How could you resolve the problem of living in a world not suited to you?

6. Suppose Jon's family had not been able to fix the "door." Write a new satisfactory ending to the story, keeping everyone involved "in character."

THE LAW

People have many different ideas of what courtrooms are like, but some of these ideas are as unreal as Perry Mason himself. Serious work goes on in these rooms. People's lives may be at stake.

Because the rights of accused people must be protected, no photographs may be taken during a trial. That is why you see artists' sketches like these on television news programs.

The two lawyers take turns questioning witnesses who were present at the scene of the crime, or who know something special about the case. Here, the prosecutor is quizzing the arresting officer.

Everyone here is playing an important role in a trial. The accused person, or defendant, is sitting with his lawyer and a member of her staff. The other table is for the prosecutor and his assistants. The assistants may be lawyers, too, or paralegal personnel. They do research and help the chief lawyers prepare their cases. Most of their work is done in law offices with the help of legal secretaries.

To make sure there is an accurate record of the trial, the court reporter takes down every word spoken in the courtroom. The reporter here is using a stenotype machine, but often court reporters use shorthand.

The woman in the robe is a judge. Her job is to act as a kind of referee between the two sides, making sure that the trial is conducted according to the law. The judge explains the law to the jury before they go to a special room to discuss the evidence.

The jury must decide, after both sides of the story have been presented, whether or not the defendant has been proved guilty beyond any reasonable doubt.

THE LAWYERS

BELVA LOCKWOOD (1830–1917)

Thousands of Cherokee Indians waited tensely for the court's decision. This was no ordinary trial—it was a hearing before the United States Supreme Court. And the lawyer for the Native Americans was Belva Lockwood. The Cherokees were suing the government for payment for lands they had given up in the peace treaty of 1835. These payments came to about one million dollars. But it was now 1905, and Mrs. Lockwood argued that the money must be paid with interest.

It did not take long for the court to reach a decision. The Cherokees were awarded the back interest. Belva Lockwood, the first woman to plead a case before the highest court in the nation, had won the largest settlement in the court's history.

Mrs. Lockwood was active in the movement to give women the vote. But she died at 87, two years before the Nineteenth Amendment was ratified.

ROBERT LAFOLLETTE BENNETT (1912–)

Born on the Oneida Indian Reservation in Wisconsin, Robert Bennett knew both the White man's world and Indian tribal tradi- tions. From his Indian mother, a teacher, he learned the importance of education in deal- ing with the day-by-day problems of his people.

Robert Bennett graduated from the Haskell Indian Junior College in Lawrence, Kansas, and began his public career as a clerk for the Bureau of Indian Affairs in Utah. Ten years later, while working in Washington, D.C., he earned his law degree. Except for his Marine Corps service, Bennett's entire career was spent working for Native Americans with the Bureau of Indian Affairs, established by the United States government to assist the tribes on the vast Indian reservations. As a result of his dedication and ability to get things done, in 1966 Robert Bennett became the first Native American Commissioner of In- dian Affairs in over 100 years.

After retiring from the Bureau, Commissioner Bennett became Director of the American In- dian Law Center at the University of New Mexico School of Law. He is now active as a consultant on American Indian affairs.

SECRETS OF A WORD FAMILY

William Jones, the language detective, discovered a kinship between ancient and modern languages. Because of this kinship, knowing a word in an ancient language may lead you to the meaning of many words in another language belonging to the same family.

The Greek, Latin, and Old English languages all belong to the Indo-European family of languages. Language scholars believe that the Indo-European people used the word *nomn* for *name*. Scholars know that the Greek word for name was *onoma*, the Latin word was *nomen*, and the Old English word was *nama*.

Descendants of Indo-European

With knowledge of the Greek, Latin, and Old English word for *name*, we can begin to build a family picture. The form of the ancient word may be somewhat different in English, but you will see how much alike they look.

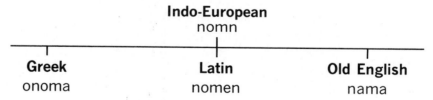

Indo-European
nomn

Greek	**Latin**	**Old English**
onoma	nomen	nama

A.   Words from Greek

Here are some of the descendants of Greek words that have found their way into modern English:

MODERN ENGLISH WORDS	GREEK PREFIXES AND MEANINGS
synonym	*syn–* "with" or "together with"
antonym	*ant–* "the opposite of"
homonym	*homo–* "the same as"
pseudonym	*pseudo–* "false"

Use one of the modern English words in **A** in the blank.
1. The writer didn't use his real name. He used a _____.
2. The word *pool*, meaning "water," is called a _____ of the word *pool*, a table game.
3. *Tall* is the _____ of *short*.
4. *Rapid* is a _____ of *swift*.

B. Words from Latin
   Here are some sentences with words that are descended from the Latin *nomen.* Discuss how each italicized word is related to the Latin word for *name.* Use a dictionary to find other words that come from the Latin word *nomen.*
1. I *nominate* Susan as class president.
2. *Nouns* and *pronouns* are used in many sentences.
3. What part of a fraction is the *denominator?*

C. Words from Old English
   Among the words descended from the Old English *nama* are *name, namely, namesake,* and *nameless.* Use each of these in a sentence of your own.

Building a Word Family Tree
   Now we can arrange the words you have studied into this kind of "family tree."

Indo-European
nomn

Greek	Latin	Old English
onoma	nomen	nama
synonym	nominate	name
antonym	noun	namely
homonym	pronoun	namesake
pseudonym	denominator	nameless

Unit 3 THE NEBULOUS DEEP

In a Million Years

While stars are watching
Man's leap
From the watery earth
To the nebulous deep,

Dolphins are talking
Dolphinese
And strange fish
Are climbing trees
On the banks of streams
By faraway seas.

O where will the dolphins be
In a million years,
And what will they be saying?
And will the fish be out of the trees
And walking the land beside the seas?

And where will man be straying?
Where will man be straying?

Stars are watching,
Stars will know,
As men and creatures
Come and go.

Claudia Lewis

Look Out over the Sea

PEARL S. BUCK

Why Does the Sea Grow Angry?

Kino lived on a farm. The farm lay on the side of a mountain in Japan. The fields were terraced by walls of stone, each one of them like a broad step up the mountain. Centuries ago Kino's ancestors had built the stone walls that held up the fields.

Above all the fields stood the farmhouse that was Kino's home. Sometimes he felt the climb was a hard one, especially when he had been working in the lowest field and he wanted his supper. But after he had eaten at night and in the morning, he was glad that he lived so high up because he could look down on the broad blue ocean at the foot of the mountain.

The mountain rose so steeply out of the ocean that there was only a strip of sandy shore at its foot. Upon this strip was the small fishing village where Kino's father sold his vegetables and rice and bought his fish. From the window of his room, Kino looked down upon the few

216

thatched roofs of the village, running in two uneven lines
on both sides of a cobbled street. These houses faced one
another, and those that stood beside the sea did not have
windows toward it. Since he enjoyed looking at the waves,
Kino often wondered why the village people did not, but
he never knew until he came to know Jiya, whose father
was a fisherman.

Jiya lived in the last house in the row of houses closer
to the ocean, and his house did not have a window
toward the sea either.

"Why not?" Kino asked him. "The sea is beautiful."

"The sea is our enemy," Jiya replied.

"How can you say that?" Kino asked. "Your father
catches fish from the sea and sells them, and that is how
you live."

Jiya only shook his head. "The sea is our enemy," he
repeated. "We all know it."

It was very hard to believe this. On hot sunny days,
when he had finished his work, Kino ran down the path
that wound through the terraces and met Jiya on the
beach. They removed their clothes, jumped into the clear
seawater, and swam far out toward a small island.

The island was full of sacred deer. They were not afraid, for no one hurt them. When they saw the two boys, they came to them, nuzzling into their hands for food. Sometimes Kino tied a little can of cakes about his waist and brought them with him to feed the deer. But now he reached high and picked the tender shoots of the rushes for them. The deer liked these very much, and they laid their soft heads against his arm in gratitude.

Kino longed to sleep on the island some night, but Jiya was never willing. Even when they spent only the afternoon there, Jiya looked often out over the sea.

"What are you looking for?" Kino asked.

"Only to see that the ocean is not angry," Jiya replied.

Kino laughed. "Silly," he said. "The ocean cannot be angry."

"Yes, it can," Jiya insisted. "Sometimes the old ocean god begins to roll in his ocean bed and to heave up his head and shoulders, and the waves run back and forth. Then he stands upright and roars, and the earth shakes under the water. I don't want to be on the island then."

"But why should he be angry with us?" Kino asked. "We are only two boys, and we never do anything to him."

"No one knows why the ocean grows angry," Jiya said anxiously.

But certainly the ocean was not angry this day. The sun sparkled deep into the clear water, and the boys swam over the silvery surface of rippling waves. Beneath them the water was miles deep. Nobody knew how deep it was, for however long the ropes that fishermen let down, weighted with iron, no bottom was ever found. Deep the water was, and the land sloped swiftly down to that fathomless ocean bed. When Kino dived, he went down—down—down, until he struck icy still water. Today when he felt the cold grasp his body, he understood why Jiya was afraid, and he darted upward to the waves and the sun.

On the beach he threw himself down and was happy again, and he and Jiya searched for pebbles, blue and emerald, red and gold. They had brought little baskets woven like bags, which they had tied with string around their waists, and these they filled with the pebbles. Jiya's mother was making a pebble path in her rock garden, and nowhere were pebbles so bright as on Deer Island.

When they were tired of the beach, they went into the pine forest behind it and looked for caves. There was one cave that they always visited. They did not dare to go too deep into it, for it stretched downward and under the ocean. They knew this, and at the far end they could see the ocean filling it like a great pool, and the tides rose and fell. The water was often phosphorescent, and it gleamed as though lamps were lit deep beneath the surface. Once a bright fish lay dead on the rocky shore. In the dark cave it glittered in their hands, but when they ran with it into the sunshine, the colors were gone, and it was gray. When they went back into the cave, it was bright again.

But however good a time they had on the island, Jiya looked often at the sun. Now he ran out on the beach and saw it sinking toward the west, and he called to Kino. "Come quickly—we must swim home."

Into the ocean, ruddy with sunset, they plunged together. The water was warm and soft and held them up, and they swam side by side across the broad channel. On the shore Jiya's father was waiting for them. They saw him standing, his hands shading his eyes against the bright sky, looking for them. When their two black heads bobbed out of the water, he shouted to them and waded out to meet them. He gave a hand to each of them, pulling them out of the white surf.

"You have never been so late before, Jiya," he said anxiously.

"We were in the cave, Father," Jiya said.

But Jiya's father held him by the shoulders. "Do not be so late," he said, and Kino, wondering, looked at him and saw that even this strong fisherman was afraid of the anger of the sea.

Something to Fear

Kino bade them good night and climbed the hill to his home and found his mother ready to set the supper on the table. The food smelled delicious—hot fragrant rice, chicken soup, brown fish. No one was worried about Kino. His father was washing himself, pouring water over his face and head with a dipper, and his little sister, Setsu, was fetching the chopsticks.

In a few minutes they were all sitting on the clean mat around a low square table, and the parents were filling the children's bowls. Nobody spoke, for it is not polite to speak until the food is served and everybody has had something to eat.

But when the supper was over and Kino's father was drinking a little hot tea out of a very small cup and his mother was gathering together the black-lacquered wood rice bowls, Kino turned to his father. "Father, why is Jiya afraid of the ocean?" he asked.

"The ocean is very big," Kino's father replied. "Nobody knows its beginning or its end."

"Jiya's father is afraid, too," Kino said.

"We do not understand the ocean," his father said.

"I am glad we live on the land," Kino went on. "There is nothing to be afraid of on our farm."

"But one can be afraid of the land, too," his father replied. "Do you remember the great volcano we visited last autumn?"

Kino did remember. Each autumn, after the harvest was in, the family took a holiday. They carried packs of food and bedding on their backs and in their hands tall staffs to help them up the mountainsides, and then, forgetting all their daily tasks, they walked to some famous spot. At home a kind neighbor tended the chickens and looked after the place. Last autumn they had gone to visit a great volcano twenty miles away. Kino had never seen it before, but he had heard of it often, and sometimes on a clear day far to the edge of the sky, if he climbed the hill behind the farm, he could see a gray, fanlike cloud. It was the smoke from the volcano, his father had told him. Sometimes the earth trembled even under the farm. That was the volcano, too.

Yes, he could remember the great yawning mouth of the volcano. He had looked down into it, and he had not liked it. Great curls of yellow and black smoke were rolling about in it, and a white stream of melted rock was crawling slowly from one corner. He had wanted to go away, and even now at night sometimes, when he was warm in his soft cotton quilt in his bed on the matting floor, he was glad the volcano was so far away and that there were at least three mountains between.

Now he looked at his father across the low table. "Must we always be afraid of something?" he asked.

His father looked back at him. He was a strong, wiry, thin man, and the muscles on his arms and legs were corded with hard work. His hands were rough, but he kept them clean, and he always went barefoot except for straw sandals. When he came into the house, he took even these off. No one wore shoes in the house. That was how the floors kept so clean.

"We must learn to live with danger," he told Kino.

"Do you mean the ocean and the volcano cannot hurt us if we are not afraid?" Kino asked.

"No," his father replied. "I did not say that. Ocean is there and volcano is there. It is true that on any day ocean may rise into storm and volcano may burst into flame. We must accept this fact, but without fear. We must say, 'Someday I shall die, and does it matter whether it is by ocean or volcano, or whether I grow old and weak?'"

"I don't want to think about such things," Kino said.

"It is right for you not to think about them," his father said. "Then do not be afraid. When you are afraid, you are thinking about them all the time. Enjoy life and do not fear death—this is the way of a good Japanese."

There was much in life to enjoy, and Kino had a good time every day. Sometimes he went fishing with Jiya and his father. It was an exciting thing to get up in the night and dress himself in his warm padded jacket tied around his waist. Even in summer the wind was cool over the sea at dawn. How exciting it was, too, to pull up the fish! At such times Kino felt Jiya was more lucky than he. Fish harvest was much easier than rice harvest. "I wish my father were a fisherman," he would tell Jiya.

Jiya shook his head. "But when the storms come, you wish yourself back upon the earth," he said. Then he laughed. "How would fish taste without rice? Think of eating only fish!"

"We need both farmers and fishermen," Jiya's father said.

On days when the sky was bright and the winds mild, the ocean lay so calm and blue that it was hard to believe that it could be cruel and angry. Yet even Kino never quite forgot that under the warm blue surface the water was cold and green. On days when the sun shone, the deep water was still. But when the deep water moved and heaved and stirred, ah, then Kino was glad that his father was a farmer and not a fisherman.

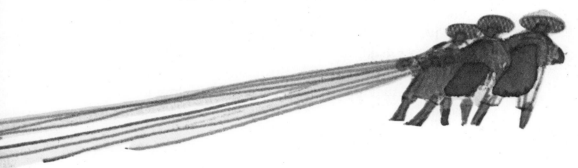

The Big Wave

And yet, one day, it was the earth that brought the big wave. Deep under the deepest part of the ocean, miles under the still green waters, fires raged in the heart of the earth. The icy cold of the water could not chill those fires. Rocks were melted and boiled under the crust of the ocean's bed, under the weight of the water, but they could not break through. At last the steam grew so strong that it forced its way through to the mouth of the volcano. That day, as he helped his father plant turnips, Kino saw the sky overcast halfway to the zenith.

"Look, Father!" he cried. "The volcano is burning again!"

His father stopped and gazed anxiously at the sky. "It looks very angry," he said. "I shall not sleep tonight." All night while the others slept, Kino's father kept watch. When it was dark, the sky was lit with red, and the earth trembled under the farmhouses. Down at the fishing village lights in the little houses showed that other fathers watched, too. For generations fathers had watched earth and sea.

Morning came, a strange fiery dawn. The sky was red and gray, and even here upon the farms, cinders and ash fell from the volcano. Kino had a strange feeling when he stepped barefoot upon the earth that it was hot under his feet. In the house his mother had taken down everything from the walls that could fall or be broken, and her few good dishes she had packed into straw in a basket and set outside.

"Will there be an earthquake, Father?" Kino asked as they ate breakfast.

"I cannot tell, my son," his father replied. "Earth and sea are struggling together against the fires inside the earth."

No fishing boats set sail that hot summer morning. There was no wind. The sea lay dead and calm, as though oil had been poured upon the waters. It was a purple-gray, suave and beautiful, but when Kino looked at it, he felt afraid.

"Why is the sea such a color?" he asked.

"Sea mirrors sky," his father replied. "Sea and earth and sky—if they work together against people, it will be dangerous indeed for us."

"Where are the gods at such a time?" Kino asked his father.

"There are times when the gods leave people to take care of themselves," his father replied. "They test us to see how able we are to save ourselves."

"And if we are not able?" Kino asked.

"We must be able," his father replied. "Fear alone makes people weak. If you are afraid, your hands tremble, your feet falter, and your brain cannot tell hands and feet what to do."

No one stirred from home that day. Kino's father sat at the door, watching the sky and the oily sea, and Kino stayed near him. He did not know what Jiya was doing, but he imagined that Jiya, too, stayed by his father.

At two o'clock the sky began to grow black. The air felt as hot as though a forest fire were burning, but there was no sign of such a fire. The glow of the volcano glared over the mountaintop, blood-red against the black. A deep-toned bell tolled over the hills.

"What is that bell?" Kino asked his father. "I never heard it before."

"It rang twice before you were born," his father replied. "It is the bell calling the people to come up out of the village and take shelter."

"Will they come?" Kino asked.

"Not all of them," his father replied. "Parents will try to make their children go, but some of the children will not want to leave their parents. Mothers will not want to leave fathers, and the fathers will stay by their boats. But some will want to be sure of life."

"I wish Jiya would come," Kino said. "Do you think he will see me if I stand on the edge of the terrace and wave a white cloth?"

"Try it," his father said.

"Come with me," Kino begged.

So Kino and his father stood on the edge of the terrace and waved. Kino took off the strip of white cloth that he wore instead of a belt and waved it high above his head.

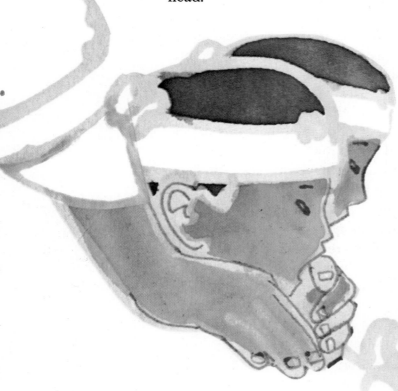

Far down the hill Jiya saw the two figures and the waving strip of white against the dark sky. He was crying as he climbed and trying not to cry. He had not wanted to leave his father, but because he was the youngest one, his older brother and his father and mother had all told him that he must go up the mountain. "We must divide ourselves," Jiya's father said. "If the ocean yields to the fires, you must live after us."

"I don't want to live alone," Jiya said.

"It is your duty to obey me, as a good Japanese son," his father told him.

Jiya had run out of the house, crying. Now when he saw Kino, he decided that he would go up the hill to the farm. Next to his own family, he loved Kino's strong father and kind mother. He had no sister of his own, and he thought Setsu was the prettiest girl he had ever seen.

Kino's father put out his hand to help Jiya up the stone wall, and Kino was just about to shout out his welcome when suddenly a hurricane wind broke out of the ocean. Kino and Jiya clung together and wrapped their arms about the father's waist.

"Look—look—what is that?" Kino screamed.

The purple rim of the ocean seemed to lift and rise against the clouds. A silver-green band of bright sky appeared like a low dawn above the sea.

"May the gods save us," Kino heard his father mutter. The bell began to toll again, deep and pleading. Ah, but would the people hear it in the roaring wind? Did they know what was about to happen? Their houses had no windows toward the sea.

Under the deep waters of the ocean, miles down under the cold, the earth had yielded at last to the fire. It groaned and split open, and the cold water fell into the middle of the boiling rocks. Steam burst out and lifted the ocean high into the sky in a big wave. It rushed toward the shore, green and solid, frothing into white at its edges. It rose, higher and higher, lifting up hands and claws.

"I must tell my father!" Jiya screamed.

But Kino's father held him fast with both arms. "It is too late," he said sternly.

And he would not let Jiya go.

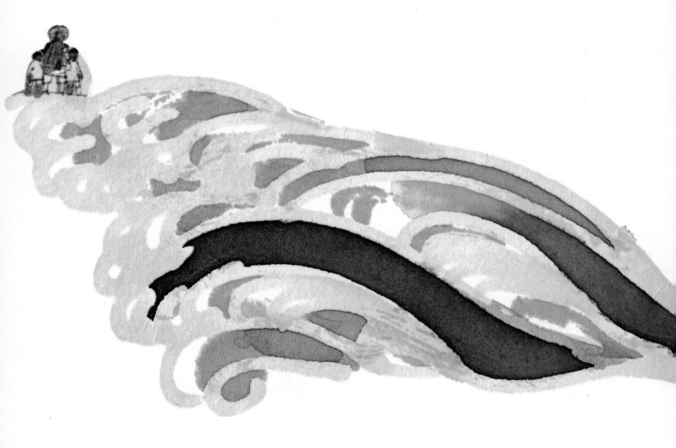

In a few seconds, before their eyes, the wave had grown and come nearer and nearer, higher and higher. The air was filled with its roar and shout. It rushed over the flat, still waters of the ocean, and before Jiya could scream again, it reached the village and covered it fathoms deep in swirling, wild water, green laced with fierce white foam. The wave ran up the mountainside. All who were still climbing the path were swept away—black, tossing scraps in the wicked waters. The wave ran up the mountain until Kino and Jiya saw the wavelets curl at the terrace walls upon which they stood. Then with a great sucking sigh, the wave swept back again, ebbing into the ocean, dragging everything with it, trees and stones and houses.

They stood, the man and the two boys, utterly silent, clinging together, facing the wave as it went away. It swept back over the village and returned slowly to the ocean, subsiding, sinking into a great stillness.

Upon the beach where the village stood, not a house remained, no wreckage of wood or fallen stone wall, no little street of shops, no docks, not a single boat. The beach was as clean of houses as if no human beings had ever lived there. All that had been was now no more.

How Wonderful Is Life

Jiya gave a wild cry, and Kino felt him slip to the ground. He was unconscious. What he had seen was too much for him. What he knew, he could not bear. His family and his home were gone.

Kino began to cry. His father stooped and gathered Jiya into his arms and carried him into the house. Kino's mother ran out of the kitchen and put down a mattress, and Kino's father laid Jiya upon it.

"It is better that he is unconscious," he said gently. "Let him remain so until his own will wakes him. I will sit by him."

"I will rub his hands and feet," Kino's mother said sadly.

Kino could say nothing. His mother left and came back in with hot rice soup, and Kino drank it. He felt warm now, and he could stop crying. But he was still frightened and sad. "What will we say to Jiya when he wakes?" he asked his father.

"We will not talk," his father replied. "We will give him warm food and let him rest. We will help him to feel he still has a home."

"Here?" Kino asked.

"Yes," his father replied. "I have always wanted another son, and Jiya will be that son. As soon as he knows that this is his home, we must help him to understand what has happened."

So they waited for Jiya to wake.

"I don't think Jiya can ever be happy again," Kino said sorrowfully.

"Yes, he will be happy someday," his father said, "for life is always stronger than death."

"He cannot forget his father and mother and his brother!" Kino exclaimed.

"He cannot and he should not forget them," Kino's father said. "Just as he lived with them alive, he will live with them dead. Someday he will accept their death as part of his life. He will weep no more. He will carry them in his memory and his thoughts. His flesh and blood are part of them. So long as he is alive, they, too, will live in him. The big wave came, but it went away. The sun shines again, birds sing, and earth flowers. Look out over the sea now!"

Kino looked out the open door, and he saw the ocean, sparkling and smooth. The sky was blue again; a few clouds on the horizon were the only sign of what had passed—except for the empty beach.

"How cruel it seems for the sky to be so clear and the ocean so calm!" Kino said.

But his father shook his head. "No, it is wonderful that after the storm the ocean grows calm and the sky is blue once more. It was not the ocean or the sky that made the evil storm."

"Who made it?" Kino asked. He let tears roll down his cheeks because there was so much he could not understand. But only his father saw them, and he understood.

"Ah, no one knows who makes evil storms," his father replied. "We only know that they come. When they come, we must live through them as bravely as we can; and after they are gone, we must feel again how wonderful is life. Every day of life is more valuable now than it was before the storm. Now we must think of Jiya. He will open his eyes at any minute, and we must be there then, you to be his brother and I to be his father. Call your mother, too, and little Setsu."

Kino ran to fetch his mother and sister, and they gathered about Jiya's bed, kneeling on the floor so as to be near him when he opened his eyes. In a few minutes, while they all watched, Jiya's eyelids fluttered on his pale cheeks, and then he opened his eyes. He did not know where he was. He looked from one face to the other as though they were strangers.

"My father—my mother—" he whispered.

Kino's mother took his hand. "I will be your mother now, dear Jiya," she said.

"I will be your father," Kino's father said.

"I am your brother now, Jiya," Kino faltered.

"Oh, Jiya will live with us," Setsu said joyfully.

Then Jiya understood. He got up from the bed and walked to the door that stood open to the sky and sea.

He looked down the hillside to the beach where the small fishing village had stood. There was only beach, and all that remained of the twenty and more houses were a few foundation posts and some big stones. The gentle little waves of the ocean were playfully carrying the light timber that had made the houses and throwing it on the sands and snatching it away again.

The family had followed Jiya, and now they stood about him. Kino did not know what to say, for his heart ached for his friend-brother. Kino's mother was wiping her eyes, and even little Setsu looked sad. But Jiya could not speak. He kept on looking at the ocean.

After many days happiness began to live in Jiya secretly, hidden inside him, in ways he did not understand or know. The good food Kino's mother gave him warmed him, and his body welcomed it and became strong. Around him the love of the four people who received him glowed like a warm and welcoming fire upon the hearth.

Reflections

1. Why didn't the fishermen's houses have windows toward the sea? Explain whether or not you think this is a good idea.

2. How did Jiya explain the big waves? Why did he think they occurred? What does the author say caused the big wave?

3. How do you feel toward Kino's father? Would you like to know a man like him? Explain.

4. Why did some people stay in the village? Why do you suppose Jiya's father made his son go up the mountain? What do you imagine the father was thinking as his son left him?

5. This story is sad, but does it leave you feeling sad? Write an explanation of why it does or does not.

Seascape Haiku

Leaping flying fish!
    Dancing for me and my boat
As I sail for home.

                —Kôson

I might feel cooler
    If I were the emperor
Of rocks in the sea.

                —Soseki

Jewels of small shells
    In ripples of sand, tangled
With kelp and rubbish.

              —Basho

    On the low-tide beach
        Everything we stoop to pick . . .
    Moves in our fingers.

             —Chiyo-Ni

Tidal Waves

HERBERT S. ZIM

You know from your own experience that pushing water in a bathtub makes waves. The great pusher on the ocean is the force of the wind. When it blows, waves begin to form and move across mile after mile of the ocean's surface.

A tidal wave or tsunami (tsoo-NAH-me), however, is not caused by the force of the wind. A tidal wave may start in any one of three ways. A large landslide in the soft deposits of mud and sand along a steep continental shelf may occur. If millions of tons of these deposits slip down, the nearby water may be given a tremendous push. The explosion of a volcano may also send tidal waves moving across the ocean. Earthquakes underneath the sea do the same thing; if an area of the ocean floor moves up or drops down rapidly, the water above the area is moved, too.

Most tidal waves are caused by earthquakes, also known as seismic disturbances. The push given to the water by an earthquake is not great when you think of the ocean as a whole. But the surface in one area only has to move up and down a few meters to start a tidal wave. From a ship in deep water, this wave may not be noticed at all.

Tidal waves are very different from wind waves. They are quite low and perhaps as much as 240 kilometers (150 miles) long. But as tsunamis come close to shore, their speed slows down and their height builds up. They may rise to over 30 meters (100 feet) high.

Only a few tidal waves may reach the shore, or there may be as many as two dozen. Tidal waves can destroy everything in one area, yet do very little damage a short distance away.

If tidal waves approach during the day, the first small waves may not be noticed by people at the beach. What does attract attention, more often, is the way the sea withdraws. It may roll back like a very low tide and expose more of the bottom than people have ever seen before, grounding small boats and leaving fish flapping on the sand. The water may recede for ten minutes or more, and this retreat, which seems like a very low tide, is the origin of the name *tidal wave*. The Japanese name *tsunami* means "a wave seen on shore, but not on the open sea."

HOKUSAI
THE GREAT WAVE

COURTESY, MUSEUM OF FINE ARTS, BOSTON

Tsunamis Cause Damage

The receding water is a warning of the tsunami to come. On some coasts it may arrive as a great churning wave. More often it is like a fast-rising tide that is in full flood about fifteen minutes after the lowest water. Each of the several waves can destroy everything in its path as it advances and retreats.

Since the beginning of history, stories of great tidal waves have appeared over and over again. Most of the damage has been along the borders of the Pacific and to its many islands, but one of the first known tsunamis took place on the island of Crete about 1400 B.C. Records tell of more than three hundred major tidal waves in which thousands of people perished.

In the past, tidal waves came without warning. Cities were destroyed overnight. Tidal waves have caused havoc from Chile, north through Peru, and up the California coast into Alaska. Japan has been hit many times, and so have Hawaii and other Pacific islands.

For example, in 1896 a tsunami in Japan destroyed 10,000 homes, killing 30,000 people. In 1946 an underwater earthquake in the Aleutian Islands sent tidal waves tearing through the Pacific. Waves over 30 meters high hit the nearby Alaskan coast. The waves rushed south and westward, reaching the Hawaiian Islands in five hours. The lower part of the town of Hilo was demolished, and many small villages on low Pacific islands were also ruined.

Tsunami Warning Systems

After the 1946 tsunami the United States government began to work on a warning system to alert Hawaii if a tidal wave approached. The job fell to the Coast and Geodetic Survey. Within two years a system was developed. Tsunamis cannot be prevented, but people can move to safety if they are warned of an approaching wave several hours in advance.

The warning system has a long name—the Seismic Sea-Wave Warning System. It is written as SSWWS, which nobody can pronounce as a word. The system goes into action whenever a seismic disturbance—an earthquake—occurs under or near the sea. The location of the disturbance and its strength are established by measuring the earthquake waves that spread rapidly through the earth's crust.

At many places delicate measuring instruments called seismographs have been set up to detect and measure earthquakes. From the record made by a moving needle, scientists at each station measure the direction and distance of the earthquake along a curve, which they draw on a map. As soon as two or three reports are in, the curves around each of the stations are plotted. The earthquake is located at the place where the curves cross. The size of the vibrations on the seismograph record tell how severe the earthquake was.

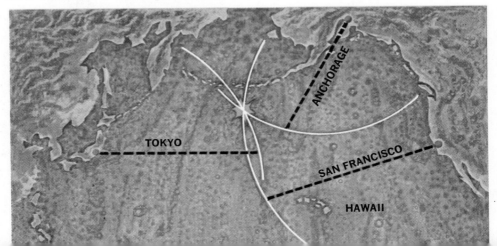

TOKYO

ANCHORAGE

SAN FRANCISCO

HAWAII

When reports indicate that the earthquake may cause a tidal wave, the central station at Hawaii radios a tsunami alert to all stations that are part of the SSWWS program. More information may come in from special tide gauges that have been set up at many places in the Pacific. Observers, especially those near the earthquake source, watch for any sign of a tidal wave.

Since the SSWWS warning system was started, a number of tidal waves have occurred. In 1952 the system had its first test. A tidal wave from the north Pacific moved south. Hawaii was warned. The waves caused much damage, but no lives were lost. Since then there have been other tidal waves, but they have killed far fewer people than before the warning system was developed.

Reflections

1. Name three forces that can cause tidal waves.
2. Why might a ship at sea not even notice a tidal wave?
3. What is the most obvious warning to people on a beach that a tidal wave is coming? About how long do they have to get out of the way?
4. What is the origin of the name *tidal wave?* What is the meaning of *tsunami?* In your opinion, which one of these terms is more accurate?
5. What is the purpose of the SSWWS? Explain how scientists cooperate to pinpoint the location of an earthquake.
6. Look back at the three illustrations for this article. Write an essay of three paragraphs, explaining how each illustration contributes to the meaning and feeling of the article.

Whale

WILLIAM JAY SMITH

When I swam underwater, I saw a Blue Whale
Sharing the fish from his dinner pail,
    In an undersea park
    With two Turtles, a Shark,
An Eel, a Squid, and a giant Snail.

When dinner was over, I saw the Blue Whale
Pick up his guests in his dinner pail,
    And swim through the park
    With two Turtles, a Shark,
An Eel, a Squid, and a giant Snail.

The Big Spring

JEAN CRAIGHEAD GEORGE

An Exhausting Trip

Off the coast of Bandon, in Oregon, a gray whale surfaced. Her seven-inch-long nostrils emerged first and blew a spout of air and water fifteen feet into the air. The column swooshed with a roar that could be heard for half a mile. Having exhaled, she then inhaled, and the breath came into her lungs with a whine like wind rushing into a tunnel. Her nostrils closed over this salty gasp. A low wall of muscle arose around the nostrils like a frown and kept the water out. She submerged.

Four seconds later, her nose, which was on the top of her head, came up again. She gave four strong blows. The waves clapped around her. She snorted at them, then headed down into the corridors of the Pacific Ocean.

The female gray whale was forty-three feet long. She weighed thirty-four tons. She was one of a group of animals that are the largest ever to live on this earth. Like all whales she was also hostess to many small beasts. On her back and over her mountain of a belly lived thousands of barnacles. They pulled their feet in and stopped kicking food into their mouths when their great hostess surfaced to breathe. They adjusted to her rising and diving, just as we adjust to the moods of the earth as it circles the sun.

This city-block-of-an-animal plunged forward for a thousand feet. Then she surfaced and peered over the ocean to make sure the other whales were traveling with her.

Beside her swam her son, a twenty-foot baby. He had been born in January in the California Bay, and now the two of them were on their way north to the Bering Sea—a long journey of seven thousand miles.

The mother plunged down into the green spring ocean and looked around. She was following a familiar canyon wall that she knew as well as you know your own street, for she had traveled along it every year for twenty years of her life. The submarine canyon was gray and dark and lay like a great highway up the continental shelf. The whale knew exactly where she was.

Ahead of her loomed a sand barrier. She quickened her pace, for she knew she was coming to a cove. Once more she blew and looked around. She saw no other gray whales and sensed she was behind the main migration. At the sandbar she tasted the silt of Coos Bay and, because she could not feel the currents from her baby, slowed down, then stopped.

Her son was looking at a giant squid. The mother attracted his attention by crunching her wide teeth and whistling, sounds familiar to her wandering son. The baby spurted to her side, eager and energetic. He whooshed friskily to the surface and peered around. He saw boats and lighthouses. This was his first trip to the summer rendezvous of the gray whales—the Bering Sea. His mother was teaching him the underwater landmarks, for in the fall he would have to travel back alone in the manner of the gray whale. Their migration was not a social affair. Although they all moved at the same time, each whale made the exhausting trip by itself.

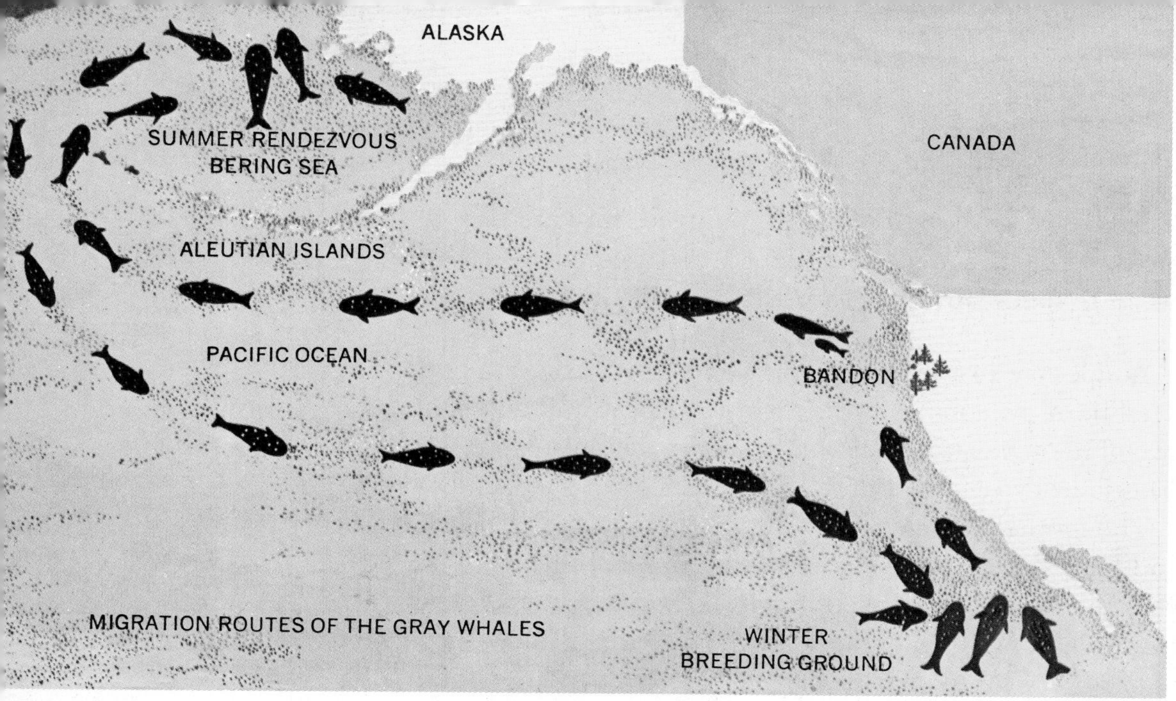
ALASKA
SUMMER RENDEZVOUS
BERING SEA
CANADA
ALEUTIAN ISLANDS
PACIFIC OCEAN
BANDON
MIGRATION ROUTES OF THE GRAY WHALES
WINTER
BREEDING GROUND

The mother whale swung over the delta at the mouth of the bay and crunched her teeth again. Her son came down to her. She was taking the water from the bay in and out of her mouth. He did likewise, and the taste of the bay was forever imprinted on his senses. Each bay and cove and canyon had to be memorized in this manner, by taste, by sight, and by currents that eddied and pulled, for each was different in every inlet along the great California coast.

The mother plunged over the sandbar. The whale child followed. For a moment they lingered in the different water pressures, feeling all the details of this place with their throat grooves, the openings under their necks that are sensitive to pressures, to currents and eddies.

The mother delayed long here as if to impress this particular spot on the youngster. From here they would head out to sea, and the underwater world of the continent would be replaced by the deeps of the Pacific. From here on it would be all pressure memories. The whale child circled gently, biting the sand, filtering the water in, and learning.

Then they hurried on—a thousand feet at a run. They swam to the edge of the continental shelf.

Suddenly the whale child looked back. He whirled in panic. Coos Bay appeared different from the north. He turned and flipped back to the sandbar, tasting the salts and minerals once more, feeling the texture of the water. When he was satisfied with his impressions, he tailed out to meet his mother. But she was gone.

The life of the gray whale is more silent than that of some of the other whales, a grind on their plankton-filtering teeth, a noisy blow, an occasional whistle. Over the sea canyon walls, ticking and rasping like the beat of a tin cup on a wooden table, came the rare "distress" sound—the clicking teeth of a baby whale.

He was lost. He surfaced, blew a great column of air and water, and pulled himself skyward so high that his whole chest was out. All he saw was a trawling boat harvesting the bottom-dwelling fish. He saw no mother. He glanced at the boat again. It was big; it might be a whale. He headed for it, spying tentatively as he went.

The boat was gray like his mother and covered with barnacles. Rising and blowing, he came up to the object. But the whale child drew back. The wooden whale was too small, the wrong design, the wrong scent, and the water that surrounded it was not warmed by the mammal body. Oil seeped from it.

The young whale fled in terror, diving into unfamiliar hills and valleys. His eyes rolled as he searched. Schools of fish felt him on their lateral lines and wheeled away. He plunged on but saw no sand barrier, tasted nothing familiar.

He cried into the ocean, tapping out his bleat that traveled swiftly for hundreds of yards and then faded against the coastal reefs.

As the sun went down, lopsided as it reached the horizon, the giant child circled and circled the empty waters. He spied out and looked until he was tired. Finally he slept. His flippers, once the feet of his land-walking ancestors, hung down into the sea. His tense nostrils were barely above the surface.

Two hours later the young whale awoke. His skin was cold, and he turned sleepily to nurse. Then he remembered his mother was not around. He swirled in panic. He breached, head in the air, fins out. He saw the land and knew this was where he must begin to retrace his steps. He swam south.

A Schedule with June

No adult gray whales eat on the long eight-month migration back and forth, nor do they eat in the bays where they give birth to their young and remate. No other beast can go so long without eating and still be active. Woodchucks, ground squirrels, and bears feed all summer and starve all winter; but they sleep during their starvation and do not use much energy. Not the gray whale. This beast swims constantly while starving, with the exception of the babies that nurse on the trip north.

And so, the giant whale child sucked in the ocean because he was hungry and weak. He filtered out the plankton through odd rows of baleen teeth that were more like sieves than teeth. Then he rolled southward in fear and fright.

At noon he found Coos Bay. He knew its taste. His mother had taught him this. Swimming to the familiar barrier, he tapped his jaws together and called. There was no answer in all the vast ocean. The young whale drifted into the cove. It was familiar. He had been born in a cove, in the low hot waters of the California Bay where flats shone white in the dry land. The young whale spied upon the shore. It was different from his first home; there were tall trees and lush plants. The strangeness alarmed him, and he submerged for his ten minutes underwater. The bars, the shallows, the light that flickered from the sun down into the bay were comforting. But he saw no whales. There had been thousands in the bay of his birth. This was a desolate cove.

The young whale felt strong instincts pulling him, and occasionally he swam to the mouth of the bay and looked north, for gray whales work on appointments with their needs. They must give birth to calves in the protected lagoons. They must depart on schedule to travel the seven thousand miles to the only food they eat—the plankton of the Bering Sea—and they must get there on time, or they starve to death. Again in the fall they must leave on schedule in order to reach the bays in time to have their babies in the protected waters. Any interference with this timing means death to the whales.

The young whale tapped his teeth and circled Coos Bay. He had been born in January, a magnificent male of sixteen feet. Upon his arrival in the whale world, he had been immediately nuzzled by his giant mother, who, without arms or feet with which to hug him, expressed her love by circling him. She led him to the surface to blow, then, tipping her body, she showed him where he would find her milk.

The rest of the two months in the lagoon were reassuring to the young whale child. Hundreds of other whales slept and rolled with him, each one awakening instinctively before the tide went out and beached him, an event which means certain death to a whale, for they are helpless on the land. The whale child learned to tell when the tide was leaving and how to avoid being stranded.

He met other young whales and, by meeting them, knew what he was.

In March there were fewer and fewer of his kind in the bay, for the great migration had started north. Finally his mother beat her tail, crunched her teeth, and led him around sandbars, over hills, and out into the sea. He stayed close to her big side. She paused beyond the bay channel to teach him the tastes and pressures of his birthplace. Then she spanked him forward to keep her schedule with the burst of spring in the Bering Sea.

WHALE MOTHER AND CHILD

The young whale felt pressures and tastes in Coos Bay similar to those he knew as an infant, and so he lingered, blowing and swirling over the bottom. By night he would swim toward the shore, and by day he would surge to the entrance, feeling the pull of his species toward the dark waters of the north. But he did not know how to go.

And so he stayed where he was.

The days passed. His mother did not return. The huge child grew weak with longing and hunger. He could not know that they had lost each other as she had spurted forward to drive a killer whale from their path. Killer whales never kill adult gray whales, but they compete for the same waters; and so to protect their rights, they molest the young. Over the eons the gray whale has learned peace by avoidance. They keep to the bottom. The killers keep to the surface.

But all life is chance. A killer whale and the whale child's mother had met, and she responded to an old instinct. She chased him. From that moment on, the separation became greater as the mother moved instinctively north, searching for her child in an effort to keep her schedule with June in the Bering Sea. And the child, following the instincts of the young, looked for familiar waters.

A week later the tired whale child came up to the shore of Coos Bay where people moved and boats were tied. In loneliness he watched the boats. They were almost as big as his mother. One night he nuzzled one. And close beside its purring motors, he fell asleep.

But as he slept, he breathed like a wind tunnel. The owner of the yacht heard the strange sound and came out to see if a storm were brewing.

He looked down into the water and saw the young whale sleeping happily against his ship. He stared again to make sure, then paced the entire length of his deck until he came to the end of the baby. An unmistakable whale tail lay under the water. He radioed the Marine Laboratory and the Fish and Wildlife Service.

At dawn the lost whale child was a captive.

The excitement was great. During the night the crew had enclosed him in a great wire fence, and they all stood and stared at him as he snapped and rolled.

Gray whales had become almost extinct in the Pacific Ocean during the whaling years in the nineteenth century, but with laws prohibiting their killing, they had increased in numbers. Nevertheless, the ships and boats on the Pacific often frightened them and diverted them from keeping their precise schedules with the plankton and the bays. And these delays spelled their death.

So the scientists in Coos Bay were thrilled to be able to study a live gray whale. They measured and weighed him. They noted the movements of the whale child, they put microphones in the water to record any sounds he might make, and they watched him judge the tide and swim to the deepest pocket of the cage when it went out. They took his temperature and analyzed his blood.

To feed him, they poured nutrients into the water that were similar to the nutrition in the plankton. The formula came from studies made on the stomachs of gray whales that had washed ashore in the past. The scientists were coming to a new understanding of this remarkable beast, and they were excited.

Meanwhile the remarkable beast grew weaker and weaker, for the plankton formula was not what he needed. He needed his mother's milk. He cried at night and eyed the people by day.

Then one night a small craft, sailing out into the ocean, was rocked by an enormous object just off the sandbar at the lighthouse. The boat was thrown off course by the swell. Its crew peered into the water to see if they had struck anything, but the sea was black. Only a trail of phosphorescent animals told them something big had passed down the channel into the bay. They gave the incident little thought, for their boat righted itself quickly and purred on out to sea.

The next morning, when the scientists came to take a cardiograph of the young whale, they were distressed to find the fence crunched as if it were paper—and the whale child gone.

Far out at sea a mother whale and her son blew four times and submerged to follow green currents in the depths of the Pacific Ocean. The mother lingered to teach her son the pressure and weight of these bleak waters. She was very patient, and her child was a serious student and obedient.

A school of sharks circled them as they plunged over the edge of the continental shelf and thundered north, for the belly of the female bore toothlike gashes—as if raked by a wire fence.

As they followed the watery highways, known only to the gray whales, the "roadsides" were spangled with the signs of spring. Diatoms bloomed, copepods glittered among the diatoms, fish glimmered as they tossed their silver eggs to the sea, and clams siphoned the bright water in and out of their valves; for it was springtime in the ocean.

Reflections

1. How did the baby whale lose his mother? Why did he return to Coos Bay?
2. What journeys must you make by yourself? How were you taught the way?
3. Although "The Big Spring" is fiction, it contains a great deal of factual information. Compare what a reference book says with what the story tells you about gray whales.
4. What do you think was the strongest instinct in the female whale in this story? In your opinion did she act intelligently? Write a short essay stating your opinions. Support them with evidence from the story.

From Owls and Crickets to Porpoises and Crabs

JEAN CRAIGHEAD GEORGE

As I sit here in my study a robin hops across my desk. He is a tame little fellow we raised when his mother was killed by a cat. Not long ago my son Luke counted all the wild animals we have had in our home. The total came to 173.

Most of these wild animals leave in autumn when the sun changes their behavior. While they are with us, however, they become characters in my books, articles, and stories.

I was born into a family of naturalists. My father is an entomologist (a person who studies insects). My brothers are ecologists. They study grizzly bears and the wildlife of the western wilderness.

When we were children our home abounded with owls,

falcons, raccoons, crickets, turtles, and dogs. My brothers and I would watch them with great curiosity as they went about their lives. Every weekend of our childhood was an adventure. Our father would take us along the Potomac River to canoe, fish, and swim. There he taught us about the plants and animals, how to make a meal off the land, and to enjoy the wild freshness of the country. From these experiences came the idea of *My Side of the Mountain,* a book which was later made into a movie.

When I was eight years old, I knew I wanted to be a writer. My third-grade teacher sent our class to the blackboard to solve arithmetic problems. I had no idea how to do my assignment, but the blackboard was before me, the chalk in my hands and I thought I should do something. I wrote a poem and sat down. Fortunately Mrs. Clark was an extraordinary teacher. She did not reprimand me, but quietly announced that I had written a lovely poem. I have been writing ever since.

"The Big Spring," is taken from *Spring Comes to the Ocean,* a book that I wrote several years ago. When I learned that spring comes to the sea just as it does to the land, I took my three children, Twig, Craig, and Luke to St. Thomas Island in the Virgin Islands to see it come. We put on snorkles and goggles and all four of us swam down among the fishes, corals, porpoises, and crabs.

Under the sea, spring was dramatic and beautiful and was suspended in a dream world of blue water and sunlit lights. Luke and Craig surfaced with living gems for my book. Twig and I swam side by side, she pointing out gleaming caverns and bespangled fish that eventually were to be part of my story. Trips to the research stations at Bimini and Woods Hole completed the background material. Then on a cold winter's night, far from the sound of the sea, I wrote *Spring Comes to the Ocean.*

A Fishy Square Dance

EVE MERRIAM

Tuna turn,
flounder round,
cuttlefish up,
halibut hold;

clam and salmon
trout about,
terrapin,
shrimp dip in;

forward swordfish,
mackerel back,
dace to the left,
ide to the right;

gallop scallop,
mussel perch,
grunnion run,
bass on down;

finnan haddie,
skate and fluke,
eel and sole,
shad and roe;

haddock, herring,
hake, squid, pike:
cod promenade
and lobster roll!

Undersea Explorer

SYLVIA EARLE

Undersea explorer Sylvia Earle once lived on the floor of the ocean for two weeks! She headed a team of four marine scientists and an engineer. Her team was part of Tektite II, an underwater exploration program. The five women ate and slept in a special building 15 meters (50 feet) below the surface of the Caribbean Sea. On page 257 (*top*), you can see Dr. Earle looking through a porthole.

(bottom) Wearing diving equipment, the aquanauts went out onto the ocean floor to study the plants and animals around them. At all times, communication with the surface was carried on from the bridge compartment. *(page 257, bottom)*

Each scientist in the program worked on a special project of her own. As a marine botanist, Dr. Earle's main interest was ocean ecology—how animals and plants

interact in ocean waters. She wanted to know why undersea plant life is so scarce in some areas.

Everywhere she looked she saw evidence of how the balance of nature can be disturbed. If large fish, like bar-racuda, are driven off or killed, the plant-eating fish they feed on will increase and this in turn causes more of the plant life to be eaten. Her findings remind us of the interdependence of all living things.

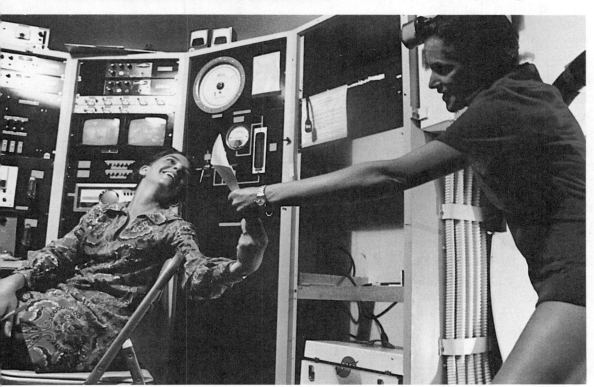

A Modern Cassandra

RACHEL CARSON (1907–1964)

More than two thousand years ago, during a war between the Greeks and the Trojans, the ancient Greeks besieged the walled city of Troy. But they could not get inside. Whereupon they built a great wooden horse and filled it with soldiers.

They wheeled the horse to the gates of the city in the dark of night and left it there. In the morning, when the Trojans saw the horse standing outside the gates of their city, they decided to bring it inside.

"Beware!" cried Cassandra, daughter of King Priam. "A terrible catastrophe will befall us if you bring this thing into our city!" But no one listened. Once inside the gates, the Greeks poured from the hollow body of the horse. The Trojans were defeated.

In 1963, another woman saw danger and issued a warning. A scientist and a writer, Rachel Carson watched as more and more chemicals were being developed to kill insects. Was no one thinking of the consequences? Useful insects as well as harmful ones were being destroyed. The chemicals were accumulating in the soil and the water. They were accumulating in the bodies of animals.

Rachel Carson called her book *Silent Spring.* For if people weren't careful, our earth would become a place where many kinds of plants and animals would die—and where no birds would sing.

The Changing Year

RACHEL CARSON

Rachel Carson was a scientist who worked for the Fish and Wildlife Service in Washington, D.C. Silent Spring *was her last book, but the book which made her famous was* The Sea Around Us. *"The Changing Year" is a small portion of that book. When you read it you will see how the pen of a skilled writer can sometimes make scientific writing sound like poetry.*

For the sea as a whole the change from day to night and from season to season has no meaning. Such changes are lost in the vastness of the ocean. But the surface waters are different. They are always changing. Sparkling in the sun, mysterious in the twilight, their moods change from hour to hour. The surface waters move with the tides. They stir to the breath of the winds. Most of all, they change with the advance of the seasons.

Spring

On land, a thousand signs tell us that spring is on the way. For spring comes to the temperate lands of our northern hemisphere in a surge of new life. Green shoots push forth, buds unfold, the birds migrate northward, a chorus of frogs rises from the wet lands. There is spring even in the different sound the wind makes as it stirs the young leaves. It is easy to suppose that at sea there can be no such feeling of advancing spring. But the signs are there, and to one who understands them, they bring the same magical sense of awakening.

In the sea, as on land, spring is a time for the renewal of

life. Before life can come, however, food must be provided. Just as land plants depend on minerals in the soil for their growth, so every plant of the sea, even the smallest, depends upon the nourishing salts or minerals in the water. Rich stores of these minerals have been gathering on the floor of the continental shelf. Some have been carried down from the land. Some have come from sea creatures, large and small, plant and animal, that have drifted down to the bottom. The waters must be deeply stirred to bring these minerals up. During the long months of winter in the temperate zones the surface waters have been absorbing the cold. Now in spring the heavy water begins to sink, slipping down and taking the place of the warmer layers below. As the warm bottom water is pushed up, it brings the minerals with it.

In the warmth of the spring sun there is a sudden awakening—the simplest plants of the sea begin to multiply. They increase with unbelievable speed. The spring sea belongs at first to the diatoms and to all the other tiny vegetables of the plankton. They cover vast areas of ocean with a living blanket of cells. Mile after mile of water may appear red or brown or green, the whole surface taking on the color of the tiny grains of coloring matter in each of the plant cells.

But plants rule the sea for only a short time. Almost at once the small animals of the plankton begin to rival them in numbers. It is the spawning time of the copepod and the glassworm, the ocean shrimp and winged snail. Now in the spring the surface waters become a vast nursery. From the continent's edge lying far below, and from the scattered shoals and banks, the eggs or young of many of the bottom animals drift up to the surface of the sea.

In the spring the sea is filled with migrating fishes. Some of them are bound for the mouths of great rivers, which they will ascend to lay their eggs. For months or years these fish have known only the vast spaces of the ocean. Now the spring sea and the maturing of their own bodies lead them back to the rivers of their birth.

Summer

When most of the spawning is over, life in the surface waters slackens to the slower pace of midsummer.

A brilliant phosphorescence often lights up the summer sea. In waters where the protozoan Noctiluca abounds, it is the chief source of this summer light. Fishes, squids, or dolphins clothe themselves in the ghostly radiance. They fill the water with racing flame. Or again the summer sea may glitter with a thousand moving pin pricks of light coming from a shoal of brilliantly phosphorescent shrimp.

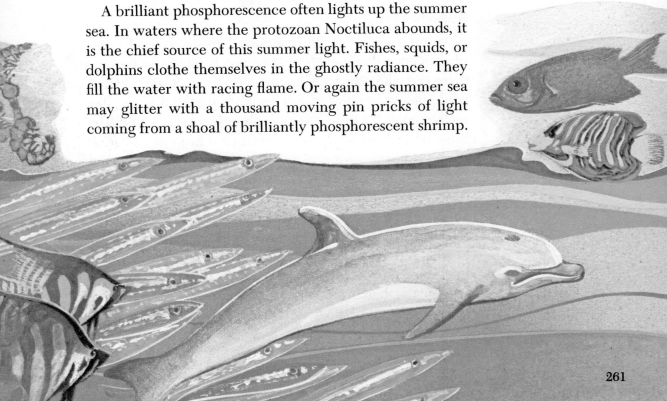

Autumn

Autumn comes to the sea with a fresh blaze of phosphorescence. Now every wave crest is aflame. Here and there the whole surface may glow with sheets of cold fire, while below, schools of fish pour through the water like molten metal. Often the phosphorescence is caused by some tiny plants which have multiplied furiously in fall as they did in the spring. Seen from the deck of a vessel at sea, it has an unearthly, disturbing quality. People are given to thinking that any light not of moon or stars or sun has a human origin. Lights on shore, lights moving over the water, mean lights kindled and controlled by other people. But here are lights that flash and fade away, lights that come and go for reasons we do not understand.

Like the blazing colors of the autumn leaves before they wither and fall, the autumn phosphorescence hints that winter is approaching. Now the flagellates and the tiny algae dwindle away to a scattered few. So do the shrimps and the copepods, the glassworms and the comb jellies. The larvae that in spring rose from the bottom have long since grown up and drifted away to take up whatever existence is their lot. Even the roving fish schools have gone from the surface waters. They have migrated into warmer latitudes or have found equal warmth in the deep, quiet waters along the edge of the continental shelf.

Winter

The surface waters now become the plaything of the winter gales. The winds build up the giant storm waves and roar along their crests, lashing the water into foam and flying spray. It seems as if life must have deserted this place forever.

But this is not true. Hopeful signs are to be found even in the grayness and bleakness of the winter sea.

On land we know that winter, though it appears life-less, is not really so. Look closely at the bare branches of a tree on which not the palest gleam of green can be seen. Spaced along each branch are the leaf buds. Concealed and safely preserved under the overlapping layers is all the spring's magic of swelling green. Pick off a piece of the rough bark of the trunk. There you will find hibernating insects. Dig down through the snow into the earth. There are the dormant seeds from which will come the grass, the herb, the oak tree.

So, too, the lifelessness of the winter sea is only seeming. Everywhere are the promises that spring will come again.

Reflections

1. What part of the sea is always changing? Why does change from season to season have no meaning for the sea as a whole?
2. What are the signs of spring in the sea? What happens to the plant life? The animal life? Where are the migrating fishes going?
3. How do you think the author's descriptions of the changing life in the sea might compare with a description you might find in an encyclopedia?
4. What happens in the sea in summer? What causes the phosphorescence and glitter that light up the summer sea?
5. How is the lighting of the sea in autumn different from that in summer?
6. What happens to the surface waters in winter?
7. Choose one of the four seasons. Write a description of the similarities between the signs of that season in the sea and on land.

Pelops and Poseidon

FRANCES CARPENTER

The story of a prince named Pelops and Poseidon, the great God of the Sea, was well known in ancient Greece. As it was told to boys and girls of those long-ago times, I will tell it to you.

A war had driven brave Pelops out of his Greek kingdom of Lydia. With ships filled with his treasures, the handsome young prince had crossed the Aegean Sea. In other parts of Greece, he would set up a new kingdom for himself. He would, he hoped, marry the beautiful Greek princess, Hippodameia, with whom he had long been in love.

Hippodameia was as fair as Aphrodite, the Goddess of Beauty and Love. So it was not at all strange that many princes like Pelops wanted her for their bride.

King Oenomaus, the father of this fair princess, however, did not want her to marry. Some said it was because he loved his daughter so much that he could not bear the thought of her ever leaving his palace.

Others said it was because of the oracle, the voice of the gods which came from the farthest depths of a cave. "When his daughter finds a husband, Oenomaus shall meet his death." This was the warning which the priest of the oracle had given that king.

So Oenomaus sent forth over the land and the sea a warning to suitors who might ask to wed Hippodameia:

"He who marries my daughter must first win over me in a chariot race. From our city of Pisa to the temple of Poseidon on the Isthmus of Corinth, we shall drive our swift steeds. A good half hour's start will I give to my daughter's suitor. But if I overtake him, my sharp spear shall pierce his heart, and he shall die."

These were fearful words. The lightning speed of this king's horses was known to all. But the beauty of Hippodameia was like that of the new moon. Her suitors did not heed the king's warning. Prince after prince came to try his luck in the race.

Always it was the same story. Four splendid horses and a fine racing chariot would be brought from the royal stables. And the young prince would drive away.

Oenomaus stayed behind to sacrifice a fat ram to his protector, Zeus. Then, standing at the side of Myrtillus, his young charioteer, Oenomaus sped away after the bold young prince.

The king's two famous mares, Psylla and Harpinna, were said to be daughters of the gods. Everyone knew they ran faster than the North Wind. Always, before the temple of Poseidon was reached, they overtook the four flying horses of the young prince.

The sharp spear of Oenomaus then flew through the air to find the heart of the unlucky suitor of Hippodameia. And next day that poor young man's skull was seen on top of a pole beside the palace gate.

Twelve such gruesome skulls were there to give warning to the young prince, Pelops. He looked long upon them. Then he turned back from that gate.

But Pelops had no thought of giving up the race. Instead, he made his way with his charioteer down to the edge of the sea. And he called on Poseidon to come forth from his palace under the waves.

When Pelops had sacrificed a handsome black bull to honor the sea god, there was a rumbling and a roaring under the waters. The waves flew apart, and out from between them rolled a splendid gold chariot. Two magnificent sea horses pulled it, and dolphins with shining scales played along in the waters on either side.

In that magnificent chariot rode mighty Poseidon, his sea crown on his head and his long beard blowing about his ruddy face in the breeze. His trident was raised high in salute to the young prince who had called him forth from his palace.

"Mighty Poseidon, Ruler of the Sea! Shaker of the Earth! Father of Swift Horses! I come to you for aid." So Pelops cried out to the friendly god.

"Speak, son of Zeus," Poseidon replied. He was fond of this handsome youth. When Pelops was still a lad, the sea god once had chosen him as his cupbearer upon Mount Olympus. Yes, he truly loved Pelops.

"Tomorrow I race with King Oenomaus, Poseidon," Pelops explained. "The prize is the hand of Hippodameia in marriage. That race I must win. But Zeus has given wings to the horses of this king. Only with your help can they be beaten. Lend me your aid, O Father of all Swift Horses."

"Zeus rides with Oenomaus, dear Pelops." The sea god shook his head. "Zeus is far mightier than is Poseidon. There will be danger for you tomorrow."

"Always there is danger, O Lord of the Sea. I must die someday. It may well be tomorrow. Or it may be another day. Give me your help, I pray, so that I may at least try to win my fair bride."

Poseidon struck the floor of his chariot with his trident. Once again the waves parted, and four magnificent horses galloped out of the sea. Behind them they drew a racing chariot that shone like the sun.

"Test your driver's skill here, before you go to the king," Poseidon advised Pelops.

So the golden chariot, behind its four galloping steeds, rolled out over the land. So fast did it go that the charioteer's breath was forced out of his body. Pelops himself had to take up the reins to finish the run. Then, like the wind, he drove off to the palace of King Oenomaus.

The king was surprised when he saw the shining gold chariot. "Surely," he thought, "those four noble steeds are the horses of Poseidon. This time I shall need Zeus by my side if I am to win."

"Hippodameia shall ride with you in the race, Pelops," Oenomaus declared. He hoped that having his princess so close would take the young man's mind off his driving. But, of course, the cunning king did not speak of this aloud.

Pelops, too, knew that he must be clever. And he thought of a plan to make his victory sure. With Hippodameia walking beside him, he went to find Myrtillus, the king's own charioteer.

"Pull out the metal wheel pins of your chariot, Myrtillus, and I will give you a rich reward," Pelops said to the young man. "Replace those metal wheel pins with pins made of stiff wax, and no one will know. During the race, the heat produced by the wheels' rolling will melt the wax. Then the king's chariot will have to stop."

At first Myrtillus would not agree to this plot. But Hippodameia added her pleading to that of Pelops. You see, at last she had fallen in love herself. To her, Prince Pelops was the husband she wanted to marry.

Myrtillus himself was young. Like almost every other man in Greece, he was under the spell of this princess's beauty. He could not refuse her. That night wax pins were put into the place of the strong wheel pins made of bronze.

The next morning the race began just as it had with the suitors whose skulls crowned the poles at the palace gates. With Hippodameia at his side, Pelops drove away from the city of Pisa.

Oenomaus quickly sacrificed the fat ram to Zeus. Then behind his two winged mares, Psylla and Harpinna, he galloped swiftly after them.

It must have taken some time for the stiff wax wheel pins to melt. The king's chariot was pulling close to that of poor Pelops. Poseidon's temple, where the race was

to end, was in sight not far ahead. Oenomaus was holding his spear ready to kill Pelops when he should pass him.

Just in time the wax melted. Without pins to hold them, the wheels of the king's chariot rolled off their axle. And in the great crash, King Oenomaus was dashed to the ground. As the oracle had warned, the cruel father came to his death on the day when his daughter found her true love.

As the husband of Hippodameia, Pelops took over the throne of Oenomaus. Many other parts of Greece did he conquer. He ruled his broad lands well. Riches poured into his treasury. All over that part of the world Pelops was known as the "One Blessed by the Gods." The great kingdom he founded was named Peloponnesus in his honor. Its people were the famed Peloponnesians.

It may have been Pelops himself who planned those very first games that honored Poseidon there on the Isthmus of Corinth. Surely he had reason to make such a festival for his protector. And surely these splendid Isthmian Games were a fit thanks offering for such a powerful god. In all that ancient world no other festivals were more magnificent, except perhaps the Olympic Games. But those games, which honored Zeus, were not begun until many years later.

Reflections

1. Who was Poseidon? Why did the Greeks honor him? Give as many details from the story as you can.
2. Why did Poseidon agree to help Pelops? Why was he doubtful about the effectiveness of his help?
3. Poseidon is said to have created the horse in the shape of breaking waves. What picture does this bring to your mind?
4. How did you feel about the outcome of the race?
5. This myth about Poseidon and Pelops is set against the background of the Isthmian Games, a forerunner of the Olympic Games. Write a report giving as much information as you can about the ancient or modern Olympic Games.

THEY WERE FIRST

MATTHEW FONTAINE MAURY (1806–1873)

Matthew Fontaine Maury has been called the "Pathfinder of the Seas" because of his work to improve ocean travel. The information he collected and published on winds and currents formed the basis for all pilot charts issued by the U.S. government. He aided in laying the first Atlantic Cable, making it possible to send and receive messages across the seas in only a few hours. In his later years he returned to his native state of Virginia and became a professor of meteorology at the Virginia Military Institute.

NAOMI JAMES (1949–   )

In her first solo venture on a sloop, Mrs. James sailed 48,000 kilometers (30,000 miles) around the world in 272 days—two days better than the record set by Sir Francis Chichester aboard the Gypsy Moth IV in 1967, eleven years earlier.

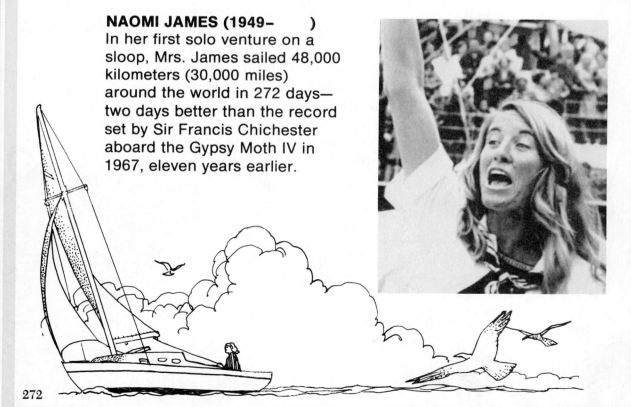

JACQUES-YVES COUSTEAU (1910–   )

When this French underwater pioneer made his first underwater movie, he found that he needed breathing equipment to make his work easier. He and an engineer invented the aqualung. In a mini-sub, he made color movies at a depth of 45 meters (150 feet). Cousteau later designed an underwater village. He believes that in the future people may be able to live underwater.

MARY MIDDLETON (1922–   )

Mary Middleton, right, and Joyce Pascoe, left, were two oceanographers assigned to sea duty from the Naval Oceanographic Office. On the USNS *Lynch,* they made chemical analyses of seawater containing plankton. They also recorded the water's depth and the contours of the ocean floor. Mary Middleton began her oceanography career as a clerk in the Navy's Oceanographic Office. Then she studied biology, physics, chemistry, and calculus to become a full-fledged oceanographer.

Earth's Deep Frontier

HELEN WOLFF VOGEL
and MARY LEONARD CARUSO

The World Ocean

So much of our world is ocean, and so little of it has been explored. Let us take a look at this region of watery mystery which surrounds us.

You could make a model of the World Ocean out of soft clay. You would shape your clay into a ball, to represent our planet, Earth; then you would punch your thumb into it good and hard, again and again until you had dug three big depressions in this clay world. These three deep holes would be like the great basins of the World Ocean which are filled with salt water: the Atlantic, the Pacific, and the Indian oceans. You could make smaller dents in your ball to show the seas, like the Mediterranean, which are arms of the World Ocean extending into the land. Some of the seas are cut off from the ocean to which they once belonged. Except for these, all the oceans and seas are connected and flow together, as Magellan's men discovered when they sailed around the world.

Your model of the world could accurately show the top layer of the World Ocean. We know where land and water meet and that three fourths of our globe is covered with salt water. But no one can tell you how deep you would have to press your thumb into the clay to show the depth of the ocean—because we still do not know. Only two percent of the bottom of the ocean has been mapped. Great mountain ranges and deep canyons have been located in the depths of the sea, but there may be others which have not been discovered yet. We know more about the face of the moon today than we know about the waters of our own planet, our "inner space."

It is only now, in the twentieth century, that we have seriously begun to explore that "inner space," to peer into the ocean depths below the reach of our fishing lines. And we are finding strange and wonderful things down there. At every depth we penetrate, we find animal life. As we probe the ocean floor, we are discovering whole areas of it that are covered with lumps of rock rich in valuable minerals. And under the water and rock of our continental shelves, we find rich wells of oil and sulfur.

There are three times as many saltwater acres as there are dry ones on our planet, and we can no longer afford to leave them unexplored and underdeveloped. We need the sea and all its treasures to take care of the people on our planet and the human beings who are born each day. If we want more of the sea's riches, we shall have to learn more about it and what it contains. Explore it we must.

People Underwater!

HELP WANTED: Daring young men and women needed to explore, study, and map Earth's last frontier, the World Ocean. Divers wanted to locate and bring up the underwater treasure hidden beneath the waves. Scientists needed to map the ocean floor and discover the natural laws which rule the sea, to name the strange fish which lie still undiscovered in its depths. Only those with curiosity and courage need apply.

Are you with us? Good. Now to explore and observe the sea. First you must put on goggles or a face mask to protect your eyes from the stinging of the salt water. Float face down in the clear waters, and you can see fish swimming below—darting silver and black streaks. If you are in the tropics, you may see them disappearing into pink and purple caves of coral. This is some of the life the sea has been hiding from us. Put rubber fins on your feet, and you can move swiftly through the water. You can dive down to explore—like a fish among the other fish—for as long as you can hold your breath.

Captain Jacques-Yves Cousteau of the French Navy used to do that in the warm waters of the Mediterranean Sea as long ago as 1943. He took along a sharp spear, too, and hunted fish. But Captain Cousteau fretted at the need to come up for air after only a few minutes underwater, so he began to search for a way that would enable him to stay below the waves longer. He wanted time to dive deeper and to see more of this new and interesting world—the "Silent World" he called it.

Cousteau could have become a helmet diver like the people who collect sponges off the ocean floor and salvage workers who dive down to work on wrecked ships. These divers wear a helmet which is connected by a long air hose to an air pump in a boat on the surface. They wear weighted shoes to help them sink down to the bottom. But this equipment prevents divers from moving around quickly or freely; they feel like a dog on a leash. Cousteau could not use a helmet for his purposes: to explore widely, to hunt swiftly.

In order to get freedom of movement underwater, there had to be some way for the diver to carry a supply of air down with him. Captain Cousteau and an engineer named Émile Gagnan finally solved this problem by strapping two tanks of compressed air onto the diver's back, enough for a two-hour stay underwater, exploring, hunting, or taking pictures. Tubes were attached to these cylinders to lead the air into the diver's face mask. A valve fed the air to him automatically as he breathed. This equipment Cousteau called an aqualung.

With aqualungs on their backs and rubber fins on their feet, people all over the world—inspired by Captain Cousteau's experiences—have begun exploring the first sixty meters (200 feet) of the ocean's depths. They are diving for lobsters, spear-fishing, observing and photographing the plants and animals hidden in the waves.

Animals of the Deep

Skin divers are getting to know the animals of the deep, eye to eye as it were. One of their most important findings is that there are many more fish in the ocean than could be told from fishing catches. Captain Cousteau, for instance, was told by marine biologists and fishermen that the liche was a rare fish which grows to only about one meter. Yet Cousteau found great numbers of liche in his underwater exploration of the Mediterranean Sea, and he frequently saw them two meters long. With the help of the divers and more efficient fishing tools, we should be able to catch these big ones which have been getting away.

What would you do, all dressed up in your skin-diving outfit, if you came across a flesh-eating shark on one of your dives? An Italian underwater expedition to the Red Sea went out looking for these terrors of the deep in order to study their behavior. The Italian divers swam down to meet tiger sharks weighing two hundred and seventy kilograms (six hundred pounds), mackerel sharks over four meters (fourteen feet), and blue sharks with six rows of teeth.

Sailors, swimmers, and fishermen claim that the shark is bold and bloodthirsty, but the divers found that sharks become very cautious when meeting humans face to face. They circled around the undersea swimmers warily, and, when the divers attacked, the sharks swiftly turned about and made off.

Another fearful-looking sea creature that has been studied by skin divers is the manta ray. These animals have a wingspread of over six meters and weigh a couple of tons. Some even have horns, so that frightened fishermen call them devilfish! Hans Habe, an Austrian skin diver, spent months photographing and observing manta rays, not from a fishing boat, but close up underwater. He discovered that this terrifying-looking monster would not eat a human being. It much prefers the tiny plants and animals which it strains out of seawater.

There are some animals, though, which skin divers dread. The moray eel lurks in dark places—caves and sunken ships—and does not like to be disturbed. Divers are careful not to poke their heads into places where a moray, with its powerful jaw full of curved teeth, may be. It is harder to avoid the sea urchins, because there are so many of them. The urchin looks like a harmless thistle, but it is covered with sharp, brittle spines, which pierce the skin, break off inside the flesh, and are more difficult to remove than splinters. If the spines are left inside the body, they can cause a bad infection. But most divers describe their underwater world as if it were safer to explore than a city . . . well, anyway, less dangerous than crossing a street against the traffic light!

SEA URCHIN

MANTA RAY

SHARK

MORAY EEL

The Deep Depths

With an aqualung, divers can explore the first layer of the World Ocean, over a hundred meters down. But the average depth of the ocean is nearly four kilometers, or over thirteen thousand feet. With echo-sounding apparatus we have discovered areas of the ocean floor that lie more than nine kilometers, or thirty thousand feet, below the waves. To explore the great deeps, divers' bodies must be protected. Otherwise the pressure of the water, which increases as they descend, will crush them to death.

In 1930 a ·solution to the pressure problem was designed and built by William Beebe, a naturalist who was studying life in the sea, and by Otis Barton, an engineer. Their machine, built for taking people down into the deep, was called the bathysphere. It was a steel ball one and a third meters wide, with walls of steel nearly four centimeters thick and windows of quartz.

Beebe and Barton squeezed themselves inside and were lowered into the depths of the Atlantic on the end of a steel-cored cable. They were able to go down a kilometer

WILLIAM BEEBE AND PARTY ON BARGE WITH BATHYSPHERE

OTIS BARTON

below the surface of the sea. Later Barton built an improved model, which he called the benthoscope. In this he managed to reach a depth of a kilometer and a half off the coast of California.

As Beebe and Barton peered through their quartz windows into those black depths that no living person had ever before penetrated, what did they see? Their greatest surprise was that there were so many creatures so far down. Below four hundred and fifty meters (fifteen hundred feet) the only light in the sea comes from the animals themselves, but there were so many phosphorescent and illuminated fish and crustaceans that Beebe compared the scene to the skies on a starry night! The bathysphere descents put an end to the ancient belief that life did not and could not exist in the great depths of the ocean.

Another explorer of the deep, deep sea was Professor Auguste Piccard, of Switzerland, who invented the bathyscaphe. This also is a steel diving ball, but it works quite differently from the Beebe and Barton machine. Piccard's bathyscaphe is not lowered on a steel cable; instead, it lowers and raises itself and can move around, propelled by battery-driven motors. Two of these bathyscaphes are the $FNRS_3$, belonging to the French Navy, and the *Trieste*, which has been bought by the United States.

THE *TRIESTE*

AUGUSTE PICCARD

Commander Georges Huout, of France, set a record in 1954 by taking the *FNRS*$_3$ down to a depth of nearly five kilometers in the Mediterranean, or 15,000 feet. This record stood until January 7, 1960, when the United States Navy proudly announced that Jacques Piccard, the inventor's son, and Lieutenant Donald Walsh in the *Trieste* had descended 24,000 feet into the Challenger Deep off the Island of Guam in the Pacific. But this amazing record stood for only two weeks. On January 23, 1960, Piccard and Walsh reached the bottom of the nearby Marianas Trench—35,800 feet below the surface of the water, almost eleven kilometers down!

What is down at that depth? Commander Huout had brought back from his descents into the depths pictures of a rare, blind fish, the beautiful benthosaurus, which rests on the bottom of the sea on three long tentacles,

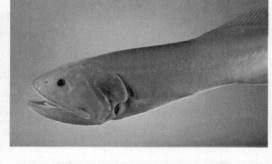

DEEP-SEA FISH

like a camera on a tripod. In all the thousands of years people have fished in the Mediterranean, no one had suspected that this unusual fish was present. Yet Huout saw many of them on every descent he made into that sea. He was amazed, too, as Dr. Beebe had been, at the great numbers of brightly illuminated fish which lit up the darkness of the deep. There were yellow lantern fish, shrimp, and what looked like fiery dragons, two meters long, whose sides flashed with blue and green lights as they swam silently past the windows of the bathyscaphe.

Otis Barton and Auguste Piccard have made it possible for biologists to observe firsthand the life in the depths. People like Dr. Beebe, trained in the science of the sea, can now go down and find out for us, at long last, what actually exists in the deepest part of the ocean.

Will you be like the four marine scientists who in 1969 set a record for underwater living by remaining submerged for sixty days? Will you become one of the pioneers of the sea who are so needed by humanity?

Reflections

1. List in chronological order the history of people's exploration of the sea. Be sure to name the different types of equipment used.
2. How did Jacques-Yves Cousteau contribute to exploration underwater?
3. What has been learned about "dangerous" sea life studied by skin divers?
4. Suppose you were a skin diver who had discovered an explanation for the belief in sea serpents. Write a report on your findings.
5. Suppose you lived in an underwater village of the future. Write a description of a typical day.

Mountain Fantasy

CLAUDIA LEWIS

I climbed, one day,
A mountain on the moon,
Bone-dry, rock-gray,
Among those crags that rise
Through starry black and airless skies,
Where meteors fall in fiery showers
And there's never a flake of cold white snow
Or rain on mountain meadow flowers.

Then I went down, down—
To the mountains deep in the sea,
Down where the scarlet fishes swim,
Far from sun
In waters dim,
    Never blue
    Never green
Where all unseen
A small white rain
Of shells
Gently falls
On those dark hills
And cones
And canyon walls—

And I marveled at the moon and sea,
And the showers of fire and shell,
And then I climbed, on the earth's shore,
A mountain I know well,

    Where sun shines down
    On cedar green and summer brown
    And the sky above
    Is blue
    And white
    In the morning light,
    And airy dark
    In the airy night.

    And there I stayed
    Through the cool, bright hours,
    Where the green trees grow
    And the mountain meadow flowers.

CUES IN WORDS AND SENTENCES

When you first learned to read, you learned to use letters as cues to sounds. You learned, too, that a capital letter may be a cue that a new sentence begins. Periods, question marks, and exclamation points are cues to show that a sentence ends. Quotation marks before and after a group of words are cues that someone's speech is being printed. There are many cues within words and within sentences that help you read. The exercises below will show you how some of these cues work.

Some Cues Within Words

1. Copy the following sentences and supply the cues needed to make them clear.

> –t –he –oment –t –appened, –he –irst
>
> –hooting –tars –ere –rossing –he –ky.
>
> –hey –ere –eginning –o –tream –cross –ike
>
> –trings –f –ewels –lung –rom –nother
>
> –lanet, –nd –veryone –as –atching –hem.

Did each person in your class choose the same letters to complete the words? Which letter would you add before –t to make a word? before –he? before –ky?

2. Copy the following sentences. Supply missing letters for each blank.

> Th–n R–y h–d a– –dea. If Anti d–d n–t
>
> ––dersta–– Engl––– w–ll –noug– to
>
> h–v– a c–nvers–t–––, th– th–ng t– do
>
> w–s to t––ch h–m!

Discuss your possible choices for letters to put in *Th–n, R–y, –dea,* and *c–nvers–t–––*. Which of the choices work to make the sentences have meaning? Does adding *and* to *Engl–* make sense in the sentence? Does adding *ish* make sense? Which of these choices, *ea* or *ou,* makes sense in the sentence when they are placed in *t––ch?* Are a few letters from each word enough to cue you to meaning, or do you need all the letters in each word?

    3.   Study the following suffixes and their meanings.

-age "collection of"	-ant "someone or something"	-ance "the action of"	-ation "the action of"
-er "a person who"	-ion "action or process"	-ment "the action of"	

    These word parts are among a group of suffixes that are used to change verbs into nouns. They signal a change in meaning. Add one of these suffixes to the italicized word in the sentences below and write a sentence using the new word. The first one is done for you.

1. Water and mud *seep* into the basement.
   Seepage causes damage.
2. Please *assist* me.
3. Do ghosts *appear* at midnight?
4. May we *celebrate* the holiday?
5. Will you *play* the game?
6. Let's *construct* a model rocket.
7. *Treat* the dog kindly.

Discuss how these suffixes act as signals to word meaning. If you have trouble, use your dictionary.

4. Discuss the following sentence pairs. What happens when we add a prefix or a suffix, or both, to the italicized word in each sentence?

1. He fell, and his clothes were covered with *grime.*
    After his fall, his clothes were *begrimed.*

2. The crates were shipped by *rail.*
    The train with the crates was *derailed.*

3. I am *able* to do that.
    I can *enable* you to do it, too.

4. I have the *power* to close the meeting.
    I am *empowered* to close the meeting.

What cue to meaning is signaled by adding *–d* or *–ed* to a verb? When *be–, de–, en–,* and *em–* are added before certain nouns or adjectives, are the new words still nouns or adjectives?

Some Cues Within Sentences
1. Where a word appears in a sentence is often a cue to sentence meaning. For example, if you find one of these words at the beginning of a sentence, what kind of sentence usually follows?

who	when	where	does
what	why	am	will
are	is	may	do

Use these words to begin some sentences you make up. Are most of your sentences questions or statements?

2. Copy the sentences below and supply a word of your own choice for each blank.

1. Two ——, a ——, and their —— were here.
2. Your —— and my —— went.
3. An —— played in our —— yesterday.
4. Some —— and a few —— passed this way.

Discuss the different words that you and your classmates used to fill the blanks. Are words like *two, a, their, your, my, an, our, some,* and *a few* cues to what follows them? How do such words determine what kinds of words will follow?

3. Supply a word for each blank below.

"—— —— ——," —— ——. "—— —— —— —— ——?"

What tells you that your first three choices are the direct speech of somebody? What choices do you have for the fourth and fifth blanks? What is a cue that tells you that your last five words must make a question?

4. Complete the sentences below by supplying a word for each blank.

If you will —— with me, I shall —— you about the movie. You may —— to see it. I have —— it twice and am —— to see it again.

What kind of words must be fitted into the blanks? Do *will, shall, may, have,* and *am* give you cues to the words you would choose for the blanks?

Words in print and the flow of words in a printed sentence give you many cues to help you read. You have been using most of these cues since you began reading. The more experience you have in reading, the easier it is for the cues to help you.

Mister Urian

Music by *Ludwig van Beethoven*   Words Translated by *Ronald Duncan*

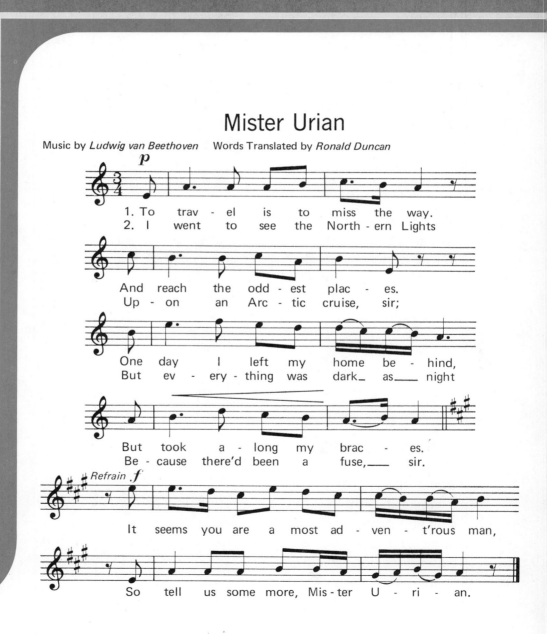

1. To trav - el is to miss the way.
2. I went to see the North - ern Lights

And reach the odd - est plac - es.
Up - on an Arc - tic cruise, sir;

One day I left my home be - hind,
But ev - ery - thing was dark_ as_ night

But took a - long my brac - es.
Be - cause there'd been a fuse,_ sir.

Refrain

It seems you are a most ad - ven - t'rous man,

So tell us some more, Mis - ter U - ri - an.

290

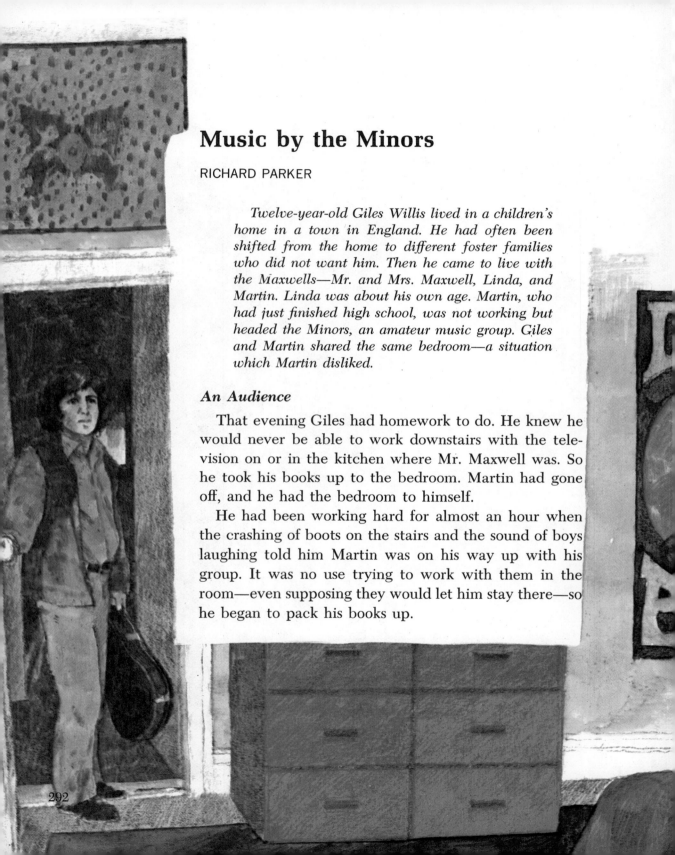

Music by the Minors

RICHARD PARKER

Twelve-year-old Giles Willis lived in a children's home in a town in England. He had often been shifted from the home to different foster families who did not want him. Then he came to live with the Maxwells—Mr. and Mrs. Maxwell, Linda, and Martin. Linda was about his own age. Martin, who had just finished high school, was not working but headed the Minors, an amateur music group. Giles and Martin shared the same bedroom—a situation which Martin disliked.

An Audience

That evening Giles had homework to do. He knew he would never be able to work downstairs with the television on or in the kitchen where Mr. Maxwell was. So he took his books up to the bedroom. Martin had gone off, and he had the bedroom to himself.

He had been working hard for almost an hour when the crashing of boots on the stairs and the sound of boys laughing told him Martin was on his way up with his group. It was no use trying to work with them in the room—even supposing they would let him stay there—so he began to pack his books up.

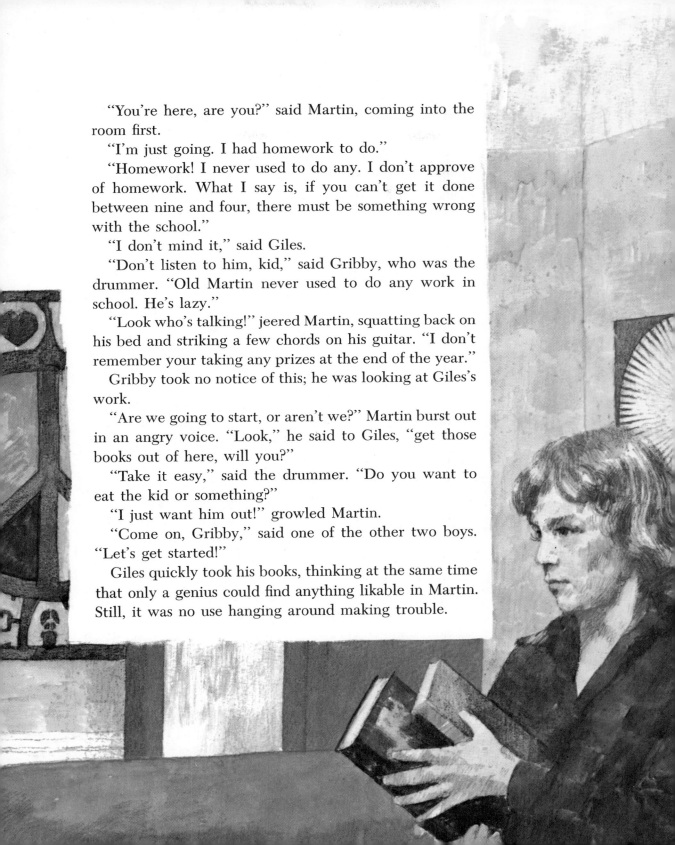

"You're here, are you?" said Martin, coming into the room first.

"I'm just going. I had homework to do."

"Homework! I never used to do any. I don't approve of homework. What I say is, if you can't get it done between nine and four, there must be something wrong with the school."

"I don't mind it," said Giles.

"Don't listen to him, kid," said Gribby, who was the drummer. "Old Martin never used to do any work in school. He's lazy."

"Look who's talking!" jeered Martin, squatting back on his bed and striking a few chords on his guitar. "I don't remember your taking any prizes at the end of the year."

Gribby took no notice of this; he was looking at Giles's work.

"Are we going to start, or aren't we?" Martin burst out in an angry voice. "Look," he said to Giles, "get those books out of here, will you?"

"Take it easy," said the drummer. "Do you want to eat the kid or something?"

"I just want him out!" growled Martin.

"Come on, Gribby," said one of the other two boys. "Let's get started!"

Giles quickly took his books, thinking at the same time that only a genius could find anything likable in Martin. Still, it was no use hanging around making trouble.

Before Giles reached the door, the drummer said to him quietly, "Hang on, kid. Why don't you stay up here awhile and listen to us? Might do us good to play to an audience. Anyway, why shouldn't you stay? It's partly your room, isn't it?"

There was a silence after he'd said this. Martin seemed on the point of some angry outburst; then he shrugged his shoulders and started fiddling with the tuning of his guitar. "Please yourself—I don't care," he muttered.

"Right. Tuck yourself away in a corner," said Gribby. "And hold onto something—we make a fair noise when we get going."

Giles got well out of everybody's way, sitting on the far side of the bed. He watched with interest as three guitars were tuned and wires plugged into them that led back to the apparatus by the wall. Gribby was setting up his drum kit, fussing a little as he made sure that each part, drum or cymbal or temple block, stood exactly the right distance from him, around in a half circle. He had a little drum break all to himself to test them out while the others were twanging notes and checking that the right amount of noise came from the two loudspeakers.

"Right, then," said Martin. "Gently for a start, eh, boys? Just a whisper on the drums. And keep it light after the intro. One, two . . ."

Three slow notes came from the lowest string of Martin's bass guitar, dropping sadly down, like weeping. The last note sounded very loud through the speakers and was held there. Giles could feel it more than he could hear it. Then there was a pause—and then the soft whisper of the brushes across the drum. The tune was played very quietly as if the sound were being carried away through the trees by the wind. Martin sang softly, as if he really were sad.

"Break it to her
Gently
Like I said.
But gently.
Tell her when I'm gone.
Tell her gently
After I've gone.
Don't think there's
Any way that you can say
Will stop her crying, but
Break it to her
Gently."

The music whispered away into silence. Giles wasn't sure whether he ought to clap or not, and while he was still wondering, the group crashed into their next number. Crashed it was. The drums went mad; the guitars throbbed like breakers pounding on the beach. The very roof seemed to be falling in on top of them. Even the words, which all the boys howled together, did not make any sort of sense, but were hurled into the air like a handful of gravel at a glass window. Giles found himself bouncing on the back of the bed in time with the beat.

He seemed to be caught up in some sort of rhythmical thunderstorm, tossed first this way by the drums then that way by the wild chords and harsh voices.

And then, suddenly, there was silence. The group seemed to droop over their instruments as if they were exhausted.

Before he realized it, Giles cried out, "That was smashing. It really was!" He still felt the excitement of it and knelt up on the bed, staring first at one boy then another.

"Well, thanks," said Martin, and it was hard to tell whether he meant it or was being his usual sarcastic self.

"Fame comes at last!" said Gribby with a grin.

They had started on a new tune when the bedroom door burst open and Mrs. Maxwell came storming into the room looking furious.

"This is a fine thing!" she exclaimed.

All the boys stopped playing and looked at her.

"Didn't you think there might be somebody who didn't like the row you were making?"

"You know what the neighbors are like," said Martin. "They grumble about anything."

"I'm sorry, Mrs. Maxwell," Gribby said. "I guess we just weren't thinking. We'll just have to give it a miss tonight and work something out tomorrow."

An Offer

Some days later, at dinner, Linda said to Giles, "Go on, Giles, why don't you tell him?"

Giles shot a quick look at Martin, who was scooping food into his mouth with quick, hungry movements. He seemed to be in a bad mood. "Not just now," Giles mumbled.

"I think you ought to tell him. He'll be pleased," Linda said loudly.

Giles tried to give her a gentle kick under the table, but she jumped in the air and shrieked as if she had a broken ankle. "What was that for?" she cried.

"I think Giles was trying to persuade you to be quiet," said Mr. Maxwell with a slight smile.

"Giles did something today, and he's got to tell Martin about it," Linda insisted.

"It's nothing to do with you," said Giles, wishing she'd stop nagging him.

"Oh, no! Not much! You've only made it so that everybody in the class will be laughing at me, that's all."

"I don't see that at all."

"Oh, don't you? Well, I'll soon show you. You only told our music teacher that Martin would bring his group down to school to play for us. And you hadn't even asked Martin first. And what's more, if I hadn't said anything about it, Martin wouldn't even have known. And anyway, he probably won't bring the group down."

Martin stood up and glared down at Giles. "You said I'd do *what?*" he demanded.

Giles was so nervous, he could hardly speak properly. He had wanted to pick just the right time to talk to Martin, but Linda had made a mess of it.

"Come on!" demanded Martin. "Spell it out. You said I'd do what?"

"It wasn't exactly the way Linda said," stammered Giles. "Mr. Marshall was saying there weren't any good tunes nowadays and that long-haired roughs just banged on guitars and shouted at the tops of their voices and . . . oh, you know the sort of thing people say."

"I'm waiting to hear what *you* said, not what people say," Martin insisted.

"Oh," said Giles, "then we got into a sort of argument, and I said your group played music that was twice as good

as any of the songs he tried to make us sing . . . and then I offered . . . well, I sort of said . . . ''

"What?" repeated Martin firmly.

Giles gulped. "I said I'd ask you to bring the Minors down to the school so that he could see what I meant, and he said he thought that was a very good idea . . . " His voice trailed away as he said this. It had seemed such a good idea at the time, but now . . .

"And you really thought," said Martin, "that the Minors would want to waste their time playing to a lot of screaming school kids? You really thought that?"

"It was an argument," mumbled Giles. "I suppose I didn't really think . . . "

"That's it, then," said Martin. "You'd better tell Mr. Marshall. And the next time maybe you won't be so ready to fix things up without finding out first."

"Now wait a minute," said Mr. Maxwell. "Giles meant it as a compliment. After all, he was sticking up for you."

"We don't need anybody to stick up for us, thanks," said Martin coldly. "I'd be much obliged if you'd all mind your own business." Then he marched out.

"There you are!" said Linda. "I knew he'd be like that."

"It might have been all right if you hadn't butted in," cried Giles.

"Giles is right," said Mr. Maxwell. "You're nothing but a mischief-maker, Linda."

"Well, I like that!" spluttered Linda.

"I think it was a very good idea," said Mrs. Maxwell. "I think Martin was most ungrateful."

"Oh," cried Linda, jumping to her feet. "You're all against me. It's not fair!" Then she jumped up and ran out of the room, slamming the door loudly behind her as she left.

"Temper!" exclaimed Mrs. Maxwell.

A *Date for the Minors*

At breakfast the next morning, Linda apologized to Giles. "You really had a good idea," she told him.

When she and Giles reached school, her friend Sandra was waiting at the gate. "Gribby asked me to give you this note," Sandra said to Giles. "He lives next door to me, you know, and he said to give it to you before we went in to school."

"Thanks," said Giles, taking the note. Then he realized it was late and hurried to make his first class, which was mathematics.

Giles had no chance to read the note until almost the end of the math class. The message was short.

> Dear Giles,
>   About your idea. We had a talk about it last night, and the rest of us like it. Not Martin, but he'll come round. Tell Mr. Marshall okay.
>
> Yours,
> Grib

Giles could hardly believe his eyes. He wrote on the bottom of the note, "Does he mean it, or is it a joke?" Later, when he had the chance, he slipped the note to Linda.

A few minutes later it came back to him. Linda had written at the very bottom. "Good old Gribby! Better tell Mr. Marshall today and set a date."

He couldn't resist letting the rest of the class know, so while the math master was at the far side of the room, he wrote a note.

> The Minors will be coming!
> Watch this space.
> Pass it on.

He passed the note and watched the reactions as each member of the class read it and then turned to him with a grin or a hand wave or even a silent cheer.

"Giles Willis!" said the master, without raising his head from the work he was marking.

"Yes, sir?"

"Is your communication strictly mathematical?"

"I beg your pardon, sir?"

"You seem to be publishing some sort of information, in other words, passing a note. Of course, I may be wrong."

"No, sir. You're not wrong."

"Will somebody be kind enough to read the note aloud? Then we'll all know the good news at once and not be kept in suspense. It will also save time."

The note made a rapid passage across the class and landed back on Giles's desk. Then Giles read the first part of the note.

The master showed immediate interest. He beamed at Giles. "Are they really?" he exclaimed. "We were very divided on that question in the staff room. Mr. Marshall was sure they wouldn't have the nerve to turn up. One or two teachers were against the whole thing. Mr. Norton, the headmaster, was in favor of the idea. In fact, I think you'd better go to see him now and tell him the good news."

Late that afternoon Gribby came to ask Giles what had happened. Giles told him that Mr. Norton wanted the Minors to play for the whole school on Friday afternoon at three o'clock.

"I haven't said anything to Martin," Giles said. "You know how he is."

Gribby laughed. "I think he just puts on an act. He's really glad about this business at school, but he wouldn't say anything to you. He'd feel too embarrassed. Leave it to me. I'll tell him about Friday."

First Public Appearance

Mr. Norton meant what he had said. The whole school was excused from the last class on Friday afternoon in order to hear Martin's group. Giles noticed, as he took his place, that the whole staff of teachers was there, too.

There was excitement in the hall. Most of the students either knew Martin or knew about him, and all certainly knew about his group. But very few had heard the group play, because it had never appeared in public.

There was not long to wait. Almost as soon as Mr. Norton had entered, the door at the back of the stage opened, and the four boys came on. Their equipment was already set up at the back. Mr. Norton stood in front of the stage and said, "We're all very grateful to these four boys for coming down this afternoon. You know them, of course. They are all former students of the school. I won't waste any more time with words but leave it to . . . the Minors!"

There was great applause. Mr. Norton grinned and sat down.

The Minors were in top form. They started off with a fast number with a tremendous beat, followed by a ballad, then went into a rhythmical piece with plenty of drums and bass guitar. Each song was greeted with ear-splitting applause. The group played on and on. It looked as if the audience would never let them stop.

After almost an hour Mr. Norton jumped up onto the stage and held up his hands for silence. At first the school went on applauding and shouting for more and taking no notice of him, but then they sank back in their seats and waited to hear what he would say.

"I must say," said Mr. Norton, "that when I arranged for these lads to play for the school, I had no idea just how good they were. Now I'll tell you something Martin Maxwell himself should have told you but was too modest to mention."

There was a mild wave of laughter at this; no one had thought of Martin as modest.

"No, I'm not joking. Martin's gruffness is really his way of covering up shyness. He didn't tell you that more than half the numbers you've just heard were written by him and Tom Gribbing."

More wild cheers. And so it went on. Mr. Norton finally let the Minors play one more number, and then the school was dismissed.

Giles was standing outside, watching the crowd streaming by, when he felt himself grabbed by the shoulders. He turned around to find Gribby.

"Thanks a lot, kid," Gribby said.

"Why me?" asked Giles.

"Well, you started it, didn't you? It was your bright idea. And now look what's happened."

"What has happened?"

"One of the chaps who sat with Mr. Norton runs the Star Hall. Mr. Norton brought him over while we were packing up our kit, and he's booked us to play for the dancing on the first Saturday of each month for the next three months."

"That's good," said Giles.

"Good? It's fabulous! What's more, he's going to pay us!"

When Giles reached home, he and Linda told Mrs. Maxwell what had happened at school, what Mr. Norton had said, and what Gribby had said afterward. They were still in the middle of it when Martin came in. He bounced into the room in a new way—not at all the usual slouching, scowling Martin.

"You heard the show?" he asked Giles.

"Yes," said Giles. "It was tremendous."

"First time we've played to a crowd," said Martin. "A bit frightening to tell you the truth. My fingers felt like boiled sausages for the first numbers. Well, you did us a bit of good with your argument with Mr. Marshall. Many thanks."

An hour later the Maxwells and Giles were sitting down to supper. It was a happy meal. Looking around him, Giles felt warm and content. He liked being in the Maxwell's house, even though Linda was her bossy self and Martin's friendly manner might not be long lasting.

One evening about a month later, Linda told Giles that Martin was happy about his job at the Star Hall and he and the group had made a recording of two tunes. That very same evening, while everyone was sitting in the living room, Martin leaped at the television set and turned it on.

"Listen!" cried Linda, pointing to the popular disc jockey on the screen.

"...and to end with," the disc jockey said, "we're going to play you a brand-new release from a brand-new group. Here it is... 'Break It to Her Gently' by the Minors."

In the room Martin conducted with the music and listened to his own voice.

"Now the neighbors will be round to congratulate us," said Mr. Maxwell.

Reflections

1. What do you think is the difference between music and noise? How would you describe "good music"?

2. How is Martin's usual gruffness explained? Do you think Gribby really understood Martin? Give reasons for your answer.

3. How do you think Martin's success will affect his personality? Do you think Martin's friendly manner towards Giles will last? Explain.

4. Martin describes his nervousness by saying, "My fingers felt like boiled sausages for the first numbers." Write a story about a time you were very nervous. Try to remember just how you felt, and then describe your feelings.

Our World of Many Images

BARTLETT HAYES

CITY INTERIOR

CHARLES SHEELER, 1883–1965

Everywhere we turn there is something different to look at. This picture
of an industrial scene is a painting, not a photograph.

WORCESTER ART MUSEUM, WORCESTER, MASSACHUSETTS

The world has always looked different to people—
depending on *when* they lived.

EARTH RISING OVER MOON'S RIM (1968)
NATIONAL AERONAUTICS AND SPACE ADMINISTRATION

In their first moon-circling voyage, the astronauts observed the world from a point of view different from anyone else before them. This picture is a glimpse of the earth from a distance of 400,000 kilometers (250,000 miles), made possible by the techniques of the modern scientist.

MAP OF THE VOYAGE
OF SIR FRANCIS DRAKE

JUDOCUS HONDIUS (jü dō'kəs hon'dē əs), 1563–1611

About four hundred years ago, an English admiral named Sir Francis Drake sailed around the earth in a daring voyage. During his time such a voyage was as daring as were the space voyages of the astronauts. A diagram, or map, of his voyage, as illustrated below, was made in London. This map does not illustrate what Drake actually saw as a camera would. It is a diagram of the whole idea of his world voyage. The idea was just as exciting for the world of the admiral's day as the camera picture, taken from the rim of the moon, was for that of the astronauts' day.

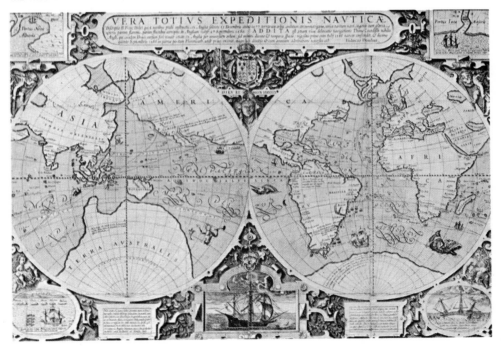

**People look at the world differently—
depending on *what* they see or imagine.**

CHILLY OBSERVATION

CHARLES S. RALEIGH, 1831–1925

Because of their inhospitable climates, both the frigid and torrid zones
were the last parts of the world to which explorers voyaged. Naturally,
each zone looked very different. When people sailed to the bleak icy zone
of the polar bear, the bear was startled to see such an unusual invasion
of his territory.

THE JUNGLE: TIGER ATTACKING A BUFFALO
HENRI ROUSSEAU (än rē′ rü sō′), 1844–1910

The artist who painted this picture had heard of dense, hot, humid jungles and wild beasts. He dreamed of tigers and buffalo and explored their jungle habitats in his artistic imagination, although he never actually ventured in them.

As people continued to explore the world, their knowledge broadened, and therefore they engaged in different kinds of activities.

DEER HUNT (detail)
PREHISTORIC ROCK DRAWING
(MAGDALENIAN PERIOD, SOUTHEAST SPAIN)

Several thousand years ago, people made these drawings on rock walls. Some scholars believe they were made for fun; others think they were made to exert magical power over wild animals and that they were intended, therefore, to help the hunters catch their prey.

GUERNICA *(mural)*

PABLO PICASSO (päb'lō pi kä'sō), 1881–1973

This painting was an important feature of the Spanish pavilion at the 1937 World's Fair in Paris. It was painted in protest against the savage air raid which destroyed the small town of Guernica during the Civil War in Spain. The frenzied horse, the tortured bull, the screaming mother —all represent the artist's angry denunciation of the deed. In contrast with the magical art of the prehistoric people, the painting helps us understand the horror of what some people have done.

ON EXTENDED LOAN TO THE MUSEUM OF MODERN ART, NEW YORK CITY, FROM THE ESTATE OF THE ARTIST

**With the growth of technical knowledge,
our world changed in appearance,
and, therefore, even our houses have become different.**

HALL OF THE ELEAZER ARNOLD HOUSE, LINCOLN, RHODE ISLAND
ARCHITECT UNKNOWN

This house was built for an early settler in New England. The large fireplace not only warmed the whole house in winter but also provided a natural place to do the cooking. The windows were small like the tiny one in the corner at the left. Very little light could come inside. The solid walls and the small windows helped keep the heat indoors in winter and outdoors in summer. The house was like a simple box, built to protect people from nature.

COURTESY OF THE SOCIETY FOR THE PRESERVATION OF NEW ENGLAND ANTIQUITIES. PHOTO: SANDAK

INTERIOR OF THE ROBINSON HOUSE, WILLIAMSTOWN, MASSACHUSETTS
MARCEL BREUER (mär sel′ broi′ ər), 1902–

A modern house also serves to protect people but, unlike the settler's house, it welcomes the beauty of nature indoors. The fireplace is merely for pleasure because, with central heating and cooling, it is not really necessary. Moreover, the stone of the fireplace and the unpainted boards of the ceiling are natural materials. Thus, the inside itself is seen as a brightly lit part of the landscape.

PHOTO: ROBERT DAMORA

As people learned to know the world,
they discovered a way to control
some of the *forces of nature.*
There were new things
such as steam engines to look at,
and art changed accordingly.

RAIN, STEAM, AND SPEED

J.M.W. TURNER, 1775–1851

Although this painting may seem to be abstract at first glance, it is actually what a camera might record. The black shape of a train rushing out of a vast, misty void and across a high bridge can barely be seen. The rain and the river represent nature uncontrolled. The steam, which propels the train, represents human control of the element—water. The second bridge, in the distance, helps define the feeling of the misty atmosphere. Both speed and space are suggested by the blurred, vaporous forms.

314

COLLECTION OF THE MUSEUM OF FINE ARTS. BOSTON. MASSACHUSETTS

Later in the nineteenth century, artists became intrigued by *scientific explanations* of light and the colors which compose it.

STONE PINE, ANTIBES

CLAUDE MONET (klōd mō nā'), 1840–1926

This bright scene is a view of a Mediterranean town. Glistening just beyond the pine tree are the sea and the town. Rising in the background are the Maritime Alps. The artist probably chose to paint this picture because of the vivid contrast between nature (represented by the tree, sea, and mountains) and civilization (represented by the town). Nevertheless, he has united people and nature by bathing both in colored light. The tiny, colored patches of paint close together depict colored beams of light. These paint patches not only give a sparkling quality to the water, the village and the sky but also represent the different colors reflected from the entire landscape.

Still other artists look at *movement* in the world as never before. The camera has helped them notice how people and things move.

DOG ON A LEASH

GIACOMO BALLA (jä'kə mō bä' lä), 1871–1958

This picture of a dog on a leash was painted more than a quarter century before the photograph of the dancer was taken. Yet the painting also shows a scientific interest in motion. By showing the dog's leash several times as it swung to and fro, the artist conveyed a sense of blurred motion. Of course, he painted the feet of the dog and of its owner in the same way.

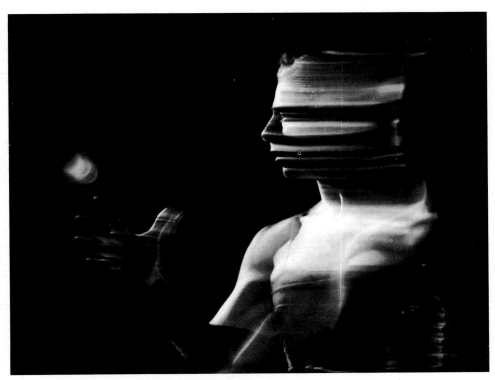

DETAIL OF ANN HALPRIN IN "ENTOMBMENT"

MILTON HALBERSTADT, 1919–

For years and years after the invention of photography, many people believed it was just a way to copy nature faithfully. They did not believe a photograph could be a work of art. Here, however, is a photograph that has artistic qualities showing a particular instant during the turning of a dancer.

319

For many years people have generally used the word *art* to mean painting, sculpture, or architecture. Today *art* can mean almost anything— at least in the eyes of some.

BROOKLYN BRIDGE
GORDON PARKS, 1913–

This is a photograph of the Brooklyn Bridge in New York City. Although many people have taken photographs of the same subject, this artist knew how to make use of light. The result is a theatrical environment. It gives the feeling that anyone who wants to can become involved with art.

The National Gallery of Art in Washington, D.C., belongs to all the people of the United States of America. The building is made of marble from Vermont, Tennessee, and Tuscany in Italy.

Walking into the Gallery, we find ourselves in a huge round room called the Rotunda. Above is a great dome, upheld by towering columns. In the center is a fountain decorated with a bronze statue of Mercury by Giovanni Bologna, an Italian sculptor. Mercury was the Roman messenger god.

There are many rooms in the Gallery, filled with some of the world's greatest masterpieces of art. The following pages give an idea of the kinds of outstanding paintings that can be seen in this great art gallery.

national gallery of art

shirley glubok

322

GINEVRA DE'BENCI
LEONARDO DA VINCI (lā ə när′ dō dä vin′ chē), 1452–1519

This calm portrait of Ginevra, the daughter of an Italian merchant, was painted about five hundred years ago. Ginevra had been ill, and her smooth face is pale. She is posed against a background of trees to show that she found great pleasure in nature. The artist, Leonardo Da Vinci, was one of the greatest painters of all time.

THE YOUTHFUL DAVID
ANDREA DEL CASTAGNO (än drā′ə del kas tan′ yō), 1423?–1457

The young biblical hero David appears as the ideal warrior in the painting on a parade shield at the left. He is about to hurl a stone with his slingshot at the giant Goliath. David has overcome his fears, fighting and winning an important battle. Goliath's head is already at David's feet. Both the heroic act and its bloody results are shown at the same time.

TOBIAS AND THE ANGEL
FILIPPINO LIPPI (fi li pē′ nō li′ pē), 1406?–1469

Tobias was also a biblical hero. He cured the blindness of his beloved old father with a miraculous fish-gall ointment. An angel who helped Tobias is leading him along, walking erect and fearless, watching over him.

SAINT GEORGE AND THE DRAGON
RAPHAEL (raf′ ē əl), 1483–1520

Saint George personified the victory of good over evil. According to legend, he was traveling along when he came upon a weeping princess about to be fed to a dragon. The knight is calm and unafraid as the rescued princess kneels in prayer behind him.

324

325

THE LUTE PLAYER

ORAZIO GENTILESCHI (jen' ti les' kē), 1563–1647

The artist's daughter, Artemisia, playing music on a lute is the subject of this painting. She is preparing for a concert. She seems to be listening to her own music as she plucks the strings. Sheet music and instruments of the period lie on the table—three recorders and a violin and bow. The girl is dressed in a bright jumper and blouse, which stand out against the dark background. Artemisia often posed for her father's pictures, and she was trained by him to be an artist herself. At that time, about three hundred and fifty years ago, it was unusual for girls to study art. Artemisia became the first woman in history to become an important painter.

A DUTCH COURTYARD

PIETER de HOOCH (pēt′ r də hōk), 1629–?1688

Dutch artists of the seventeenth century were careful observers of nature, and they often painted realistic scenes of homes and families. People in The Netherlands liked to have such scenes around them, hanging on the walls of their homes. In this Dutch courtyard the crumbling brick walls and the uneven paving are real enough to be touched. The metal breast-plate and pitcher gleam. The tower in the background shows that the courtyard is in the city of Delft, Holland. There is hardly a breath of movement in this happy scene, which makes it seem eternal, without end. One feels almost drawn into it, becoming a part of the friendly scene.

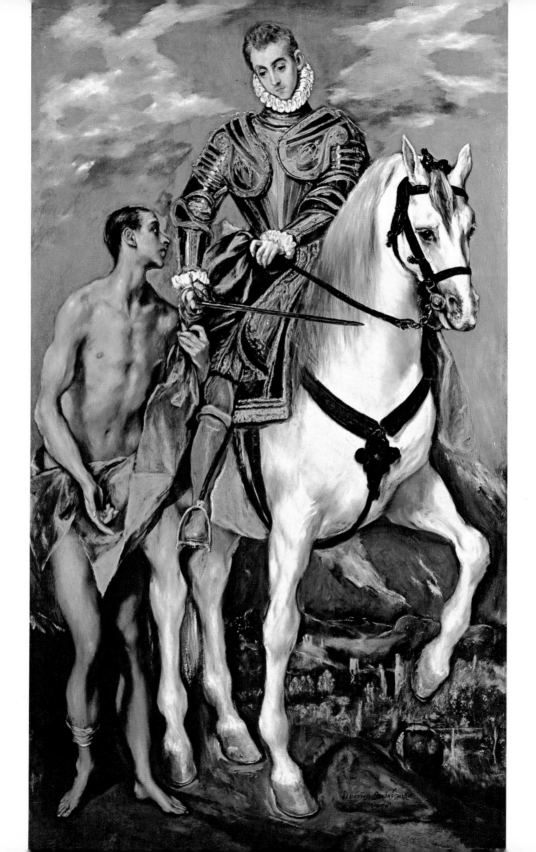

NAPOLEON IN HIS STUDY
JACQUES-LOUIS DAVID (dä vēd'), 1748–1825

This full-length portrait of the French emperor, in a typical pose, shows how the artist made Napoleon appear heroic. The portrait is filled with flattering touches: the epaulets of a general, combined with details of a guard's uniform; the Napoleonic Code of Law; the medal of the Legion of Honor, which Napoleon created. The burnt-down candles at 4:15 A.M. show that the emperor has worked all night for his subjects.

SAINT MARTIN AND THE BEGGAR
EL GRECO (grek'ō), 1541–1614

In the story behind this painting, holy mystery surrounds Martin and the beggar. Martin, a Roman soldier, shared his cloak with a naked beggar one wintry day. That night Martin had a vision of Jesus coming to him wearing half of the cloak. Because of the vision, Martin became a Christian. He later became a bishop and was finally made a saint. El Greco elongated and twisted faces and bodies to create strong drama and emotions.

PORTRAIT OF A LADY

ELISABETH VIGÉE-LEBRUN (vē zhā′ lə brün′), 1755–1842

One of the early important women artists in Europe was Elisabeth Vigée-Lebrun. By the time she was fifteen, she was supporting her family with the money she earned from her paintings. She made portraits of people all over Europe. Among her subjects were the Queen of France and the Prince of Wales in England. The name of this woman is not known. She is dressed in the latest fashion as she relaxes against the background of silk cushions.

DECIUS MUS ADDRESSING THE LEGIONS

PETER PAUL RUBENS (rüb′ənz), 1577–1640

Decius Mus, a Roman consul of the fourth century B.C., is telling his saddened troops that he is going to let himself be killed in battle. In a vision he was told that the side which sacrificed its leader would emerge victorious. This painting is a small study for a tapestry. Rubens's sketches are heroic, filled with pageantry, dramatic action, and great power.

CHILDREN PLAYING ON THE BEACH

MARY CASSATT (ka sat'), 1845–1926

Two little girls playing at the beach do not seem to know that someone is painting a picture of them. They are interested only in filling their buckets with sand. A sailboat can be seen in the distance. The artist was born in Pennsylvania but spent most of her life in Paris, France.

BREEZING UP

WINSLOW HOMER, 1836–1910

Winslow Homer was a famous American painter who was trained as an illustrator. Homer was proud of being a realist, painting things exactly as they appear. In this painting he has evoked a mood. He has portrayed the feeling of a warm sun, a fresh breeze, a swiftly moving boat. even the smell of salt in the air. The fisherman and the three boys are relaxed after the day's catch. Bright light contrasted with muted tones suggests a late summer afternoon at sunset. The position of the boat gives a sense of rapid movement as though it were about to sail out of sight.

GIRL IN A BOAT WITH GEESE

BERTHE MORISOT (bert mô rē zō'), 1841–1895

A quiet summer day with a girl rowing a boat on a lake is the subject of this painting. Three geese seem to watch her with interest while a fourth is busy with its own activity. The artist used short, rapid brush strokes to give the feeling that the light is changing.

OARSMEN AT CHATOU

AUGUSTE RENOIR (ô güst' ren wär'), 1841–1919

To capture the gay atmosphere of a pleasant holiday spot near Paris, Renoir has painted with brilliantly colored brush strokes. The colors make the light sparkle on the water and fill the air with a joyful mood. This style of painting is called Impressionism. The Impressionists liked to paint fresh, outdoor scenes, flooded with a bright sunlight.

335

BOTH MEMBERS OF THIS CLUB
GEORGE BELLOWS, 1882–1925

These two fighters locked in combat create an interesting study in opposing forces. One boxer buckles under the power of his opponent. Pain can be seen in his face as the victor springs forward to speed the defeat. This painting shows a boxing match that took place in the ring at Sharkey's Athletic Club in New York. At the time, boxing contests were only permitted if the contestants and spectators were all members of the same club. George Bellows was born in Ohio and became one of the most popular artists of his day.

These fifteen paintings are just a small sampling of the masterpieces in the National Gallery of Art. It is an important place to see on a visit to Washington, D.C.

Maria's House

JEAN MERRILL

Every Saturday, Maria got on a bus and went to the museum. There she spent the morning at an art class. One Saturday, the class was given an assignment to do at home. They were all to draw a picture of the house they lived in.

The Assignment

Maria had worried all week about the assignment. How could she do it? There was no way of making a rundown tenement building look beautiful, if you drew it the way it was.

Could she make a little watercolor painting of the inside of the apartment? Perhaps of the sunny corner of the kitchen where Mama had her spice shelf and the pots of basil and parsley growing?

But she would have to explain to Miss Lindstrom why she had drawn the inside of the house, instead of the whole house.

Maria had put off doing the assignment all week. Then the last night, Friday night, she had opened her drawing pad on the kitchen table.

She had a new set of colored markers that Mama had bought her. She wanted to do a drawing with the markers.

She tried all the colors on the cover of the pad. Then she sat for a long time, staring at a clean sheet of drawing paper. Finally, she started to draw.

She drew a large white house with picture windows. The windows looked out over a wide lawn that sloped down to a pond.

Maria sketched in a winding driveway with birch trees

on either side. To one side of the house, she drew a stone terrace and colored in some chairs, covered in a gay, striped cloth.

Mama looked over at the drawing. "Pretty," Mama nodded. "Like a picture in the magazines. But what are you drawing for the art class?"

"This is for class," Maria said.

"A magazine picture?" Mama said.

Mama was used to Miss Lindstrom's giving more interesting assignments. Things like: "A Bad Dream." Or, "The Way the World Would Look to Me, If I Were a Rabbit." Or, "The Way I Feel on the First Day of Spring."

The first time Maria came home with one of these assignments, Mama was puzzled.

"How you feel on the first day of spring?" she said. "How can you draw a feeling? Daffodils maybe. But how you feel—?"

But when Maria showed Mama her painting of lilacs in Highland Park and parents and children out walking in their best clothes, Mama said, "Ah—how you feel in the spring—nice and pretty and happy, smelling the lilacs. I see."

Mama understood about Miss Lindstrom's assignments now. She could explain to her friends all of Maria's pictures that she had pinned up in the apartment.

"Picture of a bad dream," Mama would tell Mrs. Katz. "Not what happens in the dream maybe. Just how it makes you feel. A lot of big dark shapes pressing in on you."

Mrs. Projansky from across the hall thought at first that the cabbages in the picture that Mama called "The Rabbit's World" were bushes—or big green clouds.

"Bushes!" Mama said. "Big green clouds!"

Mama explained to Mrs. Projansky that she must try to see as a rabbit would see. "To a rabbit, a cabbage would look as big as a bush."

Mama had learned a lot about art, and she knew by now that art was not like a picture in a magazine. So when she asked about the house, Maria could not lie to her.

"We have to draw a house this week," she said.

"Just a house," Mama said. "Any house? Not a house in a bad dream? In the spring? The way a house looks to a rabbit? Just a plain house?"

Maria did not answer for a minute. Then she told Mama, "It's supposed to be a picture of the house where we live."

"Oh," Mama said. She looked at Maria's picture again. "Our house?" she said.

"No," Maria said. "I can't draw our house."

"Can't draw it?" Mama said. "Before you ever went to art class, you could draw a whole block of houses burning down and five fire engines and ten police officers and a hundred people in the picture. Now you can't draw one house?"

"That's not what I mean," Maria said.

Maria tried to explain to Mama that a three-room apartment on Market Street wasn't the same as a house. And so to do the assignment, she would have to imagine a house.

"But a three-room apartment is in a house," Mama said. "So it's a big house. Apartment house. Your teacher means draw where you live."

Maria jabbed a pencil into the kitchen table.

"Oh, Mama!" she said. "This house is no good to draw. How can I make a beautiful picture of this house? I was trying to make a beautiful picture."

Mama looked down at the house Maria had drawn and shook her head.

"It's nice that art should be beautiful," Mama said. "But it should also be true. Your teacher asks you to draw what you know."

Mama pointed to the picture of the bad dream.

"When you painted the bad dream," Mama said, "did you paint Papa's bad dream? My bad dream?

"No," Mama said. "You painted your bad dream."

Maria scribbled more circles.

Mama sighed. "I am not an artist," she said. "All I know is—art must be true."

Maria Decides

Maria watched Mama packing the shirts she had been ironing all day into a carton for Papa to carry down to the Overnite Laundry. Then she looked again at the house she had drawn.

What was wrong with using her imagination? An artist should be able to imagine things, too.

But the picture did look like a magazine picture. Mama was right about that.

Maria tore the picture from her drawing pad and slipped it into her portfolio. She started another drawing.

She sketched in the outline of the house she lived in. With angry slashes of a marker, she drew the rusted fire escape zigzagging down the front of the building. She drew the sagging window frames and the crumbling cement steps leading up to the front door.

There were the broken windows in Mrs. Sedita's apartment on the ground floor. The landlord had refused to fix them, and Mrs. Sedita had had cardboard tacked over the missing panes for a year.

On the windowsill outside the Durkins' apartment, Maria drew three milk cartons. The power company kept turning off the Durkins' electricity, and Mrs. Durkin had to put her milk on the windowsill to keep it cool.

She was drawing very fast. Putting in all the things that made the building look so sad, old, tired, dirty, and ugly. Mama would see that she could not take a picture like this to Miss Lindstrom.

Maria paused and looked at her drawing.

It was 79 Market Street all right. And she hadn't had to go out and look at the building. She knew exactly how it looked.

Mama studied the picture for a long time.

"It's true," she said finally. "It's Market Street." Mama sighed. "Will you take it to art class?"

"Mama! I can't."

It was true. It was Market Street. And Maria was afraid she was going to cry.

She ripped the picture off the pad and stuffed it into her portfolio. She put away her markers and pencils, washed and went to bed.

Reflections

Which picture do you think Maria took to class? Write a paragraph giving the reasons for your decision. Remember to keep Maria's character in mind when explaining the reasons for her choice.

The Wizard of Oz

L. FRANK BAUM

Adapted by Lynne Sharon Schwartz

CHARACTERS

NARRATOR	SCARECROW	LOVELY LADY
DOROTHY	TIN WOODMAN	GLINDA, THE
WITCH OF THE	COWARDLY LION	GOOD WITCH
NORTH	SOLDIER	OF THE SOUTH
THREE MUNCHKINS	WIZARD OF OZ	AUNT EM

Scene One

(NARRATOR *enters in front of the curtain.*)

NARRATOR: Once upon a time there was a little girl named Dorothy. She lived in Kansas with her Uncle Henry, who was a farmer, and her Aunt Em, and her dog, Toto. One day they heard a low wail of the wind, and they saw the long grass bowing in waves. They heard a sharp, whistling sound in the air, and they knew that a cyclone was coming. (*Howling sound of wind.*)

Uncle Henry ran out to take care of the cattle, and Aunt Em ran to a trapdoor in the floor, calling to Dorothy to follow her. But at that moment Toto jumped out of Dorothy's arms and hid under the bed. As Dorothy reached to get him, the house shook so hard that she lost her footing and fell down on the floor. Then the house whirled around two or three times and rose slowly through the air. The house was in the exact center of the cyclone, and it was carried miles and miles up into the air. Dorothy crawled into her bed and

fell asleep. When she awoke, she found herself in a strange place. (NARRATOR *exits. Curtain rises.*)

(Setting: A field. A backdrop portrays the front of a house. Two silver shoes can be seen sticking out from under the house. DOROTHY *is standing near the doorway holding her dog, Toto.)*

DOROTHY: I wonder where I am! All I can remember is whirling around and around.

*(*WITCH OF THE NORTH *and* MUNCHKINS *enter.)*

WITCH OF THE NORTH *(Bowing):* You are welcome, most noble Sorceress, to the land of the Munchkins. We are grateful to you for having killed the Wicked Witch of the East.

DOROTHY: Oh, dear! The house must have fallen on her. Whatever shall we do?

WITCH OF THE NORTH: There is nothing to be done. She made the Munchkins her slaves. Now they are free and are grateful to you. These are three of my Munchkin friends. I am the Witch of the North.

DOROTHY: Are you a real witch?

WITCH OF THE NORTH: Yes, but I am a good witch.

DOROTHY: I thought all witches were wicked.

WITCH OF THE NORTH: Oh, no, that is a great mistake. There were four witches in all the Land of Oz, and two of them—The Witch of the North *(Points to herself)* and the Witch of the South—are good witches. The other two are wicked witches. Now that you have killed the Wicked Witch of the East, there is but one Wicked Witch left—the Wicked Witch of the West.

1ST MUNCHKIN *(Pointing at shoes under house):* Look! Look! Her feet have disappeared. *(All run to look.)*

WITCH OF THE NORTH: Now the silver shoes are yours.

DOROTHY: Thank you for the shoes. Can you help me find my way back to my Aunt Em?

WITCH OF THE NORTH: I am afraid, my dear, that you will have to stay here with us.

DOROTHY *(Starting to cry):* I want to go back to Kansas.

WITCH OF THE NORTH *(Taking off her cap and looking inside):* Perhaps we will get a magic message from the cap to help us. *(Reading.)* "Let Dorothy go to the City of Emeralds." Is your name Dorothy, my dear?

DOROTHY *(Controlling her tears):* Yes. Where is the City of Emeralds?

WITCH OF THE NORTH: It is in the center of the country and is ruled by Oz, the Great Wizard.

DOROTHY: How do I get there?

WITCH OF THE NORTH: It is a long journey, through a country that is dark and terrible. However, I will give you my charmed kiss. No one will dare injure a person who has been kissed by the Witch of the North. *(Kisses* DOROTHY *on forehead.)* The road to the City of Emeralds is paved with yellow brick, so you cannot miss it. When you reach Oz, tell the Great Wizard your story and ask him to help you. Goodbye, my dear. *(*WITCH *and* MUNCHKINS *exit.)*

DOROTHY: Goodbye, and thank you all.

> *(*DOROTHY *exits. Lights dim to show passage of time. When lights come up,* SCARECROW *stands on stool left, as if attached to pole behind stool.* DOROTHY *enters, carrying Toto. She notices* SCARECROW.*)*

DOROTHY: I'm sure I saw that Scarecrow wink at me, but it just couldn't be. After all, he's made of straw.

SCARECROW: Good day.

DOROTHY: Did you speak?

SCARECROW: Certainly. How do you do?

DOROTHY: I'm pretty well, thank you. How do you do?

SCARECROW: I'm not feeling well. It's very tedious being perched up here night and day to scare away crows.

DOROTHY: Can't you get down?

SCARECROW: No, because this pole is stuck up my back. If you will please take away the pole, I shall be greatly obliged to you. *(DOROTHY goes to SCARECROW and pretends to lift him off pole. He steps down and lowers his arms.)* Thank you very much. I feel like a new man. *(Stretches and yawns.)* Who are you, and where are you going?

DOROTHY: My name is Dorothy, and I am on my way to the Emerald City to ask the great Oz to send me back to Kansas.

SCARECROW: Where is the Emerald City? And who is Oz?

DOROTHY: Why, don't you know?

SCARECROW *(Sadly):* No, indeed. I don't know anything. You see, I am stuffed with straw, so I have no brains at all. Do you think that if I go to the Emerald City with you, Oz would give me some brains?

DOROTHY: I cannot tell, but come with me if you like.

SCARECROW: I think I shall. You see, I don't mind my legs and arms and body being stuffed, because I cannot get hurt. But I don't like to be thought a fool.

(As they talk, TIN WOODMAN enters, unseen by DOROTHY or SCARECROW. He stands at one side, with his ax raised, and groans softly. As his groans grow louder, DOROTHY looks around).

DOROTHY: I'm sure I heard someone groan. *(Sees TIN WOODMAN.)* Oh! Did you groan?

TIN WOODMAN: Yes, I did. I've been groaning for more than a year. Please get an oilcan and oil my joints. They are rusted so badly that I cannot move them at all. You

will find an oilcan right in front of my cottage a few steps farther into the woods.

DOROTHY: Very well. *(She runs offstage and returns immediately with an oilcan.)* Where shall I put the oil?

TIN WOODMAN: Oil my neck, first. (DOROTHY *does so.* SCARECROW *helps by moving* TIN WOODMAN'S *head from side to side gently.)* Now oil the joints in my arms and legs. (DOROTHY *does so.* TIN WOODMAN *sighs and lowers his ax.)* This is a great comfort. I have been holding that ax in the air ever since I rusted in a rainstorm. Thank you so much! I might have stood there forever if you had not come along. Why are you here?

DOROTHY: We are on our way to the Emerald City to see the great Oz. I want him to send me back to Kansas, and the Scarecrow wants him to put a few brains into his head.

TIN WOODMAN: Do you suppose Oz could give me a—a heart?

DOROTHY: Why, I guess so. It would be as easy as giving the Scarecrow brains.

TIN WOODMAN: True. If you will allow me to join your party, I will also go to the Emerald City and ask Oz to help me.

SCARECROW: Come along. We'd be pleased to have you. But if I were you, I should ask for brains instead of a heart, for a fool with no brains would not know what to do with a heart if he had one.

TIN WOODMAN: I shall take the heart, for brains do not make one happy, and happiness is the best thing.

(There is a loud roar, and COWARDLY LION *rushes in. He knocks over* SCARECROW *and* TIN WOODMAN. *Stunned,* DOROTHY *drops Toto, and* LION *rushes toward him.* DOROTHY *snatches him up, and slaps* LION *on nose.)*

DOROTHY: You ought to be ashamed of yourself, a big beast like you, biting a poor little dog!

LION (*Rubbing his nose*): I didn't bite him.

DOROTHY: No, but you tried to. You are a coward.

LION: I know it. I always have. But how can I help it?

DOROTHY: I'm sure I don't know. To think of your striking a poor, stuffed scarecrow! (*Helping* SCARECROW *up and patting his clothes into shape.*)

LION: Is he stuffed? That's why he went over so easily. Is the other one stuffed also?

DOROTHY (*Helping* TIN WOODMAN): No, he's made of tin.

LION: Then that's why he nearly blunted my claws.

SCARECROW: What makes you a coward?

LION: It's a mystery. All the other animals in the forest naturally expect me to be brave, because a lion is considered King of Beasts. (*Confidingly*) Actually, if the elephants and tigers and bears had ever tried to fight me, I should have run myself—I'm such a coward. (*He wipes tears from his eyes with tip of his tail.*) Whenever there is danger, my heart begins to beat fast.

TIN WOODMAN: You ought to be glad of that, for it proves you have a heart. I have no heart at all, so it cannot beat fast or slow. But I am going to ask Oz for one.

SCARECROW: And I am going to ask him to give me brains.

DOROTHY: And I am going to ask him to send Toto and me back to Kansas.

LION: Do you think Oz could give me courage?

SCARECROW: Just as easily as he can give me brains.

TIN WOODMAN: Or me a heart.

DOROTHY: Or send me back to Kansas.

LION: Then I'll go with you, for my life is simply unbearable without even a bit of courage.

DOROTHY: You will be very welcome. To Emerald City!

(*They all start to exit, as curtain falls.*)

Scene Two

(Time: A few days later. Setting: Outside of Oz's throne room. DOROTHY, SCARECROW, TIN WOODMAN, and LION enter in front of curtains, all wearing green spectacles.)

DOROTHY *(Wearily):* I thought we would never arrive.

(SOLDIER enters.)

DOROTHY: Have you seen Oz and asked him about us?

SOLDIER: Oh, no! I have never seen Oz, but I speak to him—and I gave him your message. When I mentioned your silver shoes, he was very much interested. He said he would grant you an audience, but each of you must go in alone. And you must not remove the green spectacles.

DOROTHY: Why?

SOLDIER: Because that is the rule. Otherwise the brightness and glory of Emerald City would blind you. *(Bell rings.)* That is the signal. *(To* DOROTHY*)* You must go into the throne room by yourself. *(He ushers off* SCARECROW, TIN WOODMAN, *and* LION. DOROTHY *waves to them, then faces center.* CURTAIN *opens.)*

(Setting: The throne room of Oz. There is a large, green throne at center, and suspended over it is a tremendous papier-maché head, with a mouth that moves. There is a folding screen at left. All furnishings are green. DOROTHY *walks hesitantly into room.* Oz, *hidden behind screen left, speaks as if through the head hanging over throne, manipulating mouth of head with a string as he speaks.)*

OZ *(From behind the screen):* I am Oz, the great and terrible. Who are you, and why do you seek me?

DOROTHY: I am Dorothy, the small and meek. I have come to you for help.

OZ: Where did you get the silver shoes?

DOROTHY: I got them from the Wicked Witch of the East, when my house fell on her and killed her.

OZ: What do you wish me to do?

DOROTHY: Send me back to Kansas, where my Aunt Em will be dreadfully worried over my being away so long.

OZ: Why should I do this for you?

DOROTHY: Because you are strong and I am weak; because you are a Great Wizard, and I am only a little girl.

OZ: You killed the Wicked Witch of the East, and you wear the silver shoes, which have a powerful charm. There is now but one Wicked Witch left. When you can tell me she is dead, I will send you to Kansas.

DOROTHY (*Beginning to weep*): I never killed anything willingly, and even if I wanted to, how could I kill the Wicked Witch?

OZ: I do not know, but that is my answer, and until the Wicked Witch of the West dies, you will not see your aunt again.

(DOROTHY *exits. Lights dim to show passage of time. When lights come up again, papier-maché head has been removed, and* LOVELY LADY *is sitting on throne.* SCARECROW *enters, approaches throne, and bows.*)

LADY: I am Oz, the great and terrible. Who are you, and why do you seek me?

SCARECROW: I am only a scarecrow stuffed with straw, and I have no brains. I come to you praying that you will put brains in my head instead of straw, so that I may become as much a person as any other.

LADY: This much I will promise. If you will kill the Wicked Witch of the West for me, I will bestow upon you such good brains that you will be the wisest person in all the Land of Oz.

SCARECROW: I thought you asked Dorothy to kill her.

LADY: So I did. I don't care who kills her. Until she is dead, I will not grant your wish.

(SCARECROW *exits. Lights dim. When lights come up again, Oz is sitting on throne, disguised as a horrible beast.* TIN WOODMAN *enters and bows. Oz roars.*)

OZ: I am Oz, the great and terrible. Who are you, and why do you seek me?

TIN WOODMAN: I am a woodman, and made of tin. Therefore I have no heart, and cannot love. Please give me a heart so that I may be like others.

OZ: If you indeed desire a heart, you must earn it. Help Dorothy kill the Wicked Witch of the West. I will then give you the biggest and kindest and most loving heart in all the Land of Oz.

(*He roars.* TIN WOODMAN *exits. Lights dim. When lights come up again, there is a huge ball of "fire" hanging over throne.* Oz *is concealed behind screen.* COWARDLY LION *enters timidly.*)

OZ (*From behind screen*): I am Oz, the great and terrible. Who are you, and why do you seek me?

LION: I am a cowardly lion, though I am supposed to be King of Beasts. I am frightened of everything I see, so I have come to ask if you will give me courage.

OZ: I will grant you courage only if you will do something for me. Help Dorothy kill the Wicked Witch of the West. Then I will make you the most courageous beast in all the forest. I am Oz, the great and terrible.

(*Ball of fire shakes.* LION *cringes, curtain falls.*)

Scene Three

(NARRATOR *enters in front of curtain.*)

NARRATOR: The four friends met and marveled at the many forms the Great Wizard of Oz could assume. Then together they started for the castle of the Wicked Witch of the West. Along the way they were captured by the Winged Monkeys, and Dorothy was taken prisoner by the Wicked Witch. The Witch was happy to have a new slave to clean the pots and tend the fires. But Dorothy was so angry at the mistreatment of her three friends that she threw a bucket of water on the Wicked Witch. Now water was the one thing the Wicked Witch of the West couldn't stand, and she just melted down to nothing. Dorothy took the witch's magic cap, gathered her friends, and the Winged Monkeys whisked the tired band back to the Emerald City. (*Exits.*)

(*Setting:* Oz's *throne room. As curtain rises the throne is empty.* Oz *is hidden behind screen.* DOROTHY, SCARECROW, TIN WOODMAN, *and* LION *enter.*)

DOROTHY: Phew, what a ride. I wonder where Oz is.

OZ (*From behind screen*): I am Oz, the great and terrible. Why do you seek me?

DOROTHY: Where are you? We have come to claim our rewards, O Great Oz. You promised to grant us all our wishes when the Wicked Witch was destroyed. I melted her with a bucket of water.

OZ: Dear me, how sudden. Well, come to me tomorrow, for I must have time to think it over.

TIN WOODMAN: You've had plenty of time already.

(LION *lets out a great roar so that* DOROTHY *jumps, drops Toto, and tips over the screen, revealing* Oz, *a little old man.*)

TIN WOODMAN (*Raising his ax*): Who are you?

Oz (*Fearfully*): I am Oz, the great and terrible, but don't strike me—please don't—and I'll do anything you want.

DOROTHY: I thought Oz was a great head.

SCARECROW: And I thought Oz was a lovely lady.

TIN WOODMAN: And I thought Oz was a terrible beast.

LION: And I thought he was a ball of fire.

Oz: No, you are all wrong. I'm supposed to be a Great Wizard, but I'm just a common man.

TIN WOODMAN: How shall I ever get my heart?

LION: Or I my courage?

SCARECROW: Or I my brains?

Oz: My dear friends, I pray you not to speak of these little things. Think of me, and the terrible trouble I'm in now that you have found me out.

DOROTHY: Doesn't anyone else know you're a humbug?

Oz: No one but the four of you.

SCARECROW: Really, you ought to be ashamed of yourself.

Oz: I am—I certainly am—but it was the only thing I could do. You see, I was born in Omaha—

DOROTHY: Why, that isn't very far from Kansas!

Oz: No, but it's far from here! (*Shakes his head sadly.*) I worked in a circus as a balloonist. One day the ropes of my balloon got twisted, and I floated miles through the air until I landed in this strange and beautiful country. I have been happy here. But one of my greatest fears was the Witches. That is why I was so pleased to hear that your house had fallen on the Wicked Witch of the East, and why I was so willing to promise anything if you would do away with the Wicked Witch of the West. But I cannot keep my promise to you.

SCARECROW: Can't you give me brains?

Oz: You don't need them. You are learning something every day. A baby has brains, but it doesn't know much. Experience is the only thing that brings knowledge.

SCARECROW: That may all be true, but I shall be very unhappy unless you give me brains.

OZ: Then I will try to give you brains. I cannot tell you how to use them, however. (Oz *goes to table and takes a cup filled with powder. He then goes to* SCARECROW *and pretends to pour powder into his head.*) The main ingredient is bran. Hereafter you will be a great man, for I have given you a lot of bran-new brains!

LION: Now, how about my courage?

OZ: All you need is confidence in yourself. There is no living thing that is not afraid when it faces danger. True courage is facing danger when you are afraid, and you have plenty of true courage.

LION: Perhaps I have, but I'm scared just the same. I shall really be very unhappy unless you give me the sort of courage that makes one forget he is afraid.

OZ: Very well, I will get some for you. (*Goes to table, takes green bottle, and pours contents into green dish. He offers it to* LION, *who sniffs disdainfully.*) Drink.

LION: What is it?

OZ: Well, if it were inside you, it would be courage. (LION *drinks.*) How do you feel now?

LION (*Happily*): Full of courage!

TIN WOODMAN: How about my heart?

OZ: Why, I think you are wrong to want a heart. It makes most people unhappy.

TIN WOODMAN: That must be a matter of opinion. For my part, I will bear all the unhappiness without a murmur, if you will give me a heart.

OZ: Very well. (*Goes to table, takes paper heart and pins it carefully on* TIN WOODMAN'S *chest.*) Isn't it a beauty?

TIN WOODMAN: I shall never forget your kindness.

DOROTHY: And now—how am I to get back to Kansas?

OZ (*Sighing*): I shall have to think about that for a while.

(Curtain)

Scene Four

(NARRATOR enters in front of curtain.)

NARRATOR: Oz thought for several days, and finally decided that he and Dorothy should leave in a balloon. At the moment they were to take off, she realized that she had lost Toto. She hurried through the crowd looking for him, but by the time she found him the balloon was already sailing overhead, and Oz could not bring it back. Dorothy was very sad and cried because she thought she would never get back to Kansas.

Finally, a soldier who felt sorry for Dorothy told her that Glinda, the Good Witch of the South, might help her. The road to the castle was full of dangers, but Dorothy decided to go nevertheless. And her faithful friends went along to protect her.

(NARRATOR exits, as curtain rises.)

(Time: A few days later. Setting: A room in Glinda's castle. DOROTHY, SCARECROW, TIN WOODMAN, and LION enter right. GLINDA enters left.)

GLINDA: I am Glinda, the Good Witch of the South. What can I do for you, child?

DOROTHY *(Curtsying):* My greatest wish is to get back to Kansas, for Aunt Em will certainly think something dreadful has happened to me.

GLINDA: I can help you. But you must give me the Golden Cap you took from the Wicked Witch of the West.

DOROTHY: Willingly, for it will be of no use to me now. *(Gives her cap.)*

GLINDA: I think I will need it just three times. *(To SCARECROW)* What will you do when Dorothy has left us?

SCARECROW: I will return to the Emerald City, for Oz has made me its ruler, and the people like me.

GLINDA: By the Golden Cap I shall command the Winged Monkeys to carry you again to the gates of the Emerald City, for it would be a shame to deprive the people of so wonderful a ruler. *(To* TIN WOODMAN*)* What will become of you when Dorothy leaves?

TIN WOODMAN: The Winkies, in the land of the West, were very kind to me. After the Wicked Witch of the West was melted, they asked me to rule over them.

GLINDA: My second command to the Winged Monkeys will be that they carry you safely to the land of the Winkies. Your brains may not be as large as those of the Scarecrow, but you are really much brighter than he is when you are well polished. *(To* LION*)* And what will become of you?

LION: The beasts in the forest have made me their King. If I could get back there, I would be very happy.

GLINDA: My third command to the Winged Monkeys shall be to carry you to your forest.

SCARECROW, TIN WOODMAN, LION *(Ad lib):* Thank you. You are so kind to us. *(Etc.)*

DOROTHY: You have not told me how to get back to Kansas.

GLINDA: Your silver shoes can carry you anywhere in the world. If you had known their power, you could have gone back home the very first day you came here.

SCARECROW: Then I should not have had my wonderful brains.

TIN WOODMAN: And I should not have had my lovely heart.

LION: And I should have lived a coward forever.

DOROTHY: Very true, and I am glad I was of use to my good friends. But now, I think I should like to go home.

GLINDA: Then knock your heels together three times and command the shoes to carry you wherever you wish.

DOROTHY (*Joyfully*): I shall command them at once. (*Hugs* LION, SCARECROW, *and* TIN WOODMAN.) Good-bye, goodbye, everyone. I will never forget you.

SCARECROW, TIN WOODMAN, LION (*Ad lib*): Goodbye, Dorothy.

DOROTHY (*Solemnly clicks her heels together three times*): Take me home to Aunt Em!

(*Blackout. There is a crash of thunder, and curtain quickly closes. Lights come up on apron of stage to reveal* DOROTHY *sitting on the floor, with no shoes on, holding Toto. She stands up, looking dazed.*)

DOROTHY: Good gracious, here I am in Kansas! (*Points offstage.*) And there is Uncle Henry's new farmhouse, and there are the cows in the barnyard. Oh! I've lost the silver shoes. They must have fallen off in the air.

(AUNT EM *rushes in and takes* DOROTHY *in her arms.*)

AUNT EM: My darling child! Where in the world have you been?

DOROTHY: In the land of Oz. And Toto, too. And, oh, Aunt Em, I'm so glad to be home again!

(*They embrace and exit, arm in arm.*)

THE END

Reflections

1. Do you agree with the Wizard's statement, "True courage is facing danger when you are afraid"?
2. Do you think the Wizard really helped the Scarecrow, the Tin Woodman, and the Cowardly Lion? Write an essay giving reasons for your answer.

A Joyful Noise

Lilit Gampel, noted violinist, playing before an audience of thousands.

The audience rustles in. The hundred or more musicians of the symphony orchestra tune up. But harmony, balance, melody are absent from the sounds. The order that music has only comes when the right notes mingle, when the conductor of the orchestra puts it all together in one glorious, joyful noise!

The musicians of the orchestra and their instruments have come together to play the works of famous composers. The strings—violins, violas, cellos, and bass violins—are usually the basic section. But the woodwinds, the brasses, and the percussion instruments are needed to produce the rich tapestry of sound of the modern orchestra.

The conductor enters and steps up to the podium. The baton is raised. Each section of the orchestra plays its part. And sometimes with the orchestra, there appears a guest soloist who plays on violin or piano melodies that soar above the orchestral sound.

Conductor Seiji Ozawa, leading the San Francisco Symphony Orchestra in a practice session.

357

Unit 5 THE WARRIORS

The Portrait of a Warrior

His brow is seamed with line and scar;
  His cheek is red and dark as wine;
The fires of a Northern star
  Beneath his cap of sable shine.

His right hand, bared of leathern glove,
  Hangs open like an iron gin,
You stoop to see his pulses move,
  To hear the blood sweep out and in.

He looks some king, so solitary
  In earnest thought he seems to stand,
As if across a lonely sea
  He gazed impatient of the land.

Out of the noisy centuries
  The foolish and the fearful fade;
Yet burn unquenched these warrior eyes,
  Time hath not dimmed nor death dismayed.

Walter de la Mare

Theseus and the Minotaur

CHARLES KINGSLEY

Long ago there ruled a great king in Athens called Aegeus. His son, Theseus, was a hero who had done many brave and mighty deeds.

Now the whole country was happy and at peace except for one great sorrow. Minos, king of Crete, had fought against the Athenians and had conquered them. Before returning to Crete, he had made a hard and cruel peace. Each year the Athenians were forced to send seven young men and seven maidens to be sacrificed to the Minotaur. This was a monster who lived in the labyrinth, a winding path among rocks and caves. So each spring seven youths and maidens were chosen by lot. They journeyed in a ship with black sails to the shores of Crete, to be torn in pieces by the savage Minotaur.

One spring Theseus decided to make an end of the beast and rid his father's people of this horrible evil. He went and told Aegeus that when the black-sailed ship set out the next day, he would go, too, and slay the Minotaur.

"But how will you slay him, my son?" said Aegeus. "For you must leave your club and your shield behind."

And Theseus said, "Are there no stones in that labyrinth? Have I not fists and teeth?"

Aegeus begged him not to go, but Theseus would not hear. At last Aegeus said to him, "Promise me only this. If you return in peace, take down the black sail of the ship and hoist instead a white sail, that I may know that you are safe. I shall watch for it all day upon the cliffs."

And Theseus promised and went out to the marketplace where the people drew lots for the youths and maidens who were to sail in that unhappy crew. And the people stood wailing and weeping as the lot fell on this one and on that. But Theseus strode into the midst and cried, "Here is a youth who needs no lot. I, myself, will be one of the seven."

And the herald asked in wonder, "Fair youth, do you know where you must go?"

And Theseus said, "I know. Let us go down to the black-sailed ship."

So they went down to the black-sailed ship, seven maidens and seven youths, and Theseus before them all, and the people following them, weeping. But Theseus whispered to his companions, "Have hope, for the monster cannot live forever." Then their hearts were comforted a little. But they wept as they went on board. All the isles of the Aegean Sea rang with the voice of their sorrow as they sailed on towards their deaths in Crete.

And at last they came to the palace of Minos, the great king, to whom Zeus himself taught laws. So he was the wisest of all mortal kings and conquered all the Aegean isles. His ships were as many as the sea gulls, and his palace like a marble hill.

But Theseus stood before Minos, and they looked each other in the face. And Minos ordered the captives to be taken to prison and to be cast to the monster one by one.

Then Theseus cried, "A favor, O Minos! Let me be thrown first to the beast. For I came for that very purpose, of my own will, and not by lot."

"Who art thou, then, brave youth?"

"I am the son of him whom of all men thou hatest most, Aegeus, the king of Athens, and I am come here to end this matter."

And Minos thought awhile, looking squarely at him, and he answered at last gently, "Go back in peace, my son. It is a pity that one so brave should die."

But Theseus said, "I have sworn that I will not go back till I have seen the monster face to face."

And at that Minos frowned and said, "Then thou shalt see him. Take the madman away."

And they led Theseus away into prison, with the other youths and maidens.

But Ariadne, Minos's daughter, saw him as she came out of her white stone hall. She loved him for his courage and his beauty and said, "Shame that such a youth should die!" And by night she went down to the prison and said, "Flee down to your ship at once, for I have bribed the guards before the door. Flee, you and all your friends, and go back in peace to Greece. And take me, take me with you! I dare not stay after you are gone, for my father will kill me if he knows what I have done."

And Theseus said, "I cannot go home in peace till I have seen and slain this Minotaur. I must avenge the deaths of all the youths and maidens and put an end to the terrors of my land."

"And will you kill the Minotaur? How then?"

"I know not, nor do I care. But he must be strong if he be too strong for me."

Then she loved him all the more and said, "But when you have killed him, how will you find your way out of the labyrinth?"

"I know not, neither do I care. But it must be a strange road if I do not find it out."

Then she loved him all the more and said, "Fair youth, you are too bold. But I can help you, weak as I am. I will give you a sword, and with that perhaps you may slay the beast. Also, I shall give you a clue of thread, and by that, perhaps, you may find your way out again. Only promise me that if you escape, you will take me home with you to Greece. My father will surely kill me if he knows what I have done."

Theseus took the sword and the thread. Then he swore to Ariadne that he would take her to Athens with him.

When the next evening came, the guards came in and led him away to the labyrinth.

And he went down through winding paths among the rocks, under caverns, and over heaps of fallen stone. And he turned on the left hand and on the right hand and

went up and down till his head was dizzy. But all the while he held his clue. For when he had gone in, he had fastened it to a stone and left it to unroll out of his hand as he went on. It lasted him till he met the Minotaur in a narrow chasm between black cliffs.

And when Theseus saw him, he stopped awhile, for he had never seen so strange a beast. His body was a man's; but his head was the head of a bull, and his teeth were the teeth of a lion, and with them he tore his prey. And when he saw Theseus, he roared and put his head down and rushed right at him.

But Theseus stepped aside nimbly and, as the beast passed by, cut him in the knee. Before he could turn in the narrow path, Theseus followed him and stabbed him again and again from behind till the monster fled, bellowing wildly. Never before had he felt a wound. And Theseus followed him at full speed, holding the clue of thread in his left hand.

Then on, through cavern after cavern, under dark ribs of sounding stone and up rough glens and among the sunless roots of Mount Ida and to the edge of the eternal snow went they, the hunter and the hunted, while the hills bellowed to the monster's bellow.

And at last Theseus came up with him where he lay panting on a slab among the snows and caught him by the horns. He forced the monster's head back and drove the keen sword through his throat.

Then Theseus turned and went back limping and weary, feeling his way down by the clue of thread, till he came to the mouth of the labyrinth. He saw Ariadne waiting for him. And he whispered, "It is done!" and showed her the sword. She laid her finger on her lips and led him to the prison and opened the doors. She set all the prisoners free while the guards lay sleeping heavily.

Then they fled to their ship together and leaped on board and hoisted up the sail. The night lay dark around them, so that they passed through Minos's ships and escaped all safe to Naxos; and there Ariadne became Theseus's wife.

But the fair Ariadne never came to Athens with her husband. Some say that Theseus left her sleeping on Naxos and that Dionysus, the celebration king, found her and took her up into the sky. And some say that Dionysus drove Theseus away and took Ariadne from him by force. But however that may be, in his haste or in his grief, Theseus forgot to put up the white sail.

Now Aegeus, his father, sat and watched from the cliff day after day and strained his old eyes across the sea to see the ship afar. And when he saw the black sail and not the white one, he gave up Theseus for dead. In his

grief he fell into the sea and died. So it is called the Aegean Sea to this day.

And now Theseus was king of Athens, and he guarded it and ruled it well.

Reflections

1. If you had been Aegeus, would you have let Theseus go to Crete? What conditions would have influenced your decision?
2. Minos called Theseus a "madman." Do you think he was really "mad"? Give reasons for your answer.
3. Do you think Theseus could have killed the Minotaur without Ariadne's help? Give reasons for your answer.
4. How do you think the Athenian people felt about Theseus when he returned?
5. Think back over Theseus's entire behavior in this story. Then, on the basis of each of his actions, write a description of the kind of person you think he was.
6. This story of Theseus is about a man who risked his life to save his people. Write a report about another famous man or woman who did the same.

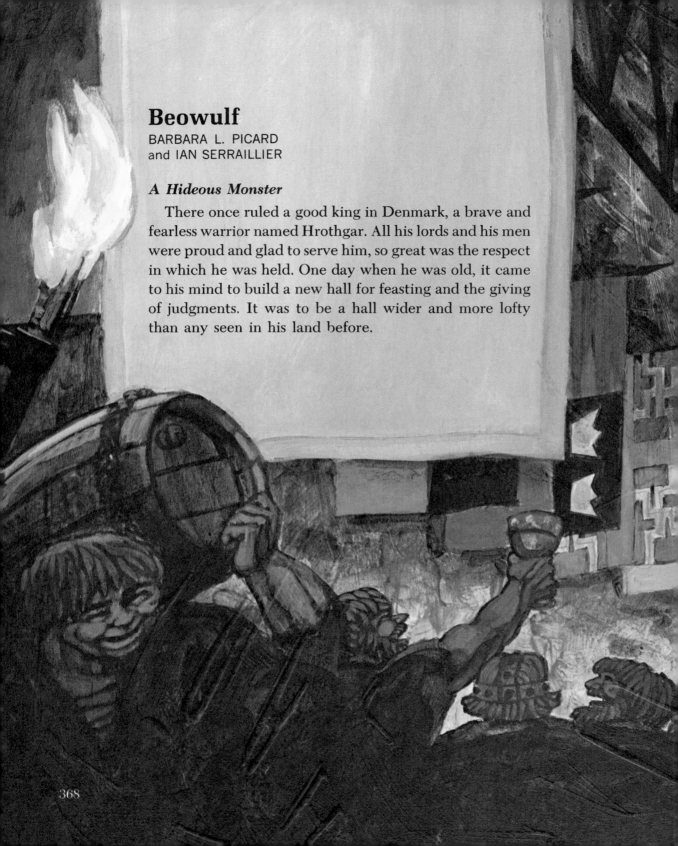

Beowulf

BARBARA L. PICARD
and IAN SERRAILLIER

A *Hideous Monster*

There once ruled a good king in Denmark, a brave and fearless warrior named Hrothgar. All his lords and his men were proud and glad to serve him, so great was the respect in which he was held. One day when he was old, it came to his mind to build a new hall for feasting and the giving of judgments. It was to be a hall wider and more lofty than any seen in his land before.

The new hall was soon built. Great and high it was, with wide gables

—its gleaming roof

Towering high to heaven—strong to withstand
The buffet of war. He called it Heorot
And lived there with his queen. At the time of feasting
He gave his followers rings and ornaments
And bracelets of bright gold, cunningly wrought,
Graved with runes and deeds of dead heroes.
Here they enjoyed feasts and high fellowship,
Story and song and the pride of armed peace.
But away in the treacherous fens, beyond the moor,
A hideous monster lurked, . . .
Grendel his name, hating the sound of the harp,
The minstrel's song, the bold merriment of men
In whose distorted likeness he was shaped
Twice six feet tall, with arms of hairy gorilla
And red ferocious eyes and ravening jaws.

Grendel came one midnight to the hall. Tall and broad he was with a skin of horny green which no sword might pierce. He strode towards Heorot through the darkness. He thrust open the door of the hall and found within a band of warriors fast asleep. In his huge clawed hands he snatched up thirty of these unhappy men and bore them off to his home in the fens, where he might tear and devour them undisturbed.

Made greedy by his success, Grendel came again the next night and slew yet more of Hrothgar's men. And after that there was no one who would sleep in the hall by night. And so it went on for twelve winters, and though brave young warriors came from other lands to slay the monster, all failed and all were slain.

Now there lived overseas
In the land of the Geats a youth of valiance abounding,
Mightiest yet mildest of men, his name Beowulf,
Who, hearing of Grendel and minded to destroy him,
Built a boat of the stoutest timber and chose him
Warriors, fourteen of the best. In shining armor
They boarded the great vessel, beached on the shingle
By the curling tide. Straightway they shoved her off.
They ran up the white sail. And the wind caught her,
The biting wind whipped her over the waves.
Like a strong bird the swan-boat winged her way
Over the gray Baltic, the wintry whale-road,
Till the lookout sighted land—a sickle of fair sand
And glittering white cliffs. The keel struck
The shingle. The warriors sprang ashore.

On the shore they were met by the old warden who
kept guard on the sea cliffs. He demanded their names
and their errand.

And Beowulf answered:
"We are from Sweden, O guardian of the shore. Fear not,
For in loyalty we come—from friendly fields
That tremble to the tale of your suffering and horror
Unspeakable. Crowding sail, hot haste we are come
With stout spears of ashwood and shields to
      protect you."
   The watchman lowered his spear, and from
      smiling lips
The wind blew to Beowulf fair words of greeting:
"Whoever serves my king is welcome here.

Come, noble warriors, let me show you the way,
And my men will look to your boat."

They left her at anchor,
The broad-bellied ship afloat on the bobbing tide,
And followed him over the cliff toward Heorot.

Outside Hrothgar's hall, Beowulf and his companions set down their shields and spears and waited. At once a herald came out to them. Beowulf told his name and asked to speak with Hrothgar. The herald went to Hrothgar with word that a band of Geats under Beowulf, the nephew of the Geatish king, had come to Denmark. The old king looked up eagerly. He bade the herald bring Beowulf to him. Beowulf went into the hall to where Hrothgar sat on his high seat.

"Greetings, King Hrothgar," said Beowulf. "I am the kinsman and warrior of King Hygelac, and I have won honor by my deeds. I have fought against giants, slain sea beasts, and taken vengeance upon those who were my country's foes. Learning that your hall is troubled by Grendel, I have come to ask that I may meet this monster alone and rid your hall of him."

Then Hrothgar stretched out his arms in welcome
And took him by the hand and said, "Beowulf,
I knew you as a child, and who has not exulted
In your fame as a fighter? It is a triumph song
That ocean thunders to her farthest shore,
It is a whisper in the frailest sea shell.
Now, like your princely father long ago,
In the brimming kindness of your heart, you have come
To deliver us."

Then they feasted, until the shadows had grown long
and the sun was setting, and an uneasiness fell upon all
the Danes.

Then the Danes
Man by man uprose and, clearing the banquet,
Brought for their guests soft couches, . . .
With fleeces of thick wool. . . .
They hurried each to his secret hiding place.

Straightway Beowulf stripped off his armor, his mailcoat,
His shining helmet. His shield and precious sword
Gave he to his servant, and in the ring of warriors
Lay down to rest. But spent as they were—
. . . —they could not sleep.
Under their fleeces in terror they sweated and trembled,
Wide-awake, till at last, outworn with weariness,
Heavy-lidded, they slept—all but Beowulf.
Alone, he watched.

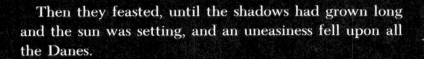

A Grisly Trophy

Over the misty moor
From the dark and dripping caves of his grim lair,
Grendel with fierce ravenous stride came stepping.
A shadow under the pale moon he moved
Toward Heorot. He beheld it from afar, the
    gleaming roof
Towering high to heaven. His tremendous hands
Struck the studded door, wrenched it from the hinges
Till the wood splintered and the bolts burst apart.
Angrily he prowled over the polished floor,
A terrible light in his eyes—a torch flaming!
As he scanned the warriors, deep-drugged in sleep,
Loud, loud he laughed, and pouncing on the nearest
Tore him limb from limb and swallowed him whole,
Sucking the blood in streams, crunching the bones.
Greedily he reached his hand for the next—little
    reckoning
For Beowulf. The youth clutched it and firmly
    grappled.

Beowulf rose and strove to drag the monster down. The sound of their struggles awoke the sleeping men. They reached for their weapons and tried in the darkness to strike at Grendel with their swords. Yet such was the thickness of his scaly skin that all weapons glanced off it harmlessly. And in the darkness, too, they feared to harm Beowulf.

As the monster grew more desperate, so his attempts to free himself grew wilder. Soon he and Beowulf were fighting all around the hall.

Spilling the benches
They tugged and heaved, from wall to wall they hurtled.
And the roof rang to their shouting, the huge hall
Rocked, the strong foundations groaned and trembled.

Yet for all his struggles, Grendel could not free himself from the mighty grip which held his arm. He gave a last despairing wrench, so that the muscles tore apart. With a terrible cry he fled, leaving one arm and the shoulder in Beowulf's grasp. Away over the moor he hastened, a great trail of blood from hall to fen showing how he had gone. Wailing and lamenting, he sank below the waters and died.

But the hero rejoiced in his triumph and wildly waved
In the air his blood-soaked trophy.

And the sun
Made glad the sky of morning. From near and far
The Danes came flocking to Heorot to behold
The grisly trophy—Grendel's giant arm
Nailed to the wall, the fingertips outspread,
With nails of sharpened steel and murderous spikes

Clawing the roof. Having drunk their fill of wonder,
Eagerly they followed his track to the lake, and there
Spellbound they stared at the water welling with blood,
Still smoking hot where down in the joyless deep
He had dived, downward to death. And they praised
    Beowulf
And swore that of all men under the sun, beyond measure
Mightiest was he and fittest to govern his people.

    Hrothgar had not thanks enough to offer Beowulf for
what he had done. "You shall be to me ever as a son,"
he said and gave him rich gifts. There were swords and
a fine helmet, eight horses, and the king's own jeweled
saddle. Gifts he gave, also, to all Beowulf's men and gold
for the kinsmen of the man who lost his life. All that day
the Danes and the Geats feasted together and rejoiced,
while the poet sang of Beowulf's deeds.

        And now the feast was ended.
With final clarion of trumpets they left the hall,
Hrothgar and his gracious queen, leading Beowulf
To a stately chamber to rest. But the Danes remained.
Clearing the banquet, they brought couches spread
With pillows and warm coverlets, and lay down,
Each with his broad shield at his head, his mailcoat,
His spear and shining helmet—as was the custom
Long ere Grendel came. Now fearless of monster,

Their minds were at ease, quiet as the summer sea,
The sparkling water, unmurmuring and serene
Under the moon. In comfort of spirit, in blessed
Trust and tranquility they sank to rest.

    Beowulf's task done in Denmark, the Geats made ready
to leave next day.

And the joyous sun, bright candle of the world,
Soared high to heaven. The meadow by the sea
Rang jubilant with prancing horses, loud
With harness bells as Beowulf marched his warriors
To the shore. And when they beheld beached
      on the shingle
The broad-bellied ship beside the curling tide,
His heart leaped for home.

    To Hrothgar, Beowulf said, "If ever you have need of
me again, good king, I shall be ready to serve you. Only
send to me, and I shall come."

    "Because of you," said Hrothgar, "there shall now be
peace between the Danes and the Geats, where formerly
there has too often been bloodshed and hatred. You have
been a good friend to me, and I sorrow to see you go.
Come again to Denmark some day. You will be welcome."
But as he spoke, Hrothgar wept, for he was old, and he
feared he would not live to see Beowulf again.

When the Danes had shoved the ship
Clear of the shingle, the warriors leaped aboard.
They ran up the white sail. And the wind caught her,
The biting wind whipped her over the waves.
Like a strong bird the swan-boat winged her way
Over the gray Baltic, the wintry whale-road,
Over the long paths of the ocean, on
And ever onward,
Till at last they beheld the shining cliffs of home.
The coastguard, spent with long weary watching,
Hailed them from afar. The keel struck the sand.
Proud, exultant, the warriors leaped to land.

Reflections

1. When Beowulf heard about Grendel, what did he decide to do? Why do you think he decided this?
2. How "real" does the fight between Beowulf and Grendel seem to you? Give reasons for your opinion.
3. This selection retells only one of several adventures of Beowulf, the hero of an epic poem dating back almost twelve hundred years. The story of Beowulf has been told and retold by each generation. Write a paragraph describing why, in your opinion, it has always been so popular.

Echoes

WALTER DE LA MARE

The sea laments
The livelong day,
Fringing its waste of sand;
Cries back the wind from the whispering shore—
No words I understand:

Yet echoes in my heart a voice,
As far, as near, as these—
The wind that weeps,
The solemn surge
Of strange and lonely seas.

Young Ladies Don't Slay Dragons

JOYCE HOVELSRUD

A dragon with exceedingly evil intentions was plaguing the Palace at Hexagon. Night and day he lurked about the courtyard walls, belching fire and smoke and roaring in a most terrible fashion. Things looked bad for the royal household.

"Mercy," said the queen.

"Dear me," said the king. "One of these days he'll get a royal blaze going, and when he does—poof! That'll be it."

"Well, what are you going to do about it?" asked the queen sharply. "I mean, you can't just sit there counting out your money and ignoring the problem."

"I have asked every brave man in the kingdom to slay the dragon," said the king. "They all said they had more important things to do."

"Nonsense," said the queen with a breathy sigh. "What could be more important than saving the palace from a monstrous dragon?"

"I'll slay the dragon," said the Princess Penelope, jumping from behind an antique suit of armor. She just

happened to hear the conversation while oiling a rusty joint.

The king blinked his eyes twice—once with shock because he was taken by surprise, and then once with pride because he was taken by his daughter's dazzling beauty. "You can't slay a dragon," he said. "Why don't you go knit a vest for the palace poodle or something?"

The princess flexed the arm of the ancient armor. "See? No more clink." She smiled.

"No more clink," said the king vacantly.

"And I just fixed the drawbridge, too," said the princess. "You won't have to worry about the clank anymore."

"Clink, clank, clunk," said the king. "I have more important worries anyway."

"I know," said Penelope. "The dragon. I said I'd slay him for you."

"Nonsense," said the king. "Young ladies don't slay dragons."

"They don't oil armor or fix drawbridges, either," said the princess matter-of-factly.

"Slaying dragons is men's work," he said finally, "and that's that."

The princess didn't really think that was that. It seemed to her that a young lady could do anything she wanted, if she set her mind to it.

She once whittled a whistle from a green willow stick when she was supposed to be sewing a fine seam.

She once built a birdhouse for the palace puffin when she was supposed to be practicing her lute lesson.

And once she even killed a mouse. She had come into the bedchamber to find her mother standing on a chair and screaming—as queens often do in the presence of mice. "Don't worry, Mother, I'll get him," Penelope said.

"Young ladies don't kill mice," the queen said. "For heaven's sake, stand on a chair and scream along with me."

But Penelope didn't stand on a chair and scream. She caught the mouse and disposed of it tidily.

Well, she would dispose of the dragon, too. And she would get some ideas on how to go about it.

She went to speak to the royal cook. "How would you slay a dragon?" she asked.

"I would cut off his head with a carving knife," said the cook. "But of course you couldn't do that."

"Why not?" asked the princess.

"Young ladies don't slay dragons," the cook said.

So she went to speak to the royal tailor. "How would you slay a dragon?" she asked.

"I would stab him through the heart with a long needle," the tailor said.

"Would you lend me a long needle?" asked the princess.

"Young ladies don't slay dragons," the tailor said. "Besides, I don't have a needle long enough."

Penelope went to speak to the royal wizard. "How would you slay a dragon?" she asked.

The royal wizard thought a long time. Then he said, "Why do you want to know?"

"Because I want to slay the dragon," Penelope said matter-of-factly.

"Well, if you really want the truth," the wizard said, "the fact is, young ladies don't slay dragons."

"Well, then," the princess said, "if a brave young man wanted to save the palace from a smoke-blowing, flame-throwing, fierce and wicked dragon, what advice would you give him?"

The royal wizard wrinkled his forehead, squinted his eyes, and made arches with his fingers while he thought. Then he said, "I would advise him to fight fire with fire."

"I see," said Penelope.

"My feet are cold," said the wizard. "Do me a favor and slide that hot bucket over here. I want to warm my toes on it."

Penelope did as he requested. "How does the bucket stay hot?" she asked.

"It's filled with a magic liquid that burns without fire," said the wizard. "I conjured it up myself."

"A good bit of magic," said Penelope admiringly. "Can you get the liquid to flame up?"

"If I want flames, I just drop a hot coal into the bucket," said the wizard. And then he fell asleep. He always fell asleep after talking three minutes, and now his three minutes were up.

But how anybody could sleep through the dragon's terrible roaring was a mystery to Penelope. And how anybody could sleep while evil threatened the palace was another mystery to her.

The wizard had given the princess an idea, though, and she tiptoed out of the room.

She found a pipe in her collection of iron and sealed it at one end. She tiptoed back to the wizard's room and filled the pipe with liquid from the magic bucket. With a pair of tongs, she took a hot coal from the fire and tiptoed away. She paused in the great hall long enough to don a suit of armor—minus the helmet that hurt her ears and hung low over her eyes. Finally she found a shield she could lift.

Then, clanking, she made her way through the courtyard to the gates.

Now the dragon was the biggest, the most ferocious dragon that ever lived. Princess Penelope didn't know that, but she rather suspected it, for why else wouldn't the brave men in the kingdom come to slay him?

And the dragon, who was also the wisest dragon that

ever lived, had a hunch someone was after him. So he crept slowly around the walls to see who it was—roaring terrible roars and belching the sky full of fire and smoke as he went.

"I wish he wouldn't smoke so much," Penelope muttered as she crept after him. Rounding the corner, she could just make out the monstrous tip of the dragon's tail disappearing around the corner ahead.

"This will never do," she said after the third corner. Turning, she crept the other way—and she met the dragon face to face!

Now, it isn't easy to describe the ferocious battle that ensued, but it went something like this.

"Stop or I'll shoot," said Penelope calmly.

"What's a nice girl like you doing out slaying dragons?" sneered the dragon as he crept toward her, blinking several times because of her dazzling beauty.

"I said, stop or I'll shoot."

"You don't shoot dragons," the dragon said, coming closer. "Everybody I ever heard of slays them with swords."

"I'm not like everybody you ever heard of," Penelope said.

"I wonder why that is," the dragon said. And though he didn't know it at the time, the dragon had spoken his last words.

Princess Penelope raised her lead pipe, ignited the liquid with her hot coal, and dealt the deadly dragon a deadly blow.

Now, nobody would believe the terrible fire that followed, so it isn't necessary to describe it. But it was like the end of the world.

At last the smoke cleared away. And there, standing among the charred remains of the world's most ferocious dragon was—the world's most handsome prince.

"I've been waiting for something like that to happen," said the prince. "You'll marry me, of course.

"I have a kingdom ten times the size of this pea patch," he added, "and it's all yours if you'll say yes."

Penelope said, "There's something you should know about me first. I wouldn't be happy just being a queen and doing queen-things. I like to fix drawbridges, build birdhouses, slay dragons—that sort of thing."

"It so happens I have bridges, birds, and dragons to spare," said the prince hopefully.

"Then my answer is 'yes'," said Penelope.

And with that they saddled up a white horse and rode off into the sunset.

Reflections

1. Why hadn't the dragon been slain?
2. How does the princess answer her father when he says, "Young ladies don't slay dragons"?
3. What do you think of Penelope? How is she unusual?
4. When Penelope becomes a queen, she will probably find new challenges to overcome. Imagine a crisis in her new life, and write a story showing how she deals with it. Try to include dialogue and clichés in your story.

Follow the Gleam

ALFRED, LORD TENNYSON

Not of the sunlight,
Not of the moonlight,
Not of the starlight,
O young Mariner,
Down to the haven,
Call your companions,
Launch your vessel,
And crowd in your canvas,
And, ere it vanishes
Over the margin,
After it, follow it,
Follow the Gleam.

387

The Challenge of the Sword
MABEL LOUISE ROBINSON

A World He Liked

Down across the sweet-smelling moors the two boys raced. The air from the sea blew them along and gave their feet the lightness of their spirit. The sun beat down on their bare heads and promised a fair day for the tournament. Arthur's pace quickened until he saw his shadow reaching past his brother's. Then he slowed down. Nothing made Kay angrier than to have Arthur pass him.

Arthur took great care not to anger Kay, his older brother. He had no fear of him, but he loved him. They had grown up together with a father who rarely bothered them. The very freedom of their life gave them a great understanding of each other.

Arthur could not know how happy it made his older brother to rule such a splendid boy. Nor would he have cared. He had the kind of world he liked to live in, and he would change nothing in it. He had a comfortable home and a father, Sir Ector, who let his boys hunt with him or by themselves. He had a strong, sound body, and now he had a chance to see the jousting at the tournament. Again his step quickened so that he almost stumbled over Kay, who had stopped short.

"I've left my sword at home!" Kay cried angrily. "You hurried me so that I forgot it. Now what can I do!"

"I'll get it for you!" Arthur had already wheeled around. "I'll have it and catch up to you before you know it!" He was off with such speed that Kay could not help but realize how much faster a runner his brother was. Now that Arthur was running as fast as he liked, he was out of sight before Kay could answer. So Kay stretched himself out in the heather to wait for Arthur to return.

Back to his home Arthur ran, across the shallow moat, and up to the great door. But the whole house was locked soundly. The dwellers had gone along with the rest of the countryside to the tournament. Now what! Kay must have his sword. He, Sir Ector's elder son, would not enter the place of the tournament without his sword by his side. For a boy like Arthur, a sword did not matter. But Kay would go no farther without his. If Kay did not go to the tournament, he would not make it easy for Arthur to go without him.

Arthur looked away from the cold granite wall out into the golden morning. He felt the deep despair of a disappointed boy. Suddenly he leaped to his feet from the stone step. What was it he had heard the knights talking about yesterday? A sword! A sword stuck in a stone! Stuck in a stone over by the cathedral. They hadn't been able to pull it out. Arthur felt the smooth hard muscles of his arm under his fingers.

"It would do no harm to try," he said. He jumped on his horse, which was grazing quietly in the meadow. "I'll pick up Kay's horse on the way back, and then we'll lose no time." He rode off toward the cathedral.

The place was deserted, for everyone had ridden away to the tournament. But there in the churchyard Arthur

saw a great stone, with an anvil of steel rising from it. In the steel had been thrust a shining sword. Arthur did not hesitate a moment. Here was a sword which even Kay would like. He did not stop to read what the letters in gold said. He seized the handle of the sword with so fierce a grip that he staggered backwards when it came out easily. He laughed aloud, tucked the sword under his cloak, and rode off at full speed.

Now the morning was right again. The air was cold on his face as he swept over the moor. Kay's horse followed close behind. Arthur lifted his voice and called, "We're coming! We're coming!" even though Kay was not within hearing distance. He had a sword for Kay. Now they could reach the tournament in time. His voice rose like a trumpet through the morning.

Kay heard and leaped to his feet. He was scowling as if he had waited longer than he could bear. Arthur rose in his stirrups, pulled the sword from under his cloak, and held it out to his brother. Kay looked so shocked that for a moment Arthur was discouraged. But then the older boy seemed to accept his explanation, and his face filled with pleasure. He leaped on his horse, and with Arthur following, they raced across the moor.

As they neared the crowd in the gathering place, Arthur saw his father first and called out to Kay, "You see, we got here as quickly as our father." Then he had to turn and follow Kay to Sir Ector's side. He sat on his horse, waiting while Kay showed his father the sword. Not until he heard the words, "Here is the sword of the stone. Now I shall be king of the land," did he straighten to attention. What was Kay talking about?

Sir Ector looked shocked. He wheeled his horse around, and called to the boys, "Come with me." Back across the moor he headed his swift horse, and the boys followed as best they could. They rode until they reached the deserted churchyard. Arthur followed his father and his brother as they rode up to the stone. Then he, too, leaned from his horse, and, for the first time, he read the words written in gold: "Whoso pulleth out this sword of this stone and anvil is rightwise king born of all England."

Arthur straightened in horror. "Now what have I done?" he thought. But he felt relief as he heard Kay telling his father that he had the sword and therefore was king of the land. Perhaps they could now settle the matter quickly and still get back in time to see the end of the jousting.

But Sir Ector still stared at his older son.

"Come with me," he commanded, and he led the boys into the cathedral. There he laid Kay's hand on a great Bible opened for the morning service. "And now, my son," he said in a voice which neither boy had ever heard or would ever disobey, "swear upon this book how you came by that sword."

At last Kay lifted his eyes. "My brother Arthur brought it to me."

"And you?" The grave look was upon Arthur now. "Where did you get this sword?"

It was not in Arthur to lie. He told freely and sorrowfully of how he had borrowed the sword for Kay and that he had not harmed it because it withdrew so easily. "See, I will put it back where it belongs," he offered. He went back outside to the stone, with his father and his brother following him, and thrust the sword back into the stone. "Nobody was here, or I would have asked permission," he explained. "You can see how easily it goes back where it belongs."

Sir Ector's face was unreadable. He turned again to Kay. "Now you shall draw the sword," he said.

Kay pulled and pulled, but the sword did not stir. He flashed an angry glance at Arthur and stepped back, rubbing his arm.

Then Sir Ector stepped up to the stone. "Now watch, Arthur." He proved to him that however hard he pulled, he could not stir the sword. "It is your turn now," he said, and he stepped back to make place for Arthur.

A Shaken World

The lad could not bear the feeling of suspense. He would get it over with quickly. "It's easy," he said. "Your hand may have slipped on the handle." He drew the sword as if it were thrust in soft clay. He started to give it to his father. But when he turned, he saw to his horrified embarrassment that his father and Kay were kneeling on the earth before him. He cried out aloud at the sight. "No! No! What does this mean? Why must you, my dear father and brother, do this thing to me?"

Sir Ector rose. Kay looked uncertain and rose, too. Then Arthur felt more comfortable. But Sir Ector was still not himself. He seemed to be feeling his way back into a past where Arthur could not follow.

At last he spoke. "No, Arthur, you are not my son," he said, and his words were cold truth in the boy's heart. "Nor is Kay your brother."

Kay not the brother whom he willingly followed? Sir Ector not his kindly father on whom he could always depend? Who then was he, a boy without a family? What had this sword, which he wanted only for Kay, done to him? His world was shaken like his heart.

Then, Sir Ector, with deep sadness at hurting the boy he loved, told Arthur about how he had come to be one of his family. For Arthur, such pain was so new and harsh that he could scarcely follow Sir Ector's words. He wanted only that the tale be done with and that they step back into the life which he knew. It could not be himself, young Arthur, who was the child of this tale!

Sir Ector spoke with words that came slowly and heavily. It was as if he drew them out of a past which he, too, had wanted to forget. Merlin, the magician, had brought a baby to him, a fair, strong boy. He told Sir Ector that it was written that he should care for him, a child of noble birth. Then Sir Ector smiled down into Arthur's unhappy face. "We could never have resisted you, my dear wife and I, even without the command of Merlin." And somehow Arthur's heart lifted a little.

So, Sir Ector and his wife had taken the child completely into their love. He was as much their own as was Kay. But now—

"But now what has come about?" cried Arthur. "I am still your son. I could belong to no one else. Let us forget the sword which has made us all this trouble and ride away to the tournament." But somehow the gay holiday was too far away even for thought. It had no part of this strange day. Arthur must listen, and finally believe.

"So finally," Sir Ector ended, "this sword has proved your royal birth. Now that you are king, I ask of you only the favor that your foster brother, Kay, shall be made manager of all your lands. I know that you will be my good and gracious lord." His voice contained simple confidence.

Then Arthur stood in sudden dignity, tall and fair. "If I ever am king," he said, and the possibility seemed far from him, "I will never fail you. You shall have of me whatever you wish. Nor shall anyone but Kay ever be manager of the lands." He was shocked at the gratitude in Kay's eyes. This story still could not be true.

But then Sir Ector led them to the archbishop. There Arthur heard the tale again and, against his own will, began to believe it. The archbishop was a kindly old man, who recognized the trouble in the boy's eyes.

"We will wait a little," he said soothingly. "On the day that all the barons are here, they shall try the sword. If they cannot move it, then Arthur shall try again. Keep your heart light, my son."

But the boyhood of young Arthur was over, and in some strange way he knew it. The people in his home seemed never to forget the sword. He found his dear mother weeping at times, and he could not comfort her. He disliked Kay's meekness. He liked much better the old relationship, where Kay tried to rule and Arthur still did as he liked. He was impatient for the day when the barons would arrive.

The day came, and it left behind many angry barons. For not one had been able even to loosen the sword. And their anger knew no bounds when a tall, straight boy stepped up to it and drew it from the stone with no effort whatsoever. Never, they said, would they be governed by a young lad not even of royal birth.

So, the archbishop postponed the decision. He put knights on guard by the sword night and day. More and more knights arrived to test their strength on the sword. Yet there it stood, except when Arthur pulled it out with such ease. Finally the disturbance grew so great that the archbishop could wait no longer. He made a public statement that the matter must be settled the next week.

The knights gathered from far and near. The archbishop saw to it that knights were near Arthur all the time, guarding against trickery. Arthur was an honest, outgoing lad who had always been trusted. This new attitude was one he did not like. By this time, too, he had a new pride in his strength. If he could draw the sword from the stone, and he knew that he could, he did not mind who else knew it. This time he looked forward to the trial, if only to settle the matter once and for all. A boy could stand just so much!

People gathered from all over the country, for the word had spread that every knight should take his turn. Not only the lords and ladies came to the trial, but the poor people came also. They were so poor that they had nothing of their own. Life had ground them down, but they still liked to watch the gleaming knights and their lovely ladies. They watched and waited. Nothing had ever come their way to help them yet, but still they hoped.

Then the trial began. Knight after knight rode up to the sword. Each one grasped it with all confidence, put into it his whole might, and left defeated. Each time a murmur like dust rose from the dark patches of the poor people watching outside the circle.

One by one, until the day grew short, the knights tried. Still no knight could stir the sword. Each one rode back and watched the next one try. And no one had stirred the sword, even to the last knight who rode away as angry as the rest.

The archbishop nodded his head to Arthur. The boy walked forward, his fair head alight in the setting sun. He stood a moment, tall and straight before the sword. Then he bent forward, pulled lightly, and stood there facing the crowd with the sword swung in his hand.

It was enough for the poor people. They had seen the miracle. Here was their lord and master. They burst into a great roar which reached across the moors to the sea. "We will have Arthur for our king and no other," they cried. "We shall slay any who would prevent his rule."

Arthur heard the deep call rolling past him like a command. He turned toward those poor people kneeling now to him and held toward them his sword. He paid little attention to the knights, who were kneeling, too. From now to the end of his reign, he promised to be the king and upholder of the poor.

Reflections

1. How did Arthur and Kay feel about each other at the beginning of the story?

2. Do you think Arthur would have tried to draw the sword had he first read the words written in gold? Why or why not?

3. Why were the poor people so interested in who would finally draw the sword from the stone?

4. Have you ever been unfairly accused of being dishonest? Describe how you felt.

5. Why was Arthur upset when he learned who he really was? Which would you like better—living a normal life or being king or queen of a country? Write a short essay giving the reasons for your choice.

Trouble in Camelot

EDWARD EAGER

It looked as though it was going to be a very uninteresting summer for Mark and his three sisters, Jane, Katharine, and Martha. Then Jane found what looked like a half of a nickel lying on the sidewalk. But this was no ordinary half of a nickel. It was a half of a magic charm. Each time one of the children made a wish, only half of it came true. They soon learned to wish for twice as much as they wanted. Each wish led them off to a world of adventure and, sometimes, trouble.

One morning it was Katharine's turn to make a wish. She held the charm in her hand and said, "I wish that we may go back twice as far as to the days of King Arthur in Camelot and see two tournaments and go on two quests and do two good deeds." And the charm worked its magic.

In the Age of Chivalry

The children found themselves in a field, where the grass seemed greener and fresher than any they had ever seen. A tall figure lay on the ground nearby, under an apple tree. It was a knight in full armor, and he was sound asleep. They knew he was asleep because Martha lifted the visor of his helmet and peeked inside. A gentle snore issued forth.

The knight's sword lay on the ground beside him, and Mark reached to pick it up. Immediately the sleeping knight awoke and sat up. He saw Mark and Jane and Katharine and Martha.

"Who be you?" he said. "Hath some grimly foe murdered me in my sleep? Am I in heaven? Be ye cherubim or seraphim?"

"We be neither," said Katharine. "And this isn't heaven. We are four children."

"Pish," said the knight. "Ye be like no children these eyes have ever beheld. Your garb is outlandish."

"People who live in tin armor shouldn't make such remarks," said Katharine.

At this moment there was an interruption. A lady came riding up on a milk-white horse. She seemed considerably excited.

"Hist, gallant knight!" she cried.

The knight rose to his feet and bowed politely. The lady began batting her eyes and looking at him in a way that made the children feel ashamed for her.

"Thank heaven I found you," she went on. "You alone of all the world can help me, if your name be Sir Launcelot, as I am let to know it is!"

The children stared at the knight, open-mouthed with awe.

"Are you really Sir Launcelot?" Mark asked him.

"That is my name," said the knight.

The four children stared at him harder. They were in the presence of Sir Launcelot of the Lake, the greatest knight in all the Age of Chivalry!

"How is Elaine?" Katharine wanted to know right away, "and little Galahad?"

"I know not the folk you mention," said Sir Launcelot.

"Oh, yes, you do, sooner or later," said Katharine. "You probably just haven't come to them yet."

"Be ye a prophetess?" cried Sir Launcelot, becoming interested. "Can ye read the future? Tell me more!"

But the lady on the milk-white horse was growing impatient. "Away, poppets!" she said, getting between the children and Sir Launcelot. "Gallant knight, I crave your assistance. In a tower nearby a dread ogre is distressing some gentlewomen. We need your help."

"Naturally," said Sir Launcelot. He whistled, and his trusty horse appeared from behind the apple tree. Sir Launcelot started to mount the horse. The four children looked at each other.

They did not like what they had seen of the lady at all, and they liked the way she had spoken to them even less. Katharine stepped forward.

"I wouldn't go if I were you," she said. "It's probably a trap."

The lady gave her an evil look.

"Even so," said Sir Launcelot, "needs must when duty calls."

Katharine drew herself up to her full four feet four. "As you noticed before, I be a mighty prophetess!" she cried. "And I say unto you, go not where this lady bids. She will bring you nothing but disaster!"

"I shall go where I please," said Sir Launcelot. "Out of the way. Never yet did Launcelot turn from a worthy quest. Out of the way."

Then Sir Launcelot and the lady began galloping down the King's Highway. Of course, it was but the work of a moment for Katharine to wish they all had horses and could follow. Immediately they had, and they did.

When they had ridden a goodly pace, they came to a dark wood, stretching along both sides of the highway. Just at the edge of the wood, the lady cried out that her horse had cast a shoe. Sir Launcelot reined in to go to her aid. The four children stopped at a safe distance.

Then, just as Sir Launcelot was dismounting, three knights rode out of the wood. One was dressed all in red, one in green, and one in black. Before the children could cry out, the knights rushed at Sir Launcelot from behind. He had no time even to touch his hand to his sword before the three knights had seized and disarmed him, bound him hand and foot, flung him across the saddle of his own horse, and galloped off into the wood with him.

The lady turned on the four children. "Ha, ha!" she cried. "Now they will take him to my castle, where he will lie in a deep dungeon and be beaten every day with thorns! And so we shall serve all knights of the Round Table who happen this way! Death to King Arthur!"

"Why, you false thing, you!" said Jane.

"I told him so!" said Katharine.

"Let's go home!" said Martha.

"No, we have to rescue him!" said Mark.

"Ho, ho!" said the lady. "Just you try it! Your magic is a mere nothing compared to mine! Know that I am the great enchantress, Morgan le Fay!"

"You would be!" said Katharine. "I remember you in the books, always making trouble. I wish you'd go jump in the lake!"

Katherine wasn't thinking of the charm when she wished this, but that didn't stop the charm. Morgan le Fay didn't go jump in the lake; she merely fell into a pool. Luckily there was a pool handy. She slid backwards off her horse and landed in it in a sitting position. And luckier still, the pool had a muddy bottom, and she stuck there long enough for Katharine to make another wish, which was that she would *stay* stuck, and unable to use any of her magic, for twice as long as necessary. This done, the children turned their horses into the wood and set about following the wicked knights.

In a Dungeon Cell

After a while, the four children came to a clearing. They saw the witch's castle rising just ahead of them. Poison ivy covered its walls. There were snakes in the moat and bats in the belfry. The four children did not like the look of it at all.

"What do we do now?" said Jane.

"Wish him free, of course," said Mark.

"Just stand out here and wish? That's too easy!" said Katharine.

"I'm not going inside that castle!" said Martha.

"Nay," said Katharine. "Ye forget that I be a mighty prophetess. Trust ye unto my clever strategy!" With that, Katharine put her hand on the charm and wished. In an instant the children found themselves in front of a heavy door at the end of a long, twisting passageway. From beyond the door came the sound of loud voices raised in something that was probably intended to be music. The children eased the door open a crack and peeked through into a large hall.

The red knight and the green knight and the black knight were enjoying a hearty meal. They were singing at the table, which was rude of them, and the words of their song were ruder still.

> "Speak roughly to our Launcelot
>   And beat him with a brier!
> And kick him in the pants a lot—
>   Of this we never tire.
>
> We've put him in a dungeon cell
> And there we'll beat him very well!
>   Clink, canikin, clink!"

The children looked at each other. "How can we get through to the dungeon with all these knights in our way?" asked Jane.

"We can wish ourselves there," said Katharine. She put her hand on the charm and wished that they were twice as far as the dungeon door and that she had two keys to the dungeon in her hand.

After that, of course, it was but a matter of turning the key, and out walked Sir Launcelot. He thanked the children quite politely, but somehow he didn't seem so happy to be free as the children had expected he would.

"You saved me by magical means?" he asked.

"That's right," said Katharine proudly. "I did it with my little charm."

"That mislikes me much," said Sir Launcelot. "I would it were otherwise."

"Well, really!" said Katharine. "I suppose you'd rather have stayed in there being beaten?"

"Sooner that," said Sir Launcelot, "than bring shame to my honor by taking unfair magical advantage of a foe, however deadly!"

"Shall I lock you up in the dungeon again?" asked Katharine, sarcastically.

"That much advantage," said Sir Launcelot, "I think I can take. Some fair jailer's daughter would probably have let me out sooner or later, anyway."

"Well," said Katharine, "is there anything else you'd like me to do?"

"Yes," said Sir Launcelot. "You might just fetch me my sword and armor."

Thoroughly cross with him by now, Katharine wished the sword and armor back on him.

"Now," said Sir Launcelot, "I shall take care of these cowardly knaves."

"Can we watch?" said Mark.

"No. Go away," said Sir Launcelot. "It makes me nervous. I want to be alone."

Katharine sighed and made a wish. Next moment the four children were on their horses once more, riding along the King's Highway.

"Now we'll never know how it ended!" complained Martha.

"He'll come out on top; trust *him!*" said Katharine. "I *do* get tired of people who are always right, all the time! Anyway, we'll be seeing him again, I imagine, at the tournament."

"Gee, yes, the tournament," said Mark. "When do you suppose it'll be?"

"Not for weeks, maybe, by the time here," said Katharine. "But for us, a mere wish on the charm . . ."

And she merely wished.

The children found themselves in a tournament field in Camelot. Trumpets were blowing, and pennons fluttered on the blue air, and armor flashed in the bright light. Gallant knights and trusty squires and faithful pages and ladies fair were crowding into the stands in hundreds to watch the chivalrous sport. The four children found seats in the front row of the grandstand and began to look around. King Arthur sat enthroned on a high platform at one end of the field. The children could see him clearly, with his kind, simple, understanding face, like the warm sun come to shine on merry England. Queen Guinevere was seated at his right, and Merlin, the magician, thin and wise and gray-bearded, at his left.

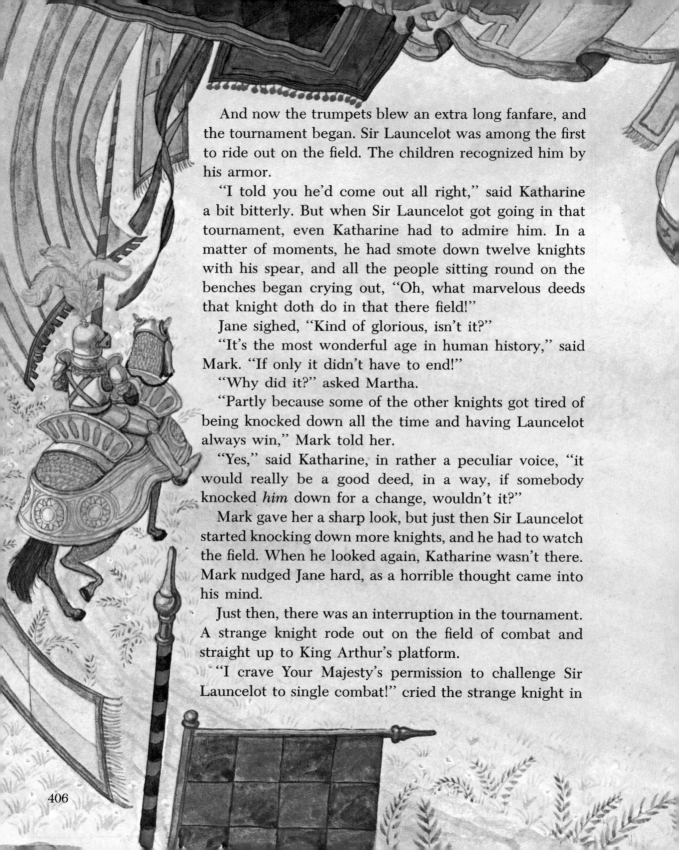

And now the trumpets blew an extra long fanfare, and the tournament began. Sir Launcelot was among the first to ride out on the field. The children recognized him by his armor.

"I told you he'd come out all right," said Katharine a bit bitterly. But when Sir Launcelot got going in that tournament, even Katharine had to admire him. In a matter of moments, he had smote down twelve knights with his spear, and all the people sitting round on the benches began crying out, "Oh, what marvelous deeds that knight doth do in that there field!"

Jane sighed, "Kind of glorious, isn't it?"

"It's the most wonderful age in human history," said Mark. "If only it didn't have to end!"

"Why did it?" asked Martha.

"Partly because some of the other knights got tired of being knocked down all the time and having Launcelot always win," Mark told her.

"Yes," said Katharine, in rather a peculiar voice, "it would really be a good deed, in a way, if somebody knocked *him* down for a change, wouldn't it?"

Mark gave her a sharp look, but just then Sir Launcelot started knocking down more knights, and he had to watch the field. When he looked again, Katharine wasn't there. Mark nudged Jane hard, as a horrible thought came into his mind.

Just then, there was an interruption in the tournament. A strange knight rode out on the field of combat and straight up to King Arthur's platform.

"I crave Your Majesty's permission to challenge Sir Launcelot to single combat!" cried the strange knight in

a voice loud enough for the children to hear clearly from where they sat. The hearts of Jane and Mark sank.

Even Martha now guessed the horrid truth. "How dare she?" she whispered.

"I don't know," said Mark.

"Wait till I get her home!" said Jane grimly.

"How call they you, strange sir?" King Arthur was saying meanwhile. "And whence do you hail?"

"They call me Sir Kath," said the strange knight, "and I hail from Toledo, Ohio."

"I know not this Toledo," said King Arthur, "but fight if you will. Let the combat begin."

The trumpets sounded, the strange knight faced Sir Launcelot, and there began the strangest combat ever witnessed by the knights of the Round, or any other, Table.

The fearless Katharine thought herself very clever at this moment. She had wished she were wearing two suits of armor and riding two horses, and she had wished she were two and a half times as tall and strong as Sir Launcelot. And immediately, here she was, wearing one suit of armor and riding one horse, and she was one and a quarter times as tall and strong.

Suddenly Sir Launcelot rode at her, struck her with his lance, and knocked her back onto her horse's tail. Then he rode at her from the opposite direction and knocked her forward on her horse's neck. The crowd roared with laughter.

With the magic charm clutched in one hot hand, Katharine shouted, "I wish I could fight ten times as well as you, you bully! Yah!" It was a cry of pure temper.

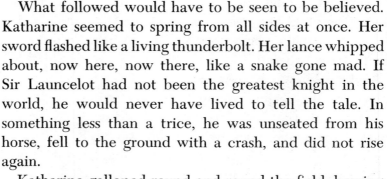

What followed would have to be seen to be believed. Katharine seemed to spring from all sides at once. Her sword flashed like a living thunderbolt. Her lance whipped about, now here, now there, like a snake gone mad. If Sir Launcelot had not been the greatest knight in the world, he would never have lived to tell the tale. In something less than a trice, he was unseated from his horse, fell to the ground with a crash, and did not rise again.

Katharine galloped round and round the field, bowing graciously to the applause of the crowd. But she soon noticed that the crowd wasn't applauding very loudly. And it was only the traitorous knights, the ones who were jealous of Launcelot, who were applauding at all. The rest of the crowd was strangely silent. For Launcelot, the flower of knighthood, the darling of the people's hearts, the greatest champion of the Round Table, had been defeated!

And it was then that the full knowledge of what she had done swept over Katharine. She, a mere girl, had defeated the greatest knight in history. But she had pretended to herself that she was doing it for a good deed, and really it had been just because she was annoyed with Launcelot for not appreciating her help enough back in Morgan le Fay's castle.

Her cheeks flamed, and she felt miserable. It was hot inside her helmet suddenly, and she dragged it off. Her long brown hair streamed down onto her shoulders, and her nine-year-old, little-girl face blinked at the astonished crowd. Those sitting nearest the ringside saw. The mean knights who were jealous of Sir Launcelot began to laugh, and mingled with the laughter were the cruel words, "Beaten by a little girl!"

A *Pattern to History*

Sir Launcelot came to and sat up. He heard the laughter. He looked at Katharine. Katharine looked away, but not before he recognized her. He got to his feet. There was silence all round the field. Even the mean knights stopped laughing. With his head held high, Sir Launcelot strode to King Arthur's platform and knelt in the dust before it. In a low voice he asked leave to go on a far quest, a year's journey at least, that he might hide his shame till, by a hundred deeds of valor, he would win back his lost honor.

King Arthur did not trust himself to speak. He nodded his consent, and Sir Launcelot walked away from the field. Katharine began to cry.

Merlin spoke a word in King Arthur's ear. King Arthur nodded. He rose, offered an arm to Guinevere, and led her from the stand. Merlin spoke another word, this time to the attendant knights. They began clearing people from the field. Presently, after what seemed like at least a year, Katharine found herself alone before Merlin. She was still crying.

Merlin looked at Katharine sternly.

"Fie on your weeping," he said. "I wot well that ye be a false enchantress, come here in this guise to defeat our champion and discredit our Table Round!"

"I'm not! I didn't!" said Katharine.

"Silence, sorceress," said Merlin. He waved his wand at her. "I command that you appear in your true form!"

Immediately Katharine wasn't tall or strong or in armor any more, but just Katharine.

Merlin looked surprised. "These fiends begin early!" he said. He waved his wand again. "I command that your allies, cohorts, aids, accomplices, and companions be brought hither to stand at your side!"

Jane and Mark and Martha appeared beside Katharine, looking nearly as unhappy and uncomfortable as she.

Merlin looked really quite startled. Then he shook his head sadly. "So young," he said, "and yet so wicked!"

"We're not!" said Martha, making a rude face.

The behavior of the others was more seemly.

"You see, sir," began Mark.

"We didn't mean to," began Jane.

"Let me," said Katharine. "I started it." And in a rush of words and tears, she told Merlin everything, beginning with the charm and her wish to travel back in time and going on to what she had hoped to do and what she'd done and where she'd gone wrong.

"Well," said Merlin, "you have succeeded in making everybody thoroughly unhappy!"

"I know," said Katharine.

"That's what comes of meddling," said Merlin. "There is a pattern to history, and when you try to change that pattern, no good may follow."

Katharine hung her head.

"However," went on Merlin, and to the surprise of the four children, he was smiling now, "all is not lost. I have a few magic tricks of my own, you know. Let me see, how shall I handle this? I *could* turn time back, I suppose, and make it as though this day had never happened, but it would take a lot out of me."

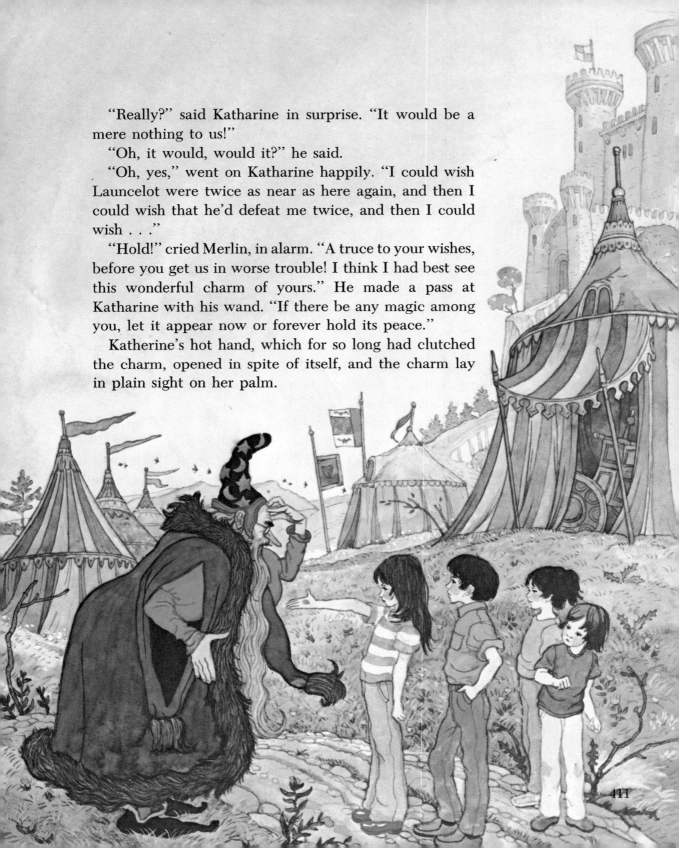

"Really?" said Katharine in surprise. "It would be a mere nothing to us!"

"Oh, it would, would it?" he said.

"Oh, yes," went on Katharine happily. "I could wish Launcelot were twice as near as here again, and then I could wish that he'd defeat me twice, and then I could wish . . ."

"Hold!" cried Merlin, in alarm. "A truce to your wishes, before you get us in worse trouble! I think I had best see this wonderful charm of yours." He made a pass at Katharine with his wand. "If there be any magic among you, let it appear now or forever hold its peace."

Katherine's hot hand, which for so long had clutched the charm, opened in spite of itself, and the charm lay in plain sight on her palm.

Merlin looked at it. His eyes widened. He swept his tall hat from his head and bowed low before the charm three times. Then he turned to the children.

"This is a very old and powerful magic," he said. "Older and more powerful than my own. It is, in fact, too powerful and too dangerous for four children, no matter how well they may intend, to have it in their keeping. I am afraid I must ask you to surrender it."

He made another pass with his wand. The charm leaped gracefully from Katharine's hand to his own.

Mark spoke. "But it came to us in our own time," he said, "and that's part of history, too, just as much as this is. Maybe we were *meant* to find it. Maybe there's some good thing we're supposed to do with it. There is a pattern to history, and when you try to change that pattern, no good may follow."

Merlin looked at him. "You are a wise child," he said.

"Just average," said Mark, modestly.

"Dear me," said Merlin. "If that be so, if all children be as sensible as you in this far future time . . ." He broke off. "What century did you say you came from?"

"We didn't," said Mark. "but it's the twentieth."

"The twentieth century," mused Merlin. "What a happy age it must be—truly the Golden Age that we are told is to come."

He stood thinking a moment. Then he smiled. "Very well. Go back to your twentieth century," he said, "and take your magic with you and do your best with it. But first I have something to say."

He held the charm at arm's length, rather as though he feared it might bite him, and addressed it with great respect.

"I wish," he said, "that in six minutes it may be as though these children had never appeared here. Except that they—and I—will remember. And I further wish that our tournament may begin all over again and proceed as originally planned by history. Only twice as much so," he added to be on the safe side.

"Now may I have it back, please?" Katharine asked when he had done.

"And I thirdly wish," he said, "for the future protection of the world from the terrible good intentions of these children, and for their protection against their own folly, that this charm may, for twice the length of time that it shall be in their hands, grant no further wishes carrying said children out of their own century and country, but that they may find whatsoever boon the magic may have in store for them in their own time and place." He put the charm into Katharine's hands. "And now you'd best be going. Because in less than a minute by my wish, it will be as though you'd never appeared here. And if you aren't home when that happens, goodness knows where you *will* be!"

"But what about the good deed I wished?" said Katharine. "Not a single one of all those I tried worked out!"

"My child," said Merlin, and his smile was very kind now, "you have done your good deed. You have brought me word that for as far into time as the twentieth century, the memory of Arthur and of the Round Table, which I helped him to create, will be living yet. And that in that far age people will still care for the ideal I began, enough to come back through time and space to try to be of service to it. You have brought me that word, and now I can finish my work in peace and know that I have done well. And if that's not a good deed, I should like to know what is. Now good-by. Wish quickly. You have exactly seventeen seconds."

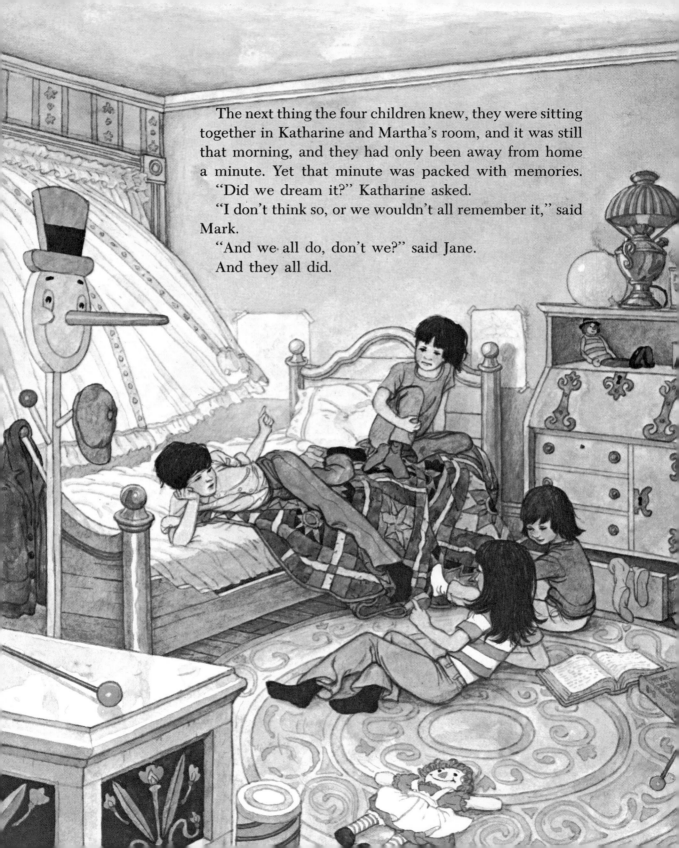

The next thing the four children knew, they were sitting together in Katharine and Martha's room, and it was still that morning, and they had only been away from home a minute. Yet that minute was packed with memories.

"Did we dream it?" Katharine asked.

"I don't think so, or we wouldn't all remember it," said Mark.

"And we all do, don't we?" said Jane.

And they all did.

"What did that last mean, that Merlin wished on the charm?" Martha wanted to know.

"It means we have to keep our wishes close to home from now on," Mark told her.

"No more travels to foreign places," said Jane, "and I was all set to take us on a pirate ship next!"

"No more olden times," said Mark, "and I've always wanted to see the Battle of Troy!"

"You might not have liked it, once you got there," said Katharine from the depths of her experience. "Traveling in olden times is hard."

"I don't care," said Martha, "I don't care if I never travel at all. I'm glad to be home. Aren't you?"

And they all were.

Reflections

1. How did Katharine feel about Launcelot after she freed him? How would you have felt? Explain why.
2. Why was everyone, except the traitorous knights, so upset about what Katharine did?
3. Who is the main character in this story? Why do you think so?
4. Do you agree with Merlin's statement that the twentieth century must be the "Golden Age"? Give reasons for your answer.
5. If you could wish yourself back to any time and place in the past, what time and place would you choose? Write an essay telling your choice and giving the reasons for it.

The Knight Whose Armor Didn't Squeak

A. A. MILNE

Of all the Knights in Appledore
   The wisest was Sir Thomas Tom.
He multiplied as far as four,
   And knew what nine was taken from
To make eleven. He could write
A letter to another Knight.

No other Knight in all the land
   Could do the things which he could do.
Not only did he understand
   The way to polish swords, but knew
What remedy a Knight should seek
Whose armor had begun to squeak.

And, if he didn't fight too much,
   It wasn't that he did not care
For blips and buffetings and such,
   But felt that it was hardly fair
To risk, by frequent injuries,
A brain as delicate as his.

His castle (Castle Tom) was set
   Conveniently on a hill;
And daily, when it wasn't wet,
   He paced the battlements until
Some smaller Knight who couldn't swim
Should reach the moat and challenge him.

Or sometimes, feeling full of fight,
   He hurried out to scour the plain;
And, seeing some approaching Knight,
   He either hurried home again,
Or hid; and, when the foe was past,
Blew a triumphant trumpet-blast.

One day when good Sir Thomas Tom
   Was resting in a handy ditch,
The noises he was hiding from,
   Though very much the noises which
He'd always hidden from before,
Seemed somehow less . . . Or was it more?

The trotting horse, the trumpet's blast,
   The whistling sword, the armor's squeak,
These, and especially the last,
   Had clattered by him all the week.
Was this the same, or was it not?
Something was different. But what?

Sir Thomas raised a cautious ear
    And listened as Sir Hugh went by,
And suddenly he seemed to hear
    (Or not to hear) the reason why
This stranger made a nicer sound
Than other Knights who lived around.

Sir Thomas watched the way he went—
    His rage was such he couldn't speak,
For years they'd call him down in Kent
    The Knight Whose Armor Didn't Squeak!
Yet here and now he looked upon
Another Knight whose squeak had gone.

He rushed to where his horse was tied;
    He spurred it to a rapid trot.
The only fear he felt inside
    About his enemy was not
"How sharp his sword?" "How stout his heart?"
But "Has he got too long a start?"

Sir Hugh was singing, hand on hip,
    When something sudden came along,
And caught him a terrific blip
    Right in the middle of his song.
"A thunderstorm!" he thought. "Of course!"
And toppled gently off his horse.

Then said the good Sir Thomas Tom,
    Dismounting with a friendly air,
"Allow me to extract you from
    The heavy armor that you wear.
At times like these the bravest Knight
May find his armor much too tight."

A hundred yards or so beyond
    The scene of brave Sir Hugh's defeat
Sir Thomas found a useful pond,
    And, careful not to wet his feet,
He brought the armor to the brink,
And flung it in . . . and watched it sink.

So ever after, more and more,
    The men of Kent would proudly speak
Of Thomas Tom of Appledore,
    "The Knight Whose Armor Didn't Squeak,"
Whilst Hugh, the Knight who gave him best,
Squeaks just as badly as the rest.

BRAVE QUEENS

ELIZABETH I, QUEEN OF ENGLAND

In the year 1588, Spain and England were at war. So far the war had been at sea. But on August 9, 1588, word came to the city of Tilbury that an invading army was approaching. Elizabeth, Queen of England rode forth to speak to her troops. Mounted on a white horse and dressed in silver armor, she was a striking figure. And her words brought forth great cheers. Here are the opening words of her speech.

My loving people,

We have been persuaded by some that are careful of our safety, to take heed how we commit ourselves to armed multitudes, for fear of treachery. But I assure you, I do not desire to live in distrust of my subjects. And therefore I am come amongst you, resolved, in the midst and heat of the battle, to live or die amongst you all; to lay down for God, for my kingdom, and for my people, my honour and my blood, even in the dust. . . .

ZENOBIA, QUEEN OF PALMYRA

In ancient times the Roman Empire ruled much of the known world. It had taken over great parts of Europe, northern Africa, and countries bordering the eastern Mediterranean Sea. But it was hard for the Romans to hold some of these lands.

One such land was Palmyra, now part of Syria. Zenobia, the queen, decided to make her country an empire independent from Rome. In 270 A.D., she rode at the head of her armies to face Aurelian, the Roman emperor who had set out from Rome to destroy her.

Zenobia threw the strength of her forces against the emperor and she defeated Aurelian. But she was finally overcome when his army lay siege to her city. During the siege, Aurelian offered favorable terms to Zenobia if she would give up without a fight. But she proudly refused in the following letter:

"It is not by writing, but by battle, that a victory over me can be won. You have dared to propose my surrender to your military might. You forget that Cleopatra preferred death to slavery. When you see me march at the head of my allies, you will not repeat your bold suggestion."

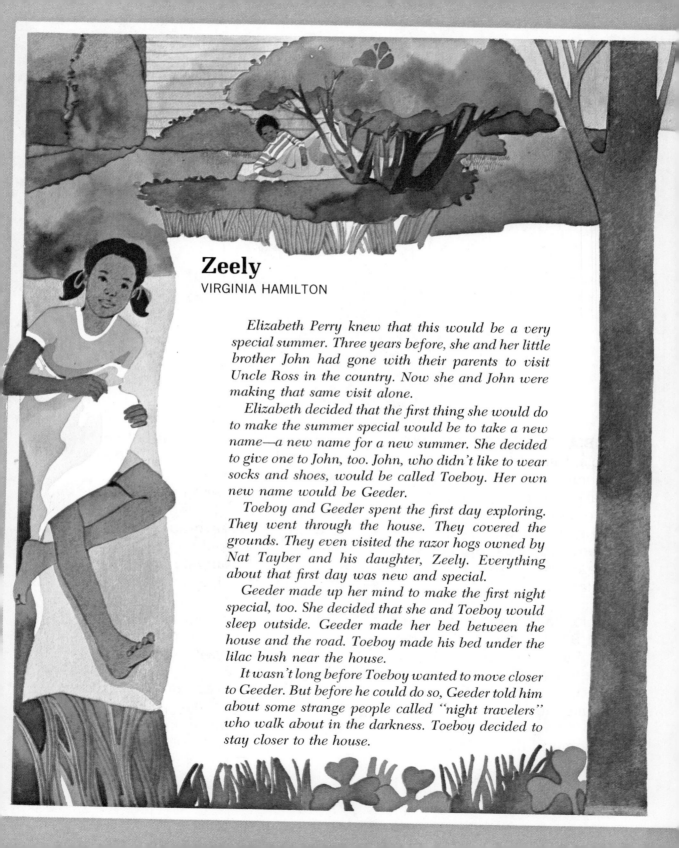

Zeely

VIRGINIA HAMILTON

Elizabeth Perry knew that this would be a very special summer. Three years before, she and her little brother John had gone with their parents to visit Uncle Ross in the country. Now she and John were making that same visit alone.

Elizabeth decided that the first thing she would do to make the summer special would be to take a new name—a new name for a new summer. She decided to give one to John, too. John, who didn't like to wear socks and shoes, would be called Toeboy. Her own new name would be Geeder.

Toeboy and Geeder spent the first day exploring. They went through the house. They covered the grounds. They even visited the razor hogs owned by Nat Tayber and his daughter, Zeely. Everything about that first day was new and special.

Geeder made up her mind to make the first night special, too. She decided that she and Toeboy would sleep outside. Geeder made her bed between the house and the road. Toeboy made his bed under the lilac bush near the house.

It wasn't long before Toeboy wanted to move closer to Geeder. But before he could do so, Geeder told him about some strange people called "night travelers" who walk about in the darkness. Toeboy decided to stay closer to the house.

Strange Sights and Sounds

A long time passed. Geeder dozed and awoke with a start. The grass beyond the tip of her toes was wet with dew. She pulled the blankets more tightly around her, tucking her feet safely inside. She had closed her eyes again when she heard a rustling sound on Leadback Road.

Some old animal, she thought. The sound grew louder, and she could not think what it was. Suddenly, what she had told Toeboy flashed through her mind.

Night travelers! She dove under the covers.

But something's happening! she told herself, poking her head out again.

It took all her courage to crawl out of the covers and the few feet over the wet grass up to the hedge. She trembled with fear but peeked through the hedge in spite of it. What she saw made her bend low, hugging the ground for protection. Truthfully, she wasn't sure what she saw. The branches of the hedge didn't allow much of a view.

Something tall and white was moving down the road. It didn't quite touch the ground. Geeder could hear no sound of footsteps. She couldn't see its head or arms. Beside it and moving with it was something that squeaked ominously. The white, very long figure made a rustling sound. It passed by toward town.

Geeder watched, moving her head ever so slowly until she could no longer see it. After waiting for what seemed hours, quaking at each sound and murmur of the night, she crept back to bed, pulling the covers over her eyes. She lay, cold and scared, unable to think and afraid even to clear her dry throat. This way, she fell asleep. She awoke in the morning, refreshed but stiff in every muscle.

Geeder lay for a moment, watching mist rise from the pink, sweet clover that sprinkled the lawn. The air smelled clean and fresh and was not yet hot from the sun.

"I've got to decide," she whispered. In the stillness, the sound of her own voice startled her. She turned carefully around to see if Toeboy had stirred. The tangled bedding deep in the lilac bush did not move.

"If I tell Toeboy about the night traveler," she whispered, "he might not want to sleep outside any more. Just think of it! Not more than a few hours ago, an awful, spooky thing walked by here!"

Geeder wasn't at all sure she wanted to sleep outside again, herself.

"Goodness knows what a night traveler will do if it sees you watching! Maybe I'd better tell Uncle Ross. . . . Maybe I shouldn't."

Geeder knew it would take her a while to figure out what course to take. Almost any minute now, the people Uncle Ross rented land to would come down the road. Uncle Ross had said they came every morning as soon as the sun was well up in the sky. It was just about time, and watching them would be something to do.

When her dew-soaked blankets grew warm from the sun, Geeder whistled for Toeboy as softly as she could. Turning around, she saw one eye peek out from the lilac bush. . . .

424

"Wake up, Toeboy!" she whispered loudly. "I think I hear them coming!"

They knelt low by the hedge. Trying not to move or blink an eye, they watched Mr. Tayber and his daughter come into view along Leadback Road. What they saw was no ordinary sight. They watched, spellbound, for nothing in the world could have prepared them for the sight of Miss Zeely Tayber.

Zeely Tayber was more than six and a half feet tall, thin and deeply dark as a pole of Ceylon ebony. She wore a long smock that reached to her ankles. Her arms, hands and feet were bare, and her thin, oblong head didn't seem to fit quite right on her shoulders.

She had very high cheekbones and her eyes seemed to turn inward on themselves. Geeder couldn't say what expression she saw on Zeely's face. She knew only that it was calm, that it had pride in it, and that the face was the most beautiful she had ever seen. . . .

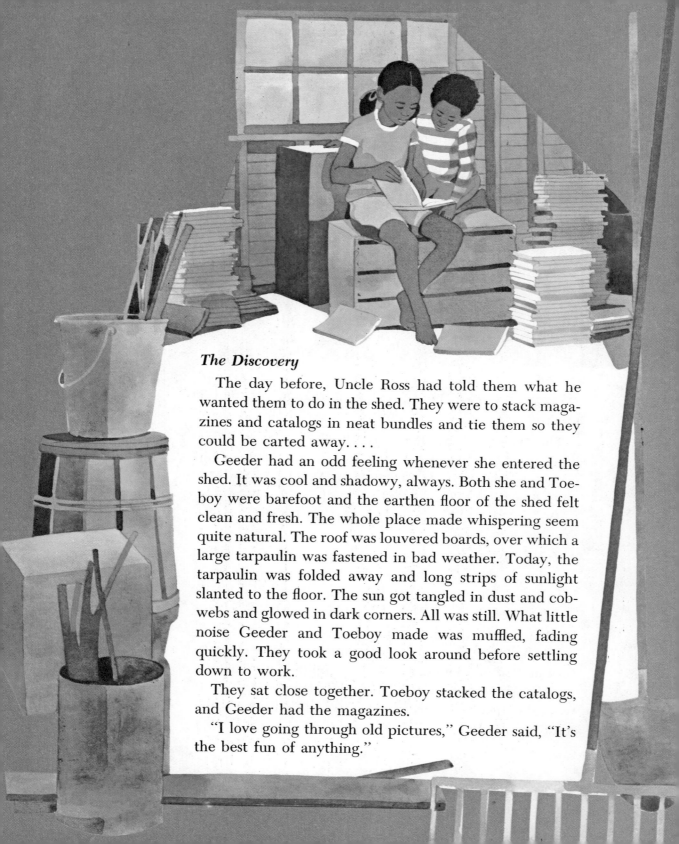

The Discovery

The day before, Uncle Ross had told them what he wanted them to do in the shed. They were to stack magazines and catalogs in neat bundles and tie them so they could be carted away. . . .

Geeder had an odd feeling whenever she entered the shed. It was cool and shadowy, always. Both she and Toeboy were barefoot and the earthen floor of the shed felt clean and fresh. The whole place made whispering seem quite natural. The roof was louvered boards, over which a large tarpaulin was fastened in bad weather. Today, the tarpaulin was folded away and long strips of sunlight slanted to the floor. The sun got tangled in dust and cobwebs and glowed in dark corners. All was still. What little noise Geeder and Toeboy made was muffled, fading quickly. They took a good look around before settling down to work.

They sat close together. Toeboy stacked the catalogs, and Geeder had the magazines.

"I love going through old pictures," Geeder said, "It's the best fun of anything."

Geeder bent low over a magazine. On her lap were two more magazines that slowly slid to the floor. She pressed her hand against the page, as if to hold on to what she saw there. Then, she sat very still and her breath came in a long, low sigh. . . .

Toeboy crept up beside her and tried taking the magazine from her, but she wouldn't let it go. He looked over her shoulder. What he saw caused him to leap away, as though he had seen a ghost.

"I knew it all the time! I knew it!" Geeder said to him.

Geeder had found something extraordinary, a photograph of an African woman of royal birth. She belonged to the Batutsi tribe. The magazine Geeder held said that the Batutsis were so tall they were almost giants. They were known all over the world as Watutsis, the word for them in the Swahili language. Except for the tribal gown the girl wore and the royal headband wound tightly around her head, she could have been Zeely Tayber standing tall and serene in Uncle Ross' west field.

Toeboy carefully read what was written under the photograph of the African girl. "Maybe Zeely Tayber is a queen," he said at last.

Geeder stared at Toeboy. It took her a few seconds to compose herself enough to say, "Well, of course, Toeboy—what do you think? I never doubted for a minute that Miss Zeely Tayber was anything else!"

She was quiet a long while then, staring at the photograph. She simply sat with her mouth open, holding the picture; not one whisper passed her lips.

Uncle Ross happened by the shed. He didn't see Geeder and Toeboy at first, they sat so still in the shadows. But soon, his eyes grew accustomed to the darkness of the shed as he peeked in and he smiled and entered. Geeder aroused herself, getting up to meet Uncle Ross. She handed him the magazine without a word. Uncle Ross carried it to the doorway. There, in the light, he stood gazing at the photograph. His face grew puzzled. Geeder was to remember all day and all night what he said that moment.

"The same nose," he muttered, "those slanted eyes . . . black, too, black as night." He looked from the photograph to Geeder, then to Toeboy and back to Geeder again. "So you believe Zeely Tayber to be some kind of royalty," he said, finally.

"There isn't any doubt that Zeely's a queen," Geeder said. Her voice was calm. "The picture is proof."

All through the summer, Geeder carried the picture with her. She longed to meet Zeely and talk to her. One afternoon, when summer was almost over, Uncle Ross brought Geeder a message from Zeely. Geeder was to meet her at two o'clock the next day at the forest. When it was time for Geeder to go, she was shaking with excitement.

She saw Zeely standing at the entrance to the forest. She was dressed in a long silk robe of many colors. She looked just like the picture of the Watutsi queen.

The Meeting

Geeder's hand shook as she gave Zeely the photograph of the Watutsi woman.

Zeely looked at the photograph. She smiled. Finally, she gave the picture back to Geeder. . . .

Carefully, Zeely ran her long fingers over her robe. "My mother's people were Watutsi people out of Africa a long time ago," she said quietly.

"Just like the lady in the picture!" Geeder said.

"Yes," said Zeely, "and I believed that through my veins ran the blood of kings and queens! So it was that my

mother came to make this robe for me," Zeely said. "I had asked her many questions about her people—I talked of nothing else for quite a while. She made this robe exactly like the ones they wore." ∴ .

Zeely laughed softly. She drew her long legs up under her chin and folded her arms around them.

Geeder watched her. Zeely's features seemed to soften and flow into the deep shadows the trees made. Her hands and forearms were hidden in the long grass around her legs. Geeder looked at Zeely's black hair, dark as night, and it became a part of the darkening leaves above her head.

Geeder said, "It's you that comes down the roadway late at night, isn't it, Miss Zeely?" She spoke into Zeely's ear.

Zeely nodded her head but did not open her eyes. "I come to look after my pigs," she said.

"And you carry a feed pail," said Geeder. "The moon going down slants on to it and it looks like it floats in the air. The moon is behind your back and so you don't have a face. It looks just like you don't have a head or any arms and you glide right above the ground."

"So," Zeely said, "you have seen me? I have seen you."

"You go by the house just before dawn," Geeder said.

"You come early in the morning, anyhow. Why must you come so way late at night?"

"And why must you sleep there in the grass," Zeely asked, "so way late at night?"

"I like the stars," Geeder said, "and the moonshine."

"I like the night," said Zeely. She opened her eyes and stretched out her legs. Her shoulders dropped forward and her head fell back, slightly, as she studied the trees.

"Where I came from," Zeely said, "Canada, there was a lake.

"Oh, it was not a large lake," she said. "You could swim it, going slowly, in about fifteen minutes. I have done that. I have swum it when there was no moon or stars to light my way. Do you know what it is like to swim at night?"

"No," Geeder said, "I don't swim well, yet."

Zeely smiled, her eyes still in the trees. "It is like no other where," she said. "It is being in something that is all movement, that you cannot see, and it ceases to be wet. You must be very calm or you will not find your way out of it."

"Is that why you like the night?" asked Geeder.

"You see," Zeely said, looking at Geeder now, "the children wouldn't often swim in that lake, even in the daytime. A tiny old woman lived beside it. She wore a big bow in her hair that was very dirty. On top of the bow she wore a man's straw hat. She walked, bent forward, with a big cane for support. Often, she cackled to herself and pointed her cane at things. The children were afraid of her but I was not. Sometimes, I'd be swimming in the lake in the daytime, and she'd come upon me. 'Zeely Tayber,' she would call, 'I see you!' And I would call back to her, 'And I see you!' Then, she would call again. 'One of these times, I'll catch you!' she would say, and she would cackle and point her cane at me.

"Oh, no," Zeely said, "I was not afraid of her like the others were. I thought of her as a friend, almost. Then . . ."

"Then, what?" Geeder said.

Zeely looked away from Geeder. Her eyes turned inward upon themselves as Geeder had seen them do before.

The Night

"One night," Zeely said, "I had finished swimming and was pulling on my clothes when I heard footsteps on the path. I heard a cackle and I knew who it was. All at once, fear took hold of me. I had not ever thought of that little woman walking around at night, you see. At that moment, I was terrified. Quickly, I gathered my clothes and stood between a bush and tree, well hidden, I thought. And there she came along the path."

"Oh," said Geeder, softly. Her eyes were wide.

"She did nothing for a moment," Zeely said. "She stood there beside the lake looking at the dark water. Then, she looked around. She went up to a stone lying there beside her and touched it with her cane. It moved. It was a turtle and it scurried into the water."

"No!" said Geeder.

"Oh, yes," Zeely said. "And there was a fallen branch, twisted upon itself there, right next to the path. Vines grew over it. She poked one vine with her cane. It rippled. It was a snake and it slithered off into a bush near where I stood."

"No!" said Geeder.

"I couldn't believe my eyes," Zeely said, "I was so amazed by what I had seen."

"You must have been just scared to death!" Geeder said. She leaned against Zeely now, looking up at her, and

Zeely leaned against Geeder. Neither realized how close they had become, sitting there under the great trees.

"I was scared," Zeely said. "The woman kept cackling. Her back was turned to me. But I must have choked out loud on my fear, for suddenly she was silent. She spun around and stood there, facing the darkness where I was hidden.

" 'Zeely Tayber,' she said, 'I see you!' And I remember, I began to cry.

" 'Zeely Tayber,' she said again. She raised her cane right at me, and she was coming toward me. I could see her bow moving in the air. Suddenly, she had me by the arms. She was cackling again—I thought she would never stop.

"At last, she spoke," Zeely said. " 'Zeely Tayber,' she said, 'you have made a poor soul happy. You are the night and I have caught you!' "

"Oh!" said Geeder. "What a thing to happen!"

"Yes," said Zeely.

"What did you do?" asked Geeder.

"Do?" Zeely asked. "I did nothing. Soon, the woman let me loose and went on her way, laughing and singing to herself. I was stunned by what she had said to me, and I stood there in the darkness for many minutes. All at once in my mind everything was as clear as day. I liked the dark. I walked and swam in the dark and because of that, I was the night!

"Finally," Zeely said, "I told my mother about what had happened. My mother said that I simply had not known darkness well enough to tell the difference between a stone and a turtle and a vine and a snake. She said the snake and turtle had been there all the time. She said that since the woman was not quite right in the head, she had decided that I was the night because my skin was so dark."

"Did you believe what your mother said?" asked
Geeder.

"I came to believe it," Zeely said. "I believe it now. But
I was sorry my mother had said what she did. It meant I
was only myself, that I was Zeely and no more."

Geeder sighed and looked down at her hands. "Things
. . . are what they are, I guess," she said, quietly.

"Yes," said Zeely. "No pretty robe was able to make me
more than what I was and no little woman could make me
the night."

"But you are different," Geeder said. "You are the most
different person I've ever talked to."

"Am I?" Zeely said, her voice kind. "And you want to
be different, too?" . . .

Geeder stopped in confusion. "I want to be . . . to
be . . ." She paused.

"Whoever it is you are when you're not being Geeder,"
Zeely said, finishing for her. "The person you are when
you're not making up stories. Not Geeder and not even
me, but yourself—is that what you want, Elizabeth?"
Zeely looked deeply at Geeder, as if the image of her were
fading away. "I stopped making up tales a long time ago,"
she said, "and now I am myself."

Geeder was so startled she could not say anything. And
the way Zeely called her Elizabeth, just as though they

were the same age, caused a pleasant, quiet feeling to grow within her. What she had promised herself at the beginning of the summer crossed Geeder's mind. *I won't be silly. I won't play silly games.*

But I was silly, she thought. I made up myself as Geeder and I made up Zeely to be a queen.

"Myself . . ." she whispered. "Yes, I guess so."

Zeely Tayber ruffled the creases from her long robe and then stood up to leave. She was tall and beautiful there, before Geeder. Her expression was soft.

"You have a most fine way of dreaming," Zeely said. "Hold on to that. But remember the turtle, remember the snake. I always have."

Geeder didn't see Zeely leave the clearing. The colors of bush and tree swam in her eyes and Zeely melted away within them.

Reflections

1. Why did Geeder have a hard time making up her mind about what to do after seeing what she thought was a night traveler?
2. Who did the traveler turn out to be? Why did she look as though she were floating?
3. Why did Geeder think that Zeely was a queen?
4. Why was Zeely sorry her mother had said what she did about her adventure?
5. How did Zeely's adventure make Geeder feel about herself?
6. What did Zeely mean when she said, "But remember the turtle, remember the snake"?
7. Pretend that you are Geeder, and that you keep a diary. Write an entry in your diary after your talk with Zeely. Remember to write your thoughts and feelings as if you were Geeder.

Childhood Days

VIRGINIA HAMILTON

Writers for young people sometimes write about what really happened to them when they were children. But more often, they write about what *could* have happened to them, what might have happened to their brothers and sisters, or their mothers, fathers, and even their ancestors. I know that while writing a story, I often do take a small amount of truth from my own life and change it into something that might have been. This is one way a writer creates fiction and I am, of course, a creative writer.

I was born and grew up in a very small, quiet town of about 4,000 people. I lived with my family on the edge of the town of Yellow Springs, Ohio, on a fifteen-acre farm. We grew almost everything we ate—tomatoes by the bushel basket, cucumbers by the truckload, corn, and beans. We raised chickens; and we raised pigs, which we butchered for the ham, bacon, and pork loin. My brothers and sisters and I could help with the farm chores if we wished, but we were never forced to work. We all simply pitched in when things needed to be done.

In summers when school was over, I was usually up and out of the house by nine o'clock in the morning. Many days, my mother wouldn't see me again until nine in the evening. But more times than not, I would disappear from home early in the morning only to reappear when I got hungry, which was about five to ten times a day.

If the day were special, like the Fourth of July, then I would hang around the house the whole day. I knew relatives would be coming to visit, and that meant that mother would bake pies, cakes, and bread. She'd take a ham or two out of the smoke house, and I would stay with her in the kitchen sniffing all of the wonderful smells and hoping I might get an early slice of cake, or ham. My mother was in a good mood on holidays just as she was at other times. As long as I helped with the dishes, she would let me taste and munch to my heart's content. Secretly, I'm sure my mother hoped to fatten me up, for I was very thin as a child.

Etta Belle Perry, my mother, was the oldest daughter of a fugitive slave. She was one of nine children, and when she grew up, she had five children of her own. I was her youngest child and spoiled by my brothers and sisters, who were from four to eight years older than I was. They always treated me with a special regard, which made me feel very important. I can recall telling my oldest sister, Nina, that one day I would write books and become famous. I must have been nine or ten years old at the time. I remember my sister saying, "Goody! Then I'll be famous, too!"

What is so nice about that is that my sister, Nina, never thought to say, "Oh, Virginia, don't be silly. You won't ever be a writer." Never was I discouraged in anything I attempted to do. Mother always said that it didn't matter to her what we became. "Just don't sit around doing

nothing," she told us. "Try things." And I certainly did.

My mother was like the earth, life-giving, and my father was like the sun around which we all revolved. He was Kenneth James Hamilton from Alton, Illinois. First and foremost, my father was a musician, although he made his living as a part-time farmer and as the service manager of a college dining hall.

Kenneth Hamilton had a beautiful antique, ivory-inlaid Gibson mandolin, which he loved to play on still summer evenings. He was an exceptionally fine mandolinist and the sound of that instrument has always had a comforting effect on me. Dad would sit on the porch with me, and while playing the mandolin, he would tell stories of his travels across America, Canada, and Alaska. He would actually change his speech patterns in order to show me how the different people he encountered spoke. I am certain that from his constant storytelling came my desire to tell my own stories.

My brother, William Levi, was also a storyteller. From the day he was born, he was called *Baby Brother* by my older brothers and sister. Later, they were to call him *Bay Bra* for short; and for years, he was known as Bay Bra all over town. My sister, Barbara, was known as *Bay Sis*, which she hated and which, now and then, I forget and still call her.

William (or Bay Bra) was four years older than I was. We were often companions, just as were Elizabeth "Geeder" Perry and John "Toeboy" Perry. But in real life, William was the leader and I was the follower.

William took me with him on his paper route on his bike in summertime and I would hold the papers for him. Even in the wintertime, I traveled the long route with him. He would pull me on his sled through deep snow and I would hold the rolled pack of papers for him on my lap.

The paper route seemed endless and each time, I nearly froze. But I never let on that my hands and feet had grown numb for fear William would send me home. I dearly loved to listen to him talk on and on about what he would do and what he would see when he grew up. William had quite an imagination. And I think that from his dreaming of what would be possible for him came my own ideas of what might be possible for me.

Perhaps now it is clearer how it happened that I would one day write a character like Geeder Perry who led *her* brother around. Geeder, then, was created, not from what happened in my own life, but from what could have happened.

As my brother, William, grew older, he found his companions among the other youths of the town. I then began to play with my cousin, Marlena, who was a year older than I. We each took turns being the leader so that everything would be fair and equal between us.

It was a fine, hot summer the time Marlena and I first went into business for ourselves. We discovered that the mustard and dandelion greens that grew wild over the fields were loved as a special delicacy by our mothers and all of their church-going friends who didn't live on farms. We picked the greens by the basketful early in the morning. We had sold about four baskets between us by early

afternoon, making fifty cents apiece. As the summer progressed, still hot and humid, we expanded our business to include cartons of strawberries, raspberries, and blackberries at fifteen cents a carton.

Barefoot and full of excitement, Marlena and I hurried down the hot highways to knock on the doors of quiet houses. Often as not, we sold all of our berries as well. At the end of the day, we each had made at least a dollar. We were millionaires! And we had an endless supply of free goods—the berries and greens growing all over our parents' farms. We seemed to have a private supply of customers because, curiously enough, no other children we knew bothered with "selling" and making money.

The pure profit we made from the sale of greens and berries we sank at once into the local movie house. We had only just discovered the horror of old and new Wolfman and Frankenstein films. A couple of times a week, we exchanged our quarters for those wonderful, terrifying movies. Always, we remembered *after* the picture that to get home we had to run more than a half-mile out of town down a pitchblack road!

Marlena and I remained inseparable throughout our

439

adolescent years. In the heat of summer, we slept out of doors. Our homes faced over a distance of fields. We had a series of signals and yodel-sounding calls which we used to communicate. In the early evening, one of us would signal to tell the other at whose house we would spend the night.

Marlena's house was the best for sleeping out because her rear yard had a small shed. We liked to sleep atop the tin roof of the shed, which grew cool with nightfall. How we ever stayed up there without sliding off, I'll never know. The shed roof had a fairly steep slant, but still we slept there and thought nothing of it.

The atmosphere of those summer nights sleeping outside naturally found its way into my books when I began to write. Marlena and I slept out, woke up in the night, just as did Geeder and Toeboy Perry. There is nothing quite like the memory of waking up before dawn, frightened, as though *something*, perhaps someone calling, had awakened me. I can feel again the dew on my blankets. The stars high above appear misty, and the moon has gone down. Insects have quieted, as though listening, also. A chill spreads up my spine; I shiver, helplessly afraid of something unseen and unknown.

More than likely a large dog from a neighboring farm had glided swiftly across Marlena's yard at the moment I awoke in the dark. And that which would have seemed familiar in daylight took on the ghostly quality of a night spirit—a *night traveler*. So it was that the night traveler in *Zeely* first became a possibility in my childhood. Then, I had awakened in the night, was frightened, and saw something made ever more huge and ghostly by my growing fear. Writers deal in possibilities—not with what is but with what could be.

In my childhood, there was no Zeely Tayber who

walked the dark roads way late at night. But there *could* have been. You see how I made a place for her in my imagination.

Zeely is a story having to do with the strength of family ties, the importance of land, and the respect of one person for another. It also tells about a young girl's growing maturity through her yearnings and her dreams. Moreover, *Zeely* reveals some of the flavor and spice of my own rural Ohio childhood. Having traveled and lived in many parts of the world, I chose in 1969 to make my permanent home in the place where I was born. My husband and I and our two children now live on one of the last sections remaining of my parents' farm.

I am fond of the land where mustard and dandelion greens grow wild. Berries ripen each late spring just the way they did in my childhood, and in my mother's childhood. Today, my own children pick the berries and stain their shirts with berry juice just as I once did. I wait for the day they discover that from a morning's work they can make a profit. But even if they choose not to go into business for themselves, I know they will remember the summers—the fine scent of heat on the air, and sleeping out in the dark of night.

Reflections

1. According to Virginia Hamilton, do writers of fiction base their stories only on things that really happened to them?
2. What role did Virginia Hamilton's family play in encouraging her dream of what she wanted to be?
3. Write a story using a person or event in your own life as a basis. Remember, your story doesn't have to tell something that really happened—just something that "could have been."

POINT OF VIEW

No one knows who wrote down the oral story of Beowulf in Old English. But whoever it was kept the point of view of the original narrator of the tale. It is the point of view of one who admired bravery and great deeds, who was familiar with the sea, and who knew the customs of Beowulf's time, centuries before.

In "Young Ladies Don't Slay Dragons," the point of view is the Princess Penelope's. The position she takes on things and events is what the story is all about.

Mabel Louise Robinson wrote "The Challenge of the Sword" from Arthur's point of view. We experience with Arthur the reactions he has when he first finds the sword and later when he accepts his role as king. Whose point of view is presented best in "Trouble in Camelot"?

Point of view has more than one definition. So far we have been talking about point of view as a character's or speaker's total position from which things and people are seen and judged. It includes the ideas and attitudes that lead to the character's opinions or actions. In "Zeely," it is from Elizabeth's (Geeder's) total position, or point of view, that the thought and action spring. And we also see how Zeely helps to change Elizabeth's original ideas and attitudes, modifying her point of view.

Most stories contain physical point of view as well. An example of this is when Geeder and Toeboy kneel by the hedge, peeking out at Zeely and her father, and a description of Zeely is given. Physical point of view, then, is the actual location of the character as something is being described. It can, of course, be fixed or moving.

Point of view can also be defined as the personal pronouns (I or we, and he, she, or they) used to tell the story or poem. The author chooses the person (first or third) that best suits the material. But we should remember that the author and the speaker are not necessarily the same. A character telling the story using the pronoun *I* does not represent the author's point of view, but the point of view of the character as the author has drawn it.

Tone is closely related to point of view. It is the "tone of voice" of the writer that gives us clues as to how we are to take the story, poem, or other writing. Edward Eager in "Trouble in Camelot," for example, treats the court of King Arthur in a humorous manner, with a mocking tone, not at all as Mabel Louise Robinson does in "The Challenge of the Sword." Her tone is interested, sympathetic. You may wish to compare the tone of "The Portrait of a Warrior" by Walter de la Mare with that of "The Knight Whose Armor Didn't Squeak" by A. A. Milne. To find tone, look carefully at the language—what is said and how it is said. Watch out for figures of speech—for similes and metaphors. The warrior's hand, for example, in the de la Mare poem, "Hangs open like an iron gin (trap)." The tone of the poem supports the third-person point of view that the warrior is fearlessness itself.

Same Subject, Different Point of View

The same subject can be treated from many points of view. Perhaps you have seen two people on a television news program arguing about something from entirely opposite viewpoints. The editorials of two newspapers may also put forth opposing points of view about a current problem or situation. Much depends on the writer's attitude and feeling toward the subject. When reading, notice which details are included and how they are arranged. Also notice in what way actions are described.

What follows is a simple illustration of how a subject can be written from various points of view. Read this familiar nursery rhyme.

Jack and Jill went up the hill
To fetch a pail of water.
Jack fell down
And broke his crown,
And Jill came tumbling after.

The point of view here is of someone who perhaps saw the event. It merely gives the facts, like a piece of reporting. The tone is objective. No feeling is shown.

A famous modern poet, Louis Untermeyer, rewrote the verse, creating the poem in the style of Walter de la Mare.

Walter de la Mare
Tells the Listener About Jack and Jill

Up to the top of the haunted turf
   They climbed on the moonlit hill.
Not a leaf rustled in the underbrush;
   Their listening air was still,

And only the noise of the water pail
   As it struck on a jutting stone,
Clattered and jarred against the silence
   As the two trod on alone.

Up to the moonlit peak they went;
   And, though not a word would they say,
Their thoughts outnumbered a poet's love-songs
   In the first green weeks of May.

The stealthy shadows crept closer;
   They clutched at the hem of Jill's gown;
And there at the very top she stumbled,
   And Jack came shuddering down.

Their cries rang out against the stillness,
   Pitiful and high and thin.
And the echoes edged back still further
   As the silence gathered them in.

We call the Untermeyer poem a parody. It was written as a humorous imitation or "takeoff" on another author's style. We have seen that subjects as well as styles of writing may be parodied. "Trouble in Camelot" parodies knighthood, for example. Untermeyer's tone in his poem is mock-solemn. The point of view is of one who is poking fun because an unimportant happening is made to appear so serious and gloomy.

From what other points of view could the Jack and Jill incident be told? The list is endless. If told from the point of view of either Jack or Jill, we would no doubt be given causes and effects and a story with much more meaning. Searching out point of view in any piece of writing is a giant step to understanding the selection as a whole.

Experimenting with Point of View

1. Prove to yourself that a narrative can be told from a number of points of view. Choose two paragraphs from the autobiographical "Childhood Days" by Virginia Hamilton. Begin, perhaps, with "Marlena and I remained inseparable throughout our adolescent years," reading through that paragraph and the one following. Note how simple, natural, and believable the *I* point of view is. Now rewrite the two paragraphs, using a third-person point of view. Become the all-knowing author, who knows everything about the characters and events. You will find you can make comments about what is happening that the *I* point of view cannot.

2. Or rewrite the two paragraphs from a *limited* third-person point of view. Pretend you are merely an observer. Be, for example, William Levi, Virginia Hamilton's brother, seeing the events from his limited observation. Unlike the third-person point of view of the author who knows everything, the character with a limited point of view cannot know what is in another character's mind.

Unit **6** AGES FAR AWAY

STONE

This is a stone, smooth and round,
  And flecked with green, that I just found.
Where did it come from? Long ago,
  Did a fierce volcano erupt and blow
This stone from its mouth—a red-hot glob
  That slowly cooled to a stoney knob?
Did waters wash it with millions of knocks,
  Grinding it smooth against other rocks?
Was it part of a mountain's growth or fall?
  Over its shape did strange things crawl?
It was old, I think, when bison and bear
  Roamed the plains, and Indians were ther
Perhaps a child then, long ago,
  Held it like this and wished to know
The story the stone keeps. Perhaps then,
  like me,
He sensed this stone's deep mystery.

Solveig Paulson Russell

The Dog of Pompeii

LOUIS UNTERMEYER

Tito and Bimbo

Tito and his dog Bimbo lived (if you could call it living) under the wall where it joined the inner gate. They really didn't live there; they just slept there. Pompeii was one of the gayest of the old Latin towns, but although Tito was never an unhappy boy, he was not exactly a merry one. The streets were always lively with shining chariots and bright red trappings; the open-air theaters rocked with laughing crowds; sham battles and athletic sports were free for the asking in the great stadium. Once a year the caesar visited the pleasure city, and the fireworks lasted for days; the sacrifices in the Forum were better than a show. But Tito saw none of these things. He was blind—had been blind from birth. He was known to everyone in the poorer quarters. But no one could say how old he was; no one remembered his parents; no one could tell where he came from.

Bimbo was another mystery. As long as people could remember seeing Tito—about twelve or thirteen years—they had seen Bimbo. Bimbo had never left his side. He was not only a dog, but nurse, pillow, playmate, mother, and father to Tito.

Did I say Bimbo never left his master? (Perhaps I had better say comrade, for if anyone was the master, it was Bimbo.) I was wrong. Bimbo did trust Tito alone exactly three times a day. It was a fixed routine, a custom understood between boy and dog since the beginning of their friendship, and the way it worked was this. Early in the morning, shortly after dawn, while Tito was still dreaming, Bimbo would disappear. When Tito awoke, Bimbo would be sitting quietly at his side, his ears cocked, his stump of a tail tapping the ground, and a fresh-baked bread—more like a large round roll—at his feet. Tito would stretch himself; Bimbo would yawn; then the boy and dog would breakfast.

At noon, no matter where they might happen to be, Bimbo would put his paw on Tito's knee, and the two of them would return to the inner gate. Tito would curl up

in the corner (almost like a dog) and sleep, while Bimbo, looking quite important (almost like a boy), would disappear again. In half an hour he'd be back with their lunch. Sometimes it would be a piece of fruit or a scrap of meat; often it was nothing but a dry crust. But sometimes there would be one of those flat rich cakes, sprinkled with raisins and sugar, that Tito liked so much.

At suppertime the same thing happened, although there was a little less of everything, for things were hard to snatch in the evening with the streets full of people. Besides, Bimbo didn't approve of too much food before going to sleep. A heavy supper made boys too restless and dogs too stodgy—and it was the business of a dog to sleep lightly, with one ear open and muscles ready for action.

But, whether there was much or little, hot or cold, fresh or dry, food was always there. Tito never asked where it came from, and Bimbo never told him. There was plenty of rainwater in the hollows of soft stones; the old egg woman at the corner sometimes gave him a cupful of strong goat's milk. So there was no danger of going hungry or thirsty. There was plenty of everything in Pompeii—if you knew where to find it—and if you had a dog like Bimbo.

As I said before, Tito was not the merriest boy in Pompeii. He could not romp with the other youngsters and play Hare-and-Hounds and I-Spy and Follow-Your-Master and Ball-Against-the-Building and Jack-Stones and Kings-and-Robbers with them. But that did not make him sorry for himself. If he could not see the sights that delighted the lads of Pompeii, he could hear and smell things they never noticed. He could really see more with his ears and nose than they could with their eyes. When he and Bimbo went out walking, he knew just where they were going and exactly what was happening.

"Ah," he'd sniff and say as they passed a handsome villa, "Glaucus Pansa is giving a grand dinner tonight. They're going to have three kinds of bread and roast pig and stuffed goose and a great stew—I think bear stew—and a fig pie." And Bimbo would note that this would be a good place to visit tomorrow.

Or, "H'm," Tito would murmur, half through his lips, half through his nostrils. "The wife of Marcus Lucretius is expecting her mother. She's shaking out every piece of goods in the house; she's going to use the best clothes —the ones she's been keeping in pine needles and camphor—and there's an extra girl in the kitchen. Come, Bimbo, let's get out of the dust!"

Or, as they passed a small but elegant dwelling behind the public baths, "Too bad! The tragic poet is ill again. It must be a bad fever this time, for they're trying smoke fumes instead of medicine. Whew! I'm glad I'm not a tragic poet!"

451

Or, as they neared the Forum, "Mm-m! What good things they have in the Macellum today!" (It really was sort of butcher-grocer-marketplace, but Tito didn't know any better. He called it the Macellum.) "Dates from Africa and salt oysters from sea caves and cuttlefish and new honey and sweet onions and—ugh!—water-buffalo steaks. Come let's see what's what in the Forum." And Bimbo, just as curious as his comrade, hurried on. Being a dog, he trusted his ears and nose (like Tito) more than his eyes. And so the two of them entered the center of Pompeii.

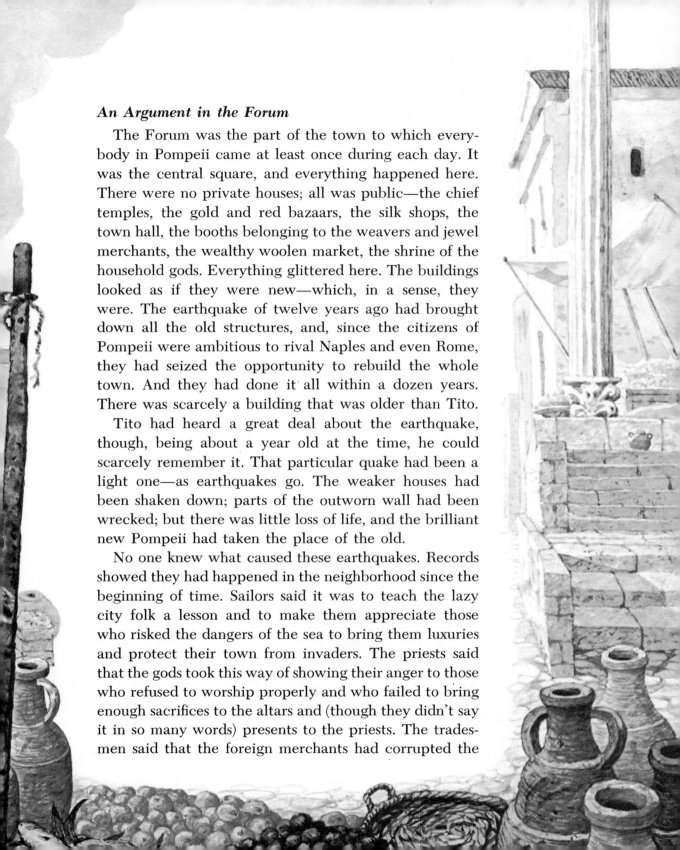

An Argument in the Forum

The Forum was the part of the town to which everybody in Pompeii came at least once during each day. It was the central square, and everything happened here. There were no private houses; all was public—the chief temples, the gold and red bazaars, the silk shops, the town hall, the booths belonging to the weavers and jewel merchants, the wealthy woolen market, the shrine of the household gods. Everything glittered here. The buildings looked as if they were new—which, in a sense, they were. The earthquake of twelve years ago had brought down all the old structures, and, since the citizens of Pompeii were ambitious to rival Naples and even Rome, they had seized the opportunity to rebuild the whole town. And they had done it all within a dozen years. There was scarcely a building that was older than Tito.

Tito had heard a great deal about the earthquake, though, being about a year old at the time, he could scarcely remember it. That particular quake had been a light one—as earthquakes go. The weaker houses had been shaken down; parts of the outworn wall had been wrecked; but there was little loss of life, and the brilliant new Pompeii had taken the place of the old.

No one knew what caused these earthquakes. Records showed they had happened in the neighborhood since the beginning of time. Sailors said it was to teach the lazy city folk a lesson and to make them appreciate those who risked the dangers of the sea to bring them luxuries and protect their town from invaders. The priests said that the gods took this way of showing their anger to those who refused to worship properly and who failed to bring enough sacrifices to the altars and (though they didn't say it in so many words) presents to the priests. The tradesmen said that the foreign merchants had corrupted the

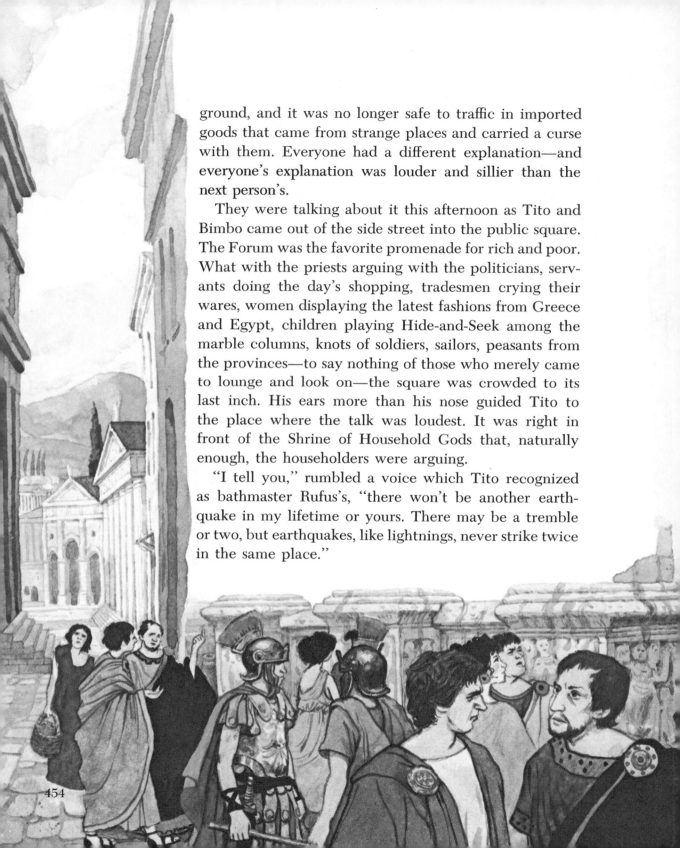

ground, and it was no longer safe to traffic in imported goods that came from strange places and carried a curse with them. Everyone had a different explanation—and everyone's explanation was louder and sillier than the next person's.

They were talking about it this afternoon as Tito and Bimbo came out of the side street into the public square. The Forum was the favorite promenade for rich and poor. What with the priests arguing with the politicians, servants doing the day's shopping, tradesmen crying their wares, women displaying the latest fashions from Greece and Egypt, children playing Hide-and-Seek among the marble columns, knots of soldiers, sailors, peasants from the provinces—to say nothing of those who merely came to lounge and look on—the square was crowded to its last inch. His ears more than his nose guided Tito to the place where the talk was loudest. It was right in front of the Shrine of Household Gods that, naturally enough, the householders were arguing.

"I tell you," rumbled a voice which Tito recognized as bathmaster Rufus's, "there won't be another earthquake in my lifetime or yours. There may be a tremble or two, but earthquakes, like lightnings, never strike twice in the same place."

"Do they not?" asked a thin voice Tito had never heard. It had a high, sharp ring to it, and Tito knew it as the accent of a stranger.

"How about the two towns of Sicily that have been ruined three times within fifteen years by the eruptions of Mount Etna? And were they not warned? And does that column of smoke that I can see above Vesuvius mean nothing?"

"That?" Tito could hear the grunt with which one question answered another. "That's always there. We use it for our weather guide. When the smoke stands up straight, we know we'll have fair weather; when it flattens out, it's sure to be foggy; when it drifts to the east—"

"Yes, yes," cut in the edged voice. "I've heard about your mountain barometer. But the column of smoke seems hundreds of feet higher than usual, and it's thickening and spreading like a shadowy tree. They say in Naples—"

"Oh, Naples!" Tito knew this voice by the little squeak that went with it. It was Attilio, the cameo cutter. "They talk while we suffer. Little help we got from them last time. Naples commits the crimes, and Pompeii pays the price. It's become a proverb with us. Let them mind their own business."

"Yes," grumbled Rufus, "and others, too."

455

"Very well, my confident friends," responded the thin voice, which now sounded curiously flat. "We also have a proverb—and it is this: Those who will not listen to humans must be taught by the gods. I say no more. But I leave a last warning. Remember the holy ones. Look to your temples. And when the smoke tree above Vesuvius grows to the shape of an umbrella pine, look to your lives."

Tito could hear the air whistle as the speaker drew his toga about him, and the quick shuffle of feet told him the stranger had gone.

"Now what," said the cameo cutter, "did he mean by that?"

"I wonder," grunted Rufus, "I wonder."

Tito wondered, too. And Bimbo, his head at a thoughtful angle, looked as if he had been doing a heavy piece of pondering. By nightfall the argument had been forgotten. If the smoke had increased, no one saw it in the dark. Besides, it was the caesar's birthday, and the town was in a holiday mood. Tito and Bimbo were among the merrymakers, dodging the charioteers who shouted at them.

They visited the uncovered theater, and, though Tito could not see the faces of the actors, he could follow the play better than most of the audience, for their attention wandered—they were distracted by the scenery, the costumes, the byplay, even by themselves—while Tito's whole attention was centered in what he heard. Then to the city walls, where the people of Pompeii watched a mock naval battle in which the city was attacked by the sea and saved after thousands of flaming arrows had been burned. Though the thrill of flaring ships and lit skies was lost to Tito, the shouts and cheers excited him as much as any, and he cried out with the loudest of them.

The End of the World

The next morning there were two of the beloved raisin and sugar cakes for his breakfast. Bimbo was unusually active and thumped his bit of a tail until Tito was afraid he would wear it out. The boy could not imagine whether Bimbo was urging him to some sort of game or was trying to say something. After a while he ceased to notice Bimbo. He felt drowsy. Last night's late hours had tired him. Besides, there was a heavy mist in the air—no, a thick fog rather than a mist—a fog that got into his throat and scraped it and made him cough. He walked as far as the marine gate to get a breath of the sea. But the blanket of haze had spread all over the bay, and even the salt air seemed smoky.

He went to bed before dusk and slept. But he did not sleep well. He had too many dreams of ships lurching in the Forum, of losing his way in a screaming crowd, of armies marching across his chest, of being pulled over every rough pavement of Pompeii.

He woke early. Or, rather, he was pulled awake. Bimbo was doing the pulling. The dog had dragged Tito to his feet and was urging the boy along. Somewhere. Where, Tito did not know. His feet stumbled uncertainly; he was still half asleep. For a while he noticed nothing except the fact that it was hard to breathe. The air was hot. And heavy. So heavy that he could taste it. The air, it seemed, had turned to powder, a warm powder that stung his nostrils and burned his sightless eyes.

Then he began to hear sounds. Peculiar sounds. Like animals under the earth. Hissings and groanings and muffled cries that a dying creature might make dislodging the stones of his underground cave. There was no doubt of it now. The noises came from beneath. He not only heard them—he could feel them. The earth twitched; the twitching changed to an uneven shrugging of the soil. Then, as Bimbo half pulled, half coaxed him across, the ground jerked away from his feet, and he was thrown against a stone fountain.

The water—hot water—splashing in his face revived Tito. He got to his feet, Bimbo steadying him, helping him on again. The noises grew louder; they came closer. The cries were even more animal-like than before, but now they came from human throats. A few people, quicker of foot and more hurried by fear, began to rush by. A family of two—then a section—then, it seemed, an army broken out of bounds. Tito, bewildered though he was, could recognize Rufus as he bellowed past him like a water buffalo gone mad. Time was lost in a nightmare.

It was then the crashing began. First a sharp crackling, like a monstrous snapping of twigs; then a roar like the fall of a whole forest of trees; then an explosion that tore earth and sky. The heavens, though Tito could not see them, were shot through with continual flickering of fire. Lightnings above were answered by thunders beneath. A house fell. Then another. By a miracle the two companions had escaped the dangerous side streets and were in a more open space. It was the Forum. They rested here a while—how long he did not know.

Tito had no idea of the time of day. He could feel it was black—an unnatural blackness. Something inside—perhaps the lack of breakfast and lunch—told him it was past noon. But it didn't matter. Nothing seemed to matter. He was getting drowsy, too drowsy to walk. But walk he must. He knew it. And Bimbo knew it; the sharp tugs told him so. Nor was it a moment too soon. The sacred ground of the Forum was safe no longer. It was beginning to rock, then to pitch, then to split. As they stumbled out of the square, the earth wriggled like a snake caught, and all the columns of the temple of Jupiter came down. It was the end of the world—or so it seemed. To walk was not enough now. They must run. Tito was too frightened to know what to do or where to go. He had lost all sense of direction. He started to go back to the inner gate; but Bimbo, straining his back to the last inch, almost pulled his clothes from him. What did the creature want? Had the dog gone mad?

Then suddenly he understood. Bimbo was telling him the way out—urging him there. The sea gate, of course. The sea gate—and then the sea. Far from falling buildings, heaving ground. He turned, Bimbo guiding him across open pits and dangerous pools of bubbling mud, away from buildings that had caught fire and were dropping their burning beams. Tito could no longer tell whether the noises were made by the shrieking sky or the agonized people. He and Bimbo ran on—the only silent beings in a howling world.

New dangers threatened. All Pompeii seemed to be thronging toward the marine gate, and, squeezing among the crowds, there was the chance of being trampled to death. But the chance had to be taken. It was growing harder and harder to breathe. What air there was choked him. It was all dust now—dust and pebbles, pebbles as large as beans. They fell on his head, his hands—pumice stones from the black heart of Vesuvius. The mountain was turning itself inside out. Tito remembered a phrase that the stranger had said in the Forum two days ago: "Those who will not listen to men must be taught by the gods." The people of Pompeii had refused to heed those warnings; they were being taught now—if it was not too late.

Suddenly it seemed too late for Tito. The red-hot ashes blistered his skin, the stinging vapors tore his throat. He could not go on. He staggered toward a small tree at the side of the road and fell. In a moment Bimbo was beside him. He coaxed. But there was no answer. He licked Tito's hands, his feet, his face. The boy did not stir. Then Bimbo did the last thing he could—the last thing he wanted to do. He bit his comrade, bit him deep in the arm. With a cry of pain, Tito jumped to his feet, Bimbo after him. Tito was in despair, but Bimbo was determined. He drove the boy on, snapping at his heels, worrying his way through the crowd; barking, baring his teeth, heedless of kicks or falling stones. Sick with hunger, half dead with fear and sulfur fumes, Tito pounded on, pursued by Bimbo. How long he never knew. At last he staggered through the marine gate and felt soft sand under him. Then Tito fainted. . . .

Someone was dashing seawater over him. Someone was carrying him toward a boat.

"Bimbo," he called. And then louder, "Bimbo!" But Bimbo had disappeared.

Voices jarred each other. "Hurry—hurry!" "To the boats!" "Can't you see the child's frightened and starving!" "He keeps calling for someone!" "Poor boy, he's out of his mind." "Here child—take this!"

They tucked him in among them. The oarlocks creaked; the oars splashed; the boat rode over toppling waves. Tito was safe. But he wept continually.

"Bimbo!" he wailed. "Bimbo! Bimbo!"

He could not be comforted.

In the Forum Once Again

Eighteen hundred years passed. Scientists were restoring the ancient city; excavators were working their way through the stones and trash that had buried the entire town. Much had already been brought to light—statues, bronze instruments, bright mosaics, household articles; even delicate paintings had been preserved by the fall of ashes that had taken over two thousand lives. Columns were dug up, and the Forum was beginning to emerge.

It was at a place where the ruins lay deepest that the director paused.

"Come here," he called to his assistant. "I think we've discovered the remains of a building in good shape. Here are four huge millstones that were most likely turned by slaves or mules—and here is a whole wall standing with shelves inside it. Why! It must have been a bakery. And here's a curious thing. What do you think I found under this heap where the ashes were thickest? The skeleton of a dog!"

"Amazing!" gasped his assistant. "You'd think a dog would have had sense enough to run away at the time. And what is that flat thing he's holding between his teeth? It can't be a stone."

"No. It must have come from this bakery. You know, it looks to me like some sort of cake hardened with the years. And, bless me, if those little black pebbles aren't raisins. A raisin cake almost two thousand years old! I wonder what made him want it at such a moment."

"I wonder," murmured the assistant.

Reflections

1. How did Tito get his food? Why is this fact important to the story?
2. What were some of the explanations for earthquakes? How did each explanation favor the one who offered it?
3. Who was the master, the dog or the boy? How does the relationship between boy and dog affect the outcome of the story?
4. In your own words, describe the earthquake. What details did Tito notice even though he was blind?
5. Do you think this story is based on fact or pure fiction? Give reasons for your opinion.
6. Look up Pompeii in an encyclopedia. Give a report to the class on what archaeologists have found there.
7. Tito was blind and an orphan. Do you think he led an unhappy life? Write a paragraph using details from the story to support your opinion.

Forever
EVE MERRIAM

My father tells me
that when he was a boy
he once crashed a ball
through a neighbor's window.

He does not mean to,
but he lies.

I know that aeons ago
the world was ice
and mud
and fish climbed out of the sea
to reptiles on land
to dinosaurs and mammals;

and I know also
that archaeologists have found
remains of ancient times
when men lived in caves
and worshiped weather.

Nonetheless I know
that my father,
a grown man,
coming home at night
with work-lines in his face
and love for me hidden behind
the newspaper in his hand,
has always been so
since the world began.

The Secrets of Minos

ALAN HONOUR

The island of Crete lies southeast of the Greek mainland, in the Mediterranean Sea. Crete was little known when an English archaeologist named Arthur Evans began to excavate. It was he who discovered that Crete was an archaeologist's paradise.

In the late 1800's Evans made many trips to Crete. There he collected seals and beads that were worn as good luck charms by many native islanders. These charms, which bore unusual inscriptions, often had been passed down in families for untold generations.

As Evans thought about what the inscriptions might mean, he remembered the ancient myths of Greece. In Homer's *Odyssey*, Crete is described as a great city, housing people of many races. It was ruled by a powerful king named Minos. Archaeologists had recently made discoveries on the mainland of Greece which hinted to Evans that Homer might prove a reliable guide to the *actual* past!

Many Greek myths recount adventures that took place on Crete. One tale may be the first record of human attempts to fly. In this legend Minos asked a clever and skillful architect, named Daedalus, to build a labyrinth for him. When the labyrinth was completed, Minos quarreled with Daedalus and threw him and his son, Icarus, into prison. While he was in prison, Daedalus made two frameworks of wings to which he fixed masses of feathers with wax. Warning his son not to fly too near the sun, Daedalus took Icarus and escaped from the prison. But Icarus forgot his father's warning. He flew too high, and the hot sun melted the wax. Icarus was dashed to the earth and killed.

According to Greek legend, Minos kept a monstrous creature called the Minotaur in the labyrinth that Daedalus had built. The Minotaur was half man and half bull. He was worshiped as a god. Every year Minos commanded the Athenian king, Aegeus, to send seven maidens and seven youths to be sacrificed to the beast. One of the best-known myths is about the Greek hero Theseus, son of Aegeus. Theseus begged to be sent to Crete to battle the Minotaur in the labyrinth.

These myths and legends raced about in Evans' mind. He knew that there is often some truth in such tales. What if a labyrinth had existed? Who could be sure that there hadn't been a king named Minos? Evans returned again and again to a curious-looking mound of earth. Here and there, outcroppings of ruined stonework dotted the mound. It seemed to Evans that the mound was an artificial, rather than a natural, formation. Perhaps this was the place to begin a search for the past.

Evans bought the land from Crete, and in 1900 he began to dig. He expected little except a pleasant summer, with the possibility of finding more charms. By summer's end he expected that he would return to England. But forty years later Arthur Evans was still hard at work on Crete.

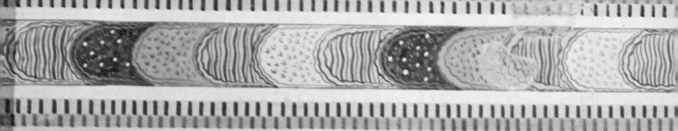

An Astounding Story

Almost with the first spade that was thrust into the earth, Arthur Evans shot back ten thousand years. When he realized that there was such wealth to be found in the earth, he gathered together a skilled team. The team changed often with the passing years, but there were always people with special knowledge of geology, art, architecture, and other fields to work with him.

A series of test pits were dug at different places on the site of the mound. The layers of earth in these pits could be read like a book by trained geologists. They would slowly be able to figure out how the layers were formed, why they differed from each other, and what natural and human events accounted for the changes.

The test pits told an astounding story. They showed immediately that the mound Evans had observed *was* artificial. The pits led Evans to believe that the site of Knossos, capital of Minos, had been continuously occupied for at least ten thousand years! The task at hand would not be to dig *into* the earth, but to peel back layers that had been built up by people for thousands of years.

The top layers of the pits, at a few feet below the surface, revealed objects of brilliant workmanship. Going on down the pit, other layers gave up pottery and utensils belonging to earlier periods. The items resembled objects painted on the walls of tombs and temples in Egypt. Since the ancient Egyptians left many dates and records,

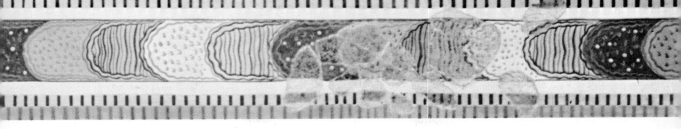

an approximate date for the pottery unearthed at Knossos could be found by comparing it with the pottery in the Egyptian wall paintings.

As layers of earth were peeled away, walls appeared close to the surface of the ground. Each basketful of earth was carefully sifted for gold beads, seals, rings, and other small objects. As the level of the earth became lower, the walls became higher. Soon it could be seen that Evans was excavating an immensely complex building. The twists and turns were labyrinthine. "This must be it!" gasped Evans. *"This must be the palace of Minos!"*

From time to time, clay tablets were unearthed. Some had pictographs, others had writing in an unknown language. It looked like writing that Evans had seen on seals on the Greek mainland. He knew that if he could understand the language, it might tell him everything he wanted to know about the mysteries of this civilization.

Fragments of frescoes once painted on plaster in glowing colors came to light. It would take time and great effort to put them together again. Carefully the pieces were lifted from their hiding places of centuries. Each piece was carefully cleaned. The room it came from was noted. Each room of the palace was given a name or a number for easy reference. Decorations on the painted fragments and examination of the bits of heads, arms, and legs told Evans that he had found an unknown civilization!

One of the most famous of all the frescoes at Knossos is known as *The Cupbearer.* Only fragments of the man's figure from the shoulders to below the waist were found, but the whole piece was put together as the experts thought it had originally been. The figure is life-sized and quite different looking from ancient Egyptians and Greeks. *The Cupbearer's* profile shows a straight nose, full lips, dark bright eyes, and a look of nobility. He wears a necklace, ear ornaments, and a bracelet. He carries a cup as an offering to the gods.

Parts of the *Bull-Jumping Fresco* were thrilling discoveries. Perhaps there was something to the legend of Theseus and the Minotaur! This fresco, painted by the ancient artists, shows slim, lifelike boy and girl acrobats grappling with fierce bulls. The acrobats call to mind the maidens and youths who were sacrificed to the Minotaur.

Myth Becomes Truth

Year after year of digging revealed a form of architecture which had never been seen before. Wood played an important part in the palace's construction. Once, in the dim past, Crete must have been well wooded. There was no doubt that the palace had been built upon the foundations of earlier structures, because changes from many periods had been made. The materials and techniques of these changes gave important clues to the time they occurred.

As each level was cleared and floors and ceilings propped up, an astounding building of at least five stories was revealed. Great light wells brought illumination to the lower levels. These light wells, centrally placed in the building, served to keep out the strong winds of winter.

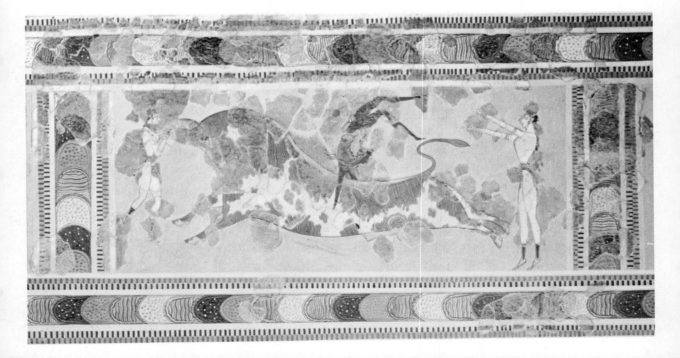

An incredibly modern way of life became evident. Pushing on, the diggers found that the palace had a servants' quarter, a throne room, storage rooms, and places for worship and bathing. Several altars were discovered, some with traces of offerings and the figurines of gods and goddesses on them. The symbol of the double ax seemed to mark royal property.

When the throne room was being excavated, traces of the outline of a wooden throne were found in what must have been its original position. A copy was made. The throne room in its restored magnificence is breathtaking. A short, crooked corridor leads off this room. It is believed to have led to the queen's apartments. Objects found in this section of the palace suggest that the queen lived in great style and cleanliness.

The palace boasted an amazingly modern drainage system. Water had been piped from natural springs on higher ground into bathrooms with elaborate baths of baked and glazed clay, beautifully designed and painted.

As the digging went on, evidence pointed to several sudden interruptions in the lives of the people. There were also signs that there had been a final, terrible disaster. The city of Knossos seems to have ceased to exist almost overnight. Artists' tools were found beside objects the artists had been making when disaster struck. There were signs that people had left household tasks, meals, and other things half finished. What had caused them to leave their homes so hurriedly, so unprepared? The reason for this sudden ending to a mighty civilization was hard to find.

Unanswered Questions

Evans feared that everything that he had unearthed might collapse unless he found a way to preserve his discoveries. He succeeded in developing a method never before employed in archaeology—the use of concrete to rebuild parts of the palace and to strengthen columns and floors. The floors at the top level of the palace were first spread with a layer of concrete. The ceilings of rooms below were thus protected and made firm. The workers moved from top to bottom, going down the stairs that had been uncovered.

Columns holding the stairs were checked for exact measurements and position. Every tiny detail of workmanship was noted and sketched. When the columns showed signs of fire or rot, they were replaced by concrete

and painted in the original colors. They looked almost exactly as they must have when Minos trod the stairway in the days of his glory.

In July 1926 the ground under Sir Arthur began to sway. He had been expecting something like this for years. The shocks grew steadily more severe. The earth began to shake, making dreadful sounds like the angry roaring of a bull! Sir Arthur, believing his new house would hold together, stayed where he was. He looked out toward the Palace of Minos and the city of Knossos.

Screams filled the darkness from a distance. A few houses collapsed, and badly damaged steeples toppled to the ground. People rushed wildly into the open spaces, frightened for their lives.

Finally the earth grew quiet. The reconstruction work had withstood the angry earth's attack. All was well at Knossos. Sir Arthur became convinced that earthquakes, together with fires, had been the main cause of the interruptions in the lives of the Minoans.

During 1935 and 1936 Sir Arthur was able to complete and publish the rest of his study of the Minoan civilization. But many questions remained unanswered. Who were these mysterious people? Where did they come from? Did they originate in North Africa as some scholars believed? Was an earthquake really the cause of their tragic fate, wiping them out overnight, or were they wiped out as the result of a great battle?

Scholars have figured out the meaning of some of the written records that were found, but these records merely listed items that were stored in the palace. So far there is no solution to the larger mysteries.

Perhaps we shall never be sure of the answers. We may never know where the Minoans came from or the true cause of their destruction. But people continue to explore, to question, and to work to find the truth.

Reflections

1. What was the great "wealth" mentioned in the second section of this article?
2. Describe the Minoan way of life, the people, and their customs. Since there were no cameras or tape recorders five thousand years ago, how can we know about the Minoans' way of life?
3. Why do you think we are interested in a vanished civilization today? What mysteries still remain about the Minoans?
4. Pretend you are a scientist from another planet. You arrive on Earth and find life totally destroyed. The only remnants of Earth's civilization that you can find are two pennies. Be a detective! Write a paper for a scientific journal describing everything you can deduce about Earth and its people from two pennies.

Finding the Past

Archeologists in their "digs" uncover the past, layer by layer, as they seek out the clues that ancient civilizations have left behind. **Divers** explore old wrecks lying on the ocean floor. **Geologists** explore the past when they investigate rock formations that give them the earth's own history. And **paleontologists** help trace the past when they bring to light the remains of ancient plants and animals.

(top) This archeologist is gently uncovering a fossil. The earth must be carefully scratched away and the fossil gently lifted from where it may have been lying for thousands, or even millions, of years. Below, a paleontologist examines a section of a skeleton. If enough other parts have been found, she will be able to put them together to reconstruct the whole animal.

477

The Subject Is People
MAY EDEL

People Are Different

When anthropologists look around at all the people of the world, they see many, many different ways of living. Some people live in tiny bands in forests or deserts. Other people live in teeming cities in thickly populated areas. Some groups are headed by warrior chiefs. In others, the priests are the chiefs. Some have no chiefs at all. There are vast empires with despotic rulers. There are tribes with councils in which everyone has a democratic voice.

There are places in the world where a man may marry many wives. There are some places where a woman has several husbands. Still other people are permitted by law to have only one mate at a time. Americans wheel babies about in baby carriages. Some people carry them in little net bags on their backs or strap them onto cradleboards. There are places where children are independent at the age of twelve, others where they must obey their fathers as long as their fathers are alive.

The differences between people are not limited just to things like language and government or ideas about children and education. They extend to the most ordinary details of everyday life.

Take a simple matter like sitting down. If you are tired, you will look about for the most comfortable chair you can find—one with cushions and arms, certainly one with a back to lean against. But members of the Bachiga tribe in Uganda would be very miserable in such a chair! They are relaxed and comfortable sitting on the ground, with

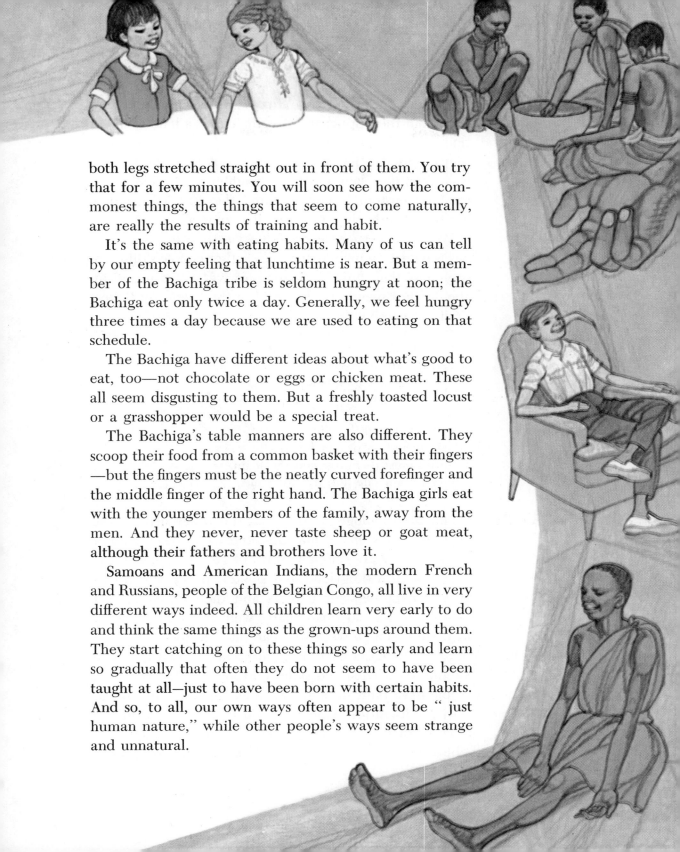

both legs stretched straight out in front of them. You try that for a few minutes. You will soon see how the commonest things, the things that seem to come naturally, are really the results of training and habit.

It's the same with eating habits. Many of us can tell by our empty feeling that lunchtime is near. But a member of the Bachiga tribe is seldom hungry at noon; the Bachiga eat only twice a day. Generally, we feel hungry three times a day because we are used to eating on that schedule.

The Bachiga have different ideas about what's good to eat, too—not chocolate or eggs or chicken meat. These all seem disgusting to them. But a freshly toasted locust or a grasshopper would be a special treat.

The Bachiga's table manners are also different. They scoop their food from a common basket with their fingers —but the fingers must be the neatly curved forefinger and the middle finger of the right hand. The Bachiga girls eat with the younger members of the family, away from the men. And they never, never taste sheep or goat meat, although their fathers and brothers love it.

Samoans and American Indians, the modern French and Russians, people of the Belgian Congo, all live in very different ways indeed. All children learn very early to do and think the same things as the grown-ups around them. They start catching on to these things so early and learn so gradually that often they do not seem to have been taught at all—just to have been born with certain habits. And so, to all, our own ways often appear to be " just human nature," while other people's ways seem strange and unnatural.

There is a tribe in Africa, for example, whose members knock out their upper front teeth. This is a kind of initiation into being a grown-up member of the tribe. Because they are used to it, they think they look much better that way. And they laugh at their neighbors who don't have the same custom. "Look at them," they say. "With those big front teeth, they look just like zebras!"

We are sometimes as prejudiced as that, too. We think our ways are "human nature" and other people's different ways less than human. Sometimes we are as mixed up about other people as the child in this poem by Robert Louis Stevenson.

> Little Indian, Sioux or Crow,
> Little frosty Eskimo,
> Little Turk or Japanese,
> O! don't you wish that you were me?
>
> You have curious things to eat,
> I am fed on proper meat;
> You must dwell beyond the foam,
> But I am safe and live at home.

The anthropologist looks at all this differently. These ways are all seen as human; otherwise they couldn't happen. They are different ways of getting along in the world, of providing food and shelter, peace and security and happiness for parents and their children. Not all ways of life do this equally well, but they must all do it well enough so people can manage to survive.

Anthropologists have a scientific name for the whole body of knowledge and skills, customs and habits which people have built up and by which they live and work. They call it *culture*. A people's culture includes all inventions, all their customs and practices, all the things they believe in—everything they have learned and pass on to their children. It includes government, art, religion, language, the way people make their living, and the way they act toward each other—even the way they express their feelings.

To the anthropologist, culture is not a jumble of queer customs. It is a whole way of life that people have built up over the hundreds of generations of their history. To understand it, anthropologists have to follow the course of human history and study the different conditions under which the people of the world have lived.

An Anthropologist at Work

I can give you some idea of how an anthropologist works by telling you what happened to me when I lived for a year among the Bachiga people of western Uganda. At that time the Bachiga people were still cut off from the modern world. Although Uganda was a British colony, there were no settlers or traders in this part of the country, only a few government officers and missionaries. There were people who had never seen a European. A few Bachiga, taught by missionaries, had learned to read and write their own language. Some of them had become Christians. But they knew very little of the outside world.

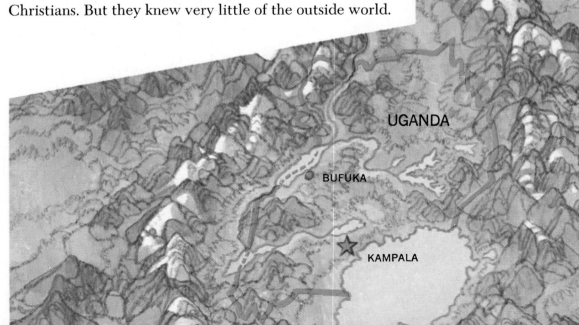

UGANDA

BUFUKA

KAMPALA

One young man who worked for me was a rare exception. He had traveled 250 miles to Kampala, the capital city of Uganda. And when he came home, even his own family thought he had become a terrible liar. He told unbelievable tales of water that ran from faucets, refrigerators, and shops with unheard-of things for sale.

The village of Bufuka, where I lived, still looked as Bachiga villages must have looked for many, many years. The grass-covered, dome-shaped huts, with their low, hooded doorways, were grouped in little clusters. Each cluster was surrounded by a hedge that formed a compound in which the cattle were kept at night. The huts were small, smoky, and dark, so in good weather everybody worked outside.

Most of the Bachiga people still dressed in cowskin and sheepskin cloaks and shirts. The tiny children wore just a grass band about their waists and perhaps a string of beads or a bracelet. Men and women alike wore their heads shaved, some with the hair all off, others with short tufts carved into swirling patterns. A few wore a more old-fashioned hairdo—heavy masses of long curls, lengthened with bits of string and decorated with beads.

The Bachiga were farmers. They grew a grain called millet for food, and their cows and sheep supplied them with clothing. They had little use for money, except for the taxes which the British government made them pay. They wanted very few store-bought goods—just soap, sometimes a blanket or two, and lengths of dull-colored cloth.

Before I could find out many of the things I wanted to know about the Bachiga people, I had to learn their language. Sometimes when you go on an expedition, you can get an interpreter to help you, but I wasn't so lucky. Only a handful of Bachiga spoke any English at all. In the beginning I did have one of them for a teacher, but for the most part I was on my own.

My next job was to win the people's confidence. I was far stranger to them than they were to me. The children were scared by the paleness of my skin and my strange clothes. They cried and ran away when I came near. At first the mothers shared their fears. They snatched up the babies and held them close while I was around. What was I doing there? How were they to be sure I meant them no harm?

Later on, when I had made many friends, they thought it was a great joke to look back at these fears and tell me about them. But in the beginning I had to work very slowly and carefully. There were even times when *I* was a little scared, myself. Late one night during my first weeks there, I heard a great din around my camp. When it turned out to be my household staff and some neighbors banging on my own pots and pans to drive away a prowling leopard from my tent, I was actually relieved.

Bufuka is a little village of about thirty-five adults, so I got to know all of them—their names, their daily round of work, their plans and problems. I attended the two weddings that took place while I was there and mourned with the women at a funeral. I talked with medicine men and priests about their work. One of them gave me a spirit horn to help me on my journey home, with careful instructions about how to feed and tend it.

My way of working was rather old-fashioned. At that time there were no tape recorders, which anthropologists

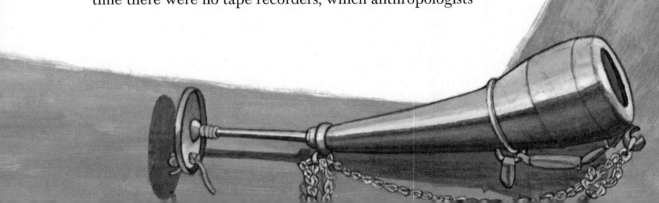

now use to bring back legends and stories and conversations. I did not even have a movie camera, which is of great scientific use. Movies and recordings can be rerun many times. Often you see and hear things you hadn't noticed the first time. Also, movies make records of things which are very hard to describe in words—dances, facial expressions, or how mothers handle their babies.

Today groups of workers often go out together. One member of the group may be a specialist in language, another in art or music; another may be more interested in different kinds of laws or tools. When groups of anthropologists work together, they can find out far more together than each person could discover alone.

Anthropologists are not interested in studying only those societies that are different from theirs. They are interested in *all humanity*. Anthropologists are trying to find out what makes Americans tick, just as they have tried to find out how and why Eskimos or East Africans live in the unique ways they do.

Reflections

1. Why was the child in Robert Louis Stevenson's poem "mixed up"? What do you think are some dangers of such beliefs?
2. What does the word *culture* mean? Do you think any one group of people can be "more cultured" than another? Explain.
3. How have anthropologists' methods changed since Dr. Edel's year with the people of Bufuka?
4. Why do you think anthropologists are interested in studying all societies?
5. What group of people would you be most interested in studying? Write a short essay explaining the reasons for your choice.

PATTERNS OF CULTURE

(bottom left) One of America's greatest anthropologists, Franz Boas believed that to really understand a culture, you had to live among its people. In this way he learned about their history, their customs, their art.

(top left) A student of Franz Boas, Dr. Ruth Benedict believed that the techniques of the anthropologist could be used to investigate modern cultures, too.

(top right) Margaret Mead was a student of both Boas and Benedict. She, too, spent many years living among people in remote villages. Here she is setting up a model of such a village for a museum exhibit.

485

How Ologbon-Ori Sought Wisdom

HAROLD COURLANDER

In a certain village there was a man named Ologbon-Ori. He himself had never been far from his village, but he had heard many travelers speak of the wonders and wisdom to be found in the outside world. Ologbon-Ori yearned to see what the world beyond the bush country was like and to obtain some of the wisdom that was to be found there. And one day after the yams had been harvested, he decided to go on a journey with his small son to find some of it.

Ologbon-Ori had things prepared. He and his son bathed and put on their finest clothes. He fed his camel and watered him. Then he mounted the camel and seated his boy behind him. His friends stood at the trail as he departed, wishing him a safe journey. Ologbon-Ori and his son rode away.

In time they came to a town. There were many buildings. Many women were going and coming with produce on their heads. In the distance there was the hum of the marketplace. Ologbon-Ori rode to where the trading was going on. He was amazed at so much activity. "See," he said to his son, "around us is wisdom in great quantities. Let us see; let us learn."

Ologbon-Ori watched all the goings-on with fascination. But soon he noticed that people were pointing at him and making comments. He listened.

"What kind of man is this?" he heard someone say. "He makes his half-starved camel carry two persons."

Someone else said: "Yes, he must come from the bush country. He has no feelings. See how exhausted his camel is."

When he had passed through the town, Ologbon-Ori said to his son: "You see, there are things to be learned in the world. I had not known it before, but a camel should not carry two people. So dismount, my son, and walk alongside."

The boy dismounted. He walked while his father rode. And in time they came to another town. As they passed through it, Ologbon-Ori marveled at the sights. But again he saw people pointing at him and making comments.

He heard one man say: "See how the father rides while he makes the small child walk. Can such a man have a heart?"

Another said: "Yes, it is so. Why should a strong man treat a boy this way?"

A third man said: "He rides as though he were an Oba and the little one his slave."

Ologbon-Ori was troubled. He stopped, saying, "The knowledge of the world is hard to learn. How could we have gotten wisdom like this in our village?"

He dismounted and put his boy on the camel. The boy rode, and the father walked, and in this manner they came to the next town. It also was full of wonders. But once again Ologbon-Ori noticed that people were talking about him.

"What is everything coming to," one man said, "when the young ride and the old must walk?"

"Yes," another said, "is there no respect any more for the aged? Since when does a child go in comfort while his father's feet are covered with dust?"

This time Ologbon-Ori was greatly perplexed. He thought about it deeply. At last he said: "There is much to learn in the outside world, things we never dreamed of in the village. How lucky we are to have made this journey. It is clear that neither of us may ride the camel, else shame comes on one or the other. Let us walk, therefore, the father and son side by side."

So, walking together and leading the camel by its halter, they arrived in the fourth town, intrigued by the wonders around them. But as it was before, so it was again. People pointed, laughed, and made remarks.

One said: "Look. A man, a boy, and a camel, walking together like friends."

Another said: "Whenever before has anyone seen such idiots? They are footsore and tired, yet they walk. Why don't they mount that camel and ride like any sensible people would do?"

This time when Ologbon-Ori stopped to consider the matter, he remained in thought a long while. At last he said: "I believe our journey has come to an end. We have learned a great thing—that the wisdom of one town is the stupidity of another. Whatever a man does to please someone will surely annoy others. Let us mount. Let us ride. Let us return whence we came." They mounted and rode back to their village in the bush country.

When they arrived, Ologbon-Ori's friends stood at the trail to greet him. They asked: "Where is it? Where is the wisdom of the world?"

Ologbon-Ori replied: "There is much wisdom to be found. I have returned with only a small portion of it. It is this:

"'Seek wisdom, but do not throw away common sense.'"

Reflections

1. This story from Africa is similar to one told in Greece. How might it happen that two very old stories from widely separated regions could be so much alike?
2. Ologbon-Ori says, "Whatever a man does to please someone will surely annoy others." Write a story using an example from your own experience to show the truth of this statement.

Post Early for Space

PETER J. HENNIKER HEATON

Once we were wayfarers, then seafarers
    then airfarers;
We shall be spacefarers soon;
Not voyaging from city to city or from
    coast to coast,
But from planet to planet and from moon to moon.

This is no fanciful flight of imagination,
No strange, incredible, utterly different thing;
It will come by obstinate thought and calculation
And the old resolve to spread an expanding wing.

We shall see homes established on distant planets,
Friends departing to take up a post on Mars;
They will have perils to meet,
    but they will meet them,
As the early settlers did on American shores.

We shall buy tickets later, as now we buy them
For a foreign vacation, reserve our seat or berth,
Then spending a holiday month on a
    moon of Saturn,
Look tenderly back to our little shining Earth.

And those who decide they will not make
    the journey
Will remember a son up there or a favorite niece,
Eagerly awaiting news from the old home-planet,
And will scribble a line to catch the post for space.

Adventure in the Outer World

SUZANNE MARTEL

Luke Goes Adventuring

"We mustn't be seen!"

The two boys looked cautiously around. Before them the white marble tunnel stretched far into the distance, bathed in a silvery light. People seldom ventured to this part of the underground city. It was too near the surface. Besides, the express trains did not stop there—which explained why Luke and Eric had traveled the last mile on the moving sidewalk.

Endlessly, noiselessly, the sidewalks glided along, side by side, one going north and the other south. Marking time on the sidewalk, the two friends slowed down, waiting for the moment when the north- and southbound expresses would pass each other and give them their opportunity.

"Here they come!" The expresses sped along at eye level, each with ten cars enclosed in a plastic tube. Three seconds later they passed. Fortunately for the boys, they were both empty, and the boys were not seen. Excursions in this part of the city would be thought suspicious.

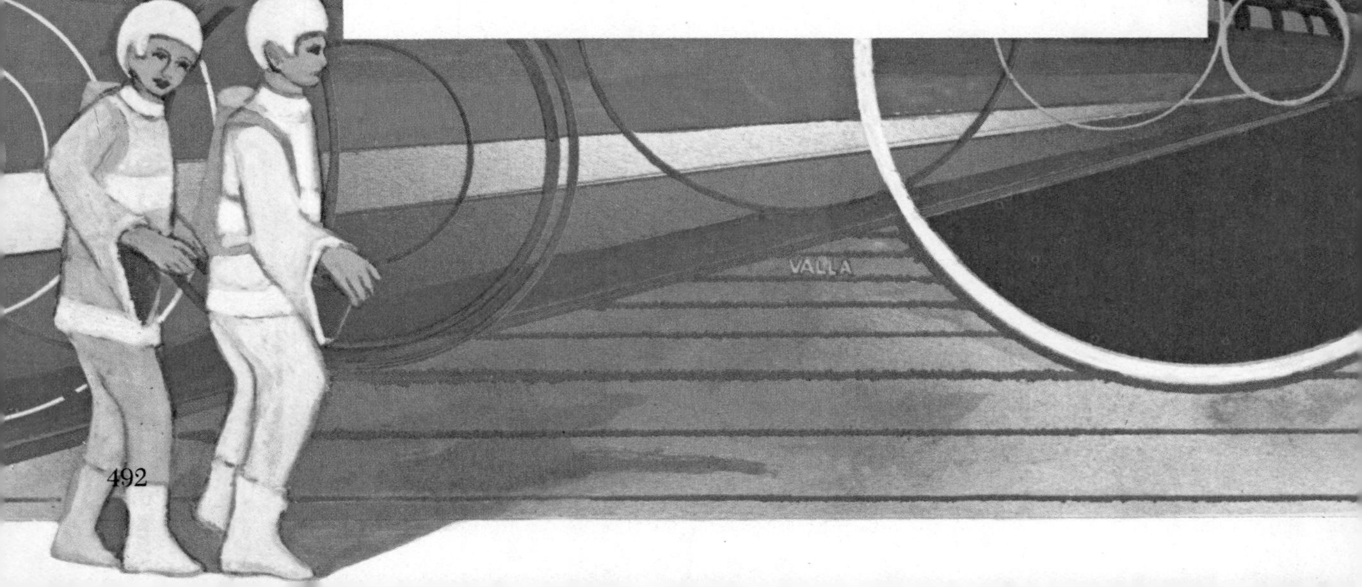

"Let's go."

Luke leaped down the marble steps, Eric behind him, and they ran at top speed down the platform. To their right was a narrow gallery barricaded at the far end by a locked gate. A complicated alarm system would alert the city immediately if invaders approached or even if some ill-advised person wanted to flee the safety of the underground city to brave the dangers outside.

In the centuries-old history of Surréal, only four men had ever illegally tried to get through the boundary gate. They had been caught, judged insane, and put into an asylum. Nothing had ever been heard of them again.

His heart thudding, Luke moved cautiously toward the gate, stopping a few feet from the electric eye which could detect his presence and set off the alarm. Ever since he was a little boy, this gate had fascinated him. Lately its spell had been so powerful that he had found himself heading for the boundary every day after school.

That is how he had discovered the secret passage and started his great adventure. He had told no one except his best friend, Eric 6 B 12.

They reached the spot where the marble slabs of the wall had split apart, leaving a narrow opening. A month earlier, Surréal had been shaken by an earthquake which had terrified the inhabitants and caused a power failure.

The synthetic air system, the very lifeblood of the city, went out of action. Things were so serious that the auxiliary motors took over for nearly twelve minutes.

Thanks to reassuring broadcasts from the Great Council, there had been little panic. Later the leaders assured the people that the seismographic instruments did not predict any future quakes. There was no need to worry. The great motors, which had worked uninterruptedly for many centuries, were running again.

But since that day the electric power had seemed weaker. At times the lights flickered and dimmed, and the moving sidewalks slowed down. As a precaution, emergency kits had been issued. Luke and Eric were wearing theirs now, light plastic tubes slung over their shoulders, each containing a gas mask and a ray helmet.

By a strange coincidence, the apparatus which was meant to help him survive under the earth was the very thing that had encouraged Luke to explore the mysteries of the outer world. Without his ray helmet he would never have dared to crawl into that pitch-black opening in the rock. Nor would he have risked the poisonous air thought to be at the surface without his gas mask.

Now he squeezed through the opening on all fours, scrambling to his feet after a few yards. Eric watched him wide-eyed, too frightened to follow.

"Hurry up, can't you?" Luke called back. "Do you want to set off the alarm?"

"I'm scared!"

Luke was merciless. "You promised to come—so *come*."

Reluctantly Eric wriggled into the dark hole. His schoolbag scraped the low ceiling, his knee became entangled in his emergency kit, and his white tunic caught on a jagged bit of rock. But Luke's calm voice reassured him.

During his daily expeditions, Luke had discovered the quickest way of getting ready. Squatting, he opened his plastic tube and put on the little white skull cap. He turned a big button on the front, and a light ray shot out, generated by his brain waves. Then he pulled a glazed mask over his forehead. It covered his nose and mouth and could provide him with enough air for six hours.

"Get ready, Eric."

Eric hung back. Like all the youngsters of Surréal, he had tried on the helmet and gas mask for fun, but he had never really expected to need them. He put the helmet on, fiddled with the button for a few seconds, and produced a ray of light.

"It's working," Luke said and grinned. "So you obviously have a brain of some kind."

Eric was adjusting the strap of his mask when Luke caught him by the arm. "First you must swear not to reveal my secret. I haven't said a word to anyone, not even my brother, Paul."

"Don't worry—I promise."

Satisfied, Luke nodded. "Now listen," he said. "I promise you there won't be the slightest danger."

"But how do you *know?*"

"Because I've proved it," Luke said confidently. "I've been coming here every day for a week, and you can see how alive I am." Taking off his schoolbag, he propped it against the wall. Under the dicta-vision rolls which contained his homework assignment, he had hidden four polythene bags. He began to cover Eric's sandals with them, tying them on with string.

"You think of everything," Eric said admiringly.

"Well, we can't take any chances," Luke said, quickly covering his own sandals. "We mustn't attract attention when we get back." In the spotless city, dusty or muddy shoes would certainly cause a sensation.

In the Outer World

Pulling Eric by the hand, Luke plunged along the narrow tunnel. To encourage his friend, he went on talking, his voice stifled by his mask. "You're going to see some real wonders. It's not a bit like they describe it in those old blue books or on the vista-screen. Outer space is wide and blue. The astral sun warms your hands, and the ground is covered with green vegetation."

The tunnel sloped upward, scarcely wide enough for the boys to get through. The climb became more and more steep. As they turned a corner, the passage opened out into a wider gallery, and a waft of cold air hit them in the face. The walls, oozing humidity, were covered with slimy moss. Eric drew back again. "What about those poisonous gases at the surface?"

Luke laughed. "That's nonsense—there aren't any. They died away years ago."

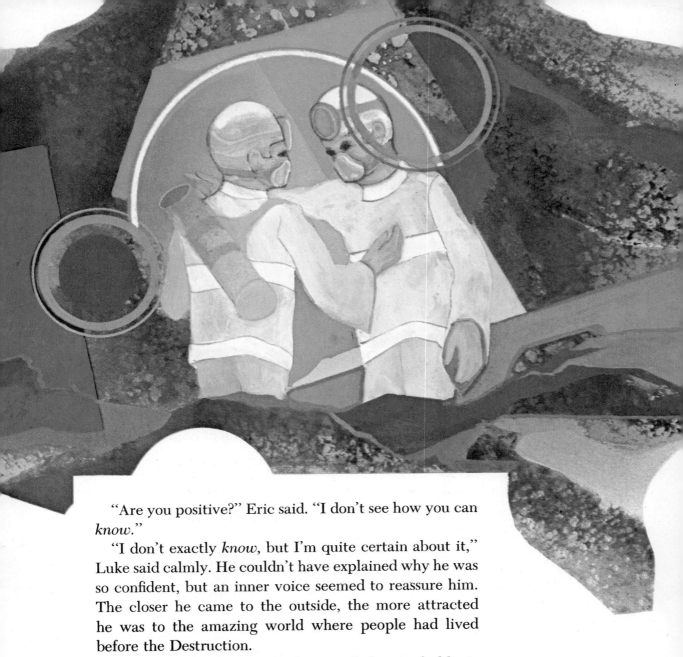

"Are you positive?" Eric said. "I don't see how you can *know*."

"I don't exactly *know*, but I'm quite certain about it," Luke said calmly. He couldn't have explained why he was so confident, but an inner voice seemed to reassure him. The closer he came to the outside, the more attracted he was to the amazing world where people had lived before the Destruction.

They plodded on, their light rays flickering feebly in the daylight. Near the exit Eric stopped short. "This must be the entrance to the old city," he said, awed.

Luke nodded. "The earthquake must have opened the passage to the boundary gate."

"Whatever made you go into the rock all by yourself?" Eric said. He had never suspected that his quiet friend could be so adventurous. Brought up in closed space, Eric didn't know what it was to suffer from claustrophobia, so he had no fear of the tunnel. But like all the youngsters of Surréal, he was terrified of the unknown.

Luke considered. "It was as if a voice were calling me," he said slowly. Looking at it through his friend's eyes, it was difficult to explain why his first expedition had seemed so natural, almost instinctive.

"It's getting cold!" Eric said, and his teeth began to chatter. Used to the uniform temperature of Surréal, he reacted quickly to the change in the atmosphere. But Luke only grinned. "Stop grumbling, can't you?" he said. "You'll be warm enough soon—maybe even a bit *too* warm."

Luke's words made Eric shudder. Hadn't he always been told that the outer world was full of poisonous gases and dangers? During the Great Destruction the entire earth had been ravaged—people, animals, and plants.

Only those who had taken refuge in the caverns under Mount Royal had been saved. A few people, foreseeing the disaster, had prepared a shelter many years before. These fortunate ones, only a few hundred, had sealed the leaden gates behind them and built a city. Above them the civilized world had perished, destroyed by the stupidity of people.

"What's that?" A strange noise, like the sound of an underground waterfall, brought them to a halt.

Even Luke was uneasy. "I don't know," he admitted. "I've never heard it before—wait here a minute." Cautiously he moved ahead to the mouth of the tunnel and stopped, startled. A little waterfall veiled the entrance, splashing softly and monotonously on the rocky floor.

When he poked his head out, he could see nothing but water falling from the sky.

Eric had no intention of being left alone in this unknown place. Hurrying after Luke, he joined him at the opening and peered through the water. "Where's all this water coming from?" he asked, leaning out of the opening and trying to see ahead. "How wet and vast it looks out here!" The first glimpse of the outside world dismayed him. Unaccustomed to long distances, his eyes could not focus properly. "I don't see any blue or green—and I'm certainly not warm yet!"

Luke seemed thunderstruck. He tried to see this way and that, but the outside world seemed one big waterfall. "I don't understand it," he muttered, brushing his wet face with his hand. Where before he had seen the sun shining in a blue sky, he saw nothing but low clouds with water pouring from them. And the trees and mountains were hidden in mist.

"This must be the atmospheric phenomenon called *rain*," Eric said learnedly. "It tells about it in the science books." He shivered. "If we catch cold, the health inspector will want to know where we've been. We'd better go back." This wet, gray land was disappointing after Luke's glowing descriptions. It wasn't worth risking the penalties of the Great Council. But he didn't want to upset Luke, so he added halfheartedly, "We can come back some other time."

Luke said nothing as they turned back into the depths of the earth, making their way toward the bright, familiar world of Surréal. His heart was heavy; he felt betrayed by this Nature whom he had been so ready to love. He had so wanted to share its beauties with Eric. But perhaps he was doomed to be forever friendless in the outer world.

Luke in the Forest

The next afternoon, right after school, Luke again made his way to the open air—to the edge of the fascinating outer world. Today the sky was heavy, but no rain was falling. He could see the edge of the forest a hundred feet below him at the foot of the mountain. The grayness reassured him more than the vivid blues and greens of his earlier expeditions. The sun did not shoot out menacing rays, the rain did not chill him, and mist shrouded the frighteningly wide horizon.

Ideal weather for an underground boy! Luke decided to venture beyond the safe threshold of the tunnel. He took a few shaky steps on the steep slope. Pebbles flew out from under his feet, and, unaccustomed to rough ground, he lost his balance and rolled to the bottom of the hill.

Looking dizzily around, he saw that he had landed near those tall, sharp-needled trees that the ancient botany books called *pines*. Putting his hand to his face, he made sure that his gas mask was secure. Picking up his ray helmet, he put it back into its plastic tube. Then he started off, taking cautious little steps and stopping every minute to consider something new. The song of a bird enchanted him, and the bird's rapid flight was even more marvelous. The deep silence of the natural world amazed him after the mechanical sounds of a world run by motors. His sandals trod lightly on the spongy earth of the pine forest. He touched the rough bark of a tree and blackened his finger in the shining gum.

Suddenly a savage-sounding cry reached his ears and froze him with fright. "Who lives on the surface of the earth? What terrible danger lurks near?" Luke was not accustomed to wide spaces, and his senses could not determine the source of the howl. He suddenly realized how far he had traveled from his protective cave. Would he perish alone without anyone ever knowing what became of him?

Luke heard sounds coming closer, branches crackling underfoot—and suddenly a great furry beast threw himself on the terrified boy and rolled him over. A long tail thrashed menacingly in the air, and a hot tongue licked his cheek. His eyes closed, and Luke waited for death.

But suddenly, from where he did not know, a feeling of security came over him. He had been terrified at first, but now he felt calm. He opened his eyes and lifted up his head as the enemy leaned over him, panting, its long tongue hanging out, its silky ears framing a long-nosed face—and its dangerous tail thrashing about.

"Don't be frightened!"

"I'm *not* frightened." Luke answered as if it were perfectly natural for someone in this supposedly uninhabited world to start a conversation with him.

"Your *thoughts* are frightened, though. I felt them!"

Luke looked at the great beast sitting beside him. "Then you must also know that by now I've stopped being frightened."

"Where are you?" asked the voice. "I don't see you anywhere."

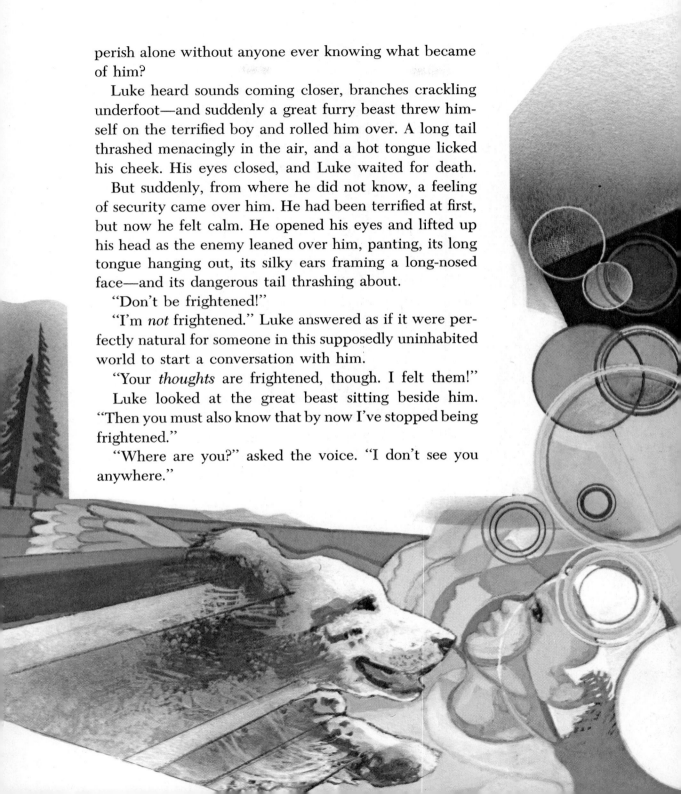

Luke snorted. "I'm here in front of you—are you blind?" He was almost ready to sympathize with this furry creature with a constantly moving tail who could not see something right under his nose. He continued questioning it. "Are there a lot of you on earth—where do you live?"

A shriek of laughter just behind him made him scramble to his feet, ready for a new attack. But there was no enemy facing him. Instead, he saw a girl as tall as himself, dressed in brown homespun, and with long red hair. She was shaking with gay but mocking laughter.

"You were talking to Bark, but he can't very well answer you."

"He was very polite, though," Luke said, annoyed as the creature bounded over to the newcomer and licked her hand.

"How funny you are," the girl said. "You have no hair, and you are wearing a mask. Did you come from the moon?"

Luke was too dumbfounded to answer. This was an astonishing moment. All the theories he had been taught since babyhood were turning out to be wrong. A world supposed to be deserted and scorched was inhabited.

Animals roamed through it, and human beings walked in its green forests.

But the girl's superior tone annoyed him, so he turned to his four-footed listener again. "Do you belong to the wolf family?" he asked politely. "Like Red Riding Hood's attacker?" Luke had a feeling that he was being rather tactless in reminding Bark of his wicked ancestor, but he wanted to show off his literary knowledge.

"He won't answer you, you know," the girl said. "He's my dog, Bark." And, as if in agreement, the dog barked shortly.

"That's what *you* think. As a matter of fact, Bark and I had a very nice chat—before you came along."

The girl shook her head. "No, you didn't! I was the one who was communicating with you. We are exchanging ideas by telepathy."

Luke, a child of the ultramodern age, was immediately interested. "Show me your apparatus, then," he said—and frowned as the girl laughed at him again.

"There isn't any apparatus. My ideas simply flash to your brain, and yours answer them. You ought to understand because you're a telepathist yourself—and quite a good one. You communicate very clearly, even from far away."

Luke flushed with pride. Nothing would have made him admit that he didn't know anything about telepathy. He was a telepathist, she said. And a good one! This strange girl was admiring him, and he certainly wasn't going to spoil it by admitting the truth.

"What's more," the girl said, dropping down beside him on the grass, "we don't even speak the same language." And for the first time Luke realized that this was true. When the girl spoke aloud, strange sounds came out of her mouth. They reminded him of the dead languages studied by his brother, Paul. But fortunately, thanks to telepathy, they could communicate even through the language barrier.

The girl flashed a friendly smile. "My name's Agatha. What's yours?"

"Luke 15 P 9. And I live in Surréal, under the mountain." He pointed to Mount Royal and the opening to the tunnel.

Agatha accepted this calmly. "I live behind the mountain myself, on the bank of the river. Our tribe settled Laurania." She leaned forward curiously. "Why are you wearing that mask? And what are you doing in these woods? Bark and I often come here, but we've never seen you before."

"This is the first time I've come down the mountain," Luke said, without telling her how he had managed it. He didn't like to explain that he was wearing a mask because the open air was poisonous. He felt that such a remark might hurt her feelings. "I'm used to synthetic air—that's why I wear a mask. Now tell me what you're doing so far from your home."

"My father and brother went out hunting, and I decided to pick some blueberries." She ran to the edge of the forest and came back, holding a leather pouch full of tiny bluish globules. "Here, do you want some?"

Luke took one courteously. Raising his mask, he gulped it down the way he gulped his tea pill.

"Go on," Agatha urged, "have some more."

"No thanks. It's not good to take more than one pill."

Agatha shrugged and went on eating berries until her mouth was stained blue. Luke was curious; he had always enjoyed getting to the bottom of things. Now he wanted to know all about these strange capsules.

"Do you find these capsules ready-made?" he asked eagerly. What a great find his discovery would be for the dietetic service! Before she could answer, he demanded, "Is that all you eat?"

Agatha stared at him, amazed. "Why no, of course not! We eat the game we catch and fish from the river—and bread, naturally."

"*Bread*? What's that?"

Agatha took a piece of bread out of her pocket, divided it into two, and gave half to Luke. He examined the dry crust and tender white crumbs.

"That's my snack," Agatha said, biting into it with her shining teeth. And Luke, who had never seen anyone eat so much in his life, feared for her health.

Always adventurous, he risked nibbling the slice of dough. But first he asked, "What's it made of?"

"It's made of flour."

"Flour? Where do you get that from?"

"From wheat! Don't you know anything?"

Luke reddened; he did not realize that what he *did* know would amaze this strange girl far more than what he *didn't* know. To hide his embarrassment, he changed the subject. "Is that a hat, that fur stuff you're wearing?"

Agatha put a hand to her head as if to find out. "Of course not," she said. "Can't you see I'm bareheaded?"

Luke began to remember his ancient history. "Then it must be fur like the skins our ancestors used to wear."

But Agatha shook her head. "You really don't know much, I see," she said. "This is *hair*." And she shook her magnificent red mop.

Luke stared at it, marveling. "Don't you—don't you ever take it off, even when you go to bed?"

Agatha smiled. "No, never. Not even on hot days in the summertime."

"It must be very hot," Luke sympathized. Actually, though it was certainly strange, he found this decoration rather pretty.

"It's no hotter than your mask."

She pointed at the dog, then, and the two friends watched Bark; he was running around, looking for a scent, drunk with space and freedom.

Different Worlds

"You live *under* the mountain?" Agatha said, as if the strangeness of such an idea had just struck her. "Under the *earth?*"

For a long time the two youngsters sat under the pines comparing their different ways of life—the scientific knowledge of Surréal, with all its restrictions, and the simplicity and freedom of Laurania. Luke told her about the origin of his people, about the Great Destruction, and how the refugees from the mountain had built a magnificent underground city. He had learned all this during his childhood, and, like a true patriot, he was quite proud of his country.

Agatha's story was simpler. She could remember only a legend about a fiery disaster and a terrible plague; it had been handed down by word of mouth. "The survivors made their homes in the devastated lands," she explained. "First they lived like animals. Then they formed bands and began to live in tribes so that they could help one another in storms and against diseases and wild animals."

"Are there many tribes like yours?" Luke asked.

Agatha considered. "Our bravest people, those who have been on long journeys, say there is a group living near the mouth of three rivers, south of here. And there may be others on a big cape, far down the river."

They didn't always understand each other clearly. Telepathy could not always cross the language barrier, and Luke's technical terms were as difficult to explain as the natural wonders that Agatha described. But the youngsters trusted each other and accepted the most surprising ideas quite calmly.

Agatha, a child of nature, could not understand how the subterranean people could be so resigned. "Hasn't anyone ever tried to get out?" she asked.

"Yes. Twice they even managed to make an opening to the outside."

"And then?" It all seemed so simple to this child of the sun.

"Well, the first time the ice-ax started a waterfall. The men were drowned, and part of the city was flooded."

"They must have been chopping under the river," Agatha said logically. "What happened the next time?"

"The next time, our Great Council studied the problem thoroughly in advance. They opened the leaden boundary gate, and volunteers went through it. They had to break through a wall of ice and snow; the air froze their lungs, and they heard the wind blowing. The Council decided that a new glacial age had begun and that the surface of the earth was uninhabitable. So everyone calmed down, and they locked the leaden gates again."

"What bad luck," Agatha said. "They must have been digging during a winter storm! Hasn't anyone tried since?"

"Not that I know of."

"Well, what made *you* come out?"

"Oh, that was just chance!" A modest boy, Luke did not want to boast. "I happened to find an opening. And I—I felt *drawn*."

"That was probably me calling you," Agatha said wisely. "I often come to this spot with Bark—and I've often wished for a friend." Gentle and more intelligent than the other children of her tribe, Agatha did not care for their primitive and noisy pastimes.

"Are there lions and tigers in these forests?" Luke asked, remembering his prehistory lessons.

Agatha shook her head. "I've never heard of any. But there are wolves and bears—and sometimes a puma."

"Aren't you afraid?" Luke, in turn, was admiring.

"No. Bark looks after me."

Just then a soft buzz from Luke's watch-radio signaled that his brother wanted to talk to him. He held the watch to his ear and heard a faint voice. "You'd better hurry home if you want to get here before the curfew!"

Luke pressed the tiny emission button twice as a sign that he had understood. He didn't want to start a conversation which would betray how far away he was.

Agatha looked interestedly at the watch. "What a funny talking bracelet! What did it say?"

"It was my brother, warning me to come home. But you were near me—couldn't you hear him?"

"Yes, quite plainly—but he was speaking to you in a foreign language."

"The same as mine," Luke said.

"Well, I couldn't understand it," Agatha said. "And, of course, your brother is not telepathic."

Luke was surprised. "Isn't everyone?" He had not realized that he possessed an exclusive talent.

His friend chuckled. "Of course not. Only a few people—I'm the only one in my family. It's a rare gift, and we don't know much about it yet. Are there many other telepathists in Surréal?"

"I've never heard of any at all," Luke answered in all honesty. A few minutes ago, he thought, he hadn't known anything about telepathy himself.

In the distance a musical sound echoed through the forest. Bark replied with a deep baying. A deep horn was blowing.

"It's the hunters coming home. I'll have to join them," Agatha said. "I'll see you tomorrow, Luke." To seal the pact, they shook hands; then each started on the path home, happy in the secret of their new friendship.

Reflections

1. How did Luke and Eric get to the outer world without being caught?

2. Using details from the story, tell what you think happened to the world as we know it.

3. Describe what you think is the everyday life of a youngster in Surréal.

4. If you were a telepathist, how do you think your life would be changed?

5. If your were Luke, would you try to get Agatha to come to Surréal? Explain why or why not.

6. Write a story about the next visit Luke takes to the outside world. Use your imagination!

PLANNING THE FUTURE

Do you live in or near a city? Can you think of things that need improving there? Is the air clean? Is it quiet, or is there too much noise? Is there convenient transportation? Are the houses comfortable to live in? Are they attractive to look at? Is there a park nearby?

These are some of the questions city planners ask. They study the needs of a community. They examine its resources. Then they draw up plans based on the amount of money the community wishes to spend.

There are many different kinds of work in this field. **Construction workers** put up buildings planned by **architects**. **Horticulturalists** follow the plans of **landscape architects** as they plant trees, shrubs, and flowers in a new park. **Traffic engineers** draw up plans for roads and subways. They put up street lights to provide safe crossings and still keep traffic moving. **Sanitary engineers** draw up plans for water and sewage disposal. The better the planning, the better and more beautiful your city will be.

THREE CITIES FOR TOMORROW

Brasília, Brazil

In 1960 Brasília replaced Río de Janeiro as the capital of Brazil. Work on this planned city started in the late 1950's and is still going on. An artificial lake borders much of the city. Note the modern design of the buildings, such as the Palace of the Congress and Senate (page 515, bottom left) and those in the background (page 515, bottom right). Behind the statue, *The Warriors* by Bruno Giorgi (page 515, top left), can be seen the Supreme Court and the museum.

Reston, Virginia

The planned community of Reston, Virginia, built in the 1960's, is neither city nor country. It includes the best parts of both types of places. The artificial lake provides recreation for all. Pedestrian malls (page 517, bottom left and top right) make cars unnecessary. High-rise apartments and single-family homes are within walking distance of the downtown area.

Islamabad, Pakistan

Islamabad, the capital of Pakistan, will be in the process of construction for many years to come. Built on hilly land a few miles north of what had been the provisional capital, Rawalpindi, the future may see the two cities joined as one. Many new government buildings are already completed and being used (page 519, bottom). And many of Islamabad's residents live in government housing (this page, bottom, and page 519, top left).

FITTING PARTS INTO A WHOLE

Meaning is a word that has many, many meanings! You know that one thing that is stressed in your study of reading is the meaning of words. Another important thing is the total meaning of a poem, a story, or an essay. The meaning of a title is important. The meaning of ideas is important. Read the following paragraph.

To see the earth as it truly is, small, blue, and beautiful in that eternal silence where it floats, is to see ourselves as riders on the earth together, brothers on that bright loveliness in the eternal cold—brothers who know they are truly brothers.

This paragraph was written by a famous poet, Archibald MacLeish. Mr. MacLeish wrote this paragraph shortly after the first American astronauts walked on the moon. He wrote it after he had seen a photograph taken of the earth from the moon. What do you think this paragraph by Mr. MacLeish means?

Meaning in Unit 1

Skim through Unit 1, "Language in Orbit." Think of the places mentioned in the unit. Is language something that ties the people of the earth together? Or does it separate the people of the earth? Does language promote friendship between people? Does the fact that William Jones, a man who lived long ago, discovered how to relate one language to others help us today? Does the work of a scientist like Von Frisch, who studied the "language" of the bees, in some way suggest, too, that bees, along with people, are riders on the earth?

Meaning in Unit 2

Turn back to the Table of Contents on pages 8 to 13. Tell why you think "All of Your Dreams" was chosen as the title of Unit 2. Does "The Dream Keeper" by Langston Hughes fit into a book called *Riders on the Earth?* How does the theme of the novel *The Forgotten Door* suggest that people are riders on the earth? Think about all the different kinds of people who ride on the earth. Do you think there are riders on other planets? What do you think they would think of us and our world?

Meaning in Unit 3

Does Unit 3, "The Nebulous Deep," add meaning to the title *Riders on the Earth?* Do the waters of the great oceans bring people and their various civilizations together——or do the waters only serve to separate people from each other? How can people work together to use the waters of the sea intelligently? Are whales and other sea animals also riders on the earth? What does the story of Poseidon suggest about the Greeks? How are people like Jacques-Yves Cousteau and Sylvia Earle helping us to ride the earth?

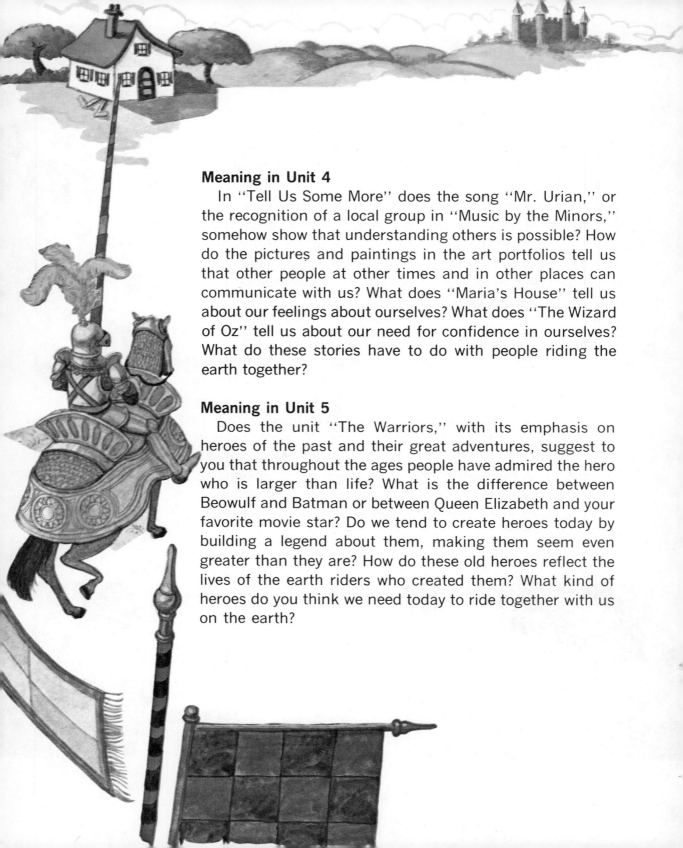

Meaning in Unit 4

In "Tell Us Some More" does the song "Mr. Urian," or the recognition of a local group in "Music by the Minors," somehow show that understanding others is possible? How do the pictures and paintings in the art portfolios tell us that other people at other times and in other places can communicate with us? What does "Maria's House" tell us about our feelings about ourselves? What does "The Wizard of Oz" tell us about our need for confidence in ourselves? What do these stories have to do with people riding the earth together?

Meaning in Unit 5

Does the unit "The Warriors," with its emphasis on heroes of the past and their great adventures, suggest to you that throughout the ages people have admired the hero who is larger than life? What is the difference between Beowulf and Batman or between Queen Elizabeth and your favorite movie star? Do we tend to create heroes today by building a legend about them, making them seem even greater than they are? How do these old heroes reflect the lives of the earth riders who created them? What kind of heroes do you think we need today to ride together with us on the earth?

Meaning in Unit 6

Does Unit 6, "Ages Far Away," suggest both past and future to you? In Louis Untermeyer's story about a boy and his dog in Pompeii, is there a message that a child and a dog today might find? Do people's loyalties remain the same, whether in the past or the present? How does this story relate to "Adventure in the Outer World"? Does the last story have a suggestion that without friendship among people, a disaster may occur? What is there in "The Secrets of Minos," with its emphasis on archaeology, to suggest that a study of the past has something to do with what we do today? Does it make a difference that the people of ancient Crete rode our earth?

Either attack or defend this statement: *Riders on the Earth* is a good title for this reader. Give your reasons.

Meaning in the Whole

Meaning may refer to many things. In one sense of the word, *meaning* summarizes and relates all the parts and pieces of one particular thing into a whole. Here, *meaning* has referred to your total experience in reading the whole book. You need to organize your thinking, to summarize, to state your views briefly and clearly when you describe the meaning of a whole book. You will be asked to do this many times. You should try to see the big picture, the whole experience, as one, although the one may have many parts.

Write a page or so on "What *Riders on the Earth* Means to Me." See how your views are similar to or different from those of your classmates.

Glossary

FULL PRONUNCIATION KEY

The pronunciation of each word is shown just after the word, in this way: **ab·bre·vi·ate** (ə brē′ vē āt).

The letters and signs used are pronounced as in the words below.

The mark ′ is placed after a syllable with primary or heavy accent, as in the example above.

The mark ′ after a syllable shows a secondary or lighter accent, as in **ab·bre·vi·a·tion** (ə brē′ vē ā′ shən).

a	hat	i	it	p	paper	v	very
ā	age	ī	ice	r	run	w	will
ä	father			s	say	y	young
		j	jam	sh	she	z	zero
b	bad	k	kind	t	tell	zh	measure
ch	child	l	land	th	thin		
d	did	m	me	ŦH	then		
		n	no			ə	represents:
e	let	ng	long	u	cup		a in about
ē	equal			u̇	full		e in taken
ėr	term	o	hot	ü	rule		i in pencil
		ō	open				o in lemon
f	fat	ô	order				u in circus
g	go	oi	oil				
h	he	ou	house				

The pronunciation key, syllable breaks, and phonetic respellings in this glossary are adapted from the second edition of the *Thorndike Barnhart Intermediate Dictionary*. Users of previous editions or of other dictionaries will find other symbols for some words.

ab·hor (ab hôr′)   to hate very much

ab·rupt·ly (ə brupt′ lē)   very suddenly

ab·stract (ab′ strakt)   not representing any real or concrete object

ac·cept (ak sept′)   to take what one is given; to agree to

ac·com·plice (ə kom′ plis)   helper, usually someone who helps one commit a crime

ac·com·plish (ə kom′ plish)   to do; to complete something hard to do

ac·cuse (ə kyūz′)   to say that someone has done something bad

ad·just (ə just′)   to change behavior in order to fit something

ad·o·les·cent (ad′ l es′ nt)   growing up from a child to an adult; youthful

a·dopt (ə dopt′)   to take for one's own

ad·vanc·ing (ad vans′ ing)   moving forward; pushing forward

Ae·ge·an (i jē′ ən)

Ae·ge·us (i jē′ əs)

af·fect (ə fekt′)   to produce some result

ag·o·nized (ag′ ə nīzd)   suffering; feeling great pain

A·leu·tian Is·lands (ə lü′ shən ī′ ləndz) chain of islands off Alaska

al·gae (al′ jē)   any of a group of water plants that are able to make their own food

al·loy (al′ oi or ə loi′)   combination of two or more metals

al·ly (al′ ī or ə lī′)   helper; someone who has the same purpose or goal

al·tar (ôl′ tər)   place of worship

al·ter (ôl′ tər)   to change; to adjust clothing to make it fit better

am·a·teur (am′ ə chər or am′ ə tər)   one who does something for fun, not for pay or profit

a·maze·ment (ə māz′mənt)   great surprise

an·a·lyze (an′ l īz)   to find out what something is really like or what it is made of

an·ces·tor (an′ ses′ tər)   earliest form of something; person from whom others come or are descended

an·cient (ān′ shənt)   very old; belonging to times long past

An·da·lu·sian (an′ də lü′ zhən)   something or someone from Andalusia, a remote part of southern Spain

an·noyed (ə noid′)   angry; upset

an·thro·pol·o·gy (an′ thrə pol′ ə jē)   study of how different people live

an·tique (an tēk′)   from times long ago; made long ago

an·vil (an′ vəl) block of iron on which metals are hammered and shaped

anx·ious·ly (angk′ shəs lē or ang′ shəs lē) in a worried way

Aph·ro·di·te (af′ rə dī′ tē)

ap·palled (ə pôld′)   horrified; very disturbed; very upset

ap·pa·ra·tus (ap′ ə rā′ təs or ap′ ə rat′ əs) any tools or equipment used to carry out some plan

ap·prox·i·mate (ə prok′ sə mit)   nearly exact or right

ap·ti·tude (ap′ tə tüd or ap′ tə tyüd)   skill; ability to do something well

a·qua·lung (ak′ wə lung′)   device that feeds air to divers from a tank that they carry on their backs, allowing them to stay underwater for a long time

ar·chae·ol·o·gist (är′ kē ol′ ə jist)   one who studies the past by digging up cities and other physical objects remaining from past civilizations

---

hat, āge, fär; let, ēqual, tėrm; it, īce; hot, ōpen, ôrder; oil, out; cup, pùt, rüle; ch, child; ng, long; sh, she; th, thin; ᴛʜ, then; zh, measure; ə represents *a* in about, *e* in taken, *i* in pencil, *o* in lemon, *u* in circus.

arch·bish·op (ärch′ bish′ əp)   very important person in the church; highest rank of bishop

ar·chi·tec·ture (är′ kə tek′ chər)   art of building; way or style of building

Ar·i·ad·ne (ar′ ē ad′ nē)

a·rise (ə rīz′)   to come from; to be caused by

ar·ti·cle (är′ tə kəl)   written composition on a special subject, found in a magazine, newspaper, or book

ar·ti·fi·cial (är′ tə fish′ əl)   not natural; made by people

as·cend (ə send′)   to go up; to climb; to rise

as·sign (ə sīn′) to give; to give one something to do

as·so·ci·a·tion (ə sō′ sē ā′ shən *or* ə sō′ shē ā′ shən)   group of people joined together for some purpose

as·tound (ə stound′)   to surprise greatly

as·tral (as′ trəl)   having to do with stars; being a star

a·sy·lum (ə sī′ ləm)   place where people who cannot take care of themselves are cared for by others

Ath·ens (ath′ ənz)   capital city of Greece

Aus·tral·ia (ô strā′ lyə)   country southeast of Asia

au·to·bi·og·ra·phy (ô′ tə bī og′ rə fē)   person's life story written by himself or herself

au·to·ma·tion (ô′ tə mā′ shən)   system in which machines do the work instead of people

aux·il·iar·y (ôg zil′ yər ē)   helping; something extra, to be used in emergencies

a·venge (ə venj′)   to get revenge for; to punish for a wrong

ax·le (ak′ səl)   bar or shaft on which a wheel turns

Ba·chi·ga (bä chē′ gä)

bade (bad)   past tense of the word *bid: The general bade his soldiers good-bye.*

Ba·ha·mas (bə hä′ məz *or* bə hā′ məz)   group of islands in the Caribbean Sea to the southeast of Florida

ba·leen (bə lēn′)   substance like horn that grows in plates in a whale's mouth and that is used to filter food from the water

Bal·tic (bôl′ tik)   body of water between Sweden and Denmark

barbed (bärbd)   having sharp points: *Barbed wire is used to keep people and animals from breaking through fences.*

bar·na·cle (bär′ nə kəl)   small shelled sea animal that attaches itself to ships, rocks, and large sea animals

ba·rom·e·ter (bə rom′ ə ter)   instrument that measures air pressure and is used to predict the weather

bar·on (bar′ ən)   nobleman of the lowest hereditary rank

bar·ri·cade (bar′ ə kād′ *or* bar′ ə kād)   to block off

bar·ri·er (bar′ ē ər)   something that separates two things

bas·il (baz′ əl)   sweet-smelling plant or herb in the same family as mint, used in cooking

ba·sin (bā′ sn)   hollow place that holds water

bath·y·scaphe (bath′ ə skaf)   ship used for underwater exploring

bath·y·spere (bath′ ə sfir′)   hollow sphere attached to a cable, holding a crew inside, which can be lowered underwater

Ba·tut·si (bä tüt′ sē)   a people who live in the countries of Rwanda and Burundi in central equatorial Africa, known for their tall stature (also known by the Swahili name, *Watutsi*)

ba·zaar (bə zär′)   street or square full of shops or outdoor booths

beaux (bō)   French: beautiful

beck·on (bec′ ən)   to make a gesture for someone to approach

Bee·be (bē′ bē)   William (Wil′ yəm)

bel·fry (bel′ frē)   tower for a bell or bells

ben·tho·scope (ben′ thə skōp)   kind of bathysphere

Ber·ing Sea (bir′ ing or ber′ ing sē)

be·stow (bi stō′)   to give as a gift

be·tray (bi trā′)   to give away a secret

be·wil·der (bi wil′ dər)   to confuse; to puzzle

bi·ol·o·gy (bī ol′ ə jē)   science of living things

birch (bėrch)   kind of tree with thin trunk and silver-gray bark

bleach·ers (blē′ chərz)   sloping stands with benches on them, and without a roof or cover

bleak (blēk)   bare; empty; cold: *The desert landscape was bleak.*

bleat (blēt)   cry made by a sheep or goat; a sound like this cry

block·bust·er (blok′ bus′ tər)   something very strong or effective

blow·er (blō′ ər)   fan; something that blows air

blunt (blunt)   to make less sharp

boo·me·rang (büm′ ə rang)   shaped piece of wood that spins and returns to the thrower after being thrown; name comes from Australia where the club is used for sport

boul·der (bōl′ dər)   large rock

brain·storm (brān′ stôrm′)   sudden good idea

breach (brēch)   to come up above the surface of the water

breath·y (breth′ ē)   marked by noisy breathing: *a breathy way of talking*

brew·ing (brü′ ing)   soaking in water and boiling

bri·er (brī′ ər)   kind of bush with thorns: *A rose bush is a brier.*

bronze (bronz)   brown metal that is a mixture of copper and tin

buf·fet (buf′ it)   hard blow; very hard punch or slap

Bu·fu·ka (bü fü′ kä)

bunt (bunt)   to hit a baseball lightly so that it falls to the ground and rolls only a short distance

cack·le (kak′ əl)   to laugh in a high or sharp way

Cae·sar (sē′ zər)   title for Roman emperor

cal·cu·lus (kal′ kyə ləs)   kind of advanced mathematics

cam·e·o (kam′ ē ō)   jewel with a design carved on it

cam·phor (kam′ fər)   chemical used to keep moths away from wool

cane (kān)   stick used for help in walking or as a decoration

cap·sule (kap′ səl)   pill; medicine inside a small gelatin case

cap·tion (kap′ shən)   words printed under a picture that explain it

car·di·o·graph (kär′ dē ə graf)   measurement of heartbeats

cast (kast)   to throw; to fling; to hurl: *I cast the fishing line over the starboard side of the boat.*

ca·the·dral (kə thē′ drəl)   very large church

cav·ern (kav′ ərn)   large cave

ce·dar (sē′ dər)   kind of evergreen tree

cen·sor·ship (sen′ sər ship)   act of interfering with the free expression of ideas in printed material

---

hat, āge, fär; let, ēqual, tėrm; it, īce; hot, ōpen, ôrder; oil, out; cup, pùt, rüle; ch, child; ng, long; sh, she; th, thin; ᵺ, then; zh, measure; ə represents *a* in about, *e* in taken, *i* in pencil, *o* in lemon, *u* in circus.

Cey·lon (si lon′) independent island country located in the Indian Ocean, off the southeastern coast of India; now known as Sri Lanka

chan·nel (chan′ l) narrow part of the ocean, lying between two wider parts

char·i·ot (char′ ē ət) two-wheeled cart pulled by horses

char·i·ot·eer (char′ ē ə tir′) one who drives a chariot

charred (chärd) burned enough to blacken; scorched

char·tered (chär′ tərd) hired: *a chartered bus, a chartered airplane*

chasm (kaz′ əm) deep crack in the earth or between two cliffs

Cher·o·kee (cher′ ə kē) Indian tribe originally from North Carolina and Tennessee now living in Oklahoma; a member of the Cherokee tribe

cher·u·bim (cher′ ə bim) cherubs; angels

Chile (chĭl′ ē) country in southwestern South America, on the Pacific coast

chiv·al·ry (shiv′ əl rē) rules and customs of knights; idea that strong people should help weak ones

chop·sticks (chop′ stiks′) two sticks, usually made of wood, used by Asians for picking up and eating food

chron·o·log·i·cal (kron′ ə loj′ ə kəl) in the order that things happened

cir·cuit (sėr′ kit) one complete closed path

civ·i·li·za·tion (siv′ ə lə zā′ shən) ways of living of a race or people; state of being civilized, not primitive

clar·i·on (klar′ ē ən) sound from a trumpet; musical salute played on a trumpet

clas·si·fied (klas′ ə fīd) sorted or arranged in groups that are alike in some way: *The classified pages in the telephone book list names according to the services the people provide.*

claus·tro·pho·bi·a (klô′ strə fō′ bē ə) fear of closed-in places

Cle·men·te (klə men′ tē) Roberto (rō ber′ tō)

clench (klench) to close tightly together

clob·ber (klob′ ər) slang for to beat badly; to hit hard

clue (klü) **1.** ball of yarn or thread **2.** something that leads one to the solution of a problem

coax (kōks) to persuade by soft words; to influence by pleasant ways

cob·bled (kob′ əld) paved with rounded stones

co·hort (kō′ hôrt) helper; companion

co·in·ci·dence (kō in′ sə dəns) two things happening at the same time by chance

col·lapse (kə laps′) to fail; to break down suddenly

col·umn (kol′ əm) **1.** slender, upright structure; anything that seems slender and upright **2.** narrow divisions of type on a page, separated by space

comb jel·lies (kōm jel′ ēz) jellyfish with comblike organs that extend in bands from their mouths to their opposite ends

com·mer·cial (kə mėr′ shəl) an advertisement

com·mit (kə mit′) to do; to perform, such as a crime

com·mit·tee (kə mit′ ē) group of people chosen to do some special thing

com·mu·ni·cate (kə myü′ nə kāt) to give or exchange information or ideas by speaking, writing, etc.

com·mu·ni·ca·tion (kə myü′ nə kā′ shən) the giving or exchanging of information or ideas by speaking, writing, etc.

com·plex (kəm pleks′ or kom′ pleks) not simple; complicated; having many parts

com·pli·ment (kom′ plə mənt) praise; saying something good about someone

com·pose (kəm pōz′) to make one's body or mind calm

com·pound (kom′ pound) fenced-in area in which people live

com·pressed (kəm presd′) pushed together in a smaller space

com·put·er (kəm pyü′ tər) machine that, given certain facts, can solve problems

con·ceal (kən sēl′)   to hide

con·cen·tra·tion   (kon′ sən trā′ shən) thinking hard about one thing; careful attention for a period of time

con·cert (kon′ sért)   musical entertainment

con·coc·tion (kon kok′ shən)   something made of many ingredients; combination of things

con·cus·sion (kən kush′ ən)   injury to the brain caused by a fall or a blow to the head

con·fi·dent (kon′ fə dənt)   sure that one is right

con·flict (kon′ flikt)   a struggle between people or ideas

con·grat·u·late (kən grach′ ə lāt)   to express pleasure to someone about something good that has happened to that person

con·jure (kon′ jər)   to cause to appear as if by magic

con·scious·ness (kon′ shəs nis)   condition or state of being aware or able to see, hear, feel, etc.

con·tain (kən tān′)   to have something inside; to have something as a part

con·ti·nent·al shelf (kon′ ti nen′ təl shelf)   shallow area of ocean near a large mass of land

con·tour (kon′ tùr)   shape

con·trib·ute (kən trib′ yüt)   to give; to add to

con·vey (kən vā′)   to communicate; to make known

Coos Bay (küs bā)

co·pe·pod (kōp′ ə pod)   kind of very small sea animal

coun·se·lor (koun′ sə lər)   wise person who gives advice

cour·i·er (kėr′ ē ər *or* kür′ ē ər)   messenger; often used as the name of a newspaper

court·yard (kôrt′ yärd′)   space partly enclosed by a building or buildings

Cous·teau   (kü stō′)   Jacques-Yves (zhäk′ ēv′)

cov·er·let (kuv′ ər lit)   blanket

cra·dle·board (krā′ dl bôrd′)   board onto which a baby is strapped

crave (krāv)   to want

cred·it (kred′ it)   honor; praise

crest (krest)   top of something; peak; summit: *the crest of the mountain*

Crete (krēt)   island in the Mediterranean southeast of Greece

cringe (krinj)   to move back because of pain or fear

crus·ta·cean (krus′ tā′ shən)   water animal with a hard shell, such as lobster, shrimp, and crab

cul·ti·vat·ed (kul′ tə vāt′ id)   grown by people; not wild

cur·few (kėr′ fyü)   fixed time at night after which everyone must be indoors

cur·rent (kėr′ ənt)   movement of water; flow of water

curve (kėrv)   baseball that is thrown to turn or swerve just before it reaches the batter   *Baseball Jargon*

cut·ter (kut′ ər)   small, lightly armed motorboat used by the Coast Guard for patrolling

cut·tle fish (kut′ l fish′)   kind of sea animal that has eight short arms with suckers, two long tentacles, and a hard inside shell

cyl·in·der (sil′ ən dər)   something shaped like a pipe or can

cym·bal (sim′ bəl)   brass plate that is struck against another or hit with a drumstick to make a ringing noise

---

hat, āge, fär; let, ēqual, tėrm; it, īce; hot, ōpen, ôrder; oil, out; cup, pùt, rüle; ch, child; ng, long; sh, she; th, thin; ᴛʜ, then; zh, measure; ə represents *a* in about, *e* in taken, *i* in pencil, *o* in lemon, *u* in circus.

Daed·a·lus (ded′ l əs)

da·ta–pro·cessed (dā′ tə *or* dat′ ə pro′ sesd)   arranged by a computer

daz·zling (daz′ ling) bright or splendid

deck (dek) floor of a ship

de·fen·sive·ly (di fen′ siv lē)   in a way intended to defend

Delft (delft)   city in Holland

de·mol·ish (di mol′ ish) to destroy

de·ni·al (di nī′ əl) a statement that something is not true

de·pict (di pikt′) to represent by drawing, painting, or describing

de·pos·it (di poz′ it)   something that has been laid down or left behind

de·pressed (di presd′) unhappy; sad

de·pres·sion (di presh′ ən) hole; an area below the surface

de·prive (di prīv′) to keep from having: *The noise deprived me of a good night's sleep.*

de·scend·ant (di sen′ dənt) person or thing that comes from something or someone else, such as a child from a parent

des·o·late (des′ ə lit) empty

de·spair·ing·ly (di sper′ ing lē *or* di spar′ ing lē) hopelessly; not believing that things will get better

des·pot·ic (di spot′ ik) having absolute power; being the only ruler, without the advice or influence of others

de·tail (di′ tāl) small or unimportant fact

de·tec·tive (di tek′ tiv) one who solves mysteries; one who searches for answers to questions

de·ter·mi·na·tion (di tér′ mə nā′ shən) firm decision to do something

dev·as·tate (dev′ ə stāt) to destroy

de·vise (di vīz′) to make up; to invent

di·a·tom (dī′ ə tom) tiny one-celled plant with a hard two-part shell

die (dē) German: the

di·e·tet·ic (dī′ ə tet′ ik) having to do with food

dig·ni·ty (dig′ nə tē) way of acting that wins the respect of others

Di·o·ny·sus (dī ə nī′ səs) Greek god of celebration

dis·as·ter (də zas′ tər) event that causes much unhappiness, destruction, or suffering

dis·be·lief (dis′ bi lēf′) feeling that something is not true

dis·dain·ful·ly (dis dān′ fəl lē) with scorn

dis·guised (dis gīzd′) made to look like something else by changes in clothes or appearance

dis·may (dis mā′) feeling of fear and hopelessness

dis·posed (dis pōzd′) got rid of

dis·tinct·ly (dis tingkt′ lē) clearly

dis·tract (dis trakt′) to turn away the attention, mind, or interest: *Kim tried to distract the baby, so he wouldn't cry for his mother.*

di·vert (də vert′) to turn aside

doe (dō) female deer

dol·phin (dol′ fən) kind of sea mammal similar to a small whale

don (don) to put on

dor·mant (dôr′ mənt) sleeping; seeming to be asleep; not awake or active

drei (drī) German: three

drie (drē) Dutch: three

drills (drilz) hits very hard *Baseball Jargon*

dum·my (dum′ ē) term used in printing to mean a model page with the reading matter and illustrations pasted into place to help the printer; a layout

dun·geon (dun′ jən) prison, especially an underground prison

ebb·ing (eb′ ing) going back; going down

eb·on·y (eb′ ə nē) wood from the tropical ebony tree, having hard dark-colored wood: *Ebony is used to make the black keys of a piano.*

ec·o·nom·ic (ē′ kə nom′ ik *or* ek′ ə nom′ ik) having to do with money, services, and goods

Ec·tor (ek′ tər)

ed·dy (ed′ ē) small current or whirlpool of water

ed·i·ble (ed′ ə bəl) fit to eat

ed·i·tor (ed′ ə tər) person in charge of a newspaper or magazine

ef·fect (ə fekt′) result

el·e·gant (el′ ə gənt) showing good taste; fancy; splendid

elon·gat·ed (i lông′ gāt′d) long and thin

em·bar·rass (em bar′ əs) to make someone feel shy or self-conscious

em·brace (em brās′) to hold in the arms; to hug

e·merge (i merj′) to come out

e·mis·sion (i mish′ ən) something given out or given off

em·phat·i·cal·ly (em fat′ ik lē) clearly; forcefully; in a way meant to stand out

en·er·get·ic (en ər jet′ ik) having energy; strong; lively

Eng·land (ing′ glənd) island country of Europe to the west of the continent

en·thralled (en thrôld′) very interested; fascinated

en·throned (en thrônd′) sitting on a throne or very fancy chair

en·thu·si·asm (en thü′ zē az′ əm) great interest; the desire to do something very much

e·on (ē′ ən) very long period of time

ep·au·lets

(ep′ ə lets) shoulder decorations worn by generals and other soldiers of high rank

Epaulet

e·rup·tion (i rup′ shən) something that bursts forth or comes out suddenly

es·tab·lish (e stab′ lish) to set up

e·ter·nal (i tėr′ nl) lasting forever; never dying or going away

Eu·rope (yür′ əp) continent east of the Atlantic Ocean and west of Asia, including the countries France, Germany, Spain, etc.

Eu·ro·pe·an (yur′ ə pē′ ən) of or having to do with Europe

e·va·sive (i vā′ siv) avoiding something

ev·i·dence (ev′ ə dens) proof; something that shows that something exists: *Skeletons have been found that give evidence that there were once dinosaurs in this country.*

e·voke (i vōk′) to call forth; to suggest

ex·ca·vate (ek′ skə vāt) to dig; to dig up

ex·ceed·ing·ly (ek sē′ ding lē) extremely; to an unusual degree; very greatly

ex·cep·tion·al (ek sep′ shə nəl) unusual; not like everything or everyone else of its kind

ex·clu·sive (ek sklü′ siv *or* ek sklü′ ziv) not shared with others; owned by only one person or thing

ex·haust·ed (eg zô′ stid) very tired; completely worn out

ex·hi·bi·tion (ek′ sə bish′ ən) show of something; public show

ex·pe·di·tion (ek′ spə dish′ ən) trip, usually to someplace far away or dangerous

ex·pen·sive (ek spen′ siv) high-priced; costly

Ex·po 67 (ek′ spō sik′ stē sev′ ən) world's fair held in Montreal, Canada, in 1967

ex·press (ek spres′) to show; to say without words

ex·ult (eg zult′) to be very glad; to rejoice

ex·ult·ant (eg zul′ tənt) rejoicing; very pleased

fab·u·lous (fab′ yə ləs) wonderful; very good

fal·ter (fôl′ tər) to fail to go straight on; to stop for a moment

fa·mil·iar·i·ty (fə mil′ yar′ ə tē) knowledge of something; being acquainted with something

---

hat, āge, fär; let, ēqual, tėrm; it, īce; hot, ōpen, ôrder; oil, out; cup, pùt, rüle; ch, child; ng, long; sh, she; th, thin; ᴛH, then; zh, measure; ə represents *a* in about, *e* in taken, *i* in pencil, *o* in lemon, *u* in circus.

fan·fare (fan′ fer or fan′ far)   short piece of trumpet music used to announce or introduce something

fang (fang)   long, pointed tooth

fas·ci·na·tion (fas′ n ā′ shən)   great interest in something

fast·ball (fast′ bôl)   baseball that is thrown very fast   *Baseball Jargon*

fath·om (faŦH′ əm)   unit, equal to six feet, used for measuring the depth of water

fawn (fôn)   young deer

fen (fen)   swamp; wet land

fe·ro·cious (fə rō′ shəs)   very fierce and dangerous

fer·ret (fer′ it)   kind of weasel that is good at finding rabbits, rats, etc.; person who is good at finding things

fic·tion (fik′ shən)   made-up story; not fact

fig·u·rine (fig′ yə rēn′)   small statue

fil·i·gree (fil′ ə grē) design made of wire; any design with open spaces

fil·ter (fil′ tər)   to pass or flow very slowly; to strain things from a liquid

Fin·land (fin′ land)   country in northern Europe

flag·el·lates (flaj′ ə lāts)   protozoans or one-celled animals with one or more long hairlike projections called flagella, which whip about rapidly to move the flagellates through the water

flank (flangk)   **1.** side of an animal **2.** to be on one or both sides of something

flash·bulb (flash′ bulb′)   electric bulb that gives out a very bright flash of light lasting for a very short time

fleece (flēs)   coat of wool cut off from a sheep

foot·ing (fút′ ing)   secure placing of the feet

fore·arms (fôr′ ärmz′)   parts of person's arms between the wrist and elbow

fo·reign·like (fôr′ ən līk)   like something from a foreign or strange country

fore·run·ner (fôr′ run′ ər)   something or someone that comes before; earlier version of something

for·lorn·ly (fôr lôrn′ lē)   hopelessly; in a lonely and sad manner

for·mu·la (fôr′ myə lə)   list of ingredients; recipe

Fo·rum (fôr′ əm)   central part of a Roman town, where public business was done

fos·ter (fô′ stər)   in the same family but not related by birth: *A foster child is one who has been adopted or taken in.*

frag·ment (frag′ mənt)   small piece of something

fra·grant (frā′ grənt)   good smelling; pleasant smelling

fres·co (fres′ kō)   painting done on plaster

fu·gi·tive (fyü′ jə tiv)   running away or having run away

ga·ble (gā′ bəl) triangular piece at the end of a pitched or slanted roof

Gag·nan (gän yän′)   Emil (ā mēl′)

Gal·a·had (gal′ ə had)

gales (gālz)   very strong winds, blowing with a speed of 51 to 100 kilometers (32 to 63 miles) per hour

gal·ler·y (gal′ ər ē)   building or room in which pictures are shown

gal·leys (gal′ ēz)   term used in printing to mean narrow pages of type used for correcting mistakes; also called *galley proofs*

gang·way (gang′ wā′)   ramp lowered from a ship to a dock

gap·ing (gāp′ ing)   staring with the mouth open

gauge (gāj)   tool for measuring

Geat (gāt)   long ago, a native of southern Sweden

Geed·er (jē′ dər)

gen·e·rate (jen′ ə rāt′) to produce: *A boiler generates steam.*

ge·o·det·ic (jē′ ə det′ ik) having to do with the measurement of the earth

ge·ol·o·gy (jē ol′ ə jē) study of the earth and the changes it has gone through

gi·gan·tic (jī gan′ tik) very big

gla·cial (glā′ shəl) having to do with glaciers, which are very large masses of ice that move down from a mountain very slowly

glass·worm (glas′ wèrm) sea animal, named for its transparency; also called *arrowworm*

glen (glen) hidden, narrow valley

glob·ule (glob′ yül) something small and round, such as a drop of liquid

glow·er (glou′ ər) to stare angrily; to scowl

glyph (glif) picture writing; writing that looks like a picture of the thing it stands for

grand·stand (grand′ stand′) seating place at an outdoor event such as a race, baseball game, etc.

gran·ite (gran′ it) kind of very hard stone

graph·ic (graf′ ik) having to do with pictures and designs

grat·i·tude (grat′ ə tüd *or* grat′ ə tyüd) thankfulness

graved (grāvd) carved

gra·zie (grät′ sē) Italian: thank you

Greek (grēk) language of Greece; coming from Greece

Gren·del (gren′ dəl)

gris·ly (griz′ lē) horrible; disgusting

Groome (grüm)

grue·some (grü′ səm) horrible; disgusting

Guam (gwäm) island in the Pacific, east of the Philippines

Guin·e·vere (gwin′ ə vir)

guise (gīz) dress, appearance, pretense

gui·tar (ge tär′) musical instrument with six strings, played with the fingers or a pick

gyp·sy (jip′ sē) person belonging to a wandering tribe of people

hab·i·tat (hab′ ə tat) place where someone or something naturally lives

hal·ter (hôl′ tər) headpiece made of rope or leather used for leading an animal

Har·pin·na (här pin′ ə)

ha·ven (hā′ vən) safe place

hav·oc (hav′ ək) great confusion and destruction

Ha·waii (hə wī′ ē) island group in the North Pacific; the 50th state of the United States

hay·wire (hā′ wīr′) broken; messed up

haze (hāz) mist; fog

head·line (hed′ līn) words printed at the top, or head, of an article that explain what the article is about

heath (hēth) open land with few trees

heck·le (hek′ əl) to tease; to try to annoy

hedge (hej) row of closely-planted small trees that form a fence or boundary

hem·i·sphere (hem′ ə sfir) half of the surface of the earth: *Both North America and South America are in the Western Hemisphere.*

Heo·rot (hē′ rot)

her·ald (her′ əld) one who brings messages and makes announcements

hes·i·tate (hez′ ə tāt) to pause; to be not sure

hi·ber·nat·ing (hī′ bər nāt ing) passing the winter in sleep or in an inactive condition

hi·er·o·glyph (hī′ ər ə glif′) piece of picture writing; one piece of Egyptian picture writing

---

hat, āge, fär; let, ēqual, tèrm; it, īce; hot, ōpen, ôrder; oil, out; cup, put, rüle; ch, child; ng, long; sh, she; th, thin; ᴛʜ, then; zh, measure; ə represents *a* in about, *e* in taken, *i* in pencil, *o* in lemon, *u* in circus.

Hi·lo (hē′ lō)

Hip·po·da·me·ia (hi pō də mē′ ə)

hive (hīv)   a house for bees

hoist (hoist)   to raise up; to lift

home·spun (hōm′ spən)   cloth made of yarn spun at home

hon·ey·comb

(hun′ ē kōm) storage place for honey, pollen, and eggs, built out of wax: *Honeycombs have six-sided cells.*

ho·ri·zon (hə rī′ zn)   line in the distance where the sky seems to touch the sea or the earth

Hroth·gar (hrōth′ gär)

hu·mid·i·ty (hyü mid′ ə tē)   dampness; amount of water in the air or on some surface

hunch (hunch)   vague feeling; suspicion (informal use of the word)

Huout (ə ü′)   George

Hur·on (hyür′ ən)

hur·ri·cane (hėr′ ə kān)   severe storm with heavy rain and strong winds

Hy·ge·lac (hē′ gə lak)

Ic·ar·us (ik′ ər əs)

i·den·ti·fy (ī den′ tə fī)   to point out; to show which is which

i·dol (ī′dl)   person or thing that is admired or loved very much

il·le·gal·ly (i lē′ gəl lē)   in a way that is against the law

il·lu·mi·nat·ed (i lü′ mə nāt id)   having a light; lighted

im·age (im′ ij)   likeness

Im·pres·sion·ist (im presh′ ə nist)   painter who tries to show the special quality of light of the scene he paints

in·au·di·ble (in ô′ də bəl)   too soft or low to be heard

in·cred·i·ble (in kred′ ə bəl)   unbelievable; too strange to believe

in·cred·u·lous (in krej′ ə ləs)   not believing something

in·di·cate (in′ də kāt)   to show; to point out

In·do–Eur·o·pe·an (in′ dō yür′ ə pē′ ən)   group of related languages that includes most of the languages of Europe, Russia, and India

in·hos·pit·a·ble (in′ ho spit′ ə bəl)   not welcoming visitors; not comfortable for visitors

i·ni·ti·a·tion (i nish′ ē ā′ shən)   ceremony admitting one into some group; entrance ceremony

in·laid (in′ lād′ *or* in lād′)   decoration or design set in the surface of something: *Her favorite present was a gold inlaid box.*

in·stinct (in′ stingkt)   something one knows without being taught; natural ability

in·stinc·tive (in stingk′ tiv)   without thinking; known without having been taught

in·ten·tions (in ten′ shənz)   plans; purposes; designs

in·ter·fer·ence (in′ tər fir′ əns)   disturbance; something that stops people from doing what they want to do

in·te·ri·or (in tir′ ē ər)   inside

in·ter·pret·er (in tėr′ prə tər)   one who translates messages; one who explains the meaning of something written or said in a foreign language

in·ter·val (in′ tər vəl)   time or space between two things

in·trigue (in trēg′)   to interest greatly

in·vad·er (in vā′ dər)   enemy that enters a place to attack it

in·va·sion (in vā′ zhən)   entering by force; attack

is·sue (ish′ ü)   to publish; to put out; to make public

Isth·mi·an (is′ mə ən)

isth·mus (is′ məs)   narrow strip of land with water on two sides

Ja·pan (jə pan′)   country of many islands, east of Asia

joust (joust *or* just) fight between two knights using long spears or lances

ju·bi·lant (jü′ bə lənt) rejoicing; very happy because of some success

judg·ment (juj′ mənt) ability to think well or to make the right choices

Ju·pi·ter (jü′ pə tər) chief Roman god

Kam·pa·la (käm pä′ lä)

keel (kēl) strip on the bottom of a ship to keep it going straight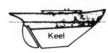

key·board (kē′ bôrd′) all the keys of something such as a piano, typewriter, etc.

kins·man (kinz′ mən) relative

knap·sack (nap′ sak′) cloth bag carried on the back

knave (nāv) tricky person

knight (nīt) man of high military rank, pledged to do good deeds in the Middle Ages

Knos·sos (nos′ əs or knos′ əs)

lab·y·rinth (lab′ ə rinth′) place through which it is hard to find one's way and in which it is easy to get lost; maze

lab·y·rin·thine (lab′ ə rin′ thən) like a labyrinth or maze; very complicated

lac·quered (lak′ ərd) covered with lacquer, a covering like paint, but smoother and shinier

lair (ler or lar) den or home of a wild animal

la·ment·ing (lə ment′ ing) crying; being sad or sorry

lar·vae (lär′ vē) undeveloped or immature forms of an animal that is different in structure from the adult form of the animal (plural of **larva**)

lat·er·al (lat′ ər əl) on the side

Lat·in (lat′ n) **1.** the language spoken in ancient Rome **2.** having to do with Rome

lat·i·tudes (lat′ ə tüdz or lat′ ə tyüdz) places or areas having a certain distance north or south from the equator, measured in degrees

Laun·ce·lot (lan′ sə lot or lôn′ sə lot)

lay·out (lā′ out′) arrangement or design for a book, newspaper, etc.

league (lēg) group of teams that play against one another

les (lā) French: the

Leu·te (loi′ tə) German: people

li·chen (lī′ kən) kind of plant, similar to moss, that grows on rocks and on trees

lieu·ten·ant (lü ten′ ənt) officer

lin·ger (ling′ gər) to stay; to stay because one does not want to leave

lin·guist (ling′ gwist) one who studies many different languages

lin·guis·tic (ling gwis′ tik) having to do with language

lin·guis·tic ge·og·ra·pher (ling gwis′ tik jē og′ rə fər) one who studies where languages are spoken and how they differ from place to place

Liv·er·pool (liv′ ər pül) seaport city in northwest England, where a certain type of rock music started

log·i·cal·ly (loj′ ə klē) reasonably; sensibly; having come to some conclusion by thought

Lon·don (lun′ dən) capital city of England

loom (lüm) to look or appear very close or high

lou·vered (lü′ vərd) made of overlapping horizontal boards set in an opening in a way that keeps out rain, but provides ventilation and light

lurked (lėrkd) moved about in a secret or sly way

---

hat, āge, fär; let, ēqual, tėrm; it, īce; hot, ōpen, ôrder; oil, out; cup, pùt, rüle; ch, child; ng, long; sh, she; th, thin; ᴛʜ, then; zh, measure; ə represents *a* in about, *e* in taken, *i* in pencil, *o* in lemon, *u* in circus.

lute (lüt)   musical instrument used in the 1500's and 1600's, played by plucking strings

lux·ur·y (luk' shər ē *or* lug' zhər ē)   something pleasant to have but not necessary

Lyd·i·a (lid' ē ə)

Ma·cel·lum (mə sel' m)

ma·dre (mä' drā)   Spanish: mother

Mag·da·le·ni·an Per·i·od (mag' də len' ē ən pir' ē əd)   late Stone Age period

ma·gi·cian (mə jish' ən)   one who can work magic

mag·nif·i·cence (mag nif' ə səns)   greatness and beauty

mag·nif·i·cent (mag nif' ə sənt)   great; wonderful

maj·es·ty (maj' ə stē)   title for a king

mam·mal (mam' əl)   warm-blooded animal that feeds its young on its own milk

man·do·lin (man' də lin' *or* man' dl ən)   musical instrument with a pear-shaped body and four or five pairs of metal strings, played with a pick

ma·nip·u·late (mə nip' yə lāt)   to handle with skill

Mar·i·an·as (mar' ē an' əz)   islands in the western Pacific

ma·rine (mə rēn')   having to do with the sea

mas·cot (mas' kot)   animal that is supposed to bring good luck

mass (mas)   a large amount or cluster of something

ma·ture (mə chùr')   to develop; to ripen

ma·tur·i·ty (mə chùr' ə tē, mə tùr' ə tē, *or* mə tyùr' ə tē)   state of reaching full development; ripeness

Med·i·ter·ra·ne·an (med' ə tə rā' nē ən)   sea between Europe and Africa

me·di·um (mē' dē əm)   something halfway between two extremes

men·ac·ing (men' is ing)   threatening

mer·ce·nar·y (mèr' sə ner' ē)   doing things only for money

mère (mer *or* mar)   French: mother

Mer·lin (mer' lən)

met·a·mor·phic (met' ə môr' fik)   rock that has changed its form

me·te·o·rol·o·gy (mē' tē ə rol' ə jē)   study of weather and the prediction of weather

mi·cro·phone (mī krə fōn)   instrument that picks up sound and allows it to be recorded or made louder

mi·gra·tion (mī grā' shən)   moving from one place to another

mil·let (mil' it)   kind of grain

mill·stone (mil'stōn') stone used to grind something, such as grain

min·er·als (min' ər əlz)   substances that are neither animal nor plant: *Salt is a very important mineral.*

min·gled (ming' gəld)   mixed in with

Min·o·an (mi nō' n)   having to do with an ancient civilization of Crete

Mi·nos (mī' nəs)

Min·o·taur (min' ə tôr)

min·strel (min' strəl)   one who invents songs and travels around singing them

mis·sion·ar·y (mish' ə ner' ē)   one who goes to a foreign country or to another people to teach religion

mist (mist)   cloud of very fine drops of water in the air or atmosphere; haze

moat (mōt) water-filled ditch around a castle to protect the castle from people who want to break in

moed·er (müd' r)   Dutch: mother

mo·not·o·nous·ly (mə not' n əs lē)   in a way that is always the same; in a boring way

Mon·tre·al (mon' trē ôl')   city in eastern Canada on the St. Lawrence River

moor (mùr)   open wasteland without many trees

mo·ray (môr' ā)   kind of eel

Mor·gan le Fay (môr' gən lə fā')

mor·tal (môr′ tl) human; having to die at some time; not living forever

mo·sa·ic (mō zā′ ik) picture made up of small pieces of stone, tile, or glass

Mount Et·na (mount et′ nə)

Mount I·da (mount ī də)

mul·ti·tudes (mul′ tə tüdz or mul′ tə tyüdz) great many; great numbers; crowds

mur·al (myür′ əl) picture painted on a wall

mut·ed (myüt id) quiet; not bright

Mut·ter (müt′ ər) German: mother

Myr·til·lus (mér til′ əs)

Na·ples (nā′ pəlz) city in southern Italy

na·tive (nā′ tiv) belonging to a particular place or person

Nax·os (nak′ sōs)

nep·o·tism (nep′ ə tiz′ əm) showing of too much favor by people in power or in high offices to relatives or close friends, especially by appointing them to desirable jobs

neu·tral (nü′ trəl) having no opinion; neither agreeing nor disagreeing

New Zea·land (nü or nyü zē′ lənd) island country in the Pacific Ocean to the southeast of Australia

nim·bly (nim′ blē) quickly and lightly; actively

nour·ish·ing (nér′ ish ing) feeding; enabling to grow

nous (nü) French: we

nu·mer·al (nü′ mər əl or nyü′ mər əl) number; way of writing a number

nurs·er·y (nér′ sər ē) room, place, or area set apart for the children's use

nu·tri·ent (nü′ trē′ ənt or nyü′ trē ənt) something used for food

nu·tri·tion (nü trish′ ən or nyü trish′ ən) food value; food

nuz·zle (nuz′ əl) to push softly with the nose

o·bliged (ə blīj′d′) bound by a favor or service

ob·long (ob′ lông) having a shape that is longer than broad

ob·sta·cle (ob′ stə kəl) something that makes it hard or impossible to do something

ob·tain (əb tān′) to get

ob·vi·ous (ob′ vē əs) clear

ob·vi·ous·ly (ob′ vē əs lē) clearly; plainly

oc·cu·pant (ok′ yə pənt) one inside; one that lives in a certain spot

o·cean·o·graph·ic (ō′ shən ə graf′ ik) having to do with the study of the ocean

Od·ys·sey (od′ ə sē) very long Greek poem about the adventures of Odysseus

Oen·o·maus (ēn′ ə məs)

o·gre (ō′ gər) monster or giant

oint·ment (oint′ mənt) oily substance used to heal or soothe

O·lym·pic (ō lim′ pik) having to do with Mount Olympus

O·lym·pics (ō lim′ piks) series of international athletic contests held every four years in a different country

O·lym·pus (ō lim′ pəs) **Mount** mountain in northeastern Greece where the Greek gods were supposed to live

om·i·nous·ly (om′ ə nəs lē) unfavorably; threateningly; menacingly: *The black clouds gathered ominously over the picnic grounds.*

o·ra·cle (ôr′ ə kəl) place where people get answers to questions from a god or a priest through whom the god speaks

or·di·nar·y (ôrd′ n er′ ē) usual; average; like most others of its kind

or·gan (ôr′ gən) part of the body that has a specific job, such as the heart

o·ri·gin (ôr′ ə jin) beginning; start

o·rig·i·nate (ə rij′ ə nāt) to begin; to start

---

hat, āge, fär; let, ēqual, tėrm; it, īce; hot, ōpen, ôrder; oil, out; cup, pùt, rüle; ch, child; ng, long; sh, she; th, thin; ᴛʜ, then; zh, measure; ə represents *a* in about, *e* in taken, *i* in pencil, *o* in lemon, *u* in circus.

or·na·ment (ôr′ nə mənt)   jewelry; something to wear because it is attractive

out·land·ish (out lan′ dish)   foreign; strange

Pa·cif·ic (pə sif′ ik)   ocean extending from North and South America to Asia and Australia

pa·dre (pä′ drā)   Spanish: father

page (pāj)   boy who is training to become a knight by acting as a knight's servant

palm (päm)   **1.** part of the inside of the hand **2.** a group of trees or shrubs grown in warm climates

pan·ic (pan′ ik)   terror or unreasoning fear

par·a·dise (par′ ə dīs)   ideal spot; heaven

par·a·sol (par′ ə sôl)   umbrella used as protection from the sun

pa·vil·ion (pə vil′ yən)   decorated temporary building; building at a fair

Pel·o·pon·ne·sus (pel ə pə nē′ səs)

Pe·lops (pel′ ops)

pen·al·ty (pen′ l tē)   punishment

pen·non (pen′ ən)   flag or banner

perched (perch′d)   seated rather high up

père (per *or* par)   French: father

per·ish (per′ ish)   to die; to cease to exist

per·plex (pər pleks′)   to confuse

Pe·ru (pə rü′)   country in northwestern South America

phe·nom·e·non (fə nom′ ə non)   unusual event; something that happens unexpectedly: *pl.* phenomena

phos·pho·res·cent (fos′ fə res′ nt)   glowing in the dark; glowing by itself

pho·tog·ra·pher (fə tog′ rə fər)   one who takes pictures with a camera

phys·ics (fiz′ iks)   study of matter and energy such as electricity, gravity, etc.

Pic·card (pē kärd′)   Auguste (ô güst′)

pic·to·graph (pik′ tə graf)   kind of writing in which the characters are pictures of what they stand for

pil·lar (pil′ ər)   pole or column used to help hold up a building

Pi·sa (pē′ zə)

plague (plāg)   deadly disease that spreads very quickly

plain·tive·ly (plān′ tiv lē)   sadly

plank·ton (plangk′ tən)   floating mass of tiny sea plants and animals

pneu·mo·nia (nü mō′ nyə *or* nyü mō′ nyə)   disease, marked by the inflammation of the lungs, that often follows a bad cold or other disease

pol·y·thene (pol′ ē thēn)   kind of plastic used for packaging and protection

Pom·peii (pom pā′)

pon·der (pon′ dər)   to think hard about something for a long time

port·fo·li·o (pôrt fō′ lē ō)   case for loose papers, drawings, and the like that can be easily carried; briefcase

pose (pōz)   position; way of holding the body

Po·sei·don (pə sīd′ n)   Greek god of the sea

pos·si·bil·i·ty (pos′ ə bil′ ə tē)   chance; something that is possible

pre·cau·tion (pri kô′ shən)   care taken to make sure of something; something done to be sure

pre·dict (pri dikt′)   to say what will happen

pre·his·tor·y (prē′ his′ tər ē)   time before written history

prej·u·dice (prej′ ə dis)   opinion formed without careful thought

pre·pos·ter·ous (pri pos′ tər əs)   silly; impossible; ridiculous

pres·sure (presh′ ər)   act of pressing or pushing; result of forcing or pushing something against something else

prim·i·tive (prim′ ə tiv)   very simple; early; uncivilized

pro·fes·sion·al (prə fesh′ ə nəl)   done by a trained person who is paid for the job rather than by an amateur

pro·file (prō′ fīl)   **1.** view from the side **2.** picture of what a person is like; list of what a person does well or badly

pro·gram (prō′ gram)   to prepare or insert a set of instructions for a computer

pro·hib·it·ing (prō hib′ it ing) forbidding; not allowing

pro·ject (prə jekt′) to throw forward

prom·e·nade (prom′ ə nād′ or prom′ ə näd′) place to stroll; place to walk for pleasure

pro·nun·ci·a·tion (prə nun′ sē ā′ shən) way of saying a word

proof·read (prüf′ rēd′) to read material that is to be printed to find errors and mark them for correction

proofs (prüfs) test printings from type: *Books, newspapers, and magazines are first seen in proofs so that errors can be found and corrected.*

pro·pel (prə pel′) to make something move

proph·et·ess (prof′ i tis) woman who can tell what will happen in the future

pro·to·zo·an Noc·ti·lu·ca (prō tə zō′ ən nok′ tə lü′ kə) one-celled plantlike sea organism that gives out light

prov·erb (prov′ ėrb′) wise saying that has been used for a long time

prov·ince (pro′ vəns) part of a country outside the capital or the largest cities

Psyl·la (sil′ ə)

puf·fin (puf′ ən) sea bird that lives in northern regions, with black and white feathers and a narrow, furrowed bill of several colors

pu·ma (pyü′ mə) large American wildcat

pum·ice (pum′ is) kind of stone made up of volcanic lava that has been mixed with gas bubbles and dried

purs·er (pėr′ sər) person on a ship who takes care of passengers and money

quartz (kwôrts) hard, transparent rock

quench (kwench) to put out or stop: *A drink of water quenched my thirst.*

quest (kwest) trip made to find something; search

ques·tion·naire (kwes′ chə ner′ or kwes′ chə nar′) list of questions used to gather information

ram·ie (ram′ ē or rām′ ē) cloth made out of ramie, a plant like hemp

rasp·ing (rasp′ ing) making a harsh scraping noise

rav·age (rav′ ij) to destroy

rav·en·ing (rav′ ə ning) ready to eat greedily

rav·en·ous (rav′ ə nəs) very hungry

rav·en·ous·ly (rav′ ə nəs lē) very hungrily; as if ready to eat

re·ac·tion (rē ak′ shən) action caused by another action; response

re·cede (ri sēd′) to go back; to go down; to get lower

reck·on (rek′ ən) to think; to figure

re·con·struc·tion (rē′ kən struk′ shən) rebuilding

re·count (ri kount′) to tell

re·cu·pe·rate (ri kyü′ pə rāt′ or ri kü′ pə rāt′) to get better; to recover from a sickness

ref·uge (ref′ yüj) shelter or protection from danger

ref·u·gee (ref′ yə jē′ or ref′ yə jē′) one who has been forced to leave a country

re·gion (rē′ jən) place; area

reign (rān) period of ruling; time during which someone is in power

re·li·a·ble (ri lī′ ə bəl) true; trustworthy

re·lief (ri lēf′) aid or help; a lessening of strain or pain

re·mote (ri mōt′) far away; distant

ren·dez·vous (rän′ də vü) meeting; appointment to meet

re·new·al (ri nü′ əl or ri nyü′ əl) state of making or being made like new

re·pel (ri pel′) to disgust; to cause dislike

re·proach·ful (ri prōch′ fəl) blaming someone for something

re·sent·ment (ri zent′ mənt) feeling that one has been hurt or treated badly

res·o·lute·ly (rez′ ə lüt′ lē) firmly; boldly

hat, āge, fär; let, ēqual, tėrm; it, īce; hot, ōpen, ôrder; oil, out; cup, pút, rüle; ch, child; ng, long; sh, she; th, thin; ŦH, then; zh, measure; ə represents a in about, e in taken, i in pencil, o in lemon, u in circus.

539

res·o·lu·tion (rez′ ə lü′ shən)   firm decision

re·solved (ri zolvd′)   made up one's mind; determined; decided

re·stric·tion (ri strik′ shən)   rule; limit

re·treat (ri trēt′)   to go back

re·veal·ing (ri vēl′ ing)   showing

rho·do·den·dron (rō′ də den′ drən) kind of bush having pink, purple, or white flowers

Rome (rōm)

rous·ing (rou′ zing)   strong; lively; exciting

rov·ing (rōv′ ing)   wandering about; wandering; roaming; rambling

runes (rünz)   letters in an alphabet used by the ancient British and Scandanavian peoples: *Runes were usually scratched or carved on stone or metal.*

rus·tling (rus′ ling)   soft noise like the sound of papers rubbing together or the wind blowing through leaves

sa·cred (sā′ krid)   holy; belonging to God

sac·ri·fice (sak′ rə fīs)   **1.** to give up or kill something or someone valuable in order to get some benefit **2.** a gift; giving up one thing to get another

sal·vage (sal′ vij)   saving or getting back things that have been lost underwater

Sa·mo·an (sə mō′ ən)   one who lives on the Samoan Islands in the South Pacific

San Juan (san wän′)   capital city and seaport of Puerto Rico

sap·phire (saf′ īr)   blue precious stone, often used in jewelry

sar·cas·tic (sär kas′ tik)   sneering; making fun of someone

sat·el·lite (sat′ l īt)   object that travels in orbit around some larger heavenly body

scald (scôld)   to burn with boiling liquid

scent·ed (sen′ tid)   having an odor; perfume

schoen·en (shẻrn′ ən)   German: beautiful

scowl·ing (skoul′ ing)   frowning; looking angry

scrap (skrap)   **1.** small piece **2.** to fight

sear (sēr)   to burn; to make something hard and smooth by heat

sec·tion (sek′ shən)   part

seis·mic (sīz′ mik)   having to do with earthquakes and movements of the earth

seis·mo·graph (sīz′ mə graf)   instrument that measures movements of the earth

ser·a·phim (ser′ ə fim)   seraphs; angels

se·rene (sə rēn′)   peaceful; calm

shaft (shaft)   long slender pole; thin beam of sunlight

shin·gle (shing′ gəl)   part of a beach covered with gravel and small stones

shoals (shōlz)   **1.** places in a body of water where the water is not very deep **2.** crowds or large groups

shrewd (shrüd)   smart about practical things

shrine (shrīn)   place where a holy thing is kept

Sic·i·ly (sis′ ə lē)   island in the Mediterranean off Italy

sick·le (sik′ əl)   tool for cutting grass and grain; something shaped like this tool; crescent

sieve (siv)   something that has holes in it that let through small things but not large ones

sight·se·er (sīt′ sē′ ər)   one who has come to look at something interesting

silt (silt)   earth or sand carried by flowing water and then dropped

sind (zint)   German: are

sin·is·ter (sin′ ə stər)   strange and frightening; dangerous

Sioux (sü)

si·phon (sī′ fən)   to pull water from one place to another

site (sīt)   place, especially a place for digging or building

skin·flint (skin′ flint′)   stingy person

slab (slab)   broad, flat piece of something

so·ci·e·ty (sə sī′ ə tē) group of people who have the same customs and way of life

sommes (sum) French: are

sor·cer·ess (sôr′ sər is) woman who can work magic

source (sôrs) place from which something comes; beginning

spawn·ing (spôn′ ing) producing young, especially from fish, frogs, and the like

spell·bound (spel′ bound′) fascinated; unable to turn away

squid (skwid) sea animal with ten legs

squire (skwīr) knight's assistant; young man who serves a knight in order to learn how to become a knight himself

stam·mer (stam′ ər) to have trouble speaking; to stutter

steal (stēl) to run to second base, third base, or home plate as the pitcher throws the ball *Baseball Jargon*

stew·ard (stü′ ərd) worker on a ship or plane

stir·rup (stėr′ əp *or* stir′ əp) rounded support for a rider's foot, attached at the end of a leather strap that hangs from the saddle

stodg·y (stoj′ ē) heavy; dull

stop·watch (stop′ woch′ *or* stop′ wôch′) watch that has a hand that can be started and stopped at any second with the press of a button, used for timing things

stow·a·way (stō′ ə wā′) one who hides on a ship or plane in order to travel without paying

strat·e·gy (strat′ ə jē) careful plan

struc·ture (struk′ chər) building; something that has been built

sub·merge (səb mėrj′) to go under water

sub·sid·ing (səb sīd′ ing) going down; becoming lower

sub·ter·ra·ne·an (sub′ tə rā′ nē ən) underground; beneath the surface of the earth

sui·tor (sü′ tər) man who asks if he can marry a woman

sup·pose (sə pōz′) to believe; to think; to imagine

sup·press (sə pres′) to hold back; to keep something from happening

sur·face (sėr′ fis) **1.** top outer part: *We walk on the surface of the earth.* **2.** of the surface; having to do with the side or face of a thing: *a surface picture.*

surge (sėrj) to rise suddenly; to move like a wave

Sur·re·ál (sə rē äl′)

sus·pense (sə spens′) unsure feeling; waiting to find out what will happen next

Swa·hi·li (swä hē′ lē) language spoken in east Africa

Swe·den (swēd′ n) country in northern Europe, one of the Scandinavian countries

Swit·zer·land (swit′ sər lənd) country in Europe east of Germany and France

sym·bol (sim′ bəl) something that stands for something else.

sym·pa·thize (sim′ pə thīz) to feel sorry for; to feel bad because someone else is hurt

syn·di·cate (sin′ də kit) group of newspapers, owned by the same person or people, that prints many of the same articles

syn·thet·ic (sin thet′ ik) not natural; manufactured: *Wool is a natural fabric; nylon is a synthetic one.*

tab·u·la·tor (tab′ yə lā′ tər) machine that does addition or arranges things or numbers in columns

tan·gle (tang′ gəl) mass of things twisted together

Tas·ma·ni·a (taz mā′ nē ə) island southeast of Australia

---

hat, āge, fär; let, ēqual, tėrm; it, īce; hot, ōpen, ôrder; oil, out; cup, pùt, rüle; ch, child; ng, long; sh, she; th, thin; ᴛʜ, then; zh, measure; ə represents *a* in about, *e* in taken, *i* in pencil, *o* in lemon, *u* in circus.

tech·ni·cal (tek′ nə kəl) involving the use of science for doing practical things

tech·nol·o·gist (tek nol′ ə jist) one who can build or make something using the techniques of science

te·di·ous (tē′ dē əs) long and tiring

te·lep·a·thy (te lep′ ə thē) exchange of thoughts without using speech or written language

tem·per·ate (tem′ pər it) not very hot or very cold in climate; mild

ten·ta·cle (ten′ tə kəl) long, slender part of an animal's body that can be used to grab and hold things

ten·ta·tive·ly (ten′ tə tiv lē) carefully; slowly, in order to be safe

term (tėrm) word; expression

ter·race (ter′ is) flat, raised piece of land near a house

tex·ture (teks′ chər) way something feels: *Sandpaper has a rough texture.*

thatched (thach′d) covered with straw or palm leaves

theme (thēm) the subject

The·se·us (thē′ sē əs *or* thē′ süs)

thrall (thrôl) slave

thresh·old (thresh′ ōld) piece of wood or stone at the bottom of a door; entrance

tides (tīdz) risings and fallings of the ocean that take place about every twelve hours, caused by the gravitational pulls of the sun and moon

ti·di·ly (tī′ dl ē) in a tidy way; neatly

to·ga (tō′ gə) outer garment worn by Roman men, made of a sheet of wool wrapped around the body

tongs (tôngz) tool with two arms that are held together with a hinge, pivot, or spring, used for grasping

tour·na·ment (tėr′ nə mənt *or* tùr′ nə mənt) contest between knights fighting for a prize; contest between many people

trag·ic (traj′ ik) very sad

trai·tor·ous (trā′ tər əs) betraying a friend

tran·quil·i·ty (trang kwil′ ə tē) peace

trans·fer·ence (tran sfer′ əns) moving something from one place to another

trans·form (tran sfôrm′) to change; to change one thing into something else

trans·late (tran slāt′ *or* tran′ slāt) to change a book, a message, etc., to another language

trans·la·tor (tran slā′ tər *or* tran′ slā tər) one who explains the meaning of something that is in a foreign language; one who changes a message from one language to another

trans·par·ent·ly (tran sper′ ənt lē) so that light shines through; so that it can be seen through

trap·door (trap dôr′) door in a floor

trawl·ing (trôl′ ing) dragging very large nets for catching fish

treach·er·ous (trech′ ər əs) not trustworthy; dangerous; tricky

treach·er·y (trech′ ər ē) disloyal behavior; breaking of faith

tre·men·dous (tri men′ dəs) very big: huge

tres (trās) Spanish: three

tres·pass·ing (tres′ pəs ing) going on someone's property without permission

tri·al (trī′ əl) **1.** the examining and deciding of a case in court **2.** a test of strength or truth, etc.

trick·le (trik′ əl) to flow or fall in drops

tri·dent (trīd′ nt) spear with three points

Tri·este (trē est′)

tri·pod (trī′ pod) stand with three legs

tri·um·phant·ly (trī um′ fənt lē) happily, because one has succeeded or been right

trois (twä) French: three

tro·phy (trō′ fē) sign of a victory; something that one has won; something that reminds one of a victory

truce (trüs) short peace; stop in the fighting or war

trudge (truj) to walk slowly and tiredly

Tus·ca·ny (tus′ kə nē)

twin·ing (twīn′ ing) twisting around

U·gan·da (ü gan′ də *or* yü gan′ də) country in East Africa

ul·tra·mod·ern (ul′ trə mod′ ərn) very modern

un·clench (un klench′) to loosen; to open something that has been tightly closed

un·con·scious·ly (un kon′ shəs lē) without thinking; as though not aware

un·in·hab·it·a·ble (un′ in hab′ ə tə bl) unfit to be lived in

un·in·hab·it·ed (un′ in hab′ ə tid) not lived in

u·nique (yü nēk′) like no other; the only one of its kind; different from all others

U·nit·ed King·dom (yü nī′ tid king′ dəm) nation made up of England, Northern Ireland, Scotland, and Wales

ut·ter·ly (ut′ ər lē) completely

va·cant·ly (vā′ kənt lē) in a way without thought or intelligence

va·der (väd′ ər) Dutch: father

vague·ly (vāg′ lē) in an unclear way

val·iance (val′ yəns) bravery; courage

valve (valv) something that controls the flow of a liquid or a gas

va·por (vā′ pər) gas; fume

var·mint (vär′ mənt) animal that causes damage; pest

Va·ter (fät′ ər) German: father

ven·ture (ven′ chər) to dare; to undertake a risk or danger

ve·ran·da (və ran′ də) large porch

ves·sel (ves′ əl) large boat or ship

Ve·su·vi·us (və sü′ vē əs)

vi·bra·tion (vī brā′ shən) movement back and forth

vi·cious (vish′ əs) fierce; dangerous; nasty

vig·or·ous·ly (vig′ ər əs lē) strongly

vil·la (vil′ ə) large house in the country

vi·sor (vī′ zər) part of a helmet that covers the face

void (void) empty space

vol·ca·no (vol kā′ nō) mountain that is very hot inside and out of which steam and melted rock sometimes come

Von Frisch (von frish′) Karl (kärl)

wail (wāl) to make a mournful sound

war·i·ly (wer′ ə lē *or* war′ ə lē) carefully; as though expecting danger

war·rant (wôr′ ənt *or* wor ənt) written order from a judge giving an official such as a sheriff or police officer a legal right to do something, such as search a house

wa·ter buf·fa·lo

(wô′ tər *or* wôt′ ər buf′ ə lō) tropical animal of Asia, sometimes used to pull plows and carry loads

Wa·tut·sis (wä tüt′ sēz) members of a people who live in the countries of Rwanda and Burundi in Africa, known for their tall stature (Swahili name for *Batutsi*)

wave·let (wāv′ lit) little wave

wea·sel·ly (wē′ zəl lē) clever and considered untrustworthy

whin·ny (hwin′ ē) to make a noise like a horse

whirl (hwėrl) to spin

whit·tled (hwit′ ld) shaped by cutting shavings or chips from wood and the like

wir (vir) German: we

---

hat, āge, fär; let, ēqual, tėrm; it, īce; hot, ōpen, ôrder; oil, out; cup, pu̇t, rüle; ch, child; ng, long; sh, she; th, thin; ᴛн, then; zh, measure; ə represents *a* in about, *e* in taken, *i* in pencil, *o* in lemon, *u* in circus.

wist·ful (wist′ fəl) sadly wishing for something one is not able to have

wiz·ard (wiz′ ərd) person thought to have magic power; magician

work·man·ship (wėrk′ mən ship) way a thing is made; skill in making a thing

wrought (rôt) made

ye (yē) you (used in speaking to more than one person)

ze·bra (zē′ brə) striped African animal, related to the horse

Zee·ly (zē′ lē)

ze·nith (zē′ nith) highest point the sun reaches in the sky; point directly over·head

Zeus (züs)